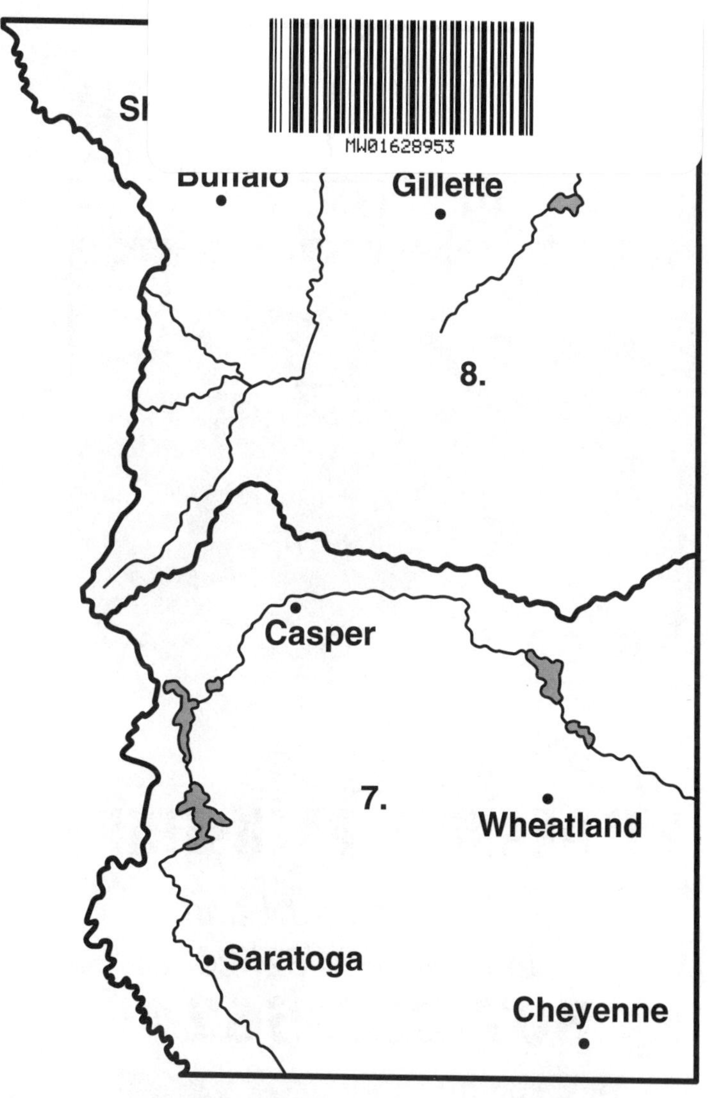

5. Chapter 5 - Green River
6. Chapter 6 - Sweetwater River
7. Chapter 7 - North Platte River
8. Chapter 8 - Northeast Wyoming

KIP CAREY'S OFFICIAL WYOMING FISHING GUIDE

ORIGINATED AS TIM KELLEY'S FISHING GUIDE IN 1954

KIP CAREY
Editor and Publisher

JILL CAREY
SUZZETTE RUMMELL
Associate Editors

MARC ALLEN
KERRI ALLEN
Graphic Design
www.horsepowerdesign.com

ISBN 0-970736-21-5

6732 West Coal Mine Ave. #230
Littleton, Colorado 80123
www.fishingcolowyo.com

Every attempt has been made to present accurate information, however situations and conditions are subject to change. This guide is intended for trip planning only, Kip Carey Publications is not responsible for mishaps, injuries, or errors in directions caused by the use of this guide for other than its intended use. Distances and elevations have been checked for accuracy but can contain errors due to estimations or rounding. The fishing regulations in this publication are current as of printing, the most current copy of the Wyoming Fishing Regulations should always be consulted for updated, complete, and current regulations.

Photo Courtesy of Rob Yingling

TABLE OF CONTENTS

PREFACE 6
COLD WATER FISH OF WYOMING 7
WARM WATER FISH OF WYOMING 17
WYOMING RECORD FISH 26
NOTES TO READERS 27
CHAPTER 1 – WIND RIVER 32
CHAPTER 2 – BIGHORN RIVER 64
CHAPTER 3 – YELLOWSTONE 94
CHAPTER 4 – SNAKE RIVER 126
CHAPTER 5 – GREEN RIVER 150
CHAPTER 6 – SWEETWATER RIVER....................196
CHAPTER 7 – NORTH PLATTE RIVER 202
CHAPTER 8 – NORTHEAST WYOMING 234
INDEX 260

DEDICATION

This book is dedicated to all those special people in my life who believe in me more than I do sometimes myself. To my children Zac, Caleb, and Mollie who each in there own special way is a big part of this book. My mother for her support and enthusiasm; and to my dad for teaching me how to fish, I only wish every child had such a great opportunity growing up. My sister Suzzette for caring and working so very hard to help make sure this book was made possible. Kevin, my brother-in-law, who I wish to thank for all those times he has dragged me through the backcountry to fish. My brother and sister, Steve and Sandy, who helped give support and prayer to keep the vision going.

Most importantly this book is dedicated to my loving wife, Jill, for who with out I would not be complete. Her patience, understanding, and sense of humor have made this book possible. I know I could not have been any more blessed in life without her by my side.

ACKNOWLEDGEMENTS

Thanks to God's grace, and the church family of Rejoice Christian Fellowship for their continual prayers for the completion of this project. A special thanks goes out to Thomas, James, Pastor George and Pastor Shawn for their continual prayers and support.
Thanks also to Marc and Kerri who spent many technical hours pulling this book together.

I wish to acknowledge Tim Kelley and the numerous people at the Wyoming Fish and Game Department, US Forest Service, Bureau of Land Management, Bureau of Reclamation, and local fishing stores who have worked hard on the completion of this guide.

PREFACE

Back in the early 1950's a professor from the University of Colorado, by the name of Tim Kelley, began the incredible task of chronicling the fishing waters of Wyoming and Colorado. Tim Kelley's vision was to chronicle all of the waters of both states in one handy guide. The resulting *Tim Kelley's Colorado and Wyoming Fishing and Hunting Guide* was published every two years starting in 1954, with the last in 1990. I was able to purchase the rights to this indispensable guide in 1999, at which time I set about updating and completing a separate guide for Colorado, which was released in 2001. This guide is the result of my belief that Wyoming deserves a separate book dedicated to all the quality waters of the state. Many times people ask me, "Have you been to all these places?". I only wish the answer was yes, but the fact of the matter is, it would take a lifetime to visit all the waters that are covered in this book. Although I have been to my share of fishing holes, the updated information in this book is made possible by the hard work and the continuing efforts of countless people, beginning with Tim Kelley; and from the wonderful people at the Wyoming Game and Fish Department, Us Forest Service, Bureau of Land Management, Bureau of Reclamation, and the National Park Service, who have helped to complete and to update the information for this book. Also contributing to the information within this guide are local anglers, local sporting good stores, and guide services from around the state. So as I continue to visit more and more of the state I hope to see you there, enjoying fishing Wyoming as much as I do!

Fish drawings on back covers and Recognizing Wyoming's Fish are used by permission from Joseph R. Tomelleri www.americanfishes.com.

Cover photo by Rick Carpenter/Lander Llama Company

RECOGNIZING WYOMING'S COLD WATER FISH

RAINBOW TROUT

The rainbow is a native of West Coast streams and was introduced in Wyoming in the 1880's. Rainbows are heavily spotted on the middle and upper body, fins and tail. A classic rainbow has a dark back, is heavily spotted, has a silverish side and a light or white belly. They are distinguished by a rose or reddish band running down their sides. Rainbow in different locations can be lighter in color tending to be more washed out, being less spotted and more silvery in color. Rainbow are an enjoyable fish to catch, they strike hard, usually make a swift run and many times leap out of the water. Brightly colored fly patterns and lures motivate rainbows. Rainbows also feed off the bottom especially in the early mornings and early evenings. Rainbow seek deeper, warmer, swift waters, although rainbows are found in some the very high cold mountain lakes. Larger rainbows are found in lower warmer bodies of water. Rainbows usually seek small headwater streams in the spring to spawn. They will scour into the gravel of a streambed where they deposit 200 to 9,000 eggs. Rainbow can live up to 11 years but most only make it to 5-6 years old in Wyoming. A **cuttbow** is a cross between a rainbow and a cutthroat. Rainbow and golden cross easily to create a highly colored rainbow hybrid with brilliant orangeish stripes along its sides. Eagle Lake rainbow were introduced from Eagle Lake in California and are best known for their long life expectancy.

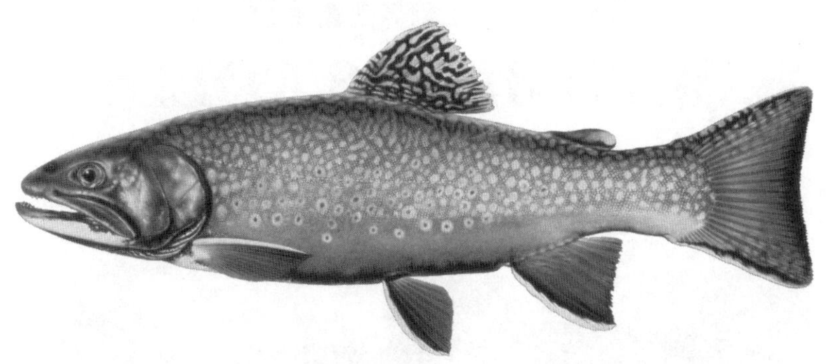

BROOK TROUT

Brook trout, or "brookies", are originally native to the eastern United States. They are now found in almost every part of the country, adapting to even the smallest of streams. Although they are spread throughout Wyoming in great numbers, being prolific reproducers, they do reach not reach large sizes in but a few of the states waters. Brook seldom reach over a half-pound. They differ from other trout mainly in the structure of a tooth bearing bone in the center of the roof of the mouth. Brook trout do not generally put up a great fight when hooked, they usually fight deep and rarely break water. The brook is very greedy and it is undoubtedly the easiest of the trout species to lure to bait or a fly. Brook trout are readily distinguished by sides spattered with red and white spots on a background of darker color. It is identified by the pure white leading edge of the lower fins and the mottled "worm track" pattern on the back. Brook trout bellies are a muted orange, during spawning the males bellies turns to a brilliant bright orange. Scales on the brook are numerous, small and deeply embedded, giving the skin a soft, fine textured appearance. They generally like spring-fed lakes and the gravelly bottom of cold-water streams with a moderate current. They are most active in 48-degree water, and cannot survive in water over 68 degrees. Look for the brook near the bottom of eddies, pools, under banks and logs, and behind rocks. In October or November, brook seek cold spring-fed tributaries with gravel bottoms to spawn. The female usually travels upstream leaving nests of 100 to 5,000 eggs in the gravel bottom along the way. Brook live about 4 years and average 7 to 10 inches.

CUTTHROAT TROUT

The cutthroat, also known as the native, is the only trout indigenous to the central Rocky Mountains. The dash of red found between the gills and the body gives the cutthroat its name. Sometimes it is necessary to separate the folds about the gills on the bottom side of the fish to see this feature. Cutthroat often are heavily spotted on a background of lighter color. There may be a reddish wash along the length of the body during spawning season. Cutthroat seem slimier than other trout because their scales are small. Cutthroat-rainbow hybrids are common, identified by having some measure of both the red slash on the throat and the rainbow stripe down the side. Found mostly in the upper stretches of cold, clear streams and mountain lakes, the cutthroat seems to do best in waters not subject to heavy silt. The range of the cutthroat has been greatly reduced throughout the West because most major streams carry a substantial silt load at some time during the year. Competition from other species has helped reduce their numbers as well. Cutthroat head for the bottom when hooked and usually fight hardest when brought in close. Flies and spinning gear are commonly used to catch them. Spawning occurs in spring from April to June, preferring clear headwater streams. They have no success reproducing in lakes without an entering stream. Four types of cutthroat are found in Wyoming; the **Snake River cutthroat** found in the Snake River drainage, the **Yellowstone cutthroat** found in the Yellowstone/Bighorn/Upper Missouri River drainage, the **Colorado River cutthroat** found in the Green River drainage, and the **Bonneville or Bear River cutthroat** found in the Bear River drainage.

BROWN TROUT

The brown trout is originally from Europe, the brown trout was introduced into the United States in 1883 and found its way to the Wyoming Rockies soon after. Two species were introduced, the Loch Leven, which came from Scotland, and the German brown. These have become hybridized to the point that it is accepted that only this mixed form exists in Wyoming. Against a golden-brown background, the brown trout has many dark spots and scattered reddish-orange specks surrounded by faint halos. Despite this, browns lack the vivid coloration of other trout. Their tail usually lacks spots and has a straight back edge from top to bottom. Browns lower fins are a pale yellow to a whitish color. Due to its hardy nature and adaptability brown often survive and flourish in streams in which other trout cannot. They are the more tolerant of high water temperatures and muddy stream conditions of all the trout species. As well, browns seem to thrive in larger bodies of slower water with deep, quiet pools. Unless they are feeding in shallow riffles, browns usually hide in heavy cover, under cut banks or deep pools. Brown trout have earned a reputation for being difficult to catch, particularly in lakes. Anglers tend to catch larger browns at night. The brown, the most predatory of trout, is ordinarily a bottom feeder. It is a shy and wary fish, and, if mature, probably "educated." Seldom does a brown rise a second time for a fly. They are also the least spectacular of the trout to catch because they do not often break water; dart and resist like other trout. When hooked, browns react stubbornly and with little finesse. During spawning, which occurs in the fall, browns prefer headwater streams from 10 to 30 feet wide. Depending on egg size, a female produces 200 to 600 eggs.

GOLDEN TROUT

Golden trout are native to the Kern River in California, and their state fish. The exact date of introduction into Wyoming is unknown but is believed to be in the early 1940's. Golden trout have an olive green back and spots on the upper dorsal fin and on their tails. They have an orange belly, yellow on their lower sides, and a reddish stripe along the middle of their sides. They are most recognized by the 10 round marks that run down their sides, called parr marks. The tips of their orange lower fins are white. Mature golden found in lakes take on a more uniform golden or yellowish color except for some light olive along their backs. Bright reddish orange stripes are found along lower sides. While golden are well adapted to live at elevations less than 10,000 feet, throughout their range in Wyoming, Idaho, California, and Washington they are almost only stocked and managed in higher elevation lakes where food sources keep them from growing larger than 10 inches. Wyoming is an exception, waters high in the Wind River, Bighorn and Absoraka mountain ranges have a higher concentration of the food golden feed upon. The golden's diet is made up of small insects, notably caddisflies, midges, terrestrial insects and small crustaceans. Golden are selective eaters, many times only feeding for short periods of time during the day. Golden will easily cross with rainbow and cutthroat, another reason they are far removed into high remote lakes. Golden can be mistaken for cutthroat if their bright coloration is not present, the difference is that golden do not have teeth on the back or base of their tongues, and white borders on their lower fins like that of a cutthroat. Golden spawn in the spring. Golden trout have not been stocked into Wyoming waters since 1995, as a result of a brood stock not being available. However, numerous self-sustaining populations of golden trout still exist throughout the state.

LAKE TROUT (MACKINAW)

The lake trout, or mackinaw, is found in deeper cold water lakes. It is the largest of all trout, reaching 60 pounds. The "laker" is an excellent food fish, although oilier than other trout. It is so closely related to brook trout that the two have been successfully crossed, resulting in a fish called a splake. A long, slender fish, the lake trout can be readily identified by its deeply forked tail. Its color varies from gray to almost black with light gray spots. Pelvic and pectoral fins are bordered in light gray. The head is long and flattened with a large, toothy mouth. These fish's eyes are set closer to the top of the head than other trout. Lake trout spend a great part of the year in deep waters, but there is a period in spring and again during fall spawning season when they move to shallower waters. Small fish make up most of the mature lake trout's diet, but some lake trout continue to eat insects throughout their lives. Because it is a cold-water fish, it is slow growing. Mature 6-year-old lake trout may average 17 inches and 1.5 pounds. Catching the lake trout requires special planning and equipment. Successful techniques vary, but for deep-water fishing try salmon eggs and sucker meat. Trolling gear usually is regarded as essential. Patience and knowledge of lake temperature stratification and currents help. Lake trout spawn at age 3 in shallow waters. In October or early November they leave 1500 to 2500 eggs in gravel beds and rocky areas. They tend to be very mobile during this time. **Splake** are a hybrid between a lake trout and a brook. Splake look very similar to brook trout in appearance except they do not have the red spots on their sides surrounded by blue halos. Splake may also exhibit more of the light color spotting on their sides, which is common to lake trout. Splake grow quicker than lake trout but do not grow as large.

GRAYLING

Grayling are a rare gamefish prized for their beauty. The grayling is a favorite of anglers who knows the species. Rising eagerly to the fly, it is not as easily hooked as trout, due partially to its smaller weaker mouth and quick movements. Part of the trout family native to the West Coast they are taken on flies and likely to jump when hooked. It will often dart repeatedly after a fly only to return swiftly to deep water without taking it. Fish using dry or wet flies, nymphs, small spinning lures, and natural bait especially salmon eggs. The grayling can be distinguished by its large, sail-like dorsal fin, patterned with green, orange or pink spots which are more evident during spawning. The males sail like dorsal fin is larger than the females. The graylings back is a darker purple, blue/black, or blue/gray color. Its sides are grayish to silver in color with purplish dark spots, with a gray to white colored belly. Grayling are more dramatically colored during spawning. Grayling may reach 20 inches and 4 pounds, but most in Wyoming do not exceed more than 1.5 pounds. Usually found in schools, grayling like cool clear lakes and streams with gravelly bottoms. Their principal food is aquatic insects, making fly fishing the most productive way to take them. Grayling will take spinners, bait or other lures. To spawn, grayling migrate to rocky tributary streams from March to June where the female lays about 6,000 eggs. The maximum life span for grayling is about 7 years. They are very slow growing and late to mature.

MOUNTAIN WHITEFISH

The mountain whitefish is a native of Wyoming found in many drainages throughout the state. Its small, weak, and delicate mouth makes it a difficult fish to hook and land. Although slightly more bony than trout, whitefish are good to eat. Many anglers smoke them. Whitefish are not a very colorful fish, best described as dirty white in color with shadings of silver and a white belly. A Patch of a light olive or muted brown may color their sides. This white, soft-fleshed fish is not easily mistaken for a trout, but it is sometimes mistaken for a grayling, especially when young. Whitefish do not have spots on their top dorsal fins, whereas grayling do. The fish's mouth and jaws are very small, requiring the use of very small hook sizes. Whitefish can reach 18 inches and 4 pounds, but most are smaller. The whitefish lives in fast, clear waters, preferring medium to large rivers with deep pools, riffles, and gravel bottoms. During the warmer summer whitefish can be found more in the riffles, retreating to the deeper pools during the winter. Whitefish largely feed on the bottom at dusk and during the night. Its main diet consists of insects, particularly caddis flies and other larvae and is in direct competition with trout for food. When fishing, try bait or flies, but take care when setting the hook, otherwise it will pull out. Whitefish also make good winter sport for ice anglers. Whitefish spawn in the fall, moving only a short distance from pools and riffles to scour out nests and lay eggs.

KOKANEE SALMON

The kokanee salmon is the landlocked cousin of the pacific sockeye salmon. Kokanee is a native word meaning “red fish”. It was introduced to Wyoming waters in the early 1950s. Since it inhabits many of the same waters as trout, it is often taken by trout anglers. The kokanee may have a few blackish spots on a rich metallic blue back. Its sides and belly are silvery in color. During its immature years, it has a weak jaw, and its scales can be removed easily. By the end of its third summer, its jaw becomes stronger. As maturity is reached by mid-fall of the third year, the kokanee goes through numerous physical changes as it prepares to spawn. The male kokanee becomes brick red, develops a hump in front of its dorsal fin, a pronounced hook in the lower jaw. The female’s color changes to a reddish gray, and in both the male and female their heads become a deep dark green color. The number of kokanee inhabiting a given body of water determines their size more so than the food supply. Studies show kokanee feed near the surface from dawn to dusk and then drops down to about 60 feet or more as night sets in. Kokanee prefer cooler waters, as temperatures rise they seek cooler and deeper waters. Kokanee feed mostly on plankton, but insects do make up a small part of their diet. Kokanee will take flies, but trolling and bait land the bulk of the catch. During the spawning season, September through November, kokanee begin to school and to swim up tributaries to spawn. As they look for spawning places they can easily be taken on egg flies. After spawning, kokanee die.

LING (BURBOT)

Ling, whose official name is burbot, is the only freshwater species of the cod fish family. Ling are closely related to haddock, pollack, and other saltwater cod species. Ling have a long slender eel-like body that is round near the tail and flat near the head. Ling's forward fins are comparably small, while the continuous and long dorsal and anal fins are almost equal in length extending down to the tail fin. The tail fin is not forked like that of all the other cold water species in Wyoming, but is round in shape. The mouth on this fish is very large, it contains many rows of small teeth which slant backward and a strong jaw to grab and hold prey. The ling has two small whiskers on its nose and another larger one on its chin, these are called barbels. Ling are dark olive color with black or yellowish mottlings on their backs and sides. Older fish may be darker and appear almost black or dark brown. Younger fish may have stomachs which are a lighter olive, brownish or pale color. Fins are generally the same color as the skin around it. Ling have very small scales which gives the skin a very smooth and slimy feel. Ling feed on nymphs and other insects when young, the adults diet is mostly other fish, but does includes fish eggs and small invertebrates. These fish are mostly night feeders, they tend to appear sluggish during the day. Ling prefer deeper and colder parts of lakes and rivers in the summer, in the winter they will move into shallow water to spawn. Ling are rare in the fact that they spawn in the middle of winter, January through March, when the water temperature is not much above freezing. Ling spawn at night in a group of 10 to 12 fish in shallow water over sand or gravel, a large mature female ling can carry more than a million eggs. Ling are from the cod family and their livers contain high levels of vitamins A and D, just like their saltwater relatives. Ice fishing is a popular way to catch ling who inhabit the Bighorn and Wind River drainages.

RECOGNIZING WYOMING'S WARM WATER FISH

BLUEGILL

The bluegill, introduced to Wyoming around the 1920s, is found in many reservoirs and low elevation streams. This scrappy little fish, also known as bream, fights deep, swimming at right angles to a rod. Pound for pound, it may well be the most sporting of freshwater fish, especially on light tackle. Known for both tenacity and an appetite limited to anything handy, bluegills are best caught in the morning or evening using light terminal tackle ranging from a cork and worm on a hook to delicate dry flies. When one bluegill is located, others are usually near by. As summer heat becomes extreme, bluegills move into deeper water and shady weed beds. Bluegill vary in coloration, but are distinguished from other sunfish relatives by the 6 to 8 vertical bars on its sides, long black earflap that has no trim and a black spot on the posterior of the dorsal fin. The maximum length is usually 12 inches weighing about one pound. Bluegill primarily feed on insects, but, when available, fish eggs or smaller fish are also a part of its diet. They tend to live and feed in shallower waters, close to shore. They are rather easy to catch and take wet or dry flies, worms, grasshoppers or other live baits. Spawning season for bluegill is from late spring through August. Closely related and very similar in looks and characteristics are the **green sunfish, rock bass** and the brightly colored **pumpkinseed.**

CRAPPIE

Crappie were introduced to Western waters in the 1880's and now is abundant in low elevation Wyoming waters. It is tolerant of warm, muddy waters. White crappie have silvery-olive sides shading into olive green on its back with eight to nine dark, vertical side bands. It usually has six distinguishing dorsal fin spines. Black crappie look very similar to white crappie except they have black spots or blotches on their sides, and more spines in their fins. White crappie are more prevalent than the closely related black crappie. In large reservoirs, crappie reach 9 to 12 inches at the mature age of 4. Crappie are attracted to submerged brushy, weedy, rocky areas. Dams of most reservoirs are favorite areas of concentration. In deep water, crappie seek irregular bottom areas, rock ledges or other types of cover where they feed on smaller fish, competing directly with bass. During summer, crappie are usually found in depths of 15 to 25 feet. Small jigs cast around submerged brush piles is an effective way to catch them. Flies or poppers fished at dusk are also reliable. Trolling or drifting with minnows in the spring is a favorite technique for catching crappie. A bobber with a small live minnow hung 5 to 8 feet below the surface is a popular method. A pork-rind hanging a foot or so below the surface often produces as well. Crappie spawn in spring, generally in water 3 to 8 feet deep. They prefer spawning sites near brush piles, stumps or rock outcroppings.

YELLOW PERCH

Yellow perch, sometimes call ring perch, have adapted well to Wyoming's lower elevation fluctuating reservoirs. It is most at home in a lake environment, but can be found in some slow moving streams. Yellow perch tend to overproduce and large fish are usually not caught. Perch rarely exceed more than 12 inches or weigh more than one pound. Young perch prefer shallows while adults prefer deeper waters. They are a favorite food of larger walleyes. Yellow perch have a white belly and golden-yellow to olive-green sides with 6 to 8 evenly spaced dark stripes. Spawning males have bright reddish-orange lower fins. They live in large schools, spending the entire day in deep waters, moving to shore to feed in the late afternoon or evening. Yellow perch are not picky eaters and will eat anything that moves. Foods include aquatic insects, clams, snails and even its own young. Small flies and spinners or natural bait fished a foot or two off the bottom are time-proven techniques. During summer, worms are often the most productive bait. If possible, fish shaded areas giving a worm some action. Large perch are often taken by trolling lures slowly near the bottom. Winter ice fishing can produce good catches, often with larger fish. When ice fishing, seek out the deepest areas of the lake. But, since the fish continue to move during winter it may be necessary to drill several holes before finding a school. A small minnow fished near the bottom is the best bet. Yellow perch spawn in spring at age three. Eggs are laid in gobs attached by ribbons to bottom vegetation. In reservoirs without rooted vegetation, eggs are laid on the bottom, drifting with water motion.

SMALL AND LARGEMOUTH BASS

The largemouth bass was the first fish introduced into Wyoming in the late 1800's. The largemouth bass is the largest member of the sunfish family. It gets its name from its upper jawbone, which extends under and behind the eye. The smallmouth bass differs from the largemouth in that its upper jaw extends to a point under the middle of the eye. The largemouth has a lustrous yellow-green body laced with dark horizontal bars. The average largemouth is 12 to 18 inches long and weighs about 2 to 3 pounds, larger ones can weigh over 5 pounds. The smallmouth bass is a golden- bronze or copper color with dark vertical bars and weighs 1 to 3 pounds. Bass are most often found in shallow, weedy lakes with soft bottoms and sparse vegetation. Young bass feed mainly on plankton; but, as it matures, its diet changes to fish, crayfish, frogs, tadpoles and larger insects. Spring is one of the best seasons for bass fishing. Work the shorelines and shallows that have shade. Try to lure them from beneath fallen trees, lily pads and boat docks. Smallmouth are attracted to rocky areas. Bass will strike throughout the day, but early morning and evening fishing is better. Bait casting and spinning are the most widely used methods for catching bass. A wide assortment of artificial lures can be used. Although bass stay deep in the summer, they lurk around submerged objects and can be caught by fishing deep with live minnows, crayfish or frogs. Most bass anglers prefer to work the shores, but many bass are taken from boats by casting toward the shore and retrieving towards the boat. Bass build nests for spawning in late May or early June.

WALLEYE

The walleye is the largest member of the North American perch family. The walleye varies in color depending on where it is found, but it is usually has a light colored belly which blends into an olive green on the sides and back. The back is crossed with 6-7 narrow dark bands. Markings on the tail and dorsal fin differentiate the walleye from its close relative, the sauger. Walleye dorsal fins have no defined rows or spots, and its tail has a silver or milky colored white tip. Distinctive characteristics include well-developed canine teeth and large eyes with milky white corneas, thus their name. Their eyes are extremely sensitive to light, so they seeks out cool, dimly lit waters during the day. At night it will prowl the shallows in search of food. Walleye can vary in length depending on the character of the water. Mature fish (about 2 years old) are usually more than 12 inches long. Walleye can obtain weights over 10 pounds. Walleye are schooling fish that stay near the bottom in both deep and shallow waters. It forages for food around sandy bars and rocky reefs and often frequents the waters off dams, particularly where lots of small fish are found. Walleyes are primarily fish eaters but also eat crayfish, frogs and snails. Trolling for walleye with artificial lures or lures combined with live and cut bait produce well. Casting with lures and live bait off sandbars and rocky reefs also gets results. Use deep and medium running lures about 6 to 18 inches off the bottom. Shortly after ice-out in early spring, walleye find a shallow, gravelly area or rocky reef to spawn. Both male and female walleye move around at this time and may be taken near the spawning areas.

NORTHERN PIKE

The northern pike is a fierce-looking predator that eats other fish up to one-half its own size and may grow 15 inches in one year. Pike feed only during daylight hours. The northern pike has a long-tapered body and pointed nose lined with needle-sharp teeth. It has light-green sides marked with white or pale yellow spots and a white or yellow belly. A mature pike weighs 5 to 20 pounds or more; pike are one of the fastest growing freshwater fish. Northern pike are a popular fish because of their size and the hard fight they put up when hooked. Pike seek shallow (1-5 ft) water with abundant vegetation during most of the year; however, they move into deeper waters during extremely warm or cold weather. The best time to hook a northern is right after the ice recedes - usually early June. Trollers working rocky points and edges of weed beds take pike on big spoons and plugs. Weedless hooks and snag-resistant gear is preferred. A steel leader is also a must to combat the mouth full of sharp teeth. Northern pike spawn immediately after the ice leaves the reservoir. Short, dense vegetation is preferred for egg laying. Currently the only place in Wyoming to catch northern pike is at Keyhole Reservoir. The Wyoming Game and Fish Department imposes a 30 inch minimum on all northern pike, this equates to an 8 to 12 pound fish.

TIGER MUSKIE

The tiger muskie is a cross between the northern pike and muskellunge, and incorporates the most desirable of its parents' characteristics. Like muskellunge, tiger muskies can potentially grow to be huge fish. They have the savage nature of the northern, making it easier to entice to a lure. Tigers go after bait with the intensity of a pike, and go airborne, fighting like the muskie. Tigers resemble muskies more than pike. The northern pike generally has horizontal rows of dots along its lengthy body. The tiger muskie and muskie have vertical markings but the tiger's are more distinctive, giving it a tiger-like striping. The general color is olive-green with yellowish-white mottling. A tiger muskie diet consists of smaller fish, and large insects. Fishing techniques that work for pike also work for tigers. Sharp teeth necessitate the need for fishing with a steel leader. This fish prefers water 15 feet deep or less, with underwater vegetation and many weeds. Tigers use the same weed patches, pockets and brush piles pike and largemouth bass prefer. Large lures, spoons and spinner baits get their attention. As a hybrid, it is sterile and does not spawn. LAK Reservoir and Grayrocks Reservoir in eastern Wyoming are the two waters in the state where tiger muskies can be caught. The Wyoming Game and Fish Department imposes a 30 inch minimum on all tiger muskies, this equates to an 8 to 12 pound fish.

CATFISH

The channel catfish is a native of Wyoming. Night fishing provides the best sport. A variety of bottom bait - night crawlers, minnows, crayfish, chicken innards and flavored dough balls - all work well. Channel catfish have a forked tail and its sides and back are a darker gray or black color on with a lighter colored stomach. Catfish have numerous "whiskers" called barbels around its mouth hence their name. Channel catfish are hearty eaters, feeding on insects, insect larvae, crayfish, worms, other fish (both dead and alive), fish eggs, and various plant materials. Mature adults feed heavily on minnows and other fish. Generally, channel catfish forage at night. Anglers who expect to take them on a regular basis must fish well into the night. Its highly developed sense of smell, touch, taste, and sight draws it to rotting chicken innards, a variety of cheeses or licorice-flavored dough balls. Large channel catfish have been caught, but few weigh over 20 pounds. Most channel cats weigh less than 5 pounds. Channel cats are attracted to muddy bottoms; however, they also frequent areas containing heavy vegetation. In reservoirs, channel catfish tend to concentrate in midsections of deep, narrow bays. Catfish spawn in the spring May through July, with the male guarding the eggs and young after they hatch. Other varieties of catfish found in Wyoming are **stonecat** and **black bullhead.**

SAUGER

Saugers are closely related to walleye and are found only in large bodies of water. Sauger will not survive in smaller bodies of water, no one is quite sure why. Unlike the walleye, sauger are able to tolerate muddier water and stronger currents in rivers. Although sauger are savage fighters, they do not get as large as their cousin the walleye, most mature fish average 1 to 2 pounds. Young sauger feed mainly on midgefly larvae and mayflies, as the fish matures its diet consists of other fish, large insects, and crayfish. This fish plies open waters looking for smaller fish to eat, almost only feeding at night. The sauger closely resembles the slender and cylindrical shape of the walleye in appearance but has a white belly that turns into an olive green color mixed with a muted yellow on its sides and back. Three to four darker patches run over the fishes back and down its sides. Saugers upper fins have rows of dark spots; the tail may have some spots present. The white belly runs all the way down to the tip of the tail, but does not form a white tip, as does the walleye. Sauger eyes are sensitive and glassy in appearance, and are found in deeper water during daylight hours. Sauger spawn at night in the spring May to June usually right after the walleye spawn.

WYOMING RECORD FISH

SPECIES	YEAR	LOCATION	WEIGHT (POUNDS)	LENGTH (INCHES)
TROUT				
BROOK	1976	GREEN RIVER LAKE	9.68	24.5
BROWN	1982	FLAMING GORGE RES.	25.81	34.25
CUTTHROAT	1959	NATIVE LAKE	15.0	32.0
GOLDEN	1948	COOK LAKE	11.25	28.0
GRAYLING	1983	MEADOW LAKE	2.36	19.62
KOKANEE	1996	FLAMING GORGE RES.	5.73	26.25
LAKE TROUT	1983	JACKSON LAKE	50.0	46.0
	1995	FLAMING GORGE RES.	50.0	48.0
RAINBOW	1969	BURNT LAKE	23.0	35.5
SPLAKE	1999	HOG PARK RES.	11.2	30.0
WHITEFISH	1977	SNAKE RIVER	4.25	21.0
SUNFISH				
BLUEGILL	1988	LAKE VIEW N. POND	1.47	10.3
GREEN	1997	POND-SHERIDAN CO.	.541	8.3
CRAPPIE				
BLACK	1997	BOYSEN RESERVOIR	2.34	15.0
WHITE	2000	GLENDO RESERVOIR	2.31	15.0
BASS				
LARGEMOUTH	1992	POND-SHERIDAN CO.	7.87	21.5
ROCK BASS	1996	POND-SHERIDAN CO.	1.29	11.0
SMALLMOUTH	1993	TONGUE RIVER	5.08	19.0
PERCH				
SAUGER	1999	BOYSEN RESERVOIR	7.4	26.2
WALLEYE	1991	BOYSEN RESERVOIR	17.42	34.0
YELLOW	1991	MARYLAND POND	2.2	16.0
PIKE				
NORTHERN	1998	KEYHOLE RESERVOIR	26.44	43.0
TIGER MUSKIE	1992	GREYROCKS RESERVOIR	29.37	49.0
CATFISH				
BULLHEAD	1987	TENSLEEP POND	2.9	15.25
CHANNEL	1993	POND-PLATTE COUNTY	24.19	34.75
FLATHEAD	1995	NORTH PLATTE RIVER	3.74	20.6
COD				
LING	1965	PILOT BUTTE RESERVOIR	19.25	44.0

NOTES TO THE READERS

I hope everyone finds this guide useful and practical. The following information should be helpful in answering questions about the guide.

MAPS – While there are general reference maps in this guide, you are encouraged to augment them with maps appropriate for your planned activity. A highway map is adequate if you intend to stay on the main roads, but a national forest map is recommended if you plan to venture off the blacktop. Make sure you have the current edition (available at rockyweb.cr.usgs.gov/forestservice/wy.html or mapping.usgs.gov/ or Washakie Range District at 307-332-5460) as many roads have been closed, new ones constructed and use restrictions have been imposed in numerous areas. If your plans involve hiking into the backcountry, a USGS (United States Geological Survey) topographic (topo) map is recommended. The 7.5 minute or 1:25,000 scale maps shows the most detail, but the 15 minute or 1:100,000 scale series maps are adequate and requires fewer maps to cover a large area (available at **www.topozone.com**, **www.mapmart.com** or 303-759-5050). Be advised that changes, mostly roads and trails, may have been made since these maps were printed. Many roads have been closed and routes of others have changed, therefore, USFS (United States Forest Service) National Forest maps are recommended for use to locate roads. Additionally several quality retail maps are available at local sporting goods stores, bait shops, and area bookstores. With your copy of the *Kip Carey's Official Wyoming Fishing Guide* and the right maps, you're ready to enjoy Wyoming's fishing to the fullest.

TIM KELLEY – Tim Kelley, teacher and fisherman, founder of the Colorado/Wyoming Fishing Guide, passed away in September of 1982, in Scottsdale Arizona. He was 75. Tim Kelley helped to produce 18 editions of the classic *Tim Kelley's Official Colorado and Wyoming Fishing Guide,* which he started producing every few years beginning in 1954. Tim Kelley's vision was to chronicle in detail all of the fishing waters in Colorado and Wyoming. The resulting guides have been a valuable resource to countless fishermen over the past 48 years, and with this new edition that tradition continues today. In 1999, I was able to obtain the rights to this great resource, with the hope to continue the work started by Tim Kelley so that you may enjoy fishing Wyoming as much as I do. *Kip Carey's Official Colorado Fishing Guide* was published in January of 2001. This edition is the first to separate Wyoming from Colorado, which I believe will be the greatest benefit to anglers throughout Wyoming.

HOW TO CATCH FISH – I can not pretend to be able to teach you how to catch fish in Colorado with a few words in the pages of this book. Even if an entire chapter was devoted to the subject it would still not prepare a person adequately enough. This guide is a "where" to fish guide, many specific books on "how" to fish exist. I will say however, if you want to catch fish in Wyoming there is a wealth of information available, probably right around the corner. Area fishing and sporting goods stores are a great place to start, fishing is their business, and they are a wealth of information. Wyoming also has numerous quality guide services which offer fishing trips which include instruction. Possibly the best way to increase your abilities is to go fishing with someone who knows how to catch fish, who knows, you just might make a friend for life.

DISCLAIMER – The information in this book is a result of information gained from the Wyoming Game and Fish Department, U.S. Forest Service, Bureau of Land Management, Bureau of Reclamation, National Park Service, local anglers, local sporting goods stores and guide services from around the state, who have helped to complete and update the information in this book. Every attempt has been made to present accurate information, however situations and conditions are subject to change. Lakes once stocked no longer are, or now they are stocked with brown instead of rainbow. Roads once opened are now closed, and public access on leased land once available is now closed. This guide is intended for trip planning only, Kip Carey Publications is not responsible for mishaps, injuries, or errors in directions caused by the use of this guide for other than its intended use. Distances and elevations have been checked for accuracy but can contain errors due to estimations or rounding. The fishing regulations in this publication are current as of printing, be sure to consult the most current copy of the Wyoming Fishing Regulations for updated information. If you find the directions, descriptions, or conditions are different than what is listed in this guide, please go to my web page at www.fishingcolowyo.com and let me know what you have found.

WHERE ARE THE FISH? – Many of the streams and lakes in this guide list several types of fish present for a particular location. A word of note: chances are at different times of the year an angler might not encounter all species listed. Remember, brown run in the fall and rainbow and cutthroat spawn in the spring, which has a definite effect on what species of trout the angler may encounter. The same is true for warm water species also, many times what you catch is just what is feeding.

TERMS AND DEFINITIONS – Throughout this guide references are made about the following terms

National Forest – Wyoming's National Forest are: Ashley (.2 million acres), Black Hills (1.25 million acres), Bighorn (1.1 million acres), Bridger – Teton (3.4 million acres), Medicine Bow (1.6 million acres), Shoshone (2.4 million acres), Targhee (1.8 million acres), and Wasatch National Forest.

Wilderness Areas – In 1964, congress passed the Wilderness Act which stated that the United States must retain pristine portions of national forests, designating them as wilderness areas. These areas, managed by the UFSF, lie in defined boundaries and must remain undisturbed. Wilderness areas are to retain their primitive status, which precludes timber cutting, road building, and any new mining activities. All Wilderness accesses is by foot or horse only. No motorized or mechanical modes of transportation are allowed. Wyoming's Wilderness areas which offer fishing opportunities are: Absaroka – Beartooth, Bridger, Cloud Peak, Encampment River, Fitzpatrick, Gros Ventre, Huston Park, Jedediah Smith, North Absaroka, Platte River, Popo Agie, Savage Run, Teton, Washakie, and Winegar Hole Wildernesses.

State Parks – Wyoming has several State Parks that offer outstanding angling possibilities. They are: Bear River, Boysen, Buffalo Bill, Curt Gowdy, Edness K. Wilkins, Glendo, Guernsey, Hot Springs, Keyhole, Seminoe, and Sinks Canyon State parks. These State Parks are managed by the Wyoming Department of State Parks and Historic Sites. In addition Big Sandy and Hawk Springs State Recreation areas are also managed by Department of State Parks and Historic Sites.

USFS – United States Forest Service – In 1905 the U.S. Forest Service was created to manage public lands in America's National Forests. The Forest Service is a Federal Agency part of the Department of Agriculture. Responsibilities include; construction and maintenance of trails and roads, operation of campgrounds, wildlife habitat management, and the protection and management of all resources on National Forest lands. In addition the United States Forest Service also manages the following Recreation Areas: Bighorn Canyon and Flaming Gorge Recreational Areas.

BLM – Bureau of Land Management – Created in the mid-1940's, the BLM is part of the Department of the Interior. The BLM is responsible for balancing the use of public land for recreation, mining, livestock grazing, and wildlife habitat on over 18 million acres in Wyoming.

Wyoming Game and Fish Department– The Wyoming Game and Fish Department is the agency responsible for regulating fishing activities, issuing fishing licenses and enforcing regulations, stocking and maintaining fish in Wyoming waters, and working hard to protect threatened and endangered fish species in the state. In 1998 the Department of Game and Fish began a lease program in which private land is leased to provide public access to enhance fishing opportunities in Wyoming. These tracts of land are located on the following: Bighorn, North Platte, Tongue, Powder, and Belle Fourche drainages.

These areas are designated as Walk In Fishing Areas, or **WIA** for short. These areas are leased from private property owners for the use of fishing only, please respect their property and take care to stay in designated areas to insure continuation of this program. For further information on this program be sure to get the current copy of the Walk-in Atlas from the Department of Game and Fish at 307-777-4600 or visit http://gf.state.wy.us/ on the web for further information.

PRIVATE PROPERTY – Private property is just that – PRIVATE. No matter how good the fishing appears to be the property is owned by someone. Wyoming has so much quality public waters to fish, please respect their rights and do not trespass. In Wyoming, landowners not only own the rivers bank, but also the land under the water. Wading, anchoring, or landing on private property is considered trespassing, and it is the responsibility of the angler to know where private and public lands are located. A recommended resource is a BLM map available for a fee (currently $4) from the BLM in Casper @ 307-261-7600.

SR, CR, FR and TR – State Road, County Road, Forest Road and Trail.

CONTACTING KIP CAREY – The best way to contact me is through my website at www.fishingcolowyo.com. You can also contact me through the U.S. Mail - Kip Carey Publications, 6732 West Coal Mine Ave. #230, Littleton, Colorado, 80123.

WIND RIVER

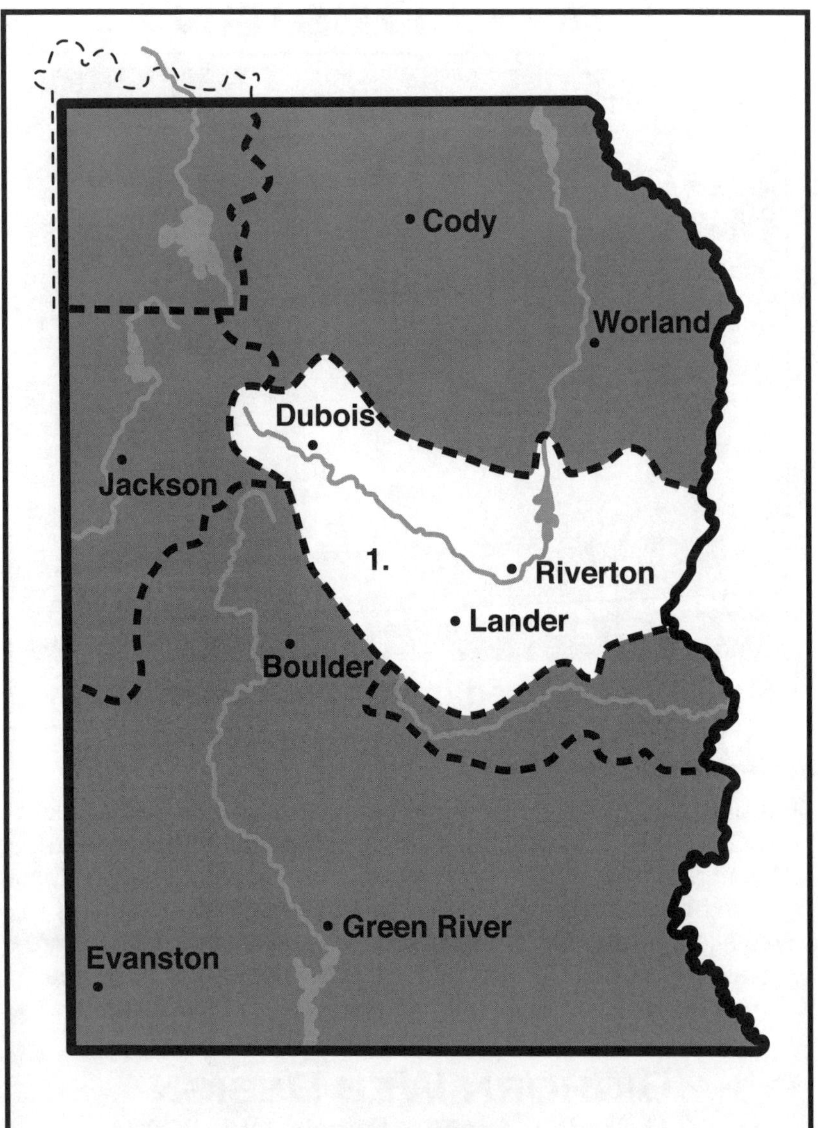

1. Wind River

WIND RIVER

The **Wind River** originates near Togwotee Pass in Shoshone National Forest. Shoshone National Forest was established in 1891 as part of the Yellowstone Timberland Reserve and consists of over 2.4 million acres of varied terrain ranging from flats of sagebrush to rugged glacier covered mountain peaks. Togwotee Pass links the Teton Valley on the west to the Wind River Valley on the east.

High on the east side of the Continental Divide in the Wind River Mountain Range southeast of Yellowstone National Park, the Wind River begins a roundabout southeasterly journey. The East Fork Wind River forms the western boundary of the Wind River Indian Reservation, draining the southern end of the Absoroka Mountain Range. The Wind River flows through the Wind River Indian Reservation, near the town of Riverton, the river swoops north where it is dammed to form Boysen Reservoir, then flows into the Owl Creek Mountains and emerges with a new name, the Bighorn River.

The primary tributaries of the Wind River are the Little Wind River from the west, and the three forks of the Popo Agie River from the southwest. Numerous small tributaries join these rivers in their upper reaches in the Fitzpatrick and Popo Agie wildernesses; offering outstanding fishing for brook, rainbow, brown, whitefish, cutthroat, and golden. In the heart of the drainage is the Wind River Indian Reservation which envelopes a major portion of the Wind River, tributary creeks, high alpine lakes, and low elevation reservoirs.

WIND RIVER HEADWATERS

From Togwotee Pass to Dubois and from there south another 44 miles, the **Wind River** closely parallels US 287. The best fishing on the main river is in the Dubois vicinity, watch for signs indicating public access. Dry flies are the angler's best bet in late summer and autumn. Rainbow, brown, cutthroat, and whitefish, averaging 14 inches but often larger, can be caught. Brook are also present and are much smaller.

Where US 287 heads south to Lander and US 26 splits east toward Riverton, the river follows US 26. It is about 75 feet wide in the Dubois area but broadens considerably as it meanders, south, east and then north. The river enters private property about 12 miles north of Dubois. South of Dubois, signs along the highway mark several access points. Check with landowners to fish the river elsewhere.

Near the top of the drainage, just east of the Continental Divide, **Wind River Lake** (9,542 ft; 6 ac) lies on the north side of US 287. There is a picnic area and easy vehicle access. The fishing is fair to good for small brook and rainbow to 9 inches. Boats with motors are prohibited.

Brooks Lake (9,050 ft; 186 ac) lies at the end of a 4.5 mile gravel road (FR 515) that exits north from US 287 about 27 miles northwest of the town of Dubois. There are camp-

Courtesy of Lander Llama Company

grounds and a lodge near the lake. The fishing is good for stocked rainbow, small brook and some splake up to 20 inches. There are also lake trout to 30 inches. The lake is stocked regularly. Boats with motors are permitted. **Brooks Lake Creek**, which flows south from the lake, offers fair to good fishing for small brook and rainbow. **Upper Brooks Lake** (9,105 ft; 25 ac), **Rainbow Lake** (9,220 ft; 24 ac), **Lower Jade Lake** (9,430 ft; 20 ac) and **Upper Jade Lake** (9,570 ft; 18 ac) lie within a 4-mile radius north of Brooks Lake and can be reached by trail. All offer good fishing. Upper Brooks Lake has small brook and rainbow, splake and cutthroat. Rainbow Lake has small brook and rainbow; Lower Jade Lake has lake trout up to 16 inches and small cutthroat, Upper Jade Lake has small cutthroat. Follow FR 515 to Brooks Lake, trailheads lead out from the northwest side of the Lower Brook Lake. Gas powered motors are prohibited in both Jade Lakes.

About 10 miles south of Togwotee Pass, **Sheridan Creek** is reached by turning west off US 287 about 18 miles northwest of the town of Dubois, just south of the Tie Hack Historical Marker. The road follows the creek for 2 miles, then becomes a trail. Fishing is fair for brook and rainbow. Fishing pressure is heavy. FR 540 (4 wheel drive) leads 5.5 miles to **Pelham Lake** (8,817 ft; 33 ac) with good fishing for cutthroat to 18 inches. The limit on trout is 2 fish, all fish less than 14 inches must be returned to the water immediately. Flies and lures only. Gas powered motors are prohibited. **Trout Creek Lake** (8,935 ft; 6 ac), with modest fishing for stocked rainbow and grayling, is reached by driving 5 miles on Sheridan Creek Road and FR 538 (4 wheel drive) 2.5 miles to the lake.

On the east side of the Wind River, **DuNoir Creek** flows south out of the Absaroka Mountains and into the Wind River from the north about 9 miles northwest of Dubois. FR 251 follows the creek for about 10 miles, mostly through private land where permission to fish is necessary. DuNoir Creek itself offers good fishing for cutthroat, and fair fishing for whitefish and brook. About 9 miles from the highway a trail forks east along **East DuNoir Creek** to **Trail Lake** (8,053 ft; 33 ac). The lake is fair for brook and rainbow. High in the drainage are the two **Watkins Lakes** (lower 9,190 ft; 5 ac, upper 9,245 ft; 4 ac), with good fishing for fishing cutthroat and brook. **Frozen Lake** (10,905 ft; 7 ac) is barren.

Located off **West DuNoir Creek** are **Murray Lake** (9,045 ft; 9 ac), **Clendenning Lake** (9,095 ft; 4 ac), **Kisinger Lakes** (9,430 to 9,485 ft; 5 to 17 ac) and several unnamed small lakes at the DuNoir headwaters which offer good to very good fishing for wily cutthroat and brook. Follow the creek north to these lakes or reach them by hiking about 8 miles east from Brooks Lake.

Warm Spring Creek is rated fair for brook to 8 inches, and possibly some small rainbow. Access is from

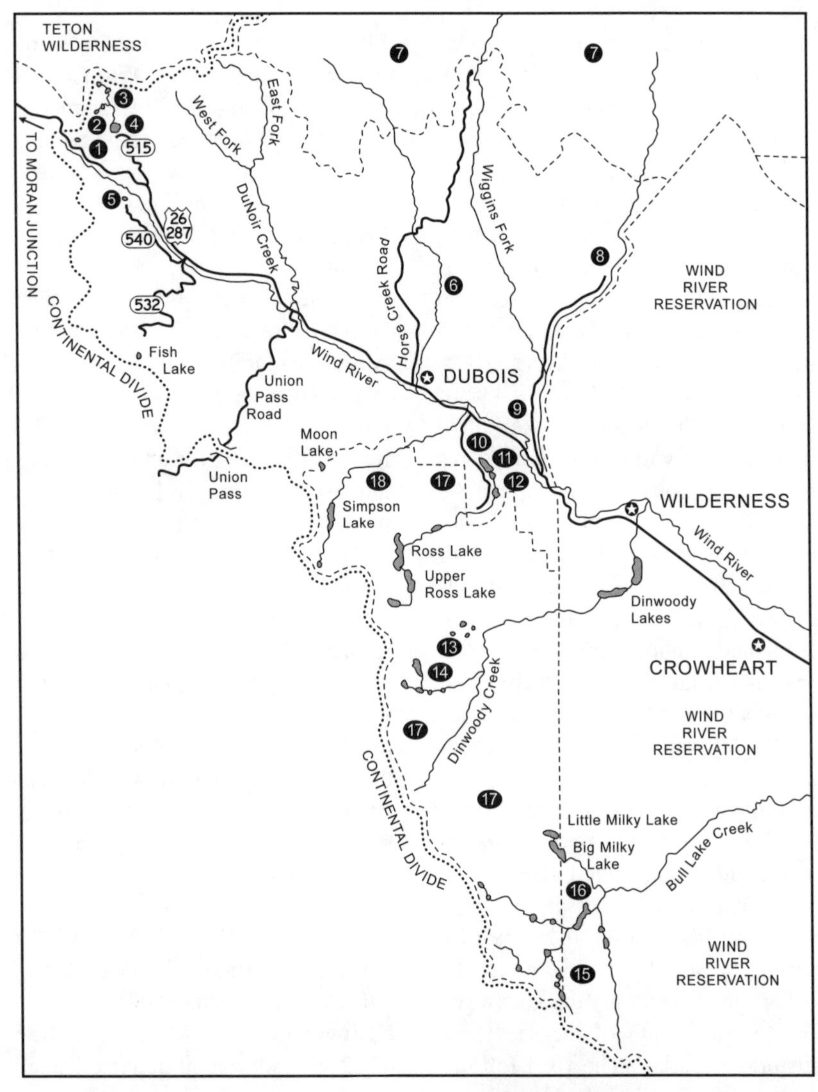

1. Wind River Lake
2. Jade Lakes
3. Rainbow Lakes
4. Brooks Lake
5. Pelham Lake
6. Horse Creek
7. Washakie Wilderness
8. East Fork Wind River
9. East Fork Road
10. Torrey Lake
11. Ring Lake
12. Trail Lake
13. Dinwoody Lakes
14. Downs Lake
15. Milky Lakes
16. Alpine Lake
17. Fitzpatrick Wilderness
18. Jakey's Fork Creek

Union Pass Road 9 miles northwest of Dubois on Highway 287. About 6 to 7 miles from the highway is Warm Springs Road to the north, which follows the creek. On Fish Creek, a tributary of Warm Springs Creek, is **Fish Lake** (9,245 ft; 19 ac) which has unusually good cutthroat fishing. The limit on trout is 3 fish. Gas powered boats are prohibited. Finding the lake may be difficult as many roads of uneven quality crisscross the area, a good map may be necessary. Roads FR 532, FR 544 and FR 534 (4 wheel drive) eventually lead to the lake.

Horse Creek, which flows into the Wind River at the town of Dubois, offers modest fishing for small brook, brown and rainbow to 8 inches. From the north side of Dubois the paved Horse Creek Road follows Little Horse Creek for several miles before becoming a good dirt road. Horse Creek Road joins Horse Creek proper after 9 miles. **Burnt Timber Lake** (9,320 ft; 3 ac) and **Carson Lake** (8,430 ft; 7 ac) are barren. **Deacon Lake** (9,540 ft; 10 ac) with small brook is 2 miles by trail off of Parque Creek Road.

Nine miles northwest of Dubois the Union Pass Road, marked by a sign, goes west from US 287. Union Pass Road provides access to some good fishing along the northern boundary of the Fitzpatrick Wilderness Area. The 4 wheel drive Moon Lake Road (FR 531) is marked by a sign on Union Pass Road. **Union Lake** (9,775 ft; 12 ac) and **Moon Lake** (9,688 ft; 60 ac) are good for brook, and some lake trout to 16 inches. Grayling have been planted in Moon. **Grass Lake** (9,615 ft; 8 ac) is fair for rainbow and small brook.

Three miles southeast of Dubois on US 287, Fish Hatchery Road (CR 241) leaves the highway west to the state fish hatchery on **Jakey's Fork Creek**. The stream is open to public fishing along the 1.5 miles to the hatchery and holds brook, brown and rainbow up to 12 inches. Jakey's Fork Creek from the upper boundary of the Dubois Hatchery downstream to the Wind River is closed to fishing from October 1 to May 31. Continuing up Jakey's Fork on the CM trail, hikers reach the Whiskey Mountain trail 6 miles in. (This approach should not be confused with the Jakey's Fork trail, which actually originates in the town of Dubois and goes to the above-mentioned Union Lake). Take a right on the Whiskey Mountain trail to reach **Soapstone Lake** (9,945 ft; 10 ac) with fair angling for brook to 9 inches. Nearby **Red Wing Lake** (9,230 ft; 5 ac), **Alice Lake** (9,180 ft; 8 ac) and **Boone Lake** (9,873 ft; 5 ac) are small lakes which have good fishing for grayling. Near the Continental Divide, 3 miles from Soapstone Lake, is **Simpson Lake** (9,725 ft; 212 ac) with 14-inch brook and cutthroat. **Long Lake** (9,821 ft; 6 ac) is barren. **Rim Lake** (10,420 ft; 22 ac), still higher, has good fishing for cutthroat and rainbow, and the two **Blanket Lakes** (upper 9,690 ft; 11 ac, lower 9,670 ft; 6 ac) north of Simpson, have good fishing for brook. Nestled right near the Continental Divide is **Marion Lake** (10,407 ft; 18 ac) with golden up to 16 inches; just below Marion are **Peat Lake** (10,355 ft; 5 ac) with small rainbow and rainbow golden crosses, and **Dyke Lake** (10,265 ft; 31 ac) with medium-size rainbow. To the south, **Lost Lake** (10,361 ft; 16 ac) has golden, **Pinto Lake** (10,348 ft; 14 ac) and **Sandra Lake** (10,275 ft; 10 ac) have cutthroat.

Torrey Creek.

A half-mile south of the Jakey's Fork turnoff on US 287 is Trail Lake Road (CR 257), a gravel road to Whiskey Basin and **Torrey Creek**, marked by a sign. The road is rough, but cars without 4 wheel drive can make it. Lower Torrey Creek is good for rainbow and brook. Upper Torrey Creek has cutthroat. The creek above Torrey Lake to the National Park Boundary is closed to fishing April 1 through May 31. **Torrey Lake** (7,411 ft; 240 ac), **Ring Lake** (7,417 ft; 108 ac) and **Trail Lake** (7,432 ft; 130 ac) can be reached by car Via CR 257. Ring Lake has good fishing for big brown, ling, rainbow and splake; Trail Lake has lake trout, some as large as 20 pounds, and good splake populations. Trail Lake also has brown and rainbow. Torrey Lake has splake, lake trout, brown, rainbow and ling. There is a crude boat ramp

Courtesy of Lander Llama Company

at Torrey Lake and boat ramps at Trail Lake and Ring Lake; motorboats are allowed. Campsites are available at Ring and Trail lakes and west of Trail Lake Ranch, which is owned by the Game and Fish Department.

Passenger vehicles can negotiate the rough road 2 miles above Trail Lake which ends at a parking area and the Torrey Creek Trailhead near the wilderness boundary. Torrey Creek Trailhead provides access to several trails including; Lake Louise Trail, Bomber Lake Trail, Whiskey Mountain Trail, and Glacier Trail.

The **Glacier Trail**, besides providing access to over 150 glaciers, is also the main access trail to the high mountain lakes in the Fitzpatrick Wilderness. The Glacier Trail leads over a saddle to the south into the Dinwoody Creek drainage, Dry Creek drainage, and on to the Dinwoody Glaciers. The Dinwoody Glaciers are among 156 glaciers in the highest reaches of the Shoshone National Forest, more than any other area in the lower 48 states. The Glacier Trail is a busy thoroughfare for horses, backpackers, and anglers. The New Glacier Trails which begins at the Torrey Creek Trailhead was constructed after a rock slide covered a lower portion of the "old trail". The new trail and the old trail do meet back up near the saddle into the Dinwoody Creek drainage.

A steep Bomber Lake Trail climbs up to Bomber Falls along **East Torrey Creek** which offers fair fishing for brook and cutthroat. There are no fish above the falls. **Bomber Lake** (10,115 ft; 42 ac) and **Turquoise Lake** (10,515 ft; 12 ac) at the headwaters are barren.

Up the very fishable **West Torrey Creek** 2.5 miles on the Lake Louise Trail is **Lake Louise** (8,380 ft; 58 ac) with small brook, rainbow, cutthroat and rainbow/cutthroat crosses. Above Lake Louise 1 mile is **Hidden Lake** (9,242 ft; 63 ac) which has fair fishing for some nice rainbow and cutthroat hybrids. Another mile is **Ross Lake** (9,675 ft; 448 ac) with excellent fishing for rainbow and rainbow/cutthroat hybrids up to 20 inches and **Upper Ross Lake** (9,738 ft; 173 ac) with cutthroat. Fishing is closed on Ross Lake south of P.J. Island and on Torrey Creek drainage above Ross Lake from January 1 through July 14. Many anglers choose to follow the Torrey Creek/Whiskey Mountain Trail 6 miles around to the north to access Ross Lake Trail and Ross Lake. **Snowband Lake** (10,400 ft; 29 ac), **Crystal Lake** (10,620 ft; 40 ac), and **Mile Long Lake** (10,270 ft; 67 ac) are barren.

EAST FORK WIND RIVER

The **East Fork Wind River** joins the main stream about 10 miles below the town Dubois. The northwestern boundary of the Wind River Reservation is the East Fork Wind River. It is good for 12-inch cutthroat, especially upstream from its confluence with the Wiggins Fork. Fishing for brown averaging 14 inches in the lower reaches can be good in the fall. Rainbow and cutthroat in the 9 to 12 inch range are also found in the lower reaches, some larger fish to 18 inches are occasionally caught. Whitefish are numerous, mostly averaging 12 inches. Upper reaches have good fishing for small cutthroat. The East Fork is easily reached from US 26-287 by a road posted "Game and Fish East Fork Elk Management Area." This road follows the creek to the north for about 20 miles, and can be hiked farther. The east bank is on the Wind River Indian Reservation; the west is a mix of state, private and federal property. Check land ownership locally and with BLM maps. A fishing permit is required to fish on the reservation side of the river, and to enter the reservation. The East Fork Wind River drainage upstream from the Wind River (including Bear Creek and Wiggins Fork, excluding Bog Lake) has a limit of 6 trout, only 2 of these can be cutthroat and only 1 can be longer than 15 inches.

Bear Creek is the middle fork of the East Fork Wind River, and is not on the Indian Reservation. The creek has good fishing for small (10-inch) cutthroat above its juncture with the East Fork Wind River, via FR 501 and 503, which are 4 wheel drive roads. Some private land does exist along the creek. **Green Lake** (9,335 ft; 6 ac) just to the north is barren.

The **Wiggins Fork** joins the East Fork Wind River to the east of the town of Dubois. The creeks upper reaches are in the National Forest and Washakie Wilderness, and are accessible from Horse Creek Road on the Horse Creek drainage to the northwest. Wiggins Fork offers excellent fishing for cutthroat, with some brown, brook and whitefish. The fish are small but plentiful, averaging 10 inches. **Bog Lakes** (upper 9,405 ft; 2 ac, lower 9,385 ft; 9 ac) are 3 miles by trail north from Horse Creek Road. The upper lake is barren, the lower lake has good fishing for rainbow and grayling. **Elk Lake** (8,075 ft; 3 ac) 0.5 miles to the east of the end of Horse Creek Road has small cutthroat. High in the wilderness by steep trails are **Snow Lake** (11,125 ft; 5 ac) and **Green Lake** (10,735 ft; 6 ac) with small cutthroat. **Sheep Lake** (11,265 ft; 2 ac) and **Emerald Lake** (10,672 ft; 7 ac) are barren.

FITZPATRICK WILDERNESS

The Fitzpatrick Wilderness lays south of the town of Dubois and west of the Wind River Reservation. The western and southern boundary of the wilderness is the Continental Divide high atop the Wind River Range. Streams flow easterly out of the Wind River Range from the Fitzpatrick Wilderness Area and into Wind River Indian Reservation where they eventually end up in the Wind River and Boysen Reservoir.

Access to the lakes in the wilderness to west of the Wind River Indian Reservation is via Glacier Trail which departs from the Torrey Creek Trailhead above Trail Lake (discussed earlier in this chapter). These lakes are several miles into the wilderness, previous planning and

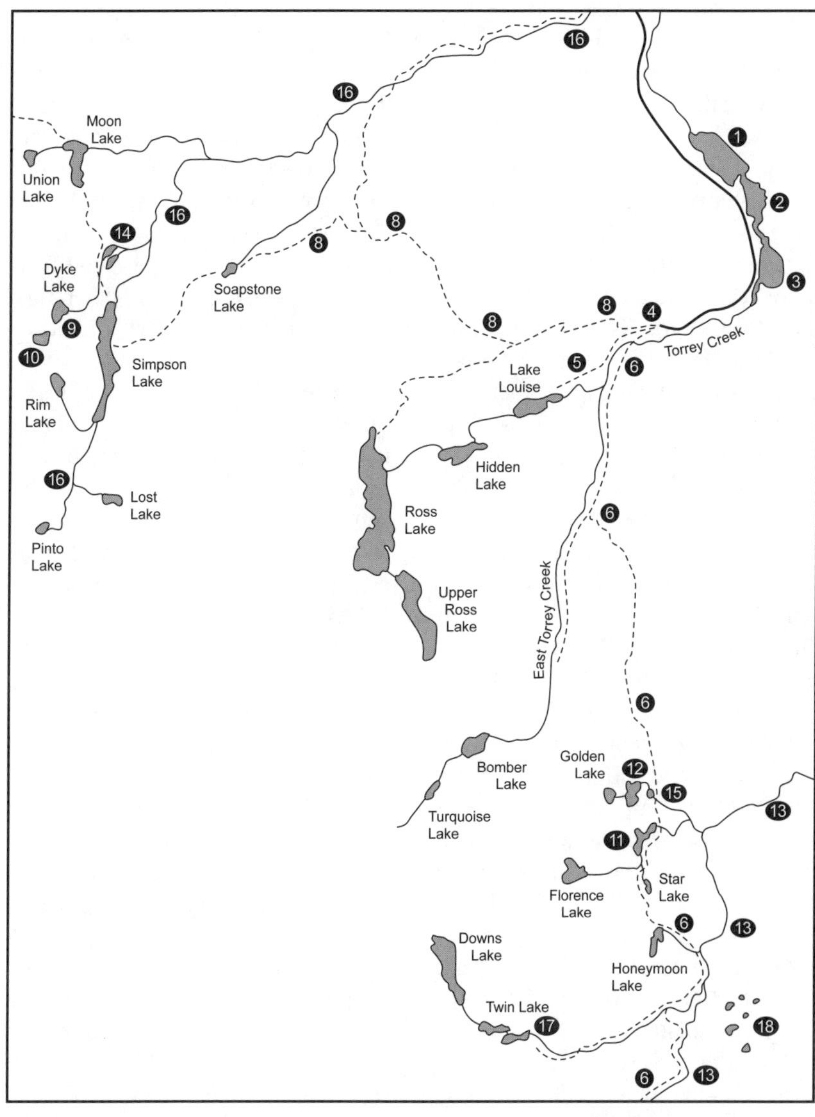

1. Torrey Lake
2. Ring Lake
3. Trail Lake
4. Torrey Creek Trailhead
5. Lake Louise Trail
6. Glacier Trail
8. Whiskey Mountain Trail
9. Peat Lake
10. Marion Lake
11. Double Lake
12. Upper Phillips Lake
13. Dinwoody Lake
14. Blanket Lakes
15. Phillips Lake
16. Jakey's Fork Creek
17. Blueberry Lake
18. Ink Wells Lakes

goods maps are a necessity.

From the Torrey Creek Trailhead, above Trail Lake, follow the Glacier Trail to the south for 9 miles to a group of small lakes. These lakes are on the Dinwoody Creek drainage and are known as the **Dinwoody Lakes** (not to be confused with the larger, more accessible Dinwoody Lakes on the reservation). **Honeymoon Lake** (9,838 ft; 18 ac) is reached by dropping down a steep embankment for moderate fishing for small to fair-size cutthroat. **Star Lake** (10,268 ft; 8 ac) has only fair fishing for 16-inch splake. **Golden Lake** (10,535 ft; 20 ac) has good sized wily golden, **Florence Lake** (10,767 ft; 43 ac) is barren. **Phillips Lake** (10,120 ft; 3 ac) and **Upper Phillips Lake** (10,230 ft; 30 ac) offer fishing for brook and cutthroat. **Double Lake** (9,945 ft; 37 ac), despite its many visitors, is very productive and offers fishing for splake, brook and cutthroat. Follow Downs Fork by horse trail and fish the water for cutthroat almost up to the large, but barren, **Downs Lake**; just below Downs Lake, two small lakes, **Twin Lake** (9,930 ft; 22 ac) and **Blueberry Lake** (9,900 ft; 19 ac) have small cutthroat. About 8 miles up the Dinwoody Creek drainage from Honeymoon Lake lie the Dinwoody Glaciers.

Dry Creek

Moving south from the Dinwoody drainage, the Dry Creek drainage has its own set of fine lakes. To reach the Dry Creek drainage continue past the Dinwoody drainage on Glacier Trail. Head up Dinwoody Creek, pick up the Ink Wells Trail and go over Horse Ridge. Topographic maps are strongly recommended. Just before the forest boundary there is a fork. One trail forks west to the **Ink Wells Lakes** (10,140 to 10,240 ft; 1 to 8 ac), a group of small lakes with good fishing for small brook. The other fork goes southwest along **Dry Creek.**

Near the reservation boundary on Dry Creek Trail are **Phillips Lake** (9,582 ft; 6 ac), **Grassy Lake** (9,623 ft; 24 ac), and **Native Lake** (9,624 ft; 50 ac) with good angling for brook and some cutthroat, rainbow and cutthroat/rainbow crosses up to 12 inches. Ponds the southeast are barren. Up Grassy Creek to the south are **Mark's Lake**, which is also barren, and **Splake Lake** (9,825 ft; 13 ac), which has splake present up to 18 inches. Further on up Dry Creek is **Marten Lake** (10,500 ft; 41 ac) and **Lake Whitney** (10,725 ft; 17 ac), both with crosses of rainbow/cutthroat and rainbow/golden to 16 inches. Other lakes in the drainage are barren.

North Fork Dry Creek above Native Lake has brook and cutthroat in its lower reaches and cutthroat in the upper reaches. **Moose Lake** (9,950 ft; 13 ac) has fair to good fishing for cutthroat under 12 inches and small brook. Further up Dry Creek 1.5 miles, **Cub Lake** (10,380 ft; 42 ac) and **Bud's Lake** (10,405 ft; 28 ac) have primarily cutthroat and maybe some cutthroat/golden crosses to 14 inches. **Don Lake** (10,475 ft; 35 ac) has good fishing for

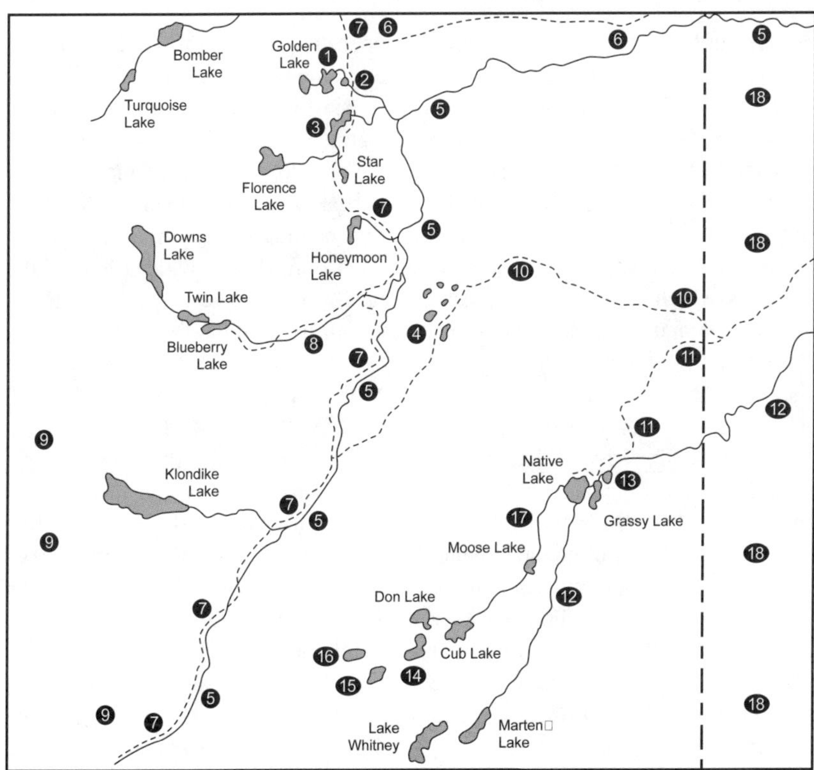

1. Upper Phillips Lake
2. Phillips Lake
3. Double Lake
4. Ink Wells Lakes
5. Dinwoody Creek
6. Dinwoody Trail
7. Glacier Trail
8. Downs Fork
9. Dinwoody Glaciers
10. Ink Wells Trail
11. Dry Creek Trail
12. Dry Creek
13. Phillips Lake
14. Bud's Lake
15. Golden Lakes
16. Lower Glacier Lake
17. North Fork Dry Creek
18. Wind River Reservation

golden/cutthroat crosses to 20 inches. Still higher, **Golden Lake** (10,530 ft; 12 ac) has healthy and wary good-sized golden. **Lower Glacier Lake** (10,670 ft; 19 ac) has moderate fishing for golden up to 14 inches.

Farther south, there are a number of lakes which drain east into Bull Lake Creek and on to the reservation. Access to this remote drainage is via the Wind River Mountains from the west. Start at Elkhart Park Trailhead (see the Green River Chapter for details), east of Pinedale, and pack in by horse or foot along the Hay Pass Trail across the Continental Divide. This arduous trip will put you among what are sometimes called the **Hay Pass Lakes**, at the headwaters of Bull Lake Creek. Among them are **Dennis Lake** (10,630 ft; 60 ac) and **Golden Lake** (10,155 ft; 20 ac) which have excellent fishing for golden up to 18 inches; **Lake Louise** (10,160 ft; 25 ac) and **Upper Golden Lake** (10,245 ft; 27 ac) have fair sized golden; **Camp Lake** is barren. Right next to the border of the Wind River Indian Reservation are two sets of **Milky Lakes**. On North Bull Lake Creek are **Little Milky Lake** (9,700 ft; 136 ac) and **Big Milky Lake** (9,635 ft; 221 ac) which have rainbow. Big Milky Lake is on the border of the Reservation and requires a permit to fish. To the south on **Middle Bull Lake Creek** are a number of lakes in the **Milky Lakes** (10,185 to 10,350 ft; 48 to 75 ac), which have cutthroat and golden. Some of these lakes are reservation waters, they are open to fishing from June 1 through September 30 and require a reservation fishing permit and recreation stamp.

For a dozen or more miles south of the lakes just described, the reservation boundary reaches all the way to the Continental Divide. Most of the headwaters of the Little Wind River are entirely on the reservation.

POPO AGIE WILDERNESS AREA

Near Bonneville Peak the reservation border leaves the Continental Divide, several of the lakes feeding the **South Fork Little Wind River** are on Forest Service land inside the Popo Agie (pronounced popo-zia) Wilderness. The Popo Agie Wilderness boundaries are the Wind River Reservation on the north and the Continental Divide on the west. There are a number of ways to reach this area - you'll need strong legs or a good horse. In any case, the fishing is worth the effort.

Access to the northern portion of the wilderness is by way of Dickinson Park. Dickinson Park provides access to several trailheads including; Bears Ears Trail and Smith Lake Trail. From Highway 287 near the town of Fort Washakie, just north of the Hines General Store and the Wind River Trading Company, the signed and paved Trout Creek Road goes west for 5 miles, watch for a gravel road (Moccasin Road) signed for Moccasin Lake. Take this road up some steep switchbacks almost 20 miles to the signed Dickinson Park

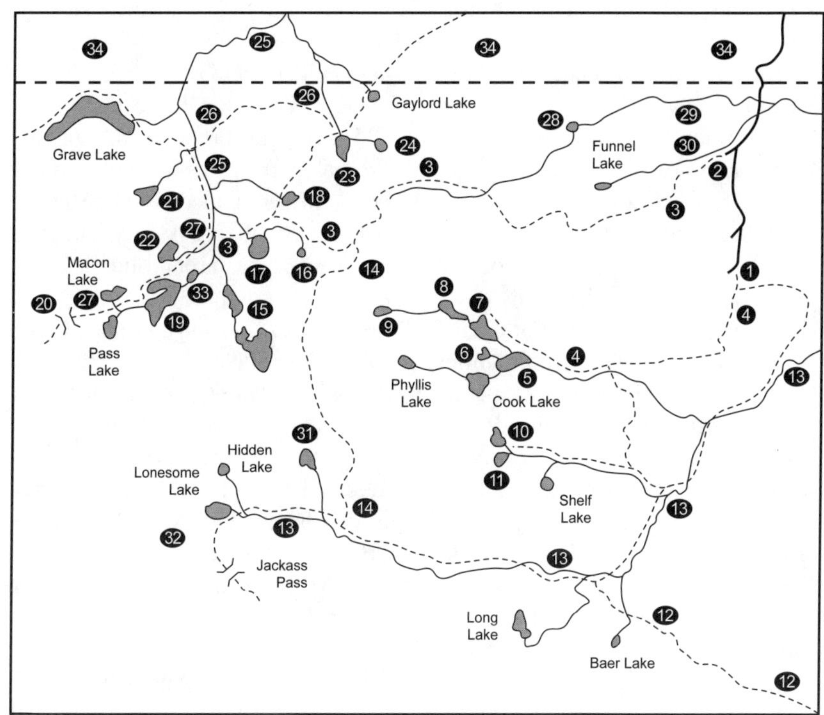

1 Dickinson Park Trailhead
2 Bears Ears Trailhead
3 Bears Ears Trail
4 Smith Lake Trail
5 Smith Lake
6 Cloverleaf Lake
7 Middle Lake
8 Cathedral Lake
9 Upper Cathedral Lake
10 High Meadow Lake
11 Cliff Lake
12 Pinto Park Trail
13 North Popo Agie River
14 Lizard Head Trail
15 South Fork Lakes
16 Little Valentine Lake
17 Valentine Lake
18 Dutch Oven Lake
19 Washakie Lake
20 Washakie Pass
21 Spearpoint Lake
22 Loch Leven Lake
23 Moss Lake
24 Little Moss Lake
25 South Fork Little Wind River
26 Moss Lake Trail
27 Washakie Trail
28 Sand Lake
29 Sand Creek
30 Ranger Creek
31 Bear Lake
32 Cirque of the Towers
33 Little Washakie Lake
34 Wind River Reservation

Road, and 2.75 miles south to trailheads at Dickinson Park.

From Dickinson Park the steep Bears Ears Trail climbs over Adams Pass to reach the **South Fork Little Wind River** after about 13 miles, and provides access to other trails and lakes. The South Fork itself has cutthroat, rainbow, golden, brook and crosses of these species in its clear, alpine waters. The South Fork Wind River flows north several miles through the wilderness area before entering into the Wind River Reservation. Please note, a permit is required to enter reservation lands.

Near the reservation border, in the wilderness area, is **Grave Lake** (9,955 ft; 202 ac) with lake trout up to 18 inches, cutthroat and an occasional golden. The small lakes above Grave Lake are barren. Four miles east, also on the reservation border, is **Gaylord Lake** (10,155 ft; 13 ac) with cutthroat to 2 pounds, some are considerably bigger. **Moss Lake** (9,965 ft; 31 ac), less than a mile south, has fair to good fishing for brook to 10 inches and some cutthroat. **Little Moss Lake** (10,360 ft; 11 ac) is barren. **Dutch Oven Lake** (10,567 ft; 12 ac), another mile south from Moss, has fair fishing for brook to 3 pounds. **Valentine Lake** (10,395 ft; 45 ac) has slow fishing for golden and cutthroat hybrids, averaging 11 inches. **Little Valentine Lake** (10,845 ft; 6 ac) has fair fishing for small golden and cutthroat. **Loch Leven Lake** (10,405 ft; 33 ac), a half-mile to the north, has hard-to-catch brown up to 18 inches, and rainbow up to 16 inches. Nearby, **Spearpoint Lake** (10,590 ft; 27 ac) has golden/rainbow hybrids to 14 inches. **Washakie Lake** (10,360 ft; 115 ac), still farther south on the Washakie Trail, has had golden/rainbow crosses landed as large as 15 pounds. Small brook are abundant. Spawning areas around this lake are closed from January to July 31 to protect the trophy fish. **Little Washakie Lake** (10,340 ft; 6 ac) below the larger lake is good for small golden/rainbow. **Macon Lake** (10,775 ft; 30 ac) has brook. **Pass Lake** (10,630 ft; 28 ac) is barren. **South Forks Lakes; Helmet Lake** (10,495 ft; 111 ac) and **Holster Lake** (10,463 ft; 36 ac) are stocked with cutthroat.

North Fork Popo Agie River

The **North Fork Popo Agie River** (pronounced popo-zia) has rainbow, brook, cutthroat and whitefish as it alternately cascades and meanders its way from the mountains. There is a good deal of summer traffic along this river (particularly mountain climbers headed for the "Cirque of Towers"). From the Dickinson Park Trailhead, Smith Lake Trail provides access to Smith Lake and other trails and lakes in the area.

Nearest to Dickinson Park are **Dickinson Creek**, **Ranger Creek,** and **Sand Creek** with brook to 7 inches. Near the headwaters of Sand Creek is **Sand Creek Lake** (9,800 ft; 9 ac) with good fishing for small brook and cutthroat. At the headwaters of Ranger Creek is **Funnel Lake**

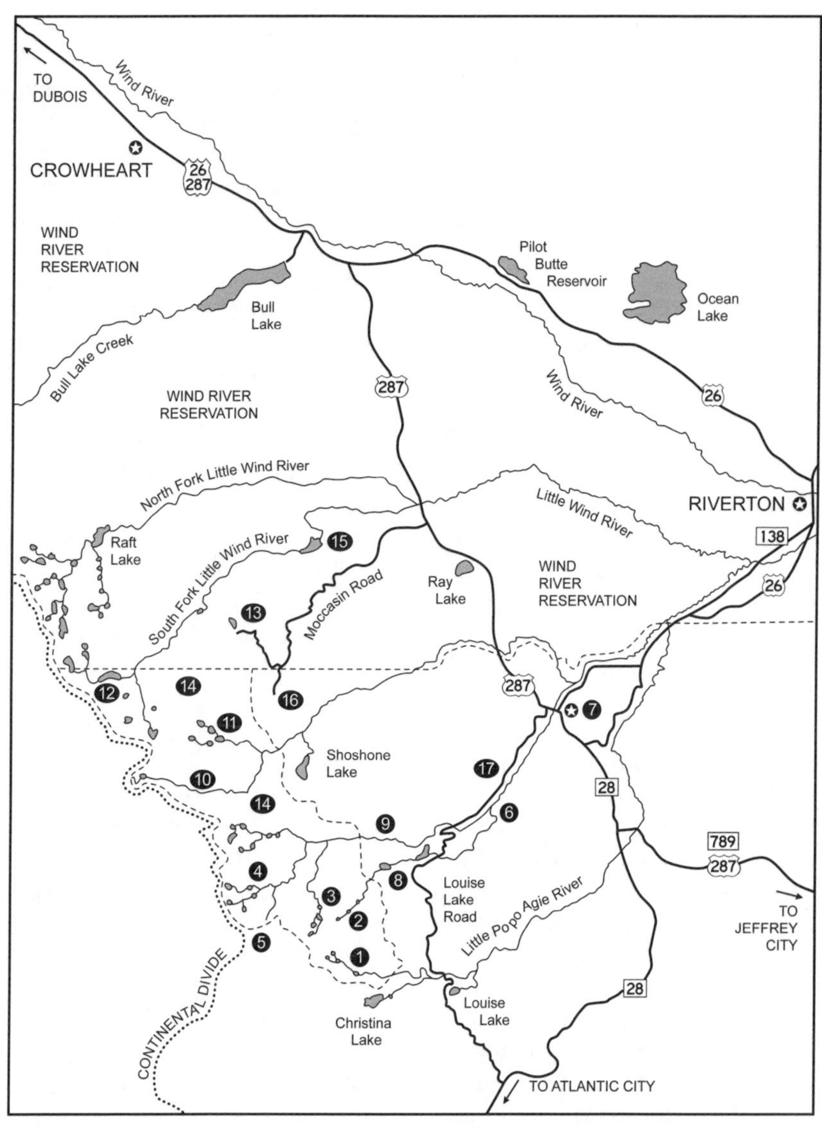

1. Atlantic Creek
2. Roaring Fork
3. Stough Lakes
4. Tayo Creek
5. Sweetwater Gap
6. Sinks Canyon
7. Lander
8. Worther Meadows Reservoir
9. Middle Popo Agie River
10. North Popo Agie River
11. Smith Lake
12. Graves Lake
13. Moccasin Lake
14. Popo Agie Wilderness

(9,890 ft; 7 ac) which is good for small brook and rainbow.

At the top of the North Fork Popo Agie drainage is **Bear Lake** (also known as **Lower Lizard Head Lake**) (10,540 ft; 25 ac) with good cutthroat fishing, and **Lonesome Lake** (10,167 ft; 30 ac) with 12-inch cutthroat and small brook. Above Lonesome Lake is **Hidden Lake** (11,000 ft; 6 ac), which is stocked with golden/rainbow crosses. The lakes are 13 miles via North Fork Trail.

Draining into the North Popo Agie from the south, requiring an 8 mile hike from Dickinson Park, are **Long Lake** (10,410 ft; 28 ac) which is barren and **Baer Lake** (9,965 ft; 8 ac), with good fishing for brook up to 2 pounds. **Echo Lakes** (East 10,091 ft; 4 ac, West 10,105 ft; 5 ac) are good for brook.

To the north, and also draining into the North Fork Popo Agie River, is **High Meadow Lake** (10,025 ft; 22 ac). It is reached by hiking from Dickinson Park to the North Popo Agie River and then along the river to the marked High Meadows Trail. Or climb over a rugged saddle, with no trail, from Cook Lake. High Meadow Lake has plentiful cutthroat up to 14 inches. **Cliff Lake** (9,897 ft; 12 ac) just to the south offers the same, plus a scenic, high waterfall. Farther down the High Meadow drainage, **Shelf Lake** (10,126 ft; 16 ac) has grayling.

Take the Smith Lake Trail to **Smith Lake** (9,748 ft; 58 ac), which has small brook, and lake trout to 20 inches. Just above Smith Lake is **Middle Lake** (9,943 ft; 43 ac), with similar fishing, and above Middle Lake is **Cathedral Lake** (9,973 ft; 30 ac), with small brook and 20-inch lake trout swimming below a spectacular sheer rock face at the western end. Nearby **Cloverleaf Lake** (9,961 ft; 10 ac) has small brook, and **Cook Lake** (10,055 ft; 38 ac) has 10-inch brook. Above Cook Lake is **Phyllis Lake** (10,555 ft; 14 ac), with more fishing for brook.

Shoshone Lake (9,490 ft; 460 ac), outside of the wilderness, drains into the North Popo Agie and has brook to 18 inches. It is a 5 mile hike from the Dickinson Trailhead. It is also accessible with a 4 wheel drive vehicle from Lander. Take the initially-paved Baldwin Creek Road west from Lander to Shoshone Lake Road. This rough, also described as terrible, 4 wheel drive road is about a 15-mile uphill drive to the lake. Shoshone Lake and **Shoshone Creek** are closed to fishing from September 1 through May 31. The limit on trout is 2 fish.

From the junction of Sand Creek the North Fork Popo Agie River leaves the National Forest and flows east to the Wind River. The lower reaches of the river form a portion of the southern boundary of the Wind River Indian Reservation north of Lander, where fishing on the reservation is open year-round. Near Lander, there is a marked public access on the North Popo Agie River, on North Second Street, 2 miles north of town.

Middle Fork Popo Agie River

Moving south, the **Middle Fork Popo Agie** emerges from the mountain in pristine Sinks Canyon State Park, 7 miles southwest of Lander. Take the Sinks Canyon Road west from Lander; there is a marked public fishing access off the road. As you enter the canyon, an area between the rise and the fall of the "sinks" is closed to fishing (from the Rise downstream to the bridge on the Sinks Canyon Road).

The river has rainbow, brown and brook in its lower reaches. Cutthroat, and grayling populations increase as altitude is gained. In the canyon a bridge spans the stream and there is a large parking area. The Middle Fork Trail leads to some excellent lake fishing. There are numerous trailheads along this road (Hwy 131), which is known as the Louis Lake or Loop Road, because it loops back to US Hwy 28 near South Pass, south of Lander.

If you want to see big brown and rainbow stop at the "Rise of the Sinks" on your way up the canyon. This is where the Middle Fork Popo Agie rises after an underground journey of less than a half-mile, and the fat trout feed there under the protective eye of park officials.

The most northerly tributary to the Middle Fork Popo Agie River is **Deep Creek**, which will be a 13-mile trek from the top of Sinks Canyon, or a few miles less if you take the Loop Road to the Worthen Reservoir Trailhead at Worthen Meadows Reservoir. Middle Fork Popo Agie River and Deep Creek have good fishing for cutthroat, brook and brown to 10 inches. Pete's Lake Trail provides access to **Pete's Lake** (9,450 ft; 41 ac) and a mile further **Twin Lakes** (9,750 and 9,775 ft; 8 and 9 ac), which are good for small brook. Both are outside of the wilderness boundary.

On the Middle Fork Trail at Three Forks Park, just within the Popo Agie Wilderness Area, take the Pinto Park Trail for access to several lakes. **Pinto Lake** (9,855 ft; 9 ac) and **Park Lake** (10,085 ft; 5 ac) have fishing for small brook. Up high, sitting below Wind River Peak, are the three **Deep Creek Lakes**. **Middle Deep Creek Lake** (10,570 ft; 36 ac) and **Upper Deep Creek Lake** (10,815 ft; 66 ac) have a few golden to 18 inches which sometimes show a curious disdain for man-made lures and flies; the **Lower Deep Creek Lake** (10,492 ft; 31 ac) has golden and golden/rainbow crosses.

Ice Creek joins Deep Creek from the south, and has small brook**.** The numerous **Ice Lakes** (10,415 to 10,465 ft; 5 to 21 ac) are at the top of the drainage. Only three of the lakes have small brook, the rest are barren.

The Middle Fork Popo Agie River, above its juncture with Deep Creek, can be followed by the Sweetwater Trail through Sweetwater Gap to the headwaters of the Sweetwater River. Near the top of the drainage the trail is joined by **Tayo Creek** which drains **Coon Lake** (10,534 ft; 31 ac), with good fishing for golden and cutthroat/golden hybrids to 17 inches; **Mountain Sheep Lake** (10,140 ft;

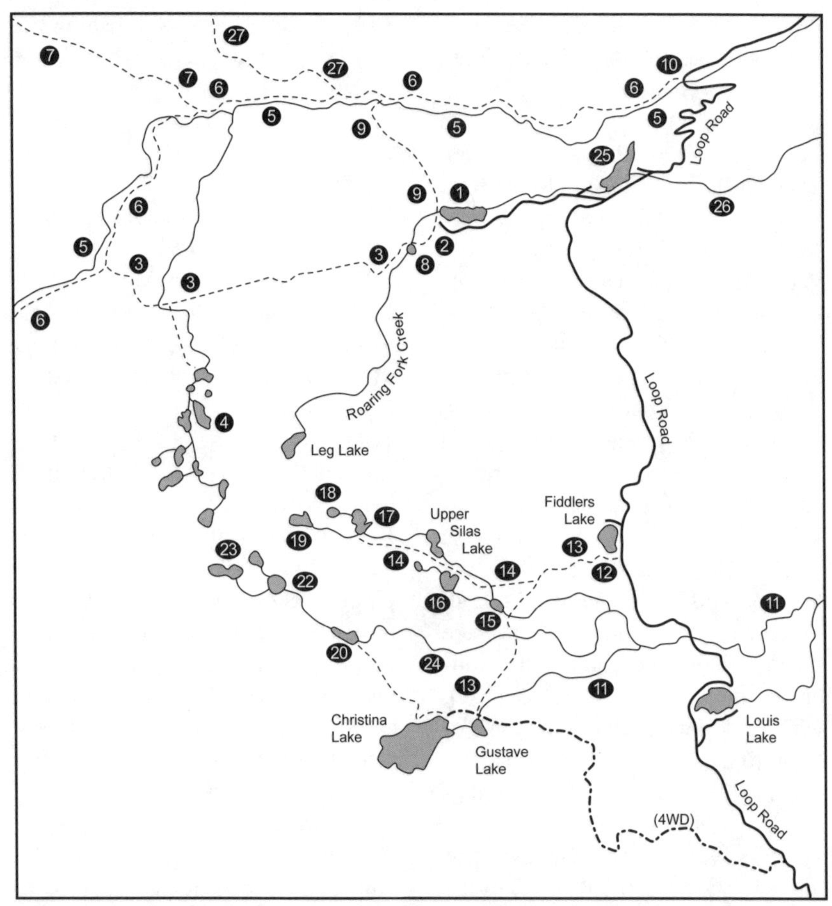

1 Worthen Reservoir
2 Worthen Reservoir Trailhead
3 Stough Creek Basin Trail
4 Stough Creek Lakes
5 Middle Fork Popo Agie River
6 Middle Fork Trail
7 Pinto Park Trail
8 Roaring Fork Lake
9 Sheep Bridge Cut Off
10 Bruce Campground
11 Little Popo Agie River
12 Fiddler Lake Trailhead
13 Christina Lake Trail
14 Silas Canyon Trail
15 Lower Silas Lake
16 Tomahawk Lake
17 Island Lake
18 Fawn Lake
19 Thumb Lake
20 Atlantic Creek Lake
21 Little Atlantic Lake
22 Windy Lake
23 Lower Saddlebags Lake
24 Atlantic Creek
25 Frye Lake Reservoir
26 Townesend Creek
27 Shoshone Lake Trail

20 ac), with the same, and **Poison Lake** (10,047 ft; 22 ac), with fair to good angling for rainbow, cutthroat and cutthroat/golden crosses to 12 inches. Just below the juncture of Tayo Creek and Middle Popo Agie, and off on a creek a quarter-mile north, is **Squirrel Lake** (9,845 ft; 7 ac), which has grayling to 16 inches.

Joining the Middle Fork from the south just below its juncture with Deep Creek is **Stough Creek**, which drains the many fine lakes in Stough Creek Basin. These lakes are easier to reach from the Loop Road, via the Stough Creek Basin Trail from Worthen Meadow Reservoir, than by hiking up the Middle Fork on the Middle Fork Trail. **Stough Creek Lakes** include; **Toadstool Lake** (10,484 ft; 22 ac) and **Upper Toadstool Lake** (10,500 ft; 5 ac) have fair to good fishing for small brook; **Big Stough Creek Lake** (10,520 ft; 28 ac) and **Little Stough Creek Lakes** (10,575 ft; 21 ac) have good fishing for brook and cutthroat. Above them, **Cutthroat Lake** (10,655 ft; 21 ac) has good fish of the same name to 18 inches; **Shoal Lake** (10,900 ft; 27 ac) has excellent brook and cutthroat fishing. **Footprint Lake** (10,645 ft; 8 ac) has cutthroat and brook, **Zigzag Lake** (10,650 ft; 9 ac) is barren, and **Blackrock Lake** (10,902 ft; 19 ac) has cutthroat.

Townsend Park provides access to **Roaring Fork Creek** and **Townsend Creek.** On Townsend Creek is **Frye Lake Reservoir** (8,485 ft; up to 95 ac), located right on the Loop Road. It is stocked with rainbow which tend to be small. Many small brook are also in the reservoir. **Worthen Meadows Reservoir** (8,830 ft; 81 ac) is reached by taking Townsend Creek Road (FR 302) west off Loop Road for about 2 miles. It provides Lander's water supply, and is stocked with rainbow and brook, up to 12 inches. A boat ramp is available. The Middle Fork Trail leaving out of Bruce Picnic Area is scenic and not too difficult to traverse; however, many people prefer to drive up the Loop Road to Worthen Meadow Reservoir and hike from it into the Middle Fork drainage via the Sheep Bridge Trailhead. A short hike up a closed jeep road from Worthen Meadow Reservoir on the Stough Creek Basin Trail is **Roaring Fork Lake** (9,023 ft; 5 ac), a shallow lake with small brook. At the headwater of Roaring Fork Creek is **Leg Lake** (10,525 ft; 36 ac) which is poor for golden to 12 inches.

Little Popo Agie River

The **Little Popo Agie River**, the third and southern most fork of this drainage, is easily accessible in its upper reaches from the Loop Road. Higher reaches of the creek have excellent fishing for small brook, some small rainbow are possible further down from Louis Lake.

Four primary drainages feed into the Little Popo Agie: **Fiddlers Creek, Silas Creek, Atlantic Creek** and **Louis Creek**. Fiddlers Creek drains **Fiddlers Lake** (9,411 ft; 56 ac), which is located 23 miles south of Lander on the Loop Road. It has

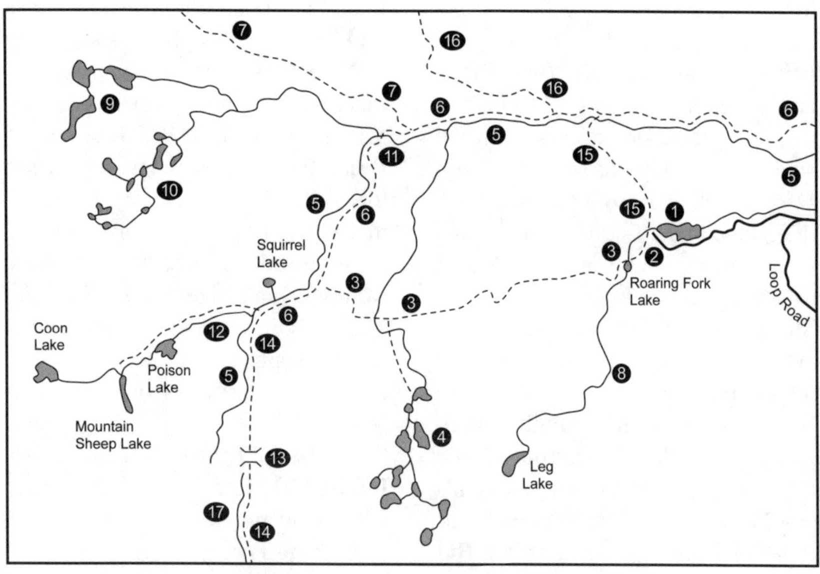

1. Worthen Reservoir
2. Worthen Reservoir Trailhead
3. Stough Creek Basin Trail
4. Stough Creek Lakes
5. Middle Fork Popo Agie River
6. Middle Fork Trail
7. Pinto Park Trail
8. Roaring Fork Creek
9. Deep Creek Lakes
10. Ice Lakes
11. Three Forks Park
12. Tayo Creek
13. Sweetwater Gap
14. Sweetwater Trail
15. Sheep Bridge Cutoff
16. Shoshone Lake Trail
17. Sweetwater River Headwaters

moderate fishing for rainbow to 14 inches and small brook. The use of gas powered boats is prohibited.

From Fiddlers Lake you can take the Christina Lake Trail, which, in 2 miles, reaches **Silas Creek**. Silas Canyon Trail leads up this drainage to **Lower Silas Lake** (9,695 ft; 7 ac) with fair fishing for small brook. About 1.5 miles up the trail is **Upper Silas Lake** (10,100 ft; 24 ac) with 10- to 12-inch brook and 13-inch cutthroat. Still higher, **Island Lake** (10,585 ft; 25 ac) has good fishing for nice cutthroat, and so does **Fawn Lake** (10,695 ft; 7 ac) just above it; **Thumb Lake** (10,980 ft; 23 ac) has poor fishing for golden up to 16 inches. A half mile above Lower Silas Lake on a small stream from the west is **Tomahawk Lake** (10,055 ft; 24 ac) with good fishing for 8- to 10-inch brook. **Little Tomahawk Lake** (10,305 ft; 4 ac) is fair for small cutthroat and brook.

Atlantic Creek, the next drainage to the south, is reached by hiking into the Popo Agie Wilderness from Christina Lake (requires 4 wheel drive) on Atlantic Lake Trail to the south or a tough 7 mile hike from Fiddlers Lake. The creek has cutthroat and brook to 10 inches. **Atlantic Creek Lake** (10,225 ft; 23 ac), 2.5 miles above Christina Lake, has small brook and feisty cutthroat to 12 inches. Draining into Atlantic Creek from the north .75 mile is **Rock Lake** (10,170 ft; 9 ac) with splake and brook to 11 inches. Above it is **Little Atlantic Lake** (10,295 ft; 7 ac), with splake to 18 inches. Up near the top of the Atlantic Creek drainage, 1.75 tough miles above Atlantic Lake, is **Windy Lake** (10,735 ft; 26 ac) and **Lower Saddlebags Lake** (11,015 ft; 14 ac) which at one time were stocked with golden, but are now barren.

To the south of the Atlantic Creek drainage off of Loop Road, Christina Lake Road (4 wheel drive), takes you to the headwaters of the Little Popo Agie at **Christina Lake** (9,948 ft; 340 ac), which has good fishing for 10-pound lake trout and brook to 12 inches. The limit on trout is 6, only 1 can be longer than 20 inches and only 2 can be lake trout. **Gustave Lake** (9,805 ft; 23 ac) is just below Christina Lake, with brook and lake trout. Gustave Lake has the same restrictions as Christina Lake.

At the extreme southern end of the Little Popo Agie River drainage is **Louis Creek** starting near the Continental Divide and rambling 8 miles to Louis Lake. The creek has fair fishing for brook. **Louis Lake** (8,561 ft; 103 ac) is located just east of the Loop Road, 27 miles from Lander. It has lake trout as big as 20 pounds; rainbow, splake, and small brook. A road runs around the southern end where there are campgrounds, boat launch ramps and a lodge.

As the Little Popo Agie drops out of the mountains, there is a good public fishing area located about 12 miles south of Lander off SR 28. Just beyond the juncture of SR 28 and Highway 287 (to Rawlins) turn right on the gravel Red Canyon Road (CR 235). There is a marked fishing

Courtesy of Lander Llama Company

access with a parking area on the left less than a mile up the road, watch for signs indicating public access. Fishing is mostly for brown and rainbow, some up to 12 inches, and small brook.

WIND RIVER INDIAN RESERVATION

The **Wind River Indian Reservation** encompass a large area (2.2 million acres) of the Wind River Mountains' eastern slope, as well as, some big lowland reservoirs and lakes. A large mountainous section in the southwest corner of the reservation, 180,387 acres, has been protected as a wilderness area since 1938. US Highway 26 from Dubois southeast to Riverton runs through the reservation and roughly parallels the Wind River. The reservation, north of the Wind River, is closed to angling and the public with the exception of Boysen Reservoir, Ocean Lake, Lake Cameahwait (Bass Lake), Middle Depression Reservoir, Pilot Butte Reservoir, and the East Fork Wind River. The reservation is the home of the Arapaho and Shoshone Indian tribes.

The Wind River Reservation offers outstanding angling opportunities. The limits and regulations on the reservation differ from those of the rest of the state, a copy of the current regulations should be consulted before fishing on reservation waters. The limit on trout (excluding lake trout) is 5 fish, only 1 can be longer than 20 inches. The limit for lake trout is 4 fish, and there is no limit on brook trout under 10 inches. The limit for ling is 2 fish, walleye/sauger is 6 fish, and there is not a limit on whitefish. A Wind River Indian Reservation Fishing Permit (resident $40, nonresident $80), in addition to a recreation stamp ($5), is required to fish and to access lands on the reservation. For a complete fee schedule and further information write, Fish and Game Office, P.O. box 217, Fort Washakie, Wyoming 82514, or call 307-332-7207. Fishing permits and recreation stamps are available at the following approved locations: Fish and Game Office, Fort Washakie; Lander Ace Hardware, Lander; The Good Place, Lander; The Tannery, Lander; Popo Agie One Stop, Lander; Ethete Store, Ethete; Trout Bait and Tackle, Ft. Washakie; Ancient Ways Taxidermy, Ft. Washakie; Maverik Store, Riverton; Rocky Mountain Sports, Riverton; K-Mart, Riverton; High Country Sporting Goods, Riverton; 789 Car/Truck Stop, Riverton; Basketeria, Pavillion; Borderline, Morton; Crowheart Store, Crowheart; Whiskey Mountain Tackle Shop, Dubois; Trail Town Supply, Shoshoni; The Fast Lane, Shoshoni; Wind river Whitewater, Thermopolis; Canyon Sporting Goods, Thermopolis; Thermopolis Hardware, Thermopolis; T's Kountry Korner, Kinnear; and The Great Outdoor Shop, Pinedale, Wyoming.

Many of the streams and some of the lakes on the reservation are not open to fishing, others, like those that follow have restrictions in place to protect the quality of fishing on the reservation. The North Fork Popo Agie River, Popo Agie River (to Hudson), Ray Lake, and Wind River Canyon are open to year around fishing. Bull Lake, Lower Bull Lake Creek, Dinwoody Lakes, and Dinwoody Creek (from Upper Dinwoody Lake to the Wind River) are open to fishing January 1 through September 30. Washakie Reservoir, Wind River (excluding the Wind River Canyon), and downstream from the confluence of the Popo Agie and Little Wind River rivers are open to fishing from April 1 through September 30. Additionally, all Roadless Area lakes and streams, Moccasin Lake, Upper Bull Lake Creek (Above the inlet of Bull Lake), and the South Fork Little Wind River (above Washakie Reservoir, and the second campground) are open to fishing June 1 through September 30. Boysen Reservoir, Ocean Lake, Lake Cameahwait (Bass Lake), Middle Depression Reservoir, Pilot Butte Reservoir, and the East Fork Wind River (west bank) are not regulated by the reservation and are open to fishing year around.

All lakes and streams on the reservation are closed to boat fishing with the exception of Bull Lake, Dinwoody Lakes, Ray Lake, Moccasin Lake (non-motorized only) and Washakie Reservoir. The use of motorized boats is not allowed in the wilderness and Roadless areas of the reservation, float tubes are allowed. Additionally many roads and trails on the reservation are closed to the public, including roads in the Roadless Area in the southwest corner of the reservation, please respect the tribes and not enter posted/closed areas.

Information about trails, lakes and creeks of the upper reaches of the Little Wind River and the reservation's back country is sketchy, reservation officials recommend the use of an outfitter for anyone unfamiliar with the area, which is remote to say the least. There are a number of access points, consult with the Tribal Fish and Game Department when planning a back country trip. In addition, lakes and streams that are open to fishing change from year to year. The regulations and descriptions give here are subject to change on a regular basis, consult a current copy of the Wind River Indian Reservation rules and regulations for updated and complete information.

About 20 miles southeast of Dubois, a rough West Dinwoody Road leaves US 26-287 near the town of Wilderness and runs south to the **Dinwoody Lakes** (lower 6,473 ft; 382 ac, upper 6,475 ft; 187 ac). Boats are allowed, and may be the best method to catch fish. Fishing is for ling, brown and lake trout. The limit for lake trout is 4 fish, only 1 can be longer than 28 inches. The lakes, and Dinwoody Creek below Upper Dinwoody Lake to the Wind River, are open to fishing from January 1 through September 30 (the creek between the lakes is closed to fishing from April 1 through May 15). Dinwoody Creek above Upper Dinwoody Lake is closed to the public.

Bob Creek enters the Wind River at Crowheart. At the upper reaches of the creek, **Little Bob Lake** (9,775 ft; 27 ac) near the headwaters, has Snake River cutthroat and brook. The lake is restricted to artificial flies and lures only; the limit on trout is 2 fish, only 1 can be longer than 15 inches. The numerous **Bob Lakes** (9,755 to 11,005 ft; 5 to 20 ac) have cutthroat and brook.

Bull Creek Drainage

Bull Lake (5,820 ft; 2383 ac) is located a couple of miles west of US 26-287, about 40 miles to the southeast of Dubois. The road to the lake, Bull Lake Road, is marked by a sign on the highway. Boats are allowed. Bull Lake has big lake trout, brown, rainbow, cutthroat, whitefish and ling. The lake has rainbow and brown to 20 inches, lake trout to 30 pounds, and large ling. The limit for lake trout is 4 fish, all lake trout 28 to 38 inches must be released; and only 1 can be over 38 inches. Above the lake, **Bull Lake Creek** has several miles of quality fly fishing waters for cutthroat and rainbow, and brown in the lower reaches below the lake. Bull Lake and Lower Bull Lake Creek are open to fishing January 1 through September 30. Upper Bull Lake Creek (above the inlet of Bull Lake) is open to fishing from June 1 through September 30.

Several lakes in the high country on the Bull Creek drainage contain fish: **Kirkland Lake** (9,955 ft; 56 ac)

Courtesy of Lander Llama Company

has fishing for lake trout; **Paradise Lakes** (upper 10,195 ft; 8 ac, lower 9,840 ft; 3 ac) have brook and rainbow; **Lydle Lake** (9,935 ft; 14 ac); and **Steamboat Lake** (10,015 ft; 41 ac) have fishing for Snake River and Yellowstone cutthroat; **Hidden Lake** (10,445 ft; 12 ac) and **Hatchet Lake** (10,470 ft; 58 ac) have good fishing for rainbow and cutthroat; **Alpine Lake** (8,950 ft; 171 ac) has cutthroat and possibly a few golden Snake River cutthroat hybrid. These lakes are very remote, hiring a guide is recommended.

North Fork Little Wind River

The North Fork Little Wind River is closed to fishing downstream from Washakie Creek to Fort Washakie. In the higher reaches of the river there are several lakes which offer fine fishing opportunities, including: **Moraine Lake** (10,400 ft; 136 ac) is at the headwaters of the North Fork Little Wind River and has fishing for Snake River cutthroat, and brook. In the area of Moraine Lake, **Lake Polaris** (10,049 ft; 48 ac), **Lake Solitude** (10,520 ft; 98 ac), **Ice Lakes** (upper 10,665 ft; 24 ac, lower 10,662 ft; 16 ac) are high lakes in the shadow of Petroleum Peak. Lake Polaris has fishing for Yellowstone and Snake River cutthroat, and brook. Lake solitude has fishing for lake trout and brook, and the Ice Lakes have Snake River Cutthroat. To the north of the headwater lakes are several more lakes, including **Wykee Lake** (9,835 ft; 42 ac) with Snake River cutthroat and brook, **Lake Kagevah** (10,555 ft; 75 ac) with cutthroat; **Sonnicant Lake** (10,098 ft; 114 ac) is a large lake with lake trout, cutthroat, and brook. Several lakes lie in the tributary to the north, including: **Lake Heebeecheeche** (10,355 ft; 78 ac) has rainbow, cutthroat, and brook; **Movo Lake** (9,360 ft; 27 ac) has rainbow and brook; the large **Raft Lake** (9,150 ft; 314 ac) has rainbow, cutthroat, brook, and lake trout. North of Raft Lake on **Wilson Creek** are several more lakes, including: **Enos Lake** (10,415 ft; 27 ac) with rainbow and Snake River cutthroat; **Tigee Lake** (10450 ft; 44 ac) with rainbow and Snake River cutthroat; and **Elk Lake** (10,580 ft; 40 ac) with fishing for Yellowstone cutthroat. South of Raft Lake are **Trail Lake** (10,590 ft; 54 ac) and **Roberts Lake** (10,735 ft; 101 ac). These lakes have Yellowstone cutthroat, Trail Lake has brook. Below Raft Lake are the two **Twin Lakes** (upper 8,842 ft; 34 ac, lower 8,840 ft; 16 ac) which have rainbow, brook, and lake trout. To the south **Shoshone Lake** (10,320 ft; 21 ac) has good fishing for brook.

South Fork Little Wind River

At the headwaters of the South Fork Little Wind River are several lakes to the south, which are outside of the reservation and in the Popo Agie Wilderness. The river flows north and into the reservation where it drains several lakes as it makes its way down to the Wind River. Inside the reservation, requiring a reservation permit, northwest of Graves

Lake is **Baptiste Lake** (10,820 ft; 172 ac) which has excellent fishing for cutthroat. Downstream from Graves Lake and to the east is **Vernal Lake** (9,925 ft; 9 ac) with fair fishing for Yellowstone cutthroat; and **Lost Lake** (9,840 ft; 15 ac) with fair fishing for cutthroat and brook.

Accessible by vehicle is **Moccasin Lake** (9,514 ft; 92 ac), which is open from June 1 until September 30, has lake trout and cutthroat. Boats are allowed on the lake, but motors are prohibited. From Highway 287 near the town of Fort Washakie, just north of the Hines General Store and the Wind River Trading Company, the signed and paved Trout Creek Road goes west for 5 miles, watch for a gravel road (Moccasin Road) signed for Moccasin Lake. Take this road up some steep switchbacks almost 20 miles to the signed Moccasin Lake Road, and 3.5 miles to the northwest to the lake. Nearby **Little Moccasin Lake** (9,350 ft; 14 ac) has Snake River cutthroat and lake trout, **Shoe Lake** (9,321 ft; 23 ac) has Snake River cutthroat, and **Long Lake** (9,320 ft; 10 ac) with Snake River cutthroat and brook.

Farther north, near the reservation headquarters at Fort Washakie, are **Washakie Reservoir** (6,339 ft; 296 ac) 6 miles west of the highway, and **Ray Lake** (5,526 ft; 459 ac) adjacent to US 287 south of Fort Washakie 4.5 miles. Washakie Reservoir has brook and cutthroat. Washakie Reservoir is open to fishing from April 1 through September 30. To reach the reservoir, from Highway 287 at Fort Washakie, take the paved South Fork Road west about 6 miles, then 3 miles by good gravel road to the reservoir. The South Fork Little Wind River, above Washakie Reservoir and the second campground is open to fishing from June 1 through September 30. Ray Lake has fishing for cutthroat, rainbow, brown, and walleye. A boat ramp is available. Ray Lake is open to year-round fishing,

EASTERN RESERVOIRS

Pilot Butte Reservoir (5,475 ft; 846 ac) is one of several large reservoirs which are along the Wind River as it makes its way through the windy flats of the Wind River Indian Reservation. Pilot Butte Reservoir offers fair fishing for rainbow, ling and yellow perch. Rainbow average 14 inches, although some are caught much larger. Wind can be a factor at Pilot Butte Reservoir. Ice fishing for large ling can be especially good during the winter. Pilot Butte Reservoir is along Hwy 26 at the town of Morton.

Ocean Lake (5,233 ft; 6162 ac) gathers water from the Riverton Reclamation Project before draining into Fivemile Creek, which runs into Boysen Reservoir. US 26 and CR 476 provides paved access on the south side of the lake, or CR 133 and 134 on the north and west sides. There are four boat launching and camping areas around the lake and a resort on the south side. From the middle of May until July this shallow lake has good fishing for walleye, yellow perch, crappie, and ling. The once-famous black crappie fishery here has declined, apparently due to the heavy siltation; with most now averaging 8 inches. Walleye range from 8 to 20 inches. Ocean Lake lies within the reservation and is managed by the Wyoming Game and Fish Department. Ocean Lake is open year round to public fishing and is not subject to reservation regulations.

Meeting the Wind River as it winds around Riverton, the **Little Wind River** and its tributaries are affected by irrigation drawdowns and offer sporadic fishing in the spring for rainbow and brook, sauger in July and August. There is some public fishing on the north side of the river at the town of Riverton, the south bank and the rest of the river requires a reservation permit to fish.

Boysen Reservoir

The Wind River turns north near the town of Riverton and empties into Boysen Reservoir. **Boysen Reservoir** (4,724 ft, 19,000 ac) and State Park collects water from the Wind River drainage, Boysen dam backs the water up behind the Owl Creek Mountain Range. The reservoir has an electricity generating station and stores water for irrigation, but it has become a popular recreation area for boaters and anglers. Walleye, perch, sauger, crappie, ling, catfish, bass, rainbow and brown inhabit the lake. Rainbow are up to 24 inches. Walleyes have been

Courtesy of Lander Llama Company

caught as large as 17 pounds. Most of the good fishing is in June and July, by trolling lures from boats. Boysen Reservoir is open to winter ice fishing, primarily for ling, perch, and walleye. The reservoir lies within the reservation and is managed by the Wyoming Game and Fish Department. Boysen Reservoir is open year round to public fishing and is not subject to reservation regulations.

US 20, from Shoshoni to Thermopolis, runs along the eastern side of the lake. Boat launching facilities are available on both sides of the lake, and campgrounds are on the east side. There also are two resorts on the lake.

West of Boysen Reservoir is **Lake Cameahwait** (4,820 ft; 464 ac) (better known as **Bass Lake**) with rainbow, yellow perch and largemouth bass. Fishing is fair for yellow perch and with bass ranging from 5 to 6 pounds. Daily limit on bass is 2 fish; of which only one may be over 15 inches, and all bass 10 to 15 inches must be released. A well-marked gravel Bass Road goes north from US 26, 5 miles west of Shoshoni to Lake Cameahwait and the west shore of Boysen Reservoir. Lodging is available and boating is allowed. **Middle Depression Reservoir** (4,945 ft; 116 ac) is west of Cameahwait via Bass Lake and Sand Mesa roads. Fishing is fair for rainbow and brown, some larger but most average 12 inches. The limit on trout is 3 fish, only 1 can be longer than 15 inches. **Sand Mesa Reservoirs #1 and #2,** listed in the Wyoming Fishing Regulations no longer offer any fishing opportunities due to lack of water.

WIND RIVER CANYON

After filling Boysen Reservoir the Wind River rambles over 10 miles through the deep **Wind River Canyon**. The sheer canyon walls are carved out of the Owl Creek Mountains by the swift Wind River. Floating is done through the canyon, but is not recommended without an experienced outfitter or guide. Highways 20 and 789 follow the river through the canyon, which is mostly on the Wind River Indian Reservation. A reservation permit is required to fish on the reservation. Private property is also encountered on the river, do not trespass on others property. Good fishing is found throughout the canyon for rainbow and brown to 22 inches, with most averaging 14 inches. Cutthroat are occasionally stocked in the 12 inch range. Walleye and ling are present as well; walleye average 16 inches and the ling are caught to 28 inches. Fishing is most productive in the early spring as moss fills the river in the summer. The Wind River exits the canyon at Wedding of the Waters where it takes on its new name - the Bighorn River. The Bighorn River and its creeks and lakes are discussed in the chapter on the Bighorn River.

BIGHORN RIVER

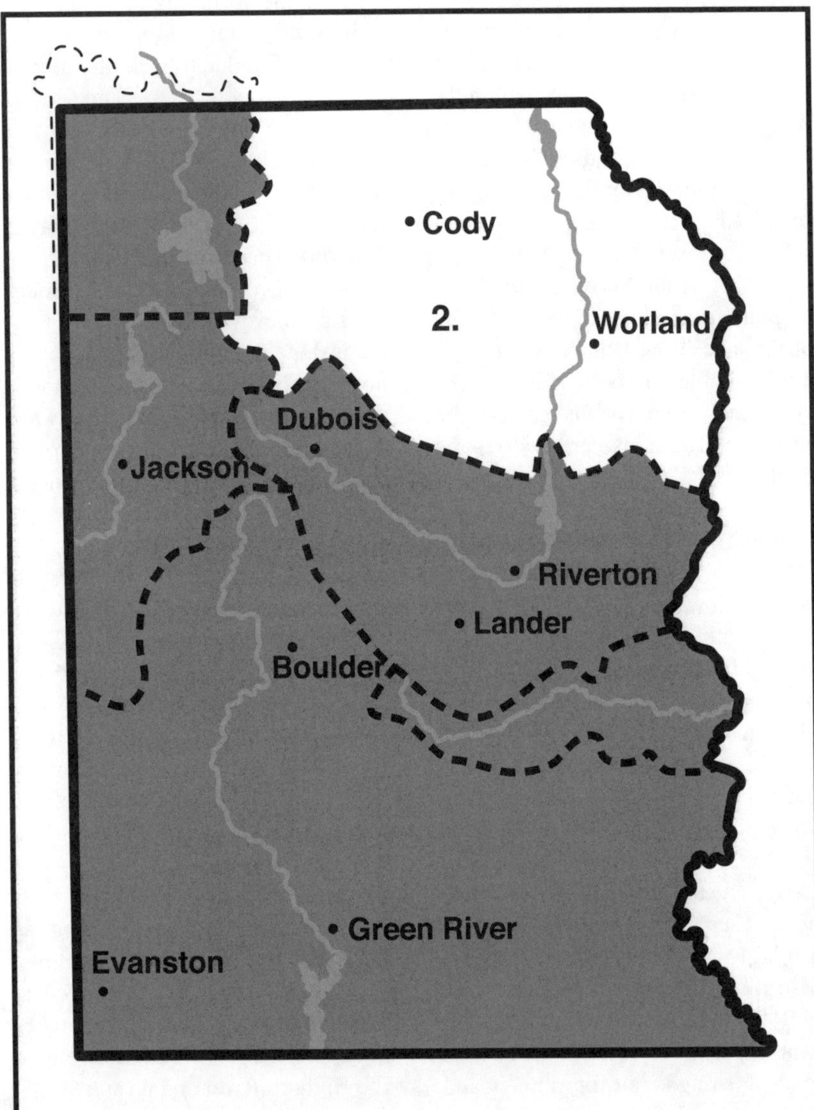

2. Bighorn River

BIGHORN RIVER

The Wind River undergoes some changes when it turns north from the town of Riverton and heads into Boysen Reservoir. It has a new direction - heading north instead of southeast. It has a different setting—after rushing clear from its snowy, mountainous beginning, it surges muddy and murky into a broad, arid plain. And finally, it gets a new name - the **Bighorn River**. The changes take place after the river leaves Boysen Reservoir and tumbles through the Owl Creek Mountains in Wind River Canyon.

Where the river emerges from the canyon south of the town of Thermopolis is called, " the Wedding of the Waters". The Shoshone Indian Tribe called the river "the Wind". The Crow Indians called it "the Bighorn." Hence, the Wedding of the Waters refers to where two "waters wed." This part of the river, north to the Wyoming-Montana border, is less known for its fishing than the Wind River. The fish are different too, second only to rainbow, many ling (burbot) are caught in this fishery. Sundry strains of cutthroat and brown, as well as, catfish are caught in the river.

The Bighorn River is one of Wyoming's most accessible rivers. From the town of Shoshoni, US 20 follows the river through the Wind River Canyon and north to the town of Greybull. There, US 310 leads to roads going to Bighorn Lake. To the west is the town of Cody, the thriving outfitting and recreation center in the Shoshone River area, and good fishing country.

As the Bighorn runs north it drains the west side of the Bighorn Mountains, which have some good lakes feeding into Shell Creek, Nowood Creek and other streams. More renowned are drainages flowing from the west out of the Absaroka Mountains, the Greybull River, North Fork Shoshone River, South Fork Shoshone River and the Clarks Fork Yellowstone River. The Clarks Fork Yellowstone River disdains an early union with the Bighorn River, turns northward into Montana and joins the Yellowstone River near Billings, Montana.

The Bighorn River runs north from the Wedding of the Waters through the towns of Thermopolis and Worland. It then empties into Bighorn Lake (also called Yellowtail Reservoir) in Bighorn Canyon National Recreation Area on the Montana-Wyoming border. There is good to excellent fishing and easy access to the river from the mouth of Wind River Canyon to SR 172. Rainbow average 12 inches, but some to 24 inches are caught. Occasionally, large brown are caught as well. Ling are plentiful and are usually caught with minnows. There are small populations of smallmouth bass and yellow perch. Cutthroat are stocked between Wind River Canyon and Worland. Moss and algae sometimes accumulate in the river during summer months, but it has little effect on the fish, just the fishing.

BIGHORN RIVER HEADWATERS

The uppermost section of the Bighorn River is a popular float-fishing destination. Floaters use the first put-in at the Wedding of the Waters Access, which is 4 miles south of the town of Thermopolis along Highway 20, and pull out 7 miles downstream at The Terraces (at Hot Springs State Park). The float is about 7 miles and takes between 3.5 and 4.5 hours. Thermopolis Bridge Access Area, located in East Thermopolis on East Broadway Street, provides bank fishing on both sides of the Bighorn River. Kirby Ditch Access, 2.5 mile down river below Hot Springs State Park, provides bank fishing along the Bighorn River. Floaters should be cautioned around Kirby Ditch, portage is necessary around the ditch diversion. To reach Kirby Ditch Access by vehicle travel north of Hot Springs State Park 2.7 miles on Upper East River Road (CR 8). Below The Terraces the next put-in/take-out is 6 miles down river at McCarthy Access Area. This is a small and difficult boat ramp, many choose to float on down a tenth of a mile to the Wakely Access. McCarthy Access is 0.75 mile north of Kirby Ditch, also on the Upper East River Road. Wakely Access, on the west side of the river, is directly below McCarthy Access. The float from The Terraces to the Wakely Access covers about 6.25 miles, which takes around 4 hours to complete. To reach the access from the town of Thermopolis, take Highway 20 north to Shaffer Drive, the access is 1 mile to the east 0.5 miles past the Wakely Ranch. Shaffer, Longwell, and Marino accesses provide bank fishing along the river, because boat launching is too difficult floaters go on down to the Skelton Access. Shaffer and Longwell accesses are located off Sunnyside Lane (CR 27), Marino Access is located off Black Mountain Road (SR 172). Floaters should be cautioned, below the Wakely Access at the Lucerne Pump Diversion, portage is required. Below the Wakely Access the next put-in/take-out is 5.25 miles down river at the Skelton Access Area. The float takes between 4 and 5 hours to complete. To reach the Skelton Access from Highway 20 at the town of Lucerne, take SR 172 (Black Mountain Road) east for 1 mile to Skelton Road (CR 21). On Skelton Road the boat ramp is just past a mile on the left, Sorenson Access Area is a tenth of a mile further on this same road. The Bighorn River from wedding of the waters downstream to the Black Mountain Road Bridge (County Road 15-172), the limit on trout is 3 fish, only 1 can be longer than 18 inches.

The Bighorn River below the Sorenson Access is not as productive as those waters upstream. The water starts to warm making a change from a cold water fishery to a warm water one. Expect less trout and more catfish, sauger, and ling. From Sorenson Access to Winchester Dam, 12 miles down river, the fishing and floating on the Bighorn River is poor and not recommended, and is further complicated by the fact there is not a public landing all the way to the town of Worland. For those choosing to float the river, a portage must be made at the Winchester Dam (Upper Hanover Canal). The fishing improves slightly in the 11.25 miles from Winchester Dam to Robertson Dam, but again there is no public access to the river. Robertson Dam also requires a portage and 6 hour float from Winchester Dam. Below Robertson Dam the next put-in/take-out is at Worland Riverside Park, on the west side of the town of Worland. The float from Robertson Dam takes about 5 hours and covers around 9 miles, a portage must be made 4 miles downstream at the Lower Hanover Canal Diversion.

BIGHORN RIVER HEADWATER TRIBUTARIES

The headwaters of the Bighorn River start at the "Wedding of the Waters" below Wind River Canyon and flow northward to the Wyoming-Montana border. The tributaries that drain into the Bighorn River come from several miles away, from the Absaroka Mountains to the west and the Bighorn Mountain Range to the east.

Below the Wedding of the Waters and the start to the Bighorn River, **Buffalo Creek** trickles in from the east. Lower reaches of the creek do not offer much in the way of fishing, but higher up, around Copper Mountain some cutthroat and small brook are present. All lakes, streams and ponds within the Buffalo Creek drainage are closed to fishing from September 1 to April 30.

Between Boysen Reservoir and the town of Thermopolis, **Owl Creek, Cottonwood Creek** and **Gooseberry Creek** flow from the west joining the Bighorn River. All three are only fair fisheries for small brook. Owl Creek and South Fork Owl Creek are the northern boundary for the Wind River Indian Reservation. **Anchor Reservoir** (6,405 ft; 174 ac) is barren, it has not been able to hold water and is used only as an irrigation reservoir.

Nowood River enters the Bighorn River at the town of Manderson, after draining most of the southern Bighorn Mountain Range. The upper reaches are known as **Nowood Creek.** The river is reached either by driving east from the town of Worland on US 16 to the town of Ten Sleep then south on Hwy 434, or, by coming north from US 20-26 east of the town of Shoshoni on the Nowood Road heading north from the town of Moneta. The most productive fishing is in the upper reaches of this creek where there are small brook and rainbow to 12 inches. Farther downstream the fishing is only fair, with a few large brown around the town of Ten Sleep.

Below Ten Sleep and north of the river is **Renner Reservoir** (4,770 ft; 45 ac). Renner Reservoir, although not much to look at, is a good bass producer. Hybrid sunfish up to a pound are also in the reservoir. The limit for largemouth bass is 6 fish; only 2 can be between 10 and 15 inches, and only one can be over 15 inches. Boats are allowed but motors over 15 horsepower are prohibited. The reservoir is 6.5 miles south of the town of Hyattville on CR 49, and 3 mile east on Renner Reservoir Access Road. Renner Reservoir fishes best from June to August.

Wyoming Game and Fish has a Walk-in Area lease on the Nowood River 8 miles west of the town of Hyattville on SR 31, the dirt access road is just past where SR 31 crosses the river. Another large Walk-in Area on the south bank of Nowood River is located just to the east of the town of Manderson off of SR 31. Check Wyoming Game and Fish Walk-in Pamphlet for more information.

The lower part of the Nowood River runs low in the summer due to irrigation diversions, however, it has some good size channel catfish. There is better fishing in the upper reaches of Nowood tributaries.

Trout Creek, Deep Creek, Lost Creek, Otter Creek and **Canyon Creek** all have good fishing for small cutthroat and brook. These creeks are south of Ten Sleep and dirt roads generally follow them. These creeks run through a patchwork of state, Bureau of Land Management and private land. Check ownership status and ask permission if necessary before fishing. A good set of maps is essential.

Ten Sleep Creek

Ten Sleep Creek enters Nowood River 24 miles east of the town of Worland on US 16. The creek, for 7 miles upstream of Ten Sleep, is on private land where permission is needed to fish for cutthroat and rainbow averaging 9 to 11 inches, and brown averaging 12 inches. Below the town of Ten Sleep, Hwy 16 follows the creek where there are a few Wyoming Game and Fish Public Access areas, watch for signs indicating public access.

Seven miles into Bighorn National Forest is the confluence of **West Ten Sleep Creek** and **East Ten Sleep Creek,** which have fair fishing for 8- to 10-inch brook. US 16 is a good road which, consequently, provides for heavy fishing pressure. Stay on Hwy 16 (3 miles along the east fork) to reach **Meadowlark Lakc** (8,468 ft; 182 ac), which has good fishing for rainbow 11 to 18 inches and some brown, cutthroat and brook up to 14 inches. Fishing pressure at Meadowlark Lake is very high. In the fall, trolling boat anglers sometimes pull in brown up to 6 pounds. There is a lodge, several picnic and campgrounds and boat rental.

A rough, 4 wheel drive FR 431 goes northeast 4 miles from Meadowlark Lake to **East Ten Sleep Lake** (9,735 ft; 45 ac), where there is fair to good fishing for cutthroat and rainbow averaging 12 inches, with some larger. A rough trail along FR 430 (rough 4 wheel drive road) and Lake McClain Trail southeast from this lake will take you 5.5 miles into Cloud peak Wilderness to **Lake McClain** (9,720 ft; 6 ac) and **Maybelle Lake** (9,625 ft; 10 ac), with cutthroat averaging 12 inches. Maybelle Lake may have larger fish. These lakes also can be reached by a

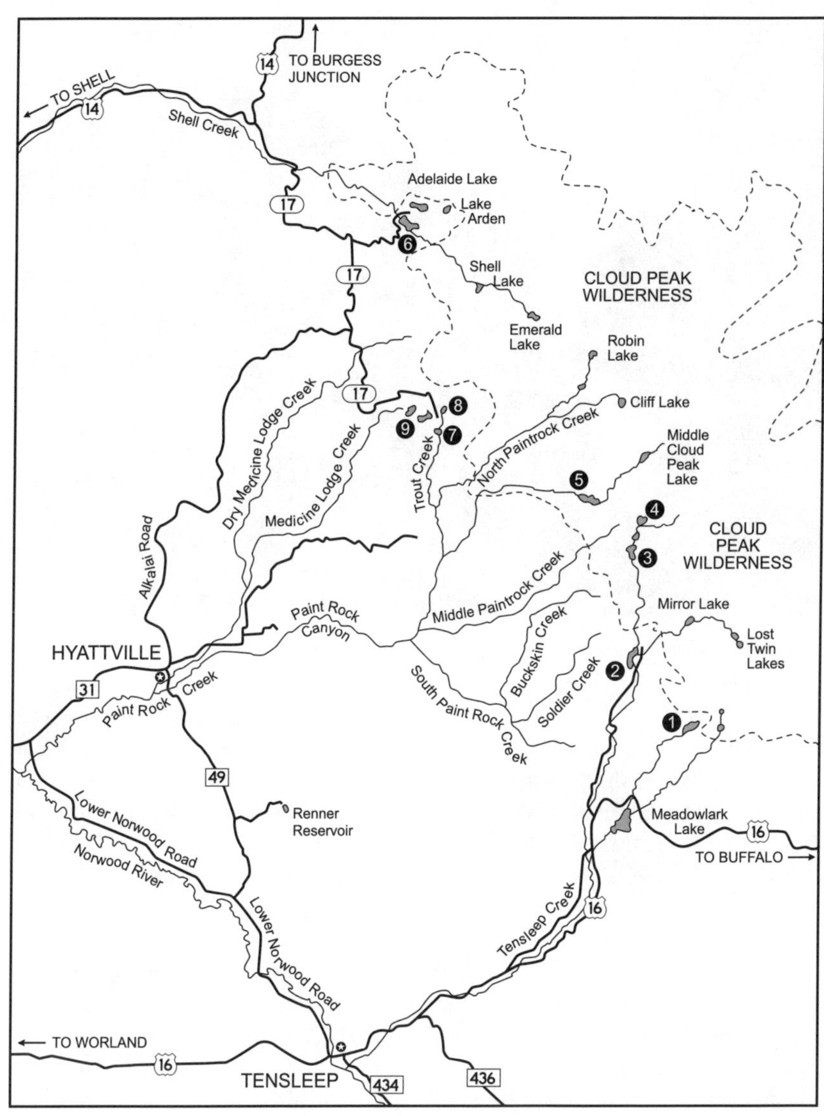

1 East Tensleep Lake
2 West Tensleep Lake
3 Lake Helen
4 Mistymoon Lake
5 Lake Solitude
6 Shell Reservoir
7 Lower Paintrock Lake
8 Upper Paintrock Lake
9 Upper and Lower Medicine Lodge Lakes

Rob Yingling/Bighorn Web Design Photo

4 wheel drive road/trail called the Baby Wagon Road. This road heads north off US 16 about 2 miles east of Meadowlark Lake. Use FR 422 and FR 419 (4 wheel drive roads), must hike the last 4.5 miles to the Maybelle and McClain lakes. Maps are a must to find these lakes.

West Ten Sleep Lake

A dirt FR 27 runs up **West Ten Sleep Creek** about 7 miles to **West Ten Sleep Lake** (9,075 ft; 42 ac), which has a campground and fair fishing for brook averaging 10 inches. Boats without motors are allowed on the lake. The road passes **Bear Lake** (8,665 ft; 7 ac) which is barren. From the West Ten Sleep Trailhead, on the east side of West Ten Sleep Lake, take the Middle Ten Sleep Trail (TR 65) northeast for 4 miles up **Middle Ten Sleep Creek** to **Mirror Lake** (9,635 ft; 11 ac) in the Cloud Peak Wilderness Area. The lake has fair to good fishing for rainbow from 14 to 18 inches, 12-inch brook and lake trout to 22 inches early in the season. Another 2 miles upstream on the Lost Twin Lakes Trail are the **Lost Twin Lakes. Upper Lost Twin Lake** (10,380 ft; 32 ac) is good for golden averaging 11 inches and the **Lower Lost Twin Lake** (10,335 ft; 29 ac) is good for Yellowstone cutthroat averaging 10 inches.

Hike north the West Ten Sleep Trailhead, from West Ten Sleep Lake, 4.5 miles on the Mistymoon Trail (TR 63) to **Lake Helen** (9,968 ft; 45 ac). Lake Helen has good fishing for small brook. The lake itself is 0.75 mile within the wilderness area. A mile north of Lake Helen, on the Mistymoon Trail, is **Lake Marion** (10,027 ft; 12 ac) with good fishing for small brook; one mile further is **Mistymoon Lake** (10,236 ft; 28 ac) with good fishing for brook 6 to 10 inches. Florence Pass Trail leads from Mistymoon Lake less than a mile east to the **Fortress Lakes** (lower 10,470 ft; 6 ac, upper 10,515 ft; 2 ac) and **Gunboat Lake** (10,550 ft; 16 ac) with good fishing for golden averaging 12 inches. This trail continues over Florence Pass to Florence Lake on the North Fork Clear Creek in the Powder River drainage (see Northeast Chapter for details).

From Mistymoon Lake trails go west and north to lakes which drain into **Paint Rock Creek**. The upper reaches of the North and South Forks of Paint Rock creeks are good for brook. The creek runs through the beautiful Paint Rock Canyon, which is rated good for rainbow and brown to 15 inches, especially in the fall and spring. The canyon is east of Hyattville on Cold Springs Road (CR 268). Paint Rock Creek Trail follows the creek through the canyon. Access to the canyon October 1 to May 10 is with landowner permission only. From the canyon to the Norwood River the creek flows through private property, permission from landowners is required. Whitefish may be found in the lower reach, brook near the headwaters. Below the town of Hyattville is a Wyoming Game and Fish Department Walk-in Area on the confluence of Paint Rock and Medicine Lodge creeks, watch for signs indicating public access off of SR 31.

Medicine Lodge Creek

Medicine Lodge Creek enters Paint Rock Creek at the town of Hyattville after draining the Medi-

Rob Yingling/Bighorn Web Design Photo

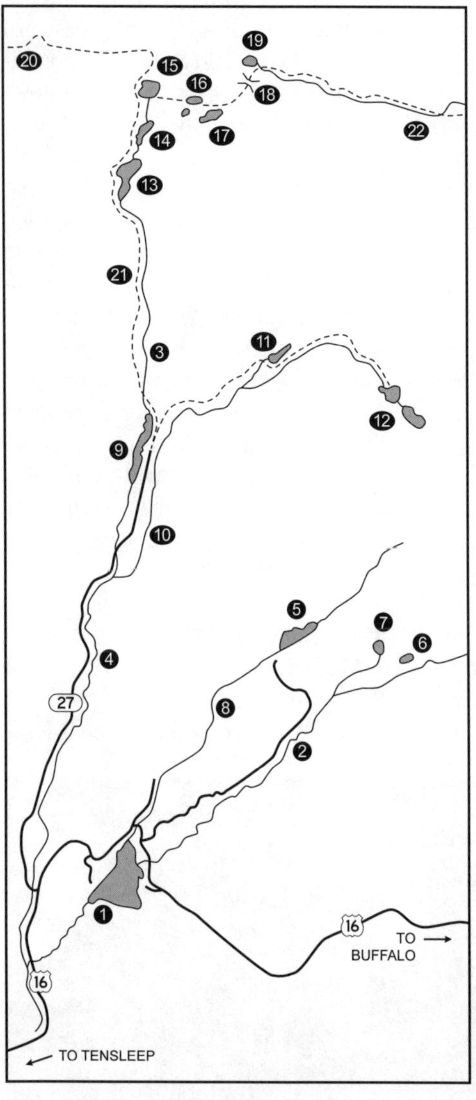

1 Meadowlark Lake
2 East Tensleep Creek
3 West Tensleep Creek
4 Tensleep Creek
5 East Tensleep Lake
6 Lake McClain
7 Maybell Lake
8 Lake Creek
9 West Tensleep Lake
10 Middle Tensleep Creek
11 Mirror Lake
12 Lost Twin Lakes
13 Lake Helen
14 Lake Marion
15 Mistymoon Lake
16 Fortress Lakes
17 Gunboat Lake
18 Florence Pass
19 Florence Lake
20 Paintrock Trail
21 Mistymoon Lake Trail
22 North Fork Clear Creek

cine Lodge Lakes high up near the Cloud Peak Wilderness. Cold Springs Road (CR 268) and FR 52 provides public access to the creek near the lower edge of Medicine Lodge Canyon. There is no defined trail up the creek through the canyon which has mostly brook to 9 inches, with some rainbow, and in the fall brown to 14 inches. Whitefish are also in the lower reaches of the creek. Upper reaches of the creek, with fishing for small brook, is from the Medicine Lodge Lake area.

The Battle Park Trailhead provides access to several lakes on the Paint Rock Creek drainage. To reach the trailhead from Highway 16, follow FR 27 to the north, and FR 24 to Battle Park Trailhead. To the east 1.25 miles is **Lily Lake** (9,547 ft; 17 ac), which has been planted with Yellowstone cutthroat. **Lake Solitude** (9274 ft; 72 ac), within the wilderness boundaries, is 6.25 miles from the Battle Park trailhead, or 9.5 miles from West Ten Sleep Lake (via Mistymoon Trail). Lake Solitude has an abundance of brook, and lake trout. The lake trout average 18 inches with some larger.

Higher in this drainage, accessible by trail to the north, is **Middle Cloud Peak Lake** (10,410 ft; 19 ac), and several other small un-named ponds which can be fair to good for golden. A mile and a half downstream from Lake Solitude, outside the wilderness, is **Grace Lake** (9,302 ft; 13 ac), with good fishing for brook to 15 inches. From Battle Park Trailhead, Grace Lake is a 4.5 mile hike on the Solitude Lake Trail. Grace Lake has a limit is 2 trout per day or in possession; all trout (including brook) less than 10 inches must be released. Fishing is allowed with artificial flies and lures only. **Lost Lake** (9,399 ft; 9 ac) has cutthroat up to 16 inches. Hike 2.75 miles north on the Solitude Lake Trail, from the Battle Park Trailhead, to a spur trail to the west that leads 0.5 miles to the lake.

North Paint Rock Creek drains a more northerly group of lakes in the wilderness area, reachable by trail from the Medicine Lodge Lakes. **Medicine Lodge Lakes** are reached from the north by taking US 14 east from Greybull up Shell Creek Canyon about 30 miles to the Cabin Creek Campground then going south approximately 20 miles on gravel FR 17 (FR17 can also be accessed via Alkali or Red Gulch roads from the west and south). There are several campgrounds in the area. The road passes barren **Round Lake** (8,635 ft; 3 ac) on the way to the Medicine Lodge Lakes. **Upper Medicine Lodge Lake** (9,265 ft; 65 ac) and **Lower Medicine Lodge Lake** (9,121 ft; 39 ac) have good fishing for rainbow and cutthroat from 10 to 12 inches, and small brook. Lower Medicine Lodge Lake is 0.5 miles by trail northwest of the upper lake. Fishing is considered better in the upper lake. Splake have been stocked into the lower lake. Near the headwaters of Medicine Lodge Creek, 4 miles by Edelman Trail, is **Horseshoe Lake** (10,052 ft; 10 ac) which has fair fishing for rainbow 6 to 13 inches. Edelman Pass Trail continues past Horseshoe Lake to Emerald Lake in the Shell Creek drainage, and over Edelman Pass into the Edelman Creek drainage of the Tongue River. Emerald lake is a hike of 5.5 miles from the Medicine Lodge Trailhead near Medicine Lodge Lakes.

Paint Rock Lakes

A half-mile to the southeast of Upper Medicine Lodge Lake, on FR 17, are the two **Paint Rock Lakes**. **Upper Paint Rock Lake** (9,259 ft;

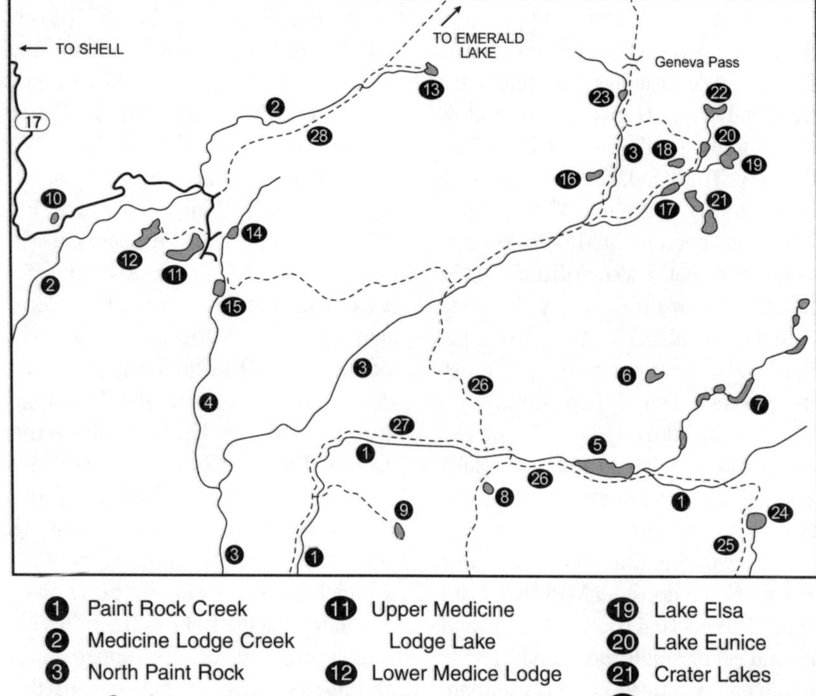

1. Paint Rock Creek
2. Medicine Lodge Creek
3. North Paint Rock Creek
4. Trout Creek
5. Lake Solitude
6. Summit Lake
7. Middle Cloud Peak Lake
8. Grace Lake
9. Lost Lake
10. Round Lake
11. Upper Medicine Lodge Lake
12. Lower Medice Lodge Lake
13. Horseshoe Lake
14. Upper Paint Rock Lake
15. Lower Paint Rock Lake
16. Granite Lake
17. Cliff Lake
18. Sheepherder Lake
19. Lake Elsa
20. Lake Eunice
21. Crater Lakes
22. Rainbow Lake
23. Robin Lake
24. Mistymoon Lake
25. Mistymoon Trail
26. Solitude Trail
27. Paint Rock Trail
28. Edelman Trail

11 ac) and **Lower Paint Rock Lake** (9,180 ft; 15 ac) are on the **Trout Creek** drainage. These lakes support an abundant population of small brook, and some small stocked rainbow in the upper lake. Fishing is considered to be better in lower lake. FR 17 ends at the lower lake and Lower Paint Rock Trailhead. The upper lake requires a hike of 0.25 miles. Cliff Lake Trail leaves the trailhead to the east into the Cloud Peak Wilderness Area, around the 9-mile mark are several high alpine lakes. Along the way, the creek itself has small brook. **Cliff Lake** (9,875 ft; 17 ac) has good fishing for brook to 11 inches, **Sheepherder Lake** (10,010 ft; 11 ac) has brook to 10 inches. Almost a half-mile northeast is **Lake Elsa**

(10,095 ft; 23 ac), and just to the southeast, **Lake Eunice** (10,072 ft; 10 ac); both are good for brook to 12 inches. To the south lie the two **Crater Lakes**, **Upper Crater Lake** (10,535 ft; 38 ac) is barren, and **Lower Crater Lake** (10,313 ft; 22 ac) supports a small population of lake trout averaging 11 inches.

Half a mile from Lake Elsa to the north is **Rainbow Lake** (10,452 ft; 10 ac) with brook to 14 inches. There are numerous smaller un-named lakes in this area with brook to 15 inches. The setting is spectacular. Geneva Pass Trail heads north over Geneva Pass to East Fork Big Goose Creek in the Tongue River drainage. To the west of the trail, **Granite Lake** (9,835 ft; 9 ac) has poor fishing for cutthroat and rainbow. **Robin Lake** (10,060 ft; 6 ac), just before the pass, has excellent fishing for 8-inch brook.

LOWER BIGHORN RIVER

Below the confluence with the Norwood River, the Bighorn River flattens out and warms up, changing the fishing from trout over to several warm water species. Catfish, ling, and sauger now dominate in the river. Sauger are found in greater numbers around Worland, catfish get bigger closer to Bighorn Lake. Sauger average 14 inches, catfish average 5 pounds. Ling to 5 pounds are generally found throughout the river. Trout are taken, but they're not as plentiful here as they are in the cooler waters upstream. BLM public accesses are located near the towns of Worland (Worland Riverside Park, Duck Swamp, and Rairden Bridge), Manderson (Manderson Highway Bridge), Basin (Basin Bridge), and Greybull (Greybull Bridge). Watch for signs indicating public access. There is also a 10-mile stretch of public fishing access just upstream of Bighorn Lake (ML Dike Boat Ramp).

Additionally, Wyoming Game and Fish has 12 Walk-in Area leases on the Bighorn River between the town of Nieber and Bighorn Reservoir, watch for signs indicating public access. Three of the leases are south of the town of Worland. Two are along Highway 20, one at a 0.25 miles and the other at 4 miles (the eastern half of this lease is accessible from SR 432 south from Worland); the other very small lease is another 0.25 south on SR 432. A small lease on the river (east bank only) is 8 miles north of Worland via highway 16 for 7.75 miles, and west on Country Lane 4 for 0.75 miles. To the south of the town of Manderson are 3 accesses to the Bighorn River, one access is directly above the town, the other 2 are along SR 433. One is 3 miles south of town off of SR 433 and Country Lane 52, the other in 7 miles south of town off of SR 433 and Country Lane 55. Directly north of the town of Manderson two small leases, at the confluence of the Bighorn and Nowood rivers, and a third access 3 miles north of Manderson via SR 31 and rough BLM roads provide access to the river. To the north of the town of Basin off of

Highway 16/20 at Country Lanes 37 and 38 dirt roads leave to the east to provide access to 0.5 miles of river. The last access is north of the town of Greybull. From Highways 16/20 travel north on CR 26 for almost 2.25 miles, cross railroad tracks on rough dirt to the east and drive 0.75 miles to the access parking. Access to these areas are subject to change, the current Wyoming Game and Fish Walk-in Areas pamphlet and a good map should be consulted for further information.

GREYBULL RIVER

With headwaters in the Shoshone National Forest, the **Greybull River** flows from the west and joins the Bighorn just south of the town of Greybull. The Greybull River, from the town of Meeteetse down to the Bighorn River is subject to heavy irrigation demands in the spring and fall, and offers limited fishing opportunities. Public access is available off of SR 120 north of Meeteetse near the junction with SR 30. Rainbow in the spring and large brown in the fall are found in the river, but fishing is considered only fair in the lower reaches. Most of lower river is on private property, with little access.

There are 4 Wyoming Game and Fish leased Walk-in Areas west of the town of Otto. Maps and Wyoming Walk-in Area pamphlets should be consulted, the following are only general directions to the Walk-in areas. Area #1 is 14 miles west of the town of Otto via SR 30 to Country Lane 40. Continue 4 miles further on this road, which changes to Lower Greybull Road, to access area #2. Areas #3 and #4 are accessible from south side of the river. From Otto travel west on Highway 30 for 8 miles to County Lane 40, from there go west 3.25 miles to CR 1, and south across the river to County Lane 40 1/2. Access #3 is down the road to the left and offers only a short stretch of the river. Access #4 is west 5 miles on County Lane 40 1/2. Watch for signs indicating Walk-in Areas. Access to these areas are subject to change, the current Wyoming Game and Fish Walk-in Areas pamphlet and a good map should be consulted for further information.

Southwest of the town of Otto, about 5.5 miles, in a very dry landscape is **Wardel Reservoir** (4,260 ft; 128 ac). Walleye predominate, with crappie and yellow perch present. Walleye are plentiful and are in the 12 to 20 inch range. Yellow perch and crappie average 5 inches. To get to the reservoir from Otto take CR 16 south, follow road to the Lane 14.5. CR16 starts out as a paved road, but before arriving at the reservoir, these roads deteriorate to a rough and somewhat bumpy road. Continue on the road above Wardel Reservoir to **Harrington Reservoir** (4,285 ft; 82 ac), which has good fishing for bass to 15 inches, bluegill and yellow perch are from 5 to 8 inches.

Better fishing, and scenery, are found in the upper reaches of the Greybull River and Wood rivers above the town of Meeteetse. The Greybull River headwaters are in the

Washakie Wilderness Area in the Absoroka Mountain Range. To reach the upper end of the Greybull River, follow Highway 290 west from the town of Meeteetse to FR 208 (dirt road) west to Jack Creek campground. The Greybull River Trail inside of the wilderness follows the river for over 16 miles of good cutthroat, and at lower elevations brown and whitefish, fishing. **Jack Creek**, **Anderson Creek**, **Cow Creek**, **Venus Creek**, **Boone Creek** and **Steer Creek** are small tributaries that offer good fishing for small cutthroat.

Wood River

Southwest of the town of Meeteetse, the **Wood River**, some 40 feet wide, flows north into the Greybull River. There is fair fishing for cutthroat, brook and whitefish on the Wood River. Take CR 290 west of Meeteetse along the Greybull River about 7 miles to the Wood River juncture then follow the Wood River south on Wood River Road. This paved, then dirt, road goes some 30 miles to the old mining town of Kirwin, surrounded by private holdings donated to the United States Forest Service in 1992.

Just inside the Shoshone National Forest boundary the **South Fork Wood River** and **Middle Fork Wood River** join the Wood River. Trails go up both forks, which have fair to good fishing for cutthroat and some brook. There are two campgrounds along the main river within the forest boundary.

About 5 miles within the forest, and 2 miles west of Brown Mountain Campground, **Jojo Creek** flows in from the north. It is a steep 4-mile trek up to **Jojo Lake** (11,275 ft; 2 ac) which is barren.

Also draining into the Greybull from the south is **Sunshine Creek**, draining the two **Sunshine Reservoirs**. Road 5XS, off CR 290 about 10 miles west of Meeteetse, provides access to **Upper Sunshine Reservoir** (6,675 ft; 1200 ac). The reservoir usually has good fishing for whitefish, Snake River and Yellowstone cutthroat to 12 inches and splake averaging 15 inches but went dry in 2001. The reservoir should be restocked as water becomes available. **Lower Sunshine Reservoir** (6,212 ft; 900 ac) is downstream of the upper reservoir alongside FR 290. Anglers usually troll with lures and bait, and the fishing is good for cutthroat and brown 16 to 24 inches, plus splake and whitefish, however, with the drought experienced in 2001 only the brown and cutthroat were able to survive. This reservoir should also be restocked as water becomes available.

Wyoming Game and Fish does have a 2 mile leased Walk-in Area on the north side of the Greybull River 11.5 miles above the town of Meeteetse at the intersection of SR 290 (Pitchfork Road) and County Road 5wt. Access to this area is subject to change, the current Wyoming Game and Fish Walk-in Areas pamphlet and a good map should be consulted for further information.

Shell Creek

Shell Creek flows west out of Bighorn National Forest and enters the Bighorn River directly below the town of Greybull. US 14 follows the stream for 22 miles from Greybull to the edge of the forest, and for another 9 miles within the forest along Shell Creek in Shell Canyon. Below the canyon there is fall fishing for brown up to 14 inches, whitefish are also in the creek nearer to the Bighorn River. The 10 miles of stream from the forest boundary to the Shell Creek Ranger Station has rainbow to 14 inches, and some brook. Above the station the stream primarily has small brook. After US 14 turns north, several gravel Forest Service roads continue south by the stream to the wilderness boundary.

At the town of Shell, **Horse Creek** flows in from the north, most of the creek is on private property. Wyoming Game and Fish has a Walk-in Area lease north of town. To reach the Walk-in Area from Shell go north 0.5 miles on Highway 14 to Horse Creek Road, follow this road 2.5 miles north to the lease where there is about 1.5 miles of leased stream.

From Shell Creek Ranger Station there are rough roads leading east, north and south to higher elevation lakes. Drive south past the station for 6 miles on gravel road FR 17 to FR 271. Most vehicles can only drive 0.5 miles on this rough road, 4 wheel drive vehicles can drive another 2.5 miles to **Shell Reservoir** (8,997 ft; 85 ac when full). The reservoir has good fishing for brook averaging 8 inches. Cross Shell Creek at the dam, and hike 0.75 mile on a rough road to **Adelaide Lake** (9,250 ft; 90 ac) which has a few rainbow to 14 inches, and brook to 10 inches. Fishing quality varies with water fluctuations. Another rough mile along the same road is **Mud Lake** (9,250 ft; 2 ac), harboring brook to 10 inches with some larger. On FR 270, from Mud Lake, to the north is **Lake Arden** (9,430 ft; 12 ac) with good fishing for brook to 10 inches.

The Shell Creek headwaters are in the Cloud Peak Wilderness Area. From Mud Lake, pick up FR 280 (rough road to the south), to Shell Creek and Shell Creek Trail. Follow the trail 3.5 miles along the creek to **Shell Lakes. Shell Lake** (9,525 ft; 32 ac) and **Little Shell Lake** (9,545 ft; 4 ac) have good fishing for small brook. Above the lakes the trail continues upstream past the **Lakes of the Rough** (9,960 to 10,250 ft; 5 ac each), which offer good fishing for Yellowstone cutthroat to 14 inches; and 3 miles to **Emerald Lake** (10,240 ft; 33 ac) at the headwaters of Shell Creek. Emerald Lake has good fishing for brook to 12 inches, rainbow somewhat larger, and a few Yellowstone cutthroat. At Emerald Lake, Shell Creek Trail ends at Edelman Pass Trail. Edelman Pass Trail to the northeast drops down into the Edelman drainage of the Tongue River, to the southwest the trail drops down to Medicine Lodge Lakes.

Willett Creek joins Shell Creek below Shell Reservoir, near the creeks headwaters is **Willet Lake** (9,305 ft; 3 ac). The creek is good for small brook, the lake is barren.

Dry Fork Granite Creek, Cedar Creek, Cottonwood Creek, Horse Creek and **Beaver Creek** on the west side of Granite Pass are creeks which may contain some small brook.

SHOSHONE RIVER

Draining Washakie Wilderness, North Absaroka Wilderness, Yellowstone National Park, and Shoshone National Forest from the west is the **Shoshone River.** The South and North forks of the Shoshone River empty into Buffalo Bill Reservoir near the town of Cody, and then flow northeast to fill Bighorn Reservoir on the Wyoming/Montana border.

The **South Fork Shoshone River** runs northeast, flowing 50 to 60 feet wide in the lower reaches of its 50-mile length of mountainous fishing waters. Below the forest boundary the river flows mostly through private land, with a couple of public access points directly above Buffalo Bill Reservoir, and several more up river. Watch for signs indicating public access. The lower reaches of the river have brown to 18 inches, some cutthroat averaging 12 inches, and whitefish averaging 12 inches. South Fork Road follows the stream for more than 30 miles before ending at the Washakie Wilderness boundary, which is just past Deer Creek campground. There are numerous private land holdings for about 12 miles into the forest. Permission from the landowners is required.

Travelling upstream, vehicle traffic ends near Deer Creek Campground. About 3 miles beyond, hikers on South Fork Trail enter the Washakie Wilderness, where the fishing tends to improve. For the next 15 miles upstream the South Fork has cutthroat 12 to 13 inches and brook averaging 9 inches, and possibly some small rainbow. The river offers fair to good fishing. Caddis, mayfly and grasshopper action is good from July into September. Above Bliss Creek Meadows there are mostly small brook.

Hardpan Creek drains barren **Hardpan Lake** (10,300 ft; 12 ac), which is just inside the Washakie Wilderness boundary on TR 766.

About 10 miles upstream from the wilderness boundary, **East Fork Creek** enters from the southeast. Four miles farther **Clark Creek** enters from the same direction. Both streams have good fishing for 14- to 16-inch cutthroat. About 3.5 miles up river from East Fork Creek a trail goes west up **Marston Creek** to Marston Pass and the Continental Divide. To the north are the headwaters of the Yellowstone River, Thorofare Plateau and Bridger Lake, on the border of Yellowstone National Park. Southwest from Marston Pass is the upper Snake River drainage. Maps show several unnamed lakes at the top of the small creeks near the headwaters of the South Shoshone River, these lakes are barren.

Also flowing into Buffalo Bill Reservoir is the **North Fork**

Shoshone River. US highways 14/16/20 follow the river for 45 miles from Buffalo Bill Reservoir to within 2 miles of the east entrance to Yellowstone National Park. The North Fork Shoshone River drainage (with the exception of Buffalo Bill Reservoir) has a limit of 3 trout, only 1 can be longer than 20 inches. The North Fork Shoshone River offers good fishing for rainbow and cutthroat, averaging 10 to 11inches, and an occasional brown during the fall spawning season. Whitefish average 8 inches. The 50-foot-wide stream varies from fast, whitewater stretches to a few deep pools. There are several well-marked public access areas along the river, and several busy campgrounds. A short stretch of the river - about a mile - between the reservoir and the first bridge upstream, the Gibbs Bridge, is closed to fishing from April 1 to July 14. Upstream from this bridge to Newton Creek (inclusive) is closed to fishing from April 1 through June 30. Rainbow from Buffalo Bill Reservoir spawn up the North Fork in April and May providing good fishing above the juncture of **Clearwater Creek**.

Among the better tributaries for fishing are **Elk Fork Creek**, entering the North Fork Shoshone River 6 miles west of the forest boundary from the southwest, with cutthroat to 13 inches; **Fishhawk Creek**, entering from the south 10 miles east of the Yellowstone entrance, has fair to good fly fishing for cutthroat, rainbow, brook and some brown. **Eagle Creek**, entering from the south 6 miles from the Yellowstone entrance, has cutthroat at the lower end and brook in the upper reaches (about 6 miles by trail).

Buffalo Bill Reservoir

Buffalo Bill Reservoir (5,387 ft; 6691 ac) is at the dammed confluence of the North and South Forks of the Shoshone River, 8 miles west of the town of Cody. It is a big and popular State Park offering rainbow, brown, cutthroat, lake trout, whitefish, carp, chubs, dace and other nongame fish. There are three boat launching ramps and several overnight camping areas in the immediate vicinity.

Fishing is usually better in early spring by trolling, and from shore. Lake trout run 17 to 25 inches and 25 pound fish have been caught. Cutthroat run 14 to 18 inches. Some big rainbow and brown are reported, but most average 15 inches. The reservoir water is used for power generation and irrigation causing considerable draw down on the reservoir in dry years. The limit on all trout is 4 fish, only one can be over 20 inches. April 1 to July 14 part of the western side of the reservoir between Rattlesnake Creek and Sheep Creek (on some maps called Spring Creek) is closed to fishing up stream to Gibbs Bridge. Below Buffalo Bill Reservoir the Shoshone River flows through the deep and rugged Shoshone Canyon on its way to the town of Cody. The canyon offers fair fishing for rainbow to 16 inches, most average 12 inches. The lower reaches of

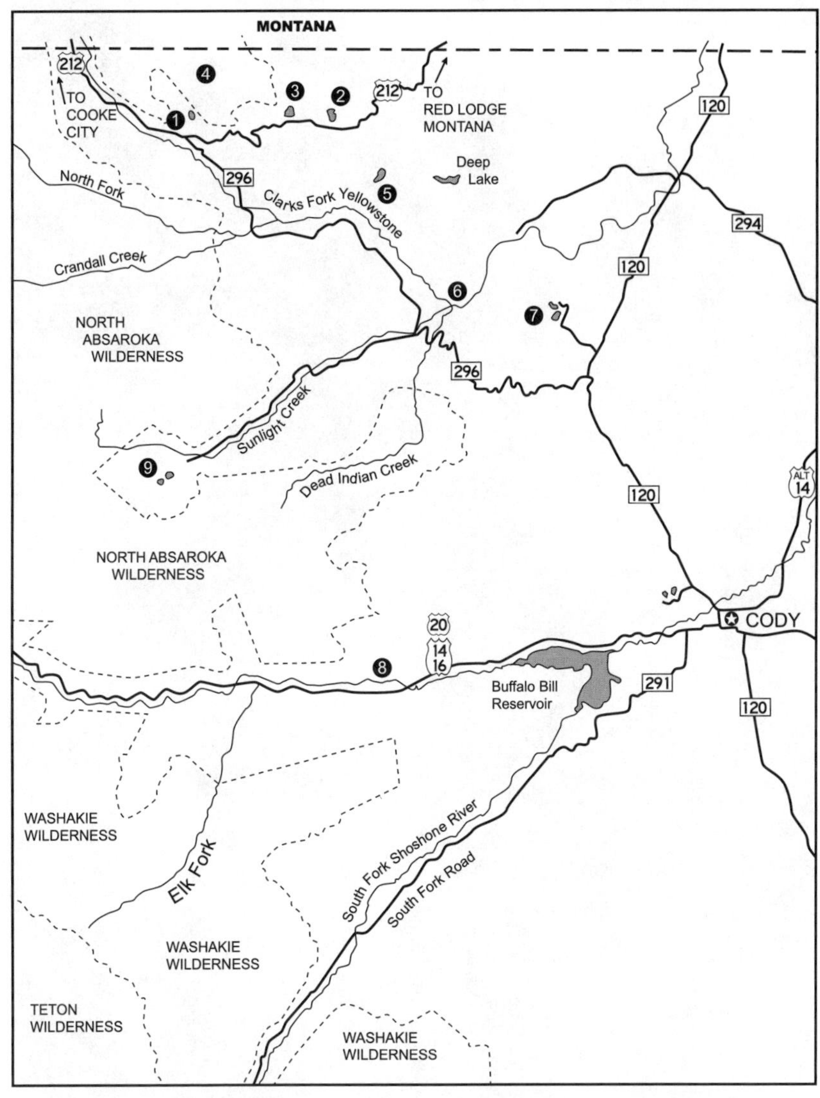

1 Lily Lake
2 Island Lake
3 Beartooth Lake
4 Absaroka - Beartooth Wilderness
5 Sawtooth Lake
6 Clarks Fork Canyon
7 Hogan and Luce Reservoirs
8 North Fork Shoshone River
9 Copper Lakes

Rob Yingling/Bighorn Web Design Photo

the canyon have easier access via CR 2ABW.

Northwest of the town of Cody about 5 miles are the **Newton Lakes** - two very popular recreation areas for swimmers, water-skiers and boaters, as well as anglers. **West Newton Lake** (5,213 ft; 31 ac) has cutthroat up to 2 pounds, most are around 13 inches, and is seasonally good fishing. There is no boat ramp, but small boats are easily launched. Motor-powered watercraft of more than 15 hp are prohibited. **East Newton Lake** (5,212 ft; 29 ac) has good fishing with rainbow, brown, and splake up to 24 inches. There are a few brook to 16 inches as well. The lake is shallow - 16 feet deep - and very productive. Waders are recommended and motor-powered watercraft of more than 15 hp are prohibited. There is a boat ramp. The lake has a special fishing regulation designed to promote trophy trout. The limit is 1 trout per day or in possession; trout less than 20 inches must be released; fishing with artificial flies and lures only.

On the south side of the town of Cody, alongside Hwy 14, is **Beck Lake** (5,085 ft; 92 ac) and Beck Lake Recreation Area. Fishing is for stocked rainbow, cutthroat, catfish, and bass. Crappie and yellow perch are also in the lake. Motorized boats are not allowed in the recreation area. The area receives heavy fishing pressure. **New Cody Reservoir** (5,138 ft; 34 ac), and **Markham Reservoir** (5,086 ft; 127 ac) are heavily stocked with rainbow and cutthroat, New Cody Reservoir is also stocked with brown.

South of the town of Cody, at the headwater of the **South Fork Sage Creek,** in the Shoshone National Forest is **Foster Reservoir** (8,750 ft; 35 ac). The reservoir has brook, but is dry most years.

From Cody US 14A follows the Shoshone River 55 miles, almost completely through private property, to Bighorn Lake. There are a couple of public access points about 5 miles down river from Cody, and a couple more near the towns of Powell and Garland. Additionally there are five Wyoming Game and Fish Walk-in Areas on the Shoshone River between the towns of Powell and Lovell. Consult Wyoming Game and Fish Walk-in Area pamphlet for specifics and detailed maps. General directions for the access areas follow, maps should be consulted for more detailed directions. Area #1, #2 and #3 are southwest of the town of Byron. Take Highway 14A west out of Byron 4.75 miles to Old US Highway 14A, go 0.75 miles southwest to Road 1, then south 1.25 miles to Lane 10 1/2. Area # 3 is along the south side of the river. Follow Lane 10 1/2 west 4.5 miles (as it changes numbers and directions several times) to the Walk-in areas #1 and #2. Walk-in Area # 4 is just southwest of the town of Byron, and area #5 is 3 miles to the southwest of Byron along Highway 14A. Area #5 accesses only a short stretch, less than a half mile, of the Shoshone River. Access to these areas are subject to change, the current Wyoming Game and Fish Walk-in Areas pamphlet and a good map should be consulted for further information.

The upper portion of the Shoshone River holds large brown to 22 inches, rainbow to 18 inches, and whitefish to 15 inches. Most fish are found in waters that are on private property, permission is required to enter private property. The lower river flattens out and the trout are replaced with warm water species, mostly large catfish.

Deaver Reservoir (4,315 ft; 68 ac) northwest of the town of Deaver has fair fishing for rainbow, cutthroat, and walleye. Boats are allowed with motors to 15 horsepower. From Deaver take SR 114 west 2.5 mile, and CR 11-1XB for 1.25 miles north to the reservoir.

Lovell Lakes (3,881 ft; 69 and 209 ac) on the south side of the town of Lovell, have plenty of suckers and carp, but no game fish.

BIGHORN LAKE

Flowing north the Bighorn River fills **Bighorn Lake** (3,645 ft; 17000 ac), also known as **Yellowtail Reservoir**, on its journey out of Wyoming into Montana. Bighorn Lake is one of the largest Reservoirs in the state, backing up 11,000 acres of water in Wyoming and 6000 acres in Montana. The lake fills a narrow, deep canyon where fish tend to hide in the canyon recesses and arms during the hot summer months, and sometimes are difficult to find.

The fish here (most caught trolling) are similar to those in the lower stretches of the river. Walleye, sauger, ling, and channel catfish. Fishing is better in early spring, before fish retreat into the canyon's nooks and crannies, or in late fall. Walleye, averaging 14 to 29 inches, are the dominant fish in the reservoir. Sauger are in the range of 12 to 24 inches. Channel catfish as large as 10 and 15 pounds are not uncommon, especially for night anglers. Ice fishing can be very productive for ling. Bighorn Lake is considered to be a warm water fishery, occasionally in the spring and fall, rainbow and brown are stocked. Bighorn Lake has special limits: trout have a limit of 5 fish (10 in possession); bass, walleye, and sauger have a limit of 6 in combination; channel catfish have a limit of 6 fish; ling have a limit of 10 fish and other game species have no limit.

To reach Bighorn Lake, take US 310 north from Greybull to Lovell, then go east on US 14A. Hwy 37, which goes north from US 14A about 3 miles east of Lovell, provides access to Horseshoe Bend Campground and a boat launch. There is also a boat ramp on the east side where the US 14A bridge crosses the lake.

Below Bighorn Lake, and across the Montana border, **Porcupine Creek** empties into the Bighorn River. The headwaters of the creek are in the Bighorn National Forest in Wyoming. Two campgrounds are near the headwaters, FR 13 provides access to Porcupine Campground and the upper portions of the creek which has small brook. Below the campground Porcupine Creek flows through the narrow, and steep Devil Canyon. The canyon can be accessed from hiking down from the campground, by hiking from Mule Creek Falls, or several rough roads to the southeast of the creek. Fishing in the canyon below **Bucking Mule Creek** is for rainbow averaging 14 inches. The canyon is steep and has rough going for most of its length. **Trout Creek** and **Deer Creek** flow into Porcupine Creek from the north near the Montana Border and offer good fishing for rainbow and small brook.

CLARKS FORK YELLOWSTONE RIVER

Clarks Fork Yellowstone River headwaters in the Beartooth Mountains near the northeast corner of Yellowstone Park just north of Cooke City, Montana. The river then dips south into Wyoming before reentering Montana to empty into the Yellowstone River near Billings. In Wyoming it offers 75 miles of river, some of it in a beautiful canyon that has earned Wyoming's only Wild and Scenic River designation. It is a popular fishing river, but the steep terrain in some sections limits access, one reason the fishing quality is high.

The Clarks Fork Yellowstone River from the Montana-Wyoming State Line downstream to the confluence of Crandall Creek (17.5 miles) offers fair to good fishing for cutthroat averaging 10 inches, and some smaller rainbow and brook. Take Hwy 120 north from Cody for 18 miles, then turning west on a road called "Sunlight Basin", "Chief Joseph Highway", or Hwy 296. Along the way, the highway runs alongside the river's upper reaches. Several campgrounds are along this stretch of river. From Wyoming-Montana State line downstream (about 19 miles) to Reef Creek, the limit is 6 trout per day or in possession; all trout more than 8 inches must be released. Fishing with artificial flies or lures only.

The middle section of the river from Crandall Creek to the national forest boundary runs through a steep canyon, with very limited access. The canyon walls are steep, and the river is 1,000 to 1,500 feet below the rim of the canyon and the road. Trails down Reef Creek and Dead Indian Creek are the two most common approaches to the river in the canyon. Once at the bottom of the canyon, Lewis and Clark Trail roughly parallels the river. The Clarks Fork River in Clark Canyon has good fishing for cutthroat and rainbow averaging 14 inches, with some large fish caught. From Reef Creek downstream to the National Forest boundary (about 19 miles) the limit on trout 2 per day or in possession; only 1 can be over 16 inches.

The chief southern tributaries of the Clarks Fork are **Crandall Creek, Sunlight Creek** and **Dead Indian Creek**. Crandall and Dead Indian creeks, except for the lower reaches, are inside North Absoroka Wilderness. Difficult trails follow these creeks, which offer good fishing for cutthroat 10 to 14 inches in the lower reaches, and small brook higher up. **Swamp Lake** (6,605 ft; 10 ac), on Corral Creek south of SR 296 via FR 128, has managed good fishing for large brook. The limit on all trout (including brook) is 2 fish, only 1 can be longer than 12 inches. Fishing is by artificial flies and lures only, and gas motors are prohibited.

A dirt road (FR 101) runs up **Sunlight Creek** to abandoned mining areas. Sunlight Creek has cutthroat 10 to 14 inches, and small brook near the headwaters. Portions of the creek are on private property, watch for signs indicating public access. The trailhead to the three **Copper Lakes** is 19 miles from Highway 296 on FR 101. Copper Lakes Trail (TR 635) leaves the road to the south leading 2 steep miles to the lakes. **Lower Copper Lake** (9,850 ft; 35 ac) offers good fishing for 10 to 14 inch Yellowstone cutthroat. **Middle Copper Lake** (10,086 ft; 5 ac) offers fair to good fishing for temperamental golden to 13 inches. **Upper Copper Lake** (10,240 ft; 7 ac) may harbor a few golden, but the lake has not been stocked since 1995 and it is doubtful the lake has fish. The hike to these lakes is difficult as it rises over 2,500 feet from the trailhead to the lower lake.

To the north of Cody 21 miles on the west windswept side of SR 120 are two reservoirs, **Hogan Reservoir** (4,840 ft; 43 ac) and **Luce Reservoir** (4,805 ft; 29 ac). Hogan Reservoir produces cutthroat and brown to 14 inches. Luce Reservoir is a good producer of rainbow to 18 inches. Fishing is catch and release, artificial flies and lures only. Take SR 120 north about 17 miles, CR 7RP travels northwest 4.5 miles to the reservoirs.

The **Clarks Fork Yellowstone River** below Clarks Canyon, from the forest boundary downstream to the Montana-Wyoming State Line, has mostly 12-inch rainbow and cutthroat and some large brown. This stretch of the river receives heavy fishing pressure. Big trout are there, but overall it's not a very productive fishery. Whitefish are also present in the 10 to 12 inch range. Numerous signed public access points are located on Highway 120, starting about 24 miles north of the town of Cody. The last access, which surrounds the Clarks Fork Fish Hatchery, is located off of Highway 120 and Old Highway 292.

BEARTOOTH LAKES

Bisected by the Montana/Wyoming border on the northern side of Clarks Fork Yellowstone River is the rugged high country of the Beartooth Plateau. The Beartooth Highway (US 212) loops to the southwest from Red Lodge, Montana into Wyoming, over Beartooth Pass (10,947 ft) and back up again to Cooke City, Montana, provides access to the lakes and streams on the plateau. It skirts a couple of the larger lakes where trails begin to over 100 lakes in more remote areas. Large areas are boggy; some are rocky, but all are very rough terrain. In recent years there has been a phenomenal growth in backpacking on the plateau, only 8 to 10 miles wide and 25 miles long. Brook were brought to the Beartooths by railroad from New England and Pennsylvania around 1900.

West of Beartooth Pass Summit-Lakes North of Highway 212

From the summit of Beartooth Pass west on Highway 212, about 6 miles, is **Long Lake** (9,660 ft; 59 ac). Long Lake is a very popular lake for brook, rainbow, and cutthroat. Above Long Lake near the highway is **Frozen Lake** (10,097 ft; 4 ac) with fair fishing for brook.

Little Bear Lake (9,555 ft; 37 ac) is on the highway a little less then a mile west from Long Lake. Little Bear Lake is also a popular lake with average fishing for brook. Above Little Bear Lake on the **Inlet Creek** drainage is **Lower Sheepeater Lake** (9,815 ft; 9 ac) and a little further **Upper Sheepeater Lake** (9,895 ft; 23 ac) both are good for small brook. Hike to these lakes from the highway or a trail from Long Lake.

Also easy to reach is Island Lake, about 2 miles east of Beartooth Lake and also on the highway. **Island Lake** (9,518 ft; 146 ac) has small brook and rainbow to 10 inches, and a campground. The stream that drains these lakes flows into the northeast corner of Beartooth Lake and is good to very good for small brook. Hike up the drainage to the lakes for beautiful scenery as well as plenty of fishing for small brook. Beauty Lake Trail goes north to several lakes. **Night Lake** (9,540 ft; 40 ac) is the first lake on the trail offering good fishing for brook to 10 inches. On a stream to the east above Night Lake 1 mile is **Snyder Lake** (10,025 ft; 11 ac) which may contain small brook, **Z Lake** (10,135 ft; 8 ac) is another 0.25 miles with fishing for rainbow. Above Z Lake is **Promise Lake** (10,235 ft; 10 ac), which is barren. Further on the Beauty Lake Trail above Night Lake is an unnamed pond which may contain small brook. On the stream coming in from the east is **Heart Lake** (10,295 ft; 37 ac), which is 1.75 tough miles above Night Lake with good fishing for small brook. The small pond above Heart Lake is barren. Back on Beauty Lake Trail the next lake in the drainage is **Flake Lake** (9,620 ft; 17 ac) with fishing for small brook. High above Flake Lake is a large unnamed lake with plenty of brook, small brook. **Wall Lake** (10,175 ft; 17 ac) is 0.25 mile further and **Snow Lake** (10,385 ft; 18 ac) is at the top of the drainage creek. Wall and Snow lakes have fair fishing for brook, with Snow Lake having better fishing. Beauty Lake Trail drops down to **Beauty Lake** (9,435 ft; 81 ac), a beautiful lake with fair fishing for small brook averaging 8 inches. On a trail .75 miles north of Beauty Lake is **Becker Lake** (9,690 ft; 73 ac), a long and narrow lake with brook and cutthroat. Below Beauty Lake is **Crane Lake** (9,350 ft; 9 ac) with brook. Continue following Beauty Lake Trail to the northwest of Beauty Lake to the first small creek coming in from the north, **Echo Lake**

(9,950 ft; 12 ac) is only a short distance up the creek. The lake is fair for small cutthroat. The Beauty Lake Trail continues over a slight saddle into the **North Beartooth Creek** drainage.

Readily accessible, and in the center of Wyoming's Beartooth Plateau area, is **Beartooth Lake** (8,901 ft; 110 ac) north of the highway. The lake receives heavy fishing pressure for rainbow, cutthroat and brook averaging 10 to 12 inches, grayling up to 15 inches at the lake's east end and lake trout as large as 20 pounds. Expect to catch a lot of small brook. There are campgrounds and boat ramps at the lake. Trial 614, Beartooth Highlakes Trail, leaves the north side of the lake to reach numerous high mountain lakes. Follow the trail 2.5 miles to the junction with Beauty Lake Trail. Following Beauty Lake Trail to the northeast 0.5 miles is **Horseshoe Lake** (9,795 ft; 14), almost connected to it to the southeast is **Marmot Lake** (9,794 ft; 2 ac), **Shallow Lake** (9,791 ft; 4 ac), and **Claw Lake** (9,709 ft; 9 ac). These lakes are excellent for small brook, Claw and Horseshoe lakes are stocked with small splake. Below Claw Lake is **Grayling Lake** (9,680 ft; 9 ac) with fishing for brook to 10 inches, but no grayling as one might think. Above Shallow Lake is **Halfmoon Lake** (9,930 ft; 3.5 ac) with brook. Directly to the north of Horseshoe Lake is **Finger Lake** (9,815 ft; 6 ac) with excellent fishing for small brook and splake. Two lakes above Finger Lake, **Lamb Lake** (9,910 ft; 2.5 ac) and **Ewe Lake** (9,915 ft; 9 ac) offer poor fishing for larger brook. Upstream and to the northwest of Finger Lake is **T Lake** (9,860 ft; 11 ac) with good fishing for small brook and stocked splake. The tributary to the north from T Lake passes two small brook ponds before leading 0.5 miles to **Gus Lake** (10,005 ft; 13 ac), which is mostly on the Montana side of the border. Gus is poor for larger brook. The tributary to the east flows 0.5 miles out of **Lonesome Lake** 10,013 ft; 33 ac) which straddles the Montana border with good fishing for brook to 12 inches. The large pond below Lonesome Lake contains brook. Returning to Beartooth Highlakes Trail, the trail continues above the junction with Beauty Lake Trail 0.5 miles to the top of a low saddle crossing over into the **Muddy Creek** drainage. **Trail Lake** (10,025 ft; 4 ac) is at the top, but does not contain fish. Less than 0.5 miles from Trail Lake is **Native Lake** (9,805 ft; 5 ac) with good fishing for stocked cutthroat. Continue on the trail for another 0.5 miles to several large and small ponds, many containing small brook. Continue along Beartooth Highlakes Trail as the trail leads down 1 mile to **Mule Lake** (9,285 ft; 9 ac) and the border of Montana. Mule is fair for small brook and cutthroat.

To the west of Beartooth Lake 5.5 miles on Highway 212 is Muddy Creek Road. Follow the road to the north to the edge of Absaroka-Beartooth Wilderness and the Muddy Creek Trailhead. After about 0.5

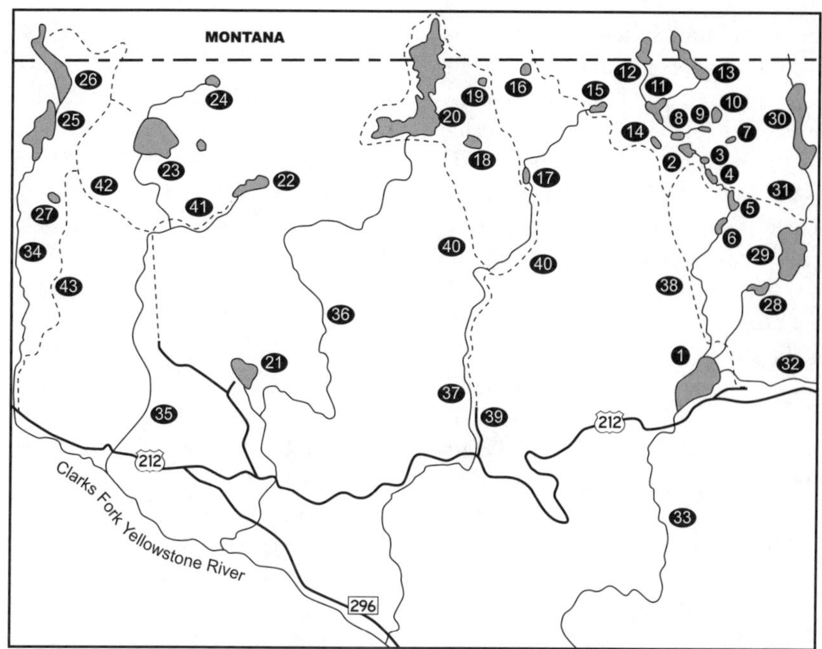

1. Beartooth Lake
2. Horseshoe Lake
3. Marmont Lake
4. Shallow Lake
5. Claw Lake
6. Grayling Lake
7. Halfmoon Lake
8. Finger Lake
9. Lamb Lake
10. Ewe Lake
11. "T" Lake
12. Gus Lake
13. Lonesome Lake
14. Trail Lake
15. Native Lake
16. Mule Lake
17. Barren
18. Elk Lake
19. Teardrop Lake
20. Granite Lake
21. Lily Lake
22. Lost Lake
23. Reno Lake
24. Little Copeland Lake
25. Ivy Lake
26. Big Moose Lake
27. Little Moose Lake
28. Crane Lake
29. Beauty Lake
30. Becker Lake
31. Beauty Lake Trail
32. Little Bear Creek
33. Beartooth Creek
34. Crazy Creek
35. Gilbert Creek
36. Lake Creek
37. Muddy Creek
38. Beartooth High Lakes Trail
39. Muddy Creek Trail
40. Granite Loop Trail
41. Lost Lake Trail
42. Reno Lake Trail
43. Crazy Lakes Trail

miles the trail splits. Take the right hand trail, Upper Granite Loop Trail, 1.5 mile to a pond which is barren, **Elk Lake** (8,905 ft; 11 ac) is situated at the base of a shallow bowl 0.75 miles to the northwest, and is barren. Upper Granite Loop Trail continues past **Teardrop Lake** (9,140 ft; 4.5 ac) with small cutthroat, to the north for access to the inlet side of Granite Lake and to the Montana border. The left fork of Muddy Creek Trail, Granite Loop Trail, climbs up a shallow canyon to the northwest. **Granite Lake** (8,625 ft; 236 ac), 2.5 miles up Granite Loop Trail, offers good fishing for small brook to 10 inches and fair fishing for rainbow and cutthroat. Granite Lake is mostly on the Wyoming side of the border and a smaller part of the north side of the lake is in Montana. Trails around the west side of the lake lead into Montana. **Lake Creek** drains Granite Lake, below the lake numerous ponds dot the map, most of the ponds on or near Lake Creek contain small brook; the creek may also contain some rainbow. Do not expect a trial down the creek.

To the west of Muddy Creek 3.5 miles on Highway 212 is Lily Lake Road. To the north on Lily Lake Road 1.75 miles is **Lily Lake** (7,675 ft; 40 ac). Lily Lake is just outside of the wilderness boundary and offers difficult fishing for brook and rainbow. Brook are small, with some to 12 inches, as are the rainbow, but some do reach 17 inches. Grayling are stocked in the lake and reach sizes to 12 inches. A rough Lily Lake Road continues a short distance to the Absaroka-Beartooth Wilderness. Follow the trailhead north about 1.5 miles to where the trail splits. The right fork, Lost Lake Trail, leads 1.5 miles to **Lost Lake** (8,240 ft; 32 ac). Lost Lake is good for small brook. The left fork, Reno Lake Trail, takes the long route to **Reno Lake** (8,250 ft; 105 ac), where there is good fishing for small brook and some rainbow to 12 inches. Above Reno Lake 1 mile to the northeast is **Little Copeland Lake** (8,615 ft; 8 ac) with good fishing for small brook. To the east of Reno Lake 1 mile on **Crazy Creek** are several lakes with larger fish. **Ivy Lake** (7,975 ft; 74 ac) is a large lake with large rainbow, but most average 12 inches, and small brook. **Big Moose Lake** (8,020 ft; 82 ac), directly above Ivy Lake, saddles the Wyoming/Montana border and offers fair fishing for rainbow, some to 20 inches, but most are smaller, and brook. Below Ivy Lake less then 0.5 miles is **Little Moose Lake** (7,995 ft; 7 ac) with difficult fishing for large cutthroat, some over 20 inches if you can entice them. The limit on trout is 6 fish, only can be over 16 inches; all trout between 10 and 16 inches must be released. Fishing is with artificial flies and lures only. These lakes can also be reached by hiking uphill 4 miles on Crazy Lakes Trail from Crazy Creek campground located on Highway 212. **Bugle Lake** (7,805 ft; 7 ac) is 1.75 cross-country miles from Ivy Lake. No trail for good fishing for small brook.

East of Beartooth Pass Summit

A few lakes of note are on the east side of Beartooth Pass. The lakes are in Wyoming, their waters drain into Montana's **Rock Creek** drainage. **Emerald Lake** (9,740 ft; 42 ac), and a fraction of the inlet of the sizable **Glacier Lake** (9,702 ft; 170 ac) are two such waters. Emerald Lake is good for small cutthroat and some brook, Glacier Lake has very big and wary cutthroat and brook (a Montana fishing license is required). Access to Emerald Lake and Glacier Lake is via roads and a steep hike from Montana. **Mirror Lake** (9,150 ft; 3.5 ac), shown on most maps, 2.5 miles to the east and south of Emerald Lake is barren. As highway 212 prepares to enter Montana on the way to Red Lodge, it passes **Twin Lakes** (lower 9,730 ft; 31 ac, upper 9,756 ft; 36 ac) which are visible from the highway. A trail leads 0.5 miles to the lower lake, where fishing is fair for brook to 11 inches. The two larger ponds above the upper lake are good for small brook.

Lakes South of Highway 212

Several lakes and creek drainages lie to the south of Highway 212 as it dips into Wyoming on its way from Red Lodge, Montana and back up again to Cooke City, Montana. Creeks drain from numerous lakes on the southern portion of the Beartooth Plateau and eventually find their way down to the Clarks Fork Yellowstone River. The south side of Highway 212 is considerablely more gentle than the north side of the road.

To the east of the summit of Beartooth Pass a trail drops down 1 mile to **Gardner Lake** (9,935 ft; 26 ac) for excellent fishing for small brook. Around the ridge to the east 1 mile is **Christmas Lake** (10,090 ft; 26 ac), which has poor fishing for cutthroat around 12 inches. These lakes are on **Littlerock Creek**, which eventually enters **Deep Lake** (7,965 ft; 308 ac) several miles down stream to the south. This lake besides being difficult to get to, is also difficult to fish. It's a tough hike out, but there are brook, 13-inch cutthroat and larger, to make it worth your effort. reach Deep Lake by following the a rough 4 wheel drive road south of Long Lake to Camp Sawtooth, followed by a rough, 3 to 5 mile (depending on the route taken) hike down a steep rim to the lake. An alternative, and as equally difficult, route is from TR 623 from the east. From the town of Clark go west on FR 121 (4 wheel drive), pick up trail TR 623 for a tough hike up Littlerock Creek to the lake. To the southwest of Gardner Lake over a low saddle is **Losekamp Lake** (9,535 ft; 16 ac). The easiest hike to the lake is 2.5 miles along TR 614 from Long Lake, for excellent fishing for small brook. Above Losekamp Lake 1-mile, **Blackstone Lake** (10,100 ft; 3 ac) is tucked up right near the summit of Beartooth Pass west of Gardner Lake. For being so near the road, the slightly larger brook in this lake require a difficult hike from any direction. Below Losekamp Lake is

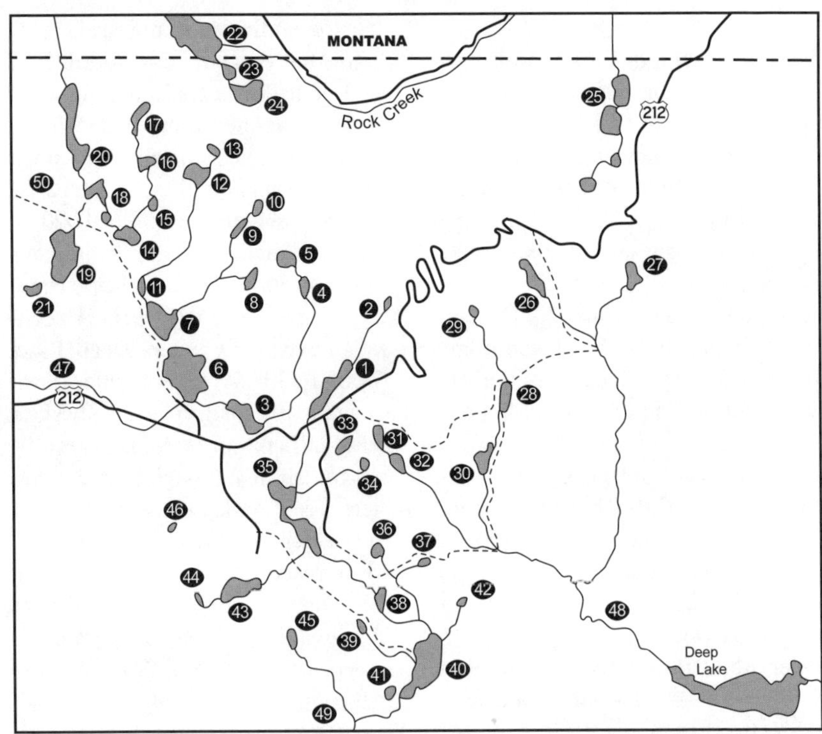

1. Long Lake
2. Frozen Lake
3. Little Bear Lake
4. Lower Sheepherder Lake
5. Upper Sheepherder Lake
6. Island Lake
7. Night Lake
8. Snyder Lake
9. "Z" Lake
10. Promise Lake
11. Unnamed Lake
12. Heart Lake
13. Barren
14. Flake Lake
15. Unnamed Lake
16. Wall Lake
17. Snow Lake
18. Unnamed Lakes
19. Beauty Lake
20. Becker Lake
21. Crane Lake
22. Glacier Lake
23. Little Glacier Lake
24. Emerald Lake
25. Twin Lakes
26. Gardner Lake
27. Christmas Lake
28. Lose Kamp Lake
29. Blackstone Lake
30. Stockade Lake
31. Hauser Lake
32. Solar Lake
33. Rainbow Lake
34. Fort Lake
35. Chain Lakes
36. Dollar Lake
37. Top Lake
38. Duck Lake
39. Lake WGN
40. Sawtooth Lake
41. Sparhawk Lake
42. Little Sawtooth Lake
43. Fantan Lake
44. Cliff Lake
45. Paradise Lake
46. Meadow Lake
47. Little Bear Creek
48. Littlerock Creek
49. Canyon Creek
50. Beauty Trail

Stockade Lake (9,412 ft; 21 ac). Stockade Lake does have 4 wheel drive access, but hiking is recommended to fish for brook. West of Stockade Lake, just 0.5 miles south of Highway 212 and on TR 614 are **Solar Lake** (9,635 ft; 9 ac) and **Hauser Lake** (9,660 ft; 12 ac) with good fishing for small brook and some stocked cutthroat. Directly west of Hauser Lake is **Rainbow Lake** (9,705 ft; 14 ac), a 0.5 miles hike from Long Lake, with good fishing for small cutthroat. To the southwest of Rainbow Lake 0.25 miles is **Fort Lake** (9,672 ft; 5 ac), with fair fishing for brook. Southwest of Fort Lake and south of Little Bear Lake on Highway 212 are the **Chain Lakes** (9,440 ft; 89 ac), which really is only one lake, with difficult marshy fishing for brook. Roads on either side of the lake provide access. Below Chain Lakes on **Canyon Creek**, are several lakes that have larger brook, larger that is than the 5-inch "small brook" found in most of the lakes on the plateau. **Dollar Lake** (9,415 ft; 9 ac), **Top Lake** (9,510 ft; 3 ac), **Duck Lake** (9,410 ft; 12 ac), and **Lake WGN** (9,505 ft; 3 ac), all are within a 1.25 miles from Chain Lakes, and have rough 4 wheel drive roads, except Lake WGN which lays to the west of this group of lakes. Below these lakes on Canyon Creek is **Sawtooth Lake** (9,225 ft; 114 ac), 4 wheel drive or hike 5 miles to the lake with good fishing for rainbow to 16 inches, 12- to 13-inch cutthroat and some brook. A few hundred feet west of Sawtooth Lake is **Sparhawk Lake** (9,235 ft; 8 ac) with good fishing for small brook. In a large marshy meadow 0.5 miles to the northeast of Sawtooth Lake is **Little Sawtooth Lake** (9,450 ft; 6 ac) with difficult fishing for 12-inch brook. About a 0.5-mile west from Little Bear Lake, on Highway 212, a dirt road leaves the highway traveling south almost 2 miles to **Fantan Lake** (9,562 ft; 43 ac) with good fishing for brook. **Cliff Lake** (9,595 ft; 4 ac) is a 0.25-mile to the west, also with brook. **Paradise Lake** (9,520 ft; 7 ac) below Fantan Lake is barren, as is **Meadow Lake** (9,845 ft; 2 ac) to the northwest.

YELLOWSTONE NATIONAL PARK

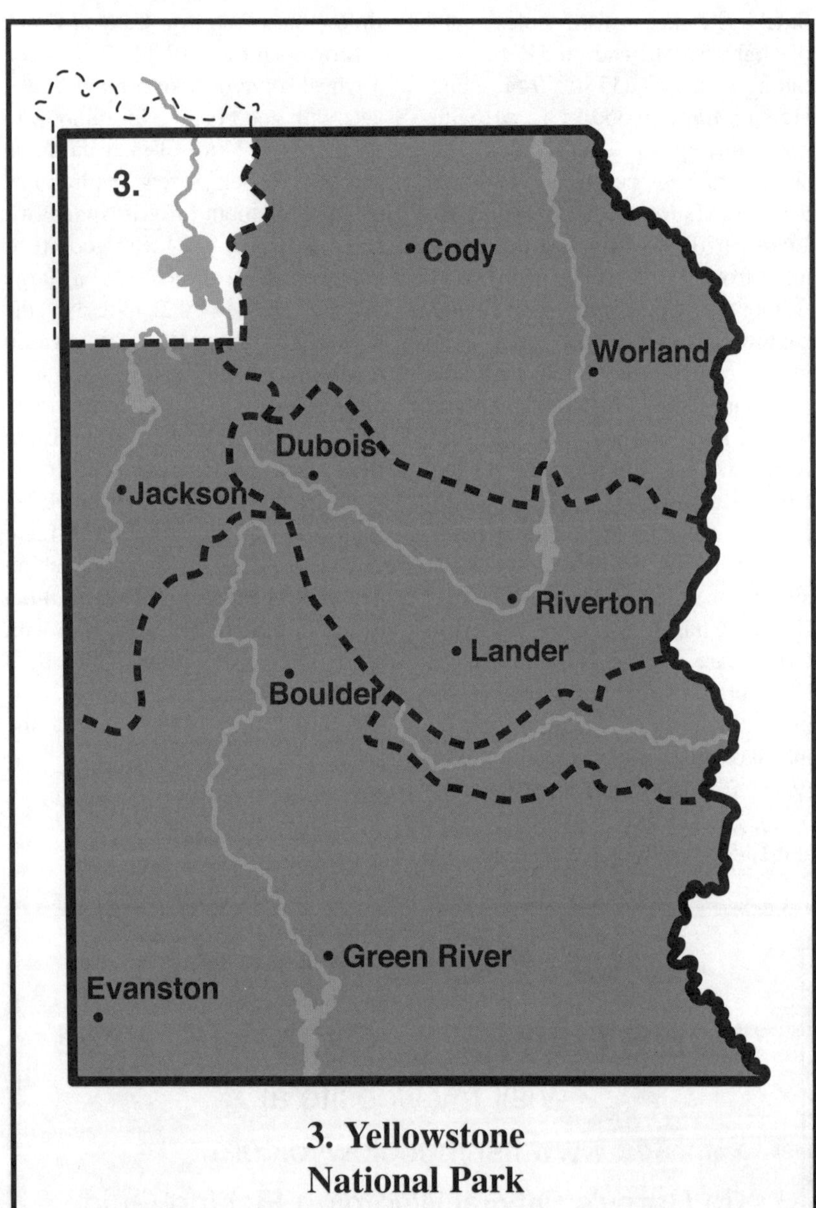

3. Yellowstone National Park

YELLOWSTONE NATIONAL PARK

The first and "original" national park, Yellowstone National Park, was established on March 1, 1872. This vast national park covers over 2.2 million acres of magnificent valleys, high mountain plateaus, deep cut canyons, awe inspiring waterfalls, hot springs, world famous geysers, numerous lakes and creeks, and a vast array of wildlife, all of which attracts over 3 million visitors annually.

Yellowstone is home to grizzly bears, wolves, elk, American bison, moose, and yes, several species of fish to tempt anglers. Native to the waters of Yellowstone National Park is the renowned Yellowstone cutthroat, along with grayling and mountain whitefish. Introduced to the waters of the park in the last 125 years, rainbow, brown, brook, and lake trout have flourished in the clear and pristine waters of the park. Only a few of the visitors to the park, less than 10 percent, come to the park to fish, most are there to see the parks incredible scenic beauty. Those that do fish, concentrate on areas in the park that have fairly easy access like Yellowstone Lake, the Yellowstone River below Yellowstone Lake, the Madison River near the Montana border, the Gibbon and Firehole rivers above Madison Junction, and Lewis and Trout lakes. Fish in these waters are fairly wary, fishing improves away from the beaten path.

Yellowstone has varied terrain stretching from a low elevation of 5,314 feet at the North Entrance, to the breathtaking elevation of 11,358 feet at Eagle Peak. Contained in the park are four major river drainages. The Snake River and its tributaries flow south out of the park into Wyoming and Idaho. The Madison River drainage covers a large part of the west side of the park. The Gallatin River drains the park's northwest corner. Finally, the Yellowstone River, the park's most famous fishing attraction, flows north into Montana. The Yellowstone River drainage includes more than half the park's 3500 square miles. A Yellowstone National Park topographic map is most helpful in locating individual creeks and lakes.

OVERVIEW OF PARK FISHING REGULATIONS

A fishing permit is required (for anyone over 12 years of age) within the parks boundaries. All native species (cutthroat, grayling, and whitefish) are catch and release only in all waters of Yellowstone National Park. Size and possession limits of non-native species (rainbow, brown, brook, and lake trout) vary by species and area. The maximum number of fish an angler can keep is five per day (not counting lake trout from Yellowstone or Heart Lakes, or brook trout from Pocket Lake) of which at least three must be brook trout. In general the following regulations apply. Parkwide the limit for rainbow is 2 fish any size, with the exception of the Madison, Firehole (and its tributaries), Belcher, and Gibbon (below Gibbon Falls) rivers where all rainbow are catch and release. The parkwide limit for brown is 2 fish any size, with the exception of the Madison, Firehole (and its tributaries), and Gibbon (below Gibbon Falls) rivers where the limit is 2 brown under 13 inches. Lewis River, below Lewis Falls, all brown are catch and release only. Parkwide the limit for brook is 5 fish any size, with the exception of Richard's Pond, Fawn Lake, and Blacktail Pond where the limit on brook is 5 fish under 13 inches. All brook caught in Pocket Lake must be kept and not returned to the water. The lake trout limit for the park is also 2 fish any size, with the exception of Yellowstone and Heart lakes where there is no size or possession limit on lake trout. All lake trout caught in Yellowstone and Heart lakes must kept or destroyed. The use of lead products and/or lead weights is prohibited. Only artificial flies and lures may be used for all waters inside the park. No natural or organic bait such as salmon eggs, worms, insects, or foodstuffs is allowed (with the exception of Gardiner River, Obsidian Creek, Panther Creek, Indian Creek, and Joffe Lake where children under 12 can fish with worms). Scented attractants are illegal. The general fishing season in Yellowstone National Park is open each day from 5 am to 10 pm beginning on the Saturday of Memorial Day weekend through, and including, the first Sunday in November. No fish snagging is allowed. The most current Yellowstone fishing regulations should be consulted before fishing in Yellowstone National Park.

All boats including canoes, pontoon, float tubes, and belly boats; require a boat permit. Boat Permits must be obtained in person at any of the following locations: South Entrance, Lewis Lake Campground, Grant Village Backcountry Office, Bridge Bay Marina and Lake Ranger Station. Non-motorized permits only may be obtained at Mammoth Backcountry Office, Canyon Backcountry Office, Northeast Entrance, and Bechler Ranger Station. Fees are charged for both motorized and non-motorized boat permits.

GALLATIN RIVER

The Gallatin River drainage covers the extreme northwest corner of Yellowstone National Park. Highway 191 meets the Gallatin about 20 miles north of the town of West Yellowstone, Montana. A few high country lakes and four major tributaries make up the fishery. Most fishing is done on the portions of the river next to the highway.

The **Gallatin River** flows north alongside Hwy 191 for about 10 miles. The better fishing occurs in this stretch where the river is a typical mountain river with varied water. The average size fish is about 11 inches. The river contains rainbow, cutthroat, brown, and whitefish. Bighorn Pass Trail follows the river to the headwaters and **Gallatin Lake** (8,825 ft; 17 ac), which is barren and no longer stocked. The river from the trailhead has fish to 10 inches for about 7 miles, until like other creeks

Rob Yingling/Bighorn Web Design Photo

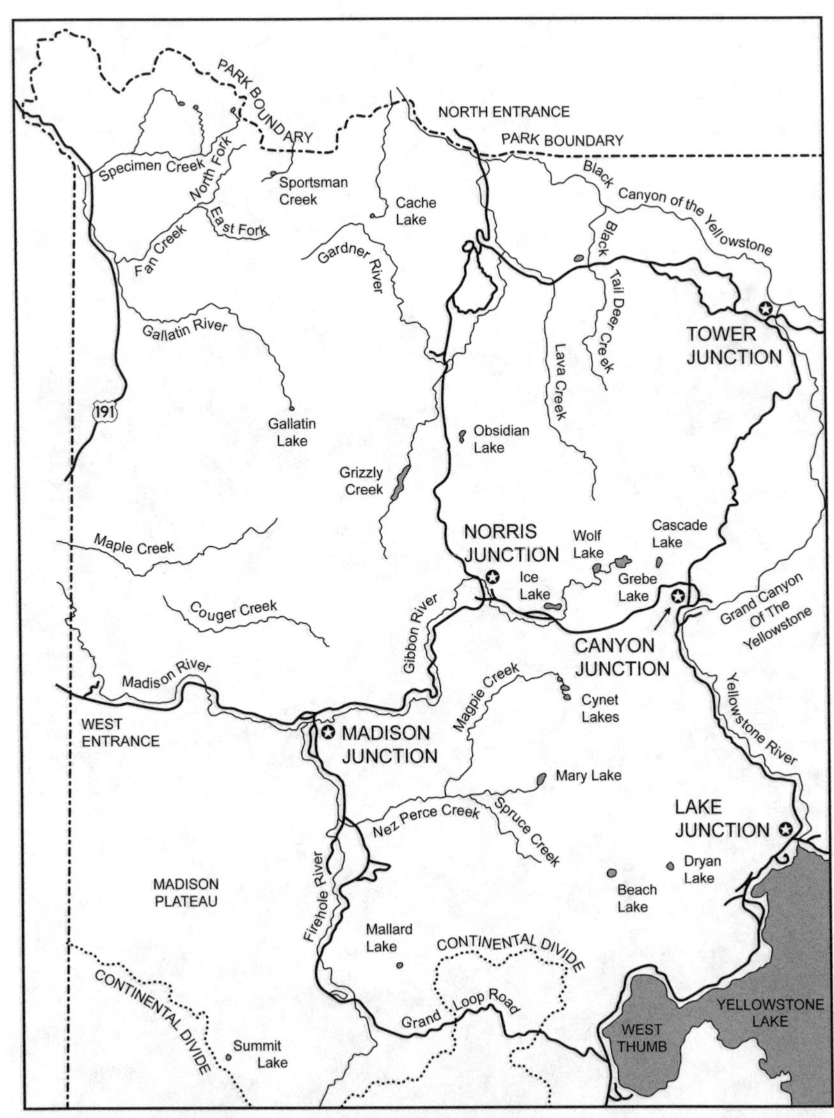

in the area, the terrain becomes to steep to support fish. **Divide Lake** (7,275 ft; 8 ac) along side US 191 is barren.

Fan Creek, one of four major tributaries, is about 2 miles downstream from where the highway meets the Gallatin River. The fishing is slow in this small creek, but the fish - cutthroat - average 9 to 11 inches. Fan Creek offers fair fishing for about 3 miles upstream from the highway before becoming to small and steep to offer much fishing.

Across from Fan Creek flowing into the Gallatin River from the west is **Bacon Rind Creek.** Brushy and small the creek is fair for small cutthroat to 9 inches. The creek offers about 3 miles of fishing within Yellowstone National Park.

Four miles downstream from Gallatin Lake Trailhead, **Specimen Creek** enters the Gallatin River. Specimen Creek is rated fair for cutthroat to 10 inches. Two miles in, the creek splits into the North and the East Forks of Specimen Creek, both are steep and rated good for small cutthroat. There are high country lakes at the heads of each the forks, which were stocked years ago but are now barren. **Shelf Lake** (9,150 ft; 6 ac) is located on one branch of the North Fork, a long 8 miles in. Another branch of the North Fork leads to **Crescent Lake** (8,580 ft; 15 ac), **Sedge Lake** (8,885 ft; 4 ac) and **Crag Lake** (8,775 ft; 6 ac), about 7 miles in. These are beautiful, but barren lakes. At the head of the east fork is **High Lake** (8,774 ft; 5 ac), about 9 miles in on a trail with significant elevation gain. High Lake has fair fishing for cutthroat to 12 inches.

Black Butte Creek is the next tributary downstream from Specimen Creek does not offer any fishing opportunities. **Daly Creek**, which is the last tributary to enter the Gallatin River before it leaves the park, is a small creek with 9- to 11-inch cutthroat and a few brown. Daly Creek joins the river about 30 miles north of the town of West Yellowstone.

MADISON RIVER

The headwaters of one of the best-known trout rivers in the country are found in Yellowstone National Park – The Madison River. The Madison River inside Yellowstone National Park, while offering superb fishing, is not as well known as the stretches of water as it travels through the state of Montana. In Yellowstone the Madison River holds brown and rainbow, and a rare grayling and brook. Rainbow are catch and release only, the limit on brown is 2 fish under 13 inches.

Northeast of the town of West Yellowstone the **Madison River** angles across the Madison Valley before leaving Yellowstone National Park. This stretch of the river is accessible from the gravel Barnes Pool Road, which is about a half-mile east from the West Entrance. Follow this road about a half-mile to the river. This area is known as "The Barns", and it's a good place to try a large nymph or streamer. Fishing "The Barnes" is for brown and rainbow to 14 inches, and whitefish to 16 inches. During spring and fall spawns larger fish swim up the river from Hebgen Lake, which is right outside of the park's boundary (in Montana). The river receives very heavy fishing pressure during spawning season where rainbow and brown average 17 inches, with some larger. Access to this portion of the Madison River and "The Barns" can also be gained from Baker's Hole Campground 3 miles north of the town of West Yellowstone on highway 191. Upstream for about a mile from the campground the river saddles the Yellowstone National Park boundary, a Montana fishing license is required to fish those waters outside the park.

To the north of the Madison Valley, Maple Creek, Duck Creek and Grayling Creek flow west out of the park directly into **Hebgen Lake** in Montana. Rainbow, brown, cutthroat and brook are the common species in all three creeks.

Maple Creek, shown on most maps as Cougar Creek, flows out of Yellowstone and into the Grayling Arm of Hebgen Lake. Maple Creek is fair for rainbow and brown to 10 inches and many smaller brook. A small tributary of Maple Creek, **Cougar Creek** above Gneiss Creek Trail is occasionally closed to fishing due to the Yellowstone Bear Management plan and below Gneiss Creek Trail offers very little fishing as Cougar Creek eventually disappears underground, despite what many maps show.

Campanula Creek, Gneiss Creek, and **Richards Creek** converge about 1 mile inside of Yellowstone to form **Duck Creek**. Fishing in these creeks is good, but difficult, for rainbow and brown to 10 inches, and small brook near the headwaters. Since many bears, including grizzlies, frequent the meadows of these creeks, caution is required. Moose also are seen here and are dangerous if surprised or approached too closely. These waters are best reached by driving about 8 miles north of West Yellowstone, Montana, on US 287. Then turn east on a dirt road, which may or may not be marked with Montana Dept of Transportation Section House. Watch for Highway Department buildings on the east side or backtrack from Duck Creek bridge to the dirt road east. Private homes are on the left as you drive in. Continue until you reach the posts marking the park boundary; follow the road to the right for Cougar Creek, left for Duck Creek. Check current park regulations on closures for these backcountry creeks as many are closed to fishing due to the Bear Management Plan.

Grayling Creek, reached via Hwy 191, is the northernmost creek in the Madison drainage within the park. Don't be fooled by the name. The creek holds mostly cutthroat, and in the lower reaches rainbow, brown and some whitefish, but no grayling. The highway follows the creek for several miles, then leaves it when the creek bends east. There is some good fishing off the road for cutthroat to 11 inches, above the road in the higher reaches fishing is good for small cutthroat. A few miles past Grayling Creek, the highway passes the barren Divide Lake and enters the Gallatin River drainage.

Madison River West Entrance to Madison Junction

The Madison River is formed from the confluence of two rivers, the Gibbon and Firehole rivers, at Madison Junction. From Grebe Lake near Canyon, the Gibbon River flows through high meadows and down over Gibbon Falls to meet the Firehole River. The Firehole River headwaters are Madison Lake near Shoshone Lake, flowing north through one of the park's most extensive thermal areas. From there the river rushes through Firehole Canyon and meets the Gibbon at Madison Junction. Their confluence forms the Madison River. The Madison River is restricted to fly-fishing only. Anglers may keep 2 brown under 13 inches in the Madison River proper.

The Madison River is about 75 feet wide as it flows west through the park toward the West Entrance. West Entrance Road closely follows the river for about 14 miles to Madison Junction. The river is heavily fished for rainbow and brown to 13 inches, whitefish to 15 inches, and small brook. **Harlequin Lake** (6,885 ft; 9 ac) along side the river is barren, as is, **Big Bear Lake** (8,005 ft; 19 ac) high up on the Madison Plateau.

GIBBON RIVER

The **Gibbon River**, 38 miles of river averaging 25 feet in width, on the whole provides fair to good fishing for rainbow, brown, brook, whitefish, and some grayling.

Two of Yellowstone's best grayling waters are at the headwaters of the Gibbon River: **Grebe Lake** (8,035 ft; 133 ac) and **Wolf Lake** (8,005 ft; 38 ac). Grebe Lake has grayling from 10 to 12 inches, and rainbow to 18 inches, but most are in the 12-inch range. Wolf Lake is rated good for grayling and rainbow to 12 inches. Grebe can be reached by an easy 3-mile trail beginning 3 miles west of Canyon on the Grebe Lake Trailhead. **Ice Lake** (7,885 ft; 48 ac) is subject to winterkill and offers no fishing. From the Ice Lake Trailhead, 3 miles east of Norris on the road to Canyon, Ice Lake is 0.25 mile. Wolf Lake is 3 miles farther, and Grebe Lake is 1 mile more.

Solfatara Creek enters the Gibbon at Norris, and is reached by trail from the ranger station. It is fair for small brook.

The upper reaches of the Gibbon River are loosely followed for 4 miles by Norris Canyon Road from Norris Junction to Virginia Meadows near the headwaters. In the upper reaches, from Solfatara Creek at Norris Meadow to Grebe Lake, fishing is for 10 to 12 inch rainbow and a some grayling to 10 inches, and small brook closer to Solfatara Creek.

From Norris Junction to Madison Junction the Gibbon River increases in size and offers challenging fishing for larger fish. Brook to 10 inches are found in the reaches around Norris Junction; fishing is for 10- to 12-inch brown and small brook in the meadow sections of Elk Park and Gibbon Meadows, 3 miles west of Norris on Madison Junction Road. Larger fish are taken below Gibbon Falls. Rainbow average 13 inches with a few larger, brook and an infrequent grayling are caught to 10 inches, and closer to Madison Junction whitefish to 10 inches may be present. **Nymph Lake** (7,520 ft; 13 ac) along side Grand Loop Road is barren.

The **Gibbon River**, below Gibbon Falls, is restricted to fly-fishing only. Anglers may keep 2 brown under 13 inches in the Gibbon River proper, all rainbow are catch and release only.

FIREHOLE RIVER

The headwaters of the Firehole River can be found at **Madison Lake** (8,210 ft; 2 ac), located a few miles west of Shoshone Lake. Madison Lake is barren, and the river below the lake all the way to Old Faithful has poor fishing for small brook. **Spring Creek**, a tributary that follows the Old Faithful Road near the barren **Scaup Lake** (7,925 ft; 5 ac) enters the Firehole about 1.5 miles in from the road. Spring Creek provides fair fishing for small brook.

The Firehole River is closed to fishing for about 1.5 miles above and below Old Faithful. A transformation begins as the Firehole flows past Old Faithful and the underlying thermal features in the area. The river picks up warm water overflow from the thermals along with minerals that are beneficial to insect growth. For the next 12 miles, the Firehole provides some of the most challenging dry-fly fishing and some of the most unique fishing experiences found anywhere. In those 12 miles, the river is generally a flat, meadow river. Fishing there requires stealth, long leaders and small flies. The rewards can be great, as there are very large rainbow and brown here, however most average about 12 inches. Geysers, hot springs and fumaroles along the river create an atmosphere not found elsewhere. They also create hazards, and anglers should take care where they wade in the river and watch where they walk on the bank. The Firehole River becomes more normal again as it flows through the 2-mile-long Firehole Canyon, after which it joins with the Gibbon River to form the Madison River.

In **Firehole Canyon**, anglers will find pocket water and deep swift runs. Here streamers and nymphs work well, and, although there are not as many large fish, it is good fishing. Avoid the swimming hole near the top of the canyon. Fishing success in all parts of the Firehole River tends to drop off in July and August due to warm water temperatures. The fishing on the river resumes in autumn as the water temperature starts to cool.

The Firehole River proper is restricted to fly-fishing only. Anglers may keep 2 brown under 13 inches in the Firehole River Proper and its tributaries, all rainbow are catch and release only.

Two tributaries enter the Firehole in the Biscuit Basin area, 14 miles from Madison Junction. **Iron Spring Creek** enters above the bridge, and the **Little Firehole River** enters below the bridge. Both offer good fishing for 9- to 11-inch rainbow, brown and brook, with the possibility of larger fish close to the Firehole River. The Little Firehole River is considered better, however Iron Spring Creek holds bigger fish during hot summer months, but they are difficult to catch. **West Fork Iron**

Springs Creek, a tributary of Iron Spring Creek, enters at Black Sand Geyser Basin. The creek is considered fair for smaller rainbow and brown. **Summit Lake** (8,560 ft; 26 ac), in the backcountry southwest of Biscuit Basin, **Mallard Lake** (8,060 ft; 30 ac) and **Teal Lake** (8,430 ft; 10 ac), east of Biscuit Basin, are barren.

North of Midway Geyser Basin, the Firehole River leaves the main highway. Access is from Fountain Freight Road, which exits 5.5 miles south of Madison Junction. This road ends at **Goose Lake** (7,220 ft; 37 ac), a small lake with rainbow to 14 inches. **Feather Lake** (7,215 ft; 18 ac) and **Lower Basin Lake** (7,240 ft; 7 ac) are barren. West of the lakes, **Fairy Creek** parallels the road on its way to the Firehole River below Ojo Caliente Spring. The creek is only about 5 feet wide, but holds some small rainbow and brown. **Sentinel Creek** entering 0.25 mile downstream from the west is a meandering meadow creek 6 to 10 feet wide with fair fishing for small rainbow and brown.

The major tributary of the Firehole River is **Nez Perce Creek**, which enters near the Fountain Freight Road exit. A fairly shallow creek, 15 feet wide, it is rated poor for 9- to 11-inch rainbow, brown and brook. Three tributaries enter the Nez Perce starting about 5 miles in by trail. **Magpie Creek, Spruce Creek** and **Cowan Creek** are fair for small brook. At the headwaters of Magpie Creek, **Cygnet Lakes** (8,300 ft; 5 to 11 ac) are barren. Above Cowan Creek confluence, Nez Perce Creek and its headwater lake, **Mary Lake** (8,260 ft; 19 ac), are barren.

YELLOWSTONE RIVER

The **Yellowstone River** drainage is the most extensive in the park. Beginning at the southeast corner of the park, the river winds through the Thorofare Region, one of the most remote and scenic areas in the park. On its arduous journey the river pauses momentarily to fill Yellowstone Lake, a primary attraction for anglers. From Fishing Bridge at the lake's outlet, the river flows along the Grand Loop Road.

From its roadside run, the Yellowstone breaks free of civilization at Canyon, site of the spectacular Upper and Lower Falls, and flows north through some of the most rugged country in the park, the Grand Canyon of the Yellowstone River. There are few tributaries here and little water close to any roads.

The Yellowstone briefly meets civilization again just east of Tower Junction. The river then flows through the Black Canyon of the Yellowstone on its way to Gardiner, Montana, near the north entrance to the park. A major tributary, the Lamar River, has its confluence in this section.

From Gardner, the Yellowstone flows west for a few miles on the northern boundary before leaving the park. Fishing here requires a Montana fishing license. There are a few minor tributaries. The Gardner River is an extensive watershed that enters the Yellowstone just south of the North Entrance.

Yellowstone River Headwaters

To get to the remote headwaters of the Yellowstone River requires an effort no matter how you look at the situation. The headwaters of the Yellowstone are remote to say the least; most of the area is a minimum 20 miles from anywhere. The Yellowstone River humble beginnings start high up near the continental divide in the Teton Wilderness and are surrounded by the Washakie Wilderness Area to the east and Yellowstone National Park to the north. The river flows north from the Teton Wilderness into the southeast corner of Yellowstone National Park, and on northward to Yellowstone Lake. There are no roads in this area, however several trails provide access to the headwaters; Thorofare Trail from East Entrance Road, Trail Creek Trail from Heart Lake to the west, South Boundary Trail from the South Entrance, Pacific Creek Trail over Two Ocean Pass, Pass Creek and Butte Creek trails from the Shoshone River to the east. The following discussion of the upper Yellowstone River will follow the most popular route via Thorofare Trail beginning at East Entrance Road on the east side of Yellowstone Lake.

The Thorofare Trailhead (10 miles southeast from Fishing Bridge on East Entrance Road) provides access the headwaters of the Yellowstone River. The trail runs 32 miles to the south boundary of the park. At 1.5 miles from the trailhead the trail crosses Cub Creek. **Cub Creek** is the first of several creeks that enter Yellowstone Lake on the east shore, south of the highway. At the 3-mile point, the trail crosses **Clear Creek**, a major creek for spawning cutthroat that flows from near **Sylvan Lake** (8,420 ft; 25 ac). Clear Creek is excellent for 7 to 8-inch cutthroat, Cub and Clear Creeks are closed to fishing until August 11.

The next creek south is **Meadow Creek**, near Park Point. The inlet area can be good, particularly early in the season for cutthroat (check with current park regulations for closures). At 9 miles, the trail crosses **Columbine Creek**, which is good for small cutthroat. Along the Southeast Arm of Yellowstone Lake, the trail reaches **Beaver Dam Creek**, 17 miles in. Beaver Dam Creek is considered excellent for cutthroat averaging 12 inches. **Rocky Creek**, a tributary 2 miles upstream, is good for 10-inch cutthroat.

At this point the Thorofare Trail heads in a southerly direction, climbing toward the headwaters of the Yellowstone River and into some of the most remote and wild areas in the park. The main river is excellent fishing, cutthroat average 9 inches, with spawning cutthroat averaging 14 to 16 inches. Many small creeks enter the river along this valley. **Badger Creek, Phlox Creek**, and **Lynx Creek** enter from the west. **Cabin Creek, Trappers Creek, Mountain Creek** (and its tributary **Howell Creek**), **Cliff Creek** and **Escarp-**

ment Creek enter from the east side. All are good for small cutthroat. **Thorofare Creek** flows into the Yellowstone just inside the south boundary, 32 miles by trail from the East Entrance Road. The creek provides excellent fishing for cutthroat to 16 inches during spawning, 10 inches is the average during other seasons. The tributaries of Thorofare Creek, **Hidden Creek**, **Open Creek**, **Pass Creek**, and **Butte Creek** offer good fishing for small cutthroat. Thorofare Creek and the tributaries are all inside the Teton Wilderness Area.

Near the confluence of Thorofare Creek and the Yellowstone River, in the Teton Wilderness is **Bridger Lake** (7,850 ft; 101 ac). Fishing is better in the spring for cutthroat to 15 inches. Above Bridger Lake the upper reaches of the Yellowstone River are small and offer fishing for only small cutthroat. The lower reaches of **Atlantic Creek,** which is about a half mile above Bridger Lake, can be good for spawning cutthroat to 15 inches early in the year coming up from the Yellowstone Lake. After the spawning season cutthroat to 6 inches are more common. **Note: The Yellowstone River drainage upstream from the Yellowstone National Park boundary has a limit of 2 fish, only 1 can be longer than 20 inches.**

Yellowstone Lake

The most prominent body of water in the park is **Yellowstone Lake** (7,733 ft; around 84,320 ac). Yellowstone Lake is large, with 110 miles of shoreline and a surface area of 136 square miles. Yellowstone Lake is also North America's largest mountain lake. At this elevation the lake remains ice-locked about half the year, thawing out around the end of May. The lake, its inlet creeks, and the Yellowstone River downstream to the Upper Falls represent the largest pure-strain cutthroat fishery in the world. The lake is not open to fishing until June 15 to protect spawning fish. Creeks coming into the lake are closed until July 15; Cub and Clear creeks are closed until August 11. Cutthroat in the lake average 15 inches, but can be up to 21 inches. Around thirty years ago lake trout were "mischievously introduced" into the lake by "persons unknown", causing possible harm to the native Yellowstone cutthroat population. The full impact of this action may not be fully realized for several years into the future. The lake trout have flourished in the deep waters of Yellowstone Lake, as much of the lake is over 225 feet deep. Lake trout average 18 to 20 inches, with many larger taken. Park rules require the destruction of any lake trout caught in Yellowstone Lake, and there is not a possession limit on lake trout. The lake also supports a large sucker population. Many areas along the shore are wadeable, and fly fishers enjoy casting for cruising trout. Grand Loop Road closely follows the northwest, north, and northeast sides of the lake affording many opportunities to fish the lake. Check with Grant Village or Fishing Bridge

Visitor centers for further information. The shoreline from West Thumb Geyser Basin to little Thumb Creek is closed to fishing, as are the Bridge Bay and Grant Village marinas and harbors. Boating is allowed with a required permit, and some areas of the lake are restricted. Check with the park service for current boating and fishing regulations. Afternoons can be windy on the lake making mornings and early evenings the best time to fish.

South of Yellowstone Lake

Trail Creek, the outlet of **Trail Lake** (7,748 ft; 56 ac), flows from the south into the bottom of the Southeast Arm of Yellowstone Lake. Both the lake and the creek are good for 10- to 12-inch cutthroat. Access is by Trail Creek Trail, which begins near Cabin Creek, 20 miles in by Thorofare Trail. Obviously it is a remote area. Trail Creek is about 2 miles from **Cabin Creek**; Trail Lake is 1 mile upstream from the creek crossing. About 6 miles farther west is **Chipmunk Creek,** which also flows into the South Arm of Yellowstone Lake. The creek has cutthroat that average 10 inches. **Passage Creek**, a tributary, has smaller fish. On the Promontory, the extension of land separating the Southeast Arm and the South Arm, is **Adler Lake** (7,752 ft; 112 ac), which has small cutthroat to 12 inches. Four more miles brings the angler to **Grouse Creek**, a small creek holding 8 to 10-inch trout. All the creeks in this area are frequented by grizzlies, especially during the cutthroat spawn when the bears help themselves to the fishing. Trail Creek Trail continues over the Continental Divide to Outlet Lake (See the Snake River section of this chapter for further details) and down to the Heart Lake area.

Between the South Arm and West Thumb, **Delusion Lake** (7822 ft; 573 ac) is barren. On the east shore of West Thumb, **Solution Creek** enters the lake. The creek provides very good fishing for cutthroat. **Riddle Lake** (8,585 ft; 86 ac), at the headwaters of Solution Creek, is difficult to fish and is rated poor for cutthroat averaging 12 inches. The lake and the upper reaches of the creek are usually reached by a 2.5 mile trail from the east end of the Grant Campground.

West of Yellowstone Lake

On the west shore between Grant Village and Fishing Bridge, **Big Thumb Creek**, just north of Grant Village; **Arnica Creek**, 6 miles north of West Thumb Junction; **Weasel Creek**, 2 miles south of Bridge Bay and **Bridge Creek**, just south of Bridge Bay; all offer fair to good fishing for small cutthroat. The rest of the small creeks on the west shore are spawning creeks that have no year-round resident fish populations. **Duck Lake** (7,795 ft; 27 ac) a mile northwest of the town of West Thumb contains a few large cutthroat, but is not stocked. Fishing is questionable as the lake as no spawning creeks to support the replenishment of more fish. **Chickadee Lake**

(8,305 ft; 22 ac), **Beach Lake** (8,155 ft; 78 ac), **Dryad Lake** (8,305 ft; 33 ac) and **Nuthatch Lake** (8,350 ft; 12 ac) are barren.

North of Yellowstone Lake

Beginning at Fishing Bridge (the lake's outlet and once-famous fishing spot that has been closed to all angling) the road toward the East Entrance provides access to several creeks as it follows the north shore of Yellowstone Lake. The road crosses **Pelican Creek** 1.4 miles from the bridge. This is a good spot to see moose, but a poor place to fish since the creek is closed for the first 2 miles above Yellowstone Lake. It is better to take the trail from near Indian Pond, about 3 miles from the bridge. Pelican Creek contains large spawning cutthroat early in the spring, but fishing is poor for small cutthroat after the spawning season. There is often high bear activity in the drainage. Two tributaries, **Raven Creek** and **Astringent Creek** are good for small cutthroat.

Indian Pond (7,765 ft; 24 ac) on the south side of the East Entrance Road, 3.1 miles east of Fishing Bridge, is still referred to as Squaw Lake on some maps. Indian Pond has poor for fishing for cutthroat. Nearby, **Beach Springs Lake** (7,740 ft; 32 ac) is a barren thermal lake.

About 8 miles from the bridge, **Sedge Creek** enters Yellowstone Lake. The creek flows out of **Turbid Lake** (7,837 ft; 68 ac), a barren thermal lake 2 miles in by trail. Sedge Creek above Turbid Lake, and **Bear Creek** which is another inlet creek to Turbid Lake, have small cutthroat. These creeks are often closed as part of the bear management plan.

Shortly after it crosses Sedge Creek, the road leaves the lake and begins to climb Sylvan Pass. About 13 miles from Fishing Bridge, the road crosses **Cub Creek**, a small creek holding 10-inch trout. **Clear Creek**, a major creek for spawning cutthroat that flows from near Sylvan Lake. Clear Creek is excellent for 7 to 8-inch cutthroat, Cub and Clear Creeks are closed to fishing until August 11. About 3 miles farther, **Sylvan Lake** (8,420 ft; 28 ac) lies just south of the road. The lake doesn't open to fishing until July 15 for 10-inch cutthroat. On the other side of Sylvan Pass and out of the Yellowstone River drainage, **Middle Creek** flows alongside the highway as it nears the East Entrance and flows out of the park into the North Fork Shoshone River. The upper reaches contain small brook, fishing the lower reaches near the North Fork Shoshone is for cutthroat averaging 10 inches.

Eleanor Lake (8,450 ft 2 ac) on the south side of the East Entrance Highway, 7.6 miles west of the East Entrance, is barren.

Yellowstone River - Yellowstone Lake to Tower

More than 20,000 anglers fish the **Yellowstone River** annually, most of them concentrate on the 9 miles of river from Lake Junction to Canyon. Some sections are closed and posted.

The remaining miles of the Yellowstone within the park are in rugged backcountry. Beginning at the outlet of Yellowstone Lake at Fishing Bridge, the river is large; much of it is also deep and swift. It is necessary to wade the river in order to fish it properly, and chest waders are best. Because of the depth and swiftness of the current and the loose bottom gravel in many parts, caution is required.

The Yellowstone River from **Fishing Bridge** near Lake Junction to **Chittenden Bridge** near Canyon, does not open to fishing until July 15 to protect spawning cutthroat. Several areas in this stretch of river are closed to fishing; from the outlet buoy above Fishing Bridge downstream for 1 mile, Le Hardy Rapids, a small section of the river above Buffalo Ford Picnic Area, and 6-mile section of Hayden Valley from Sulphur Cauldron to Alum Creek.

The Yellowstone River below Yellowstone Lake offers 14 miles of fishing and is very popular, with best results early in the season. Stoneflies are effective early in the season, later angling requires matching caddis and mayfly hatches carefully. Later in the season, the fishing can be tough but the rewards are high. Fish average about 15 inches, and 20-inch cutthroat are caught regularly.

Several tributaries enter the Yellowstone from Fishing Bridge to Canyon, but most of them are in the Hayden Valley, which is closed to fishing, as are the creeks. These include **Alum Creek**, **Trout Creek** and **Elk Antler Creek** from the west, and **Sour Creek** and **Cottongrass Creek** from the east. All contain small cutthroat. **Wrangler Lake** (7,875 ft; 32 ac), near Sour Creek, is barren, as is **Dewdrop Lake** (8,180 ft; 9 ac). Just below LeHardy Rapids, 3 miles from Lake Junction, **Thistle Creek** enters from the east. The creek contains 9- to 11-inch trout, but since the Yellowstone River cannot be crossed safely nearby, the creek can only be reached by walking down the Howard Eaton Trail from Fishing Bridge or by crossing the Yellowstone at Buffalo Ford (5 miles north of Lake Junction) and walking upstream. **Otter Creek** enters the Yellowstone River from the west about 12.5 miles north of Lake Junction. A shallow creek averaging 10 to 15 feet in width, it is poor to fair for small cutthroat. **Cascade Creek** meets the Yellowstone near the Lower Falls. Fishing is for small cutthroat, and an occasional grayling which drifts down from Cascade Lake. Two trails lead to **Cascade Lake** (7,986 ft; 21 ac), which is good to excellent for cutthroat and grayling from 10 to 12 inches, some larger. Howard Eaton Trail follows Cascade Creek from Norris Canyon Road for 2.5 miles to the lake. Another 2.5-mile trail to the lake begins at the picnic area 1.25 miles north of Canyon. The trail continues on to Grebe and Wolf lakes, which also have grayling (see Madison River section).

From Canyon to Tower Junction, the Yellowstone River flows through

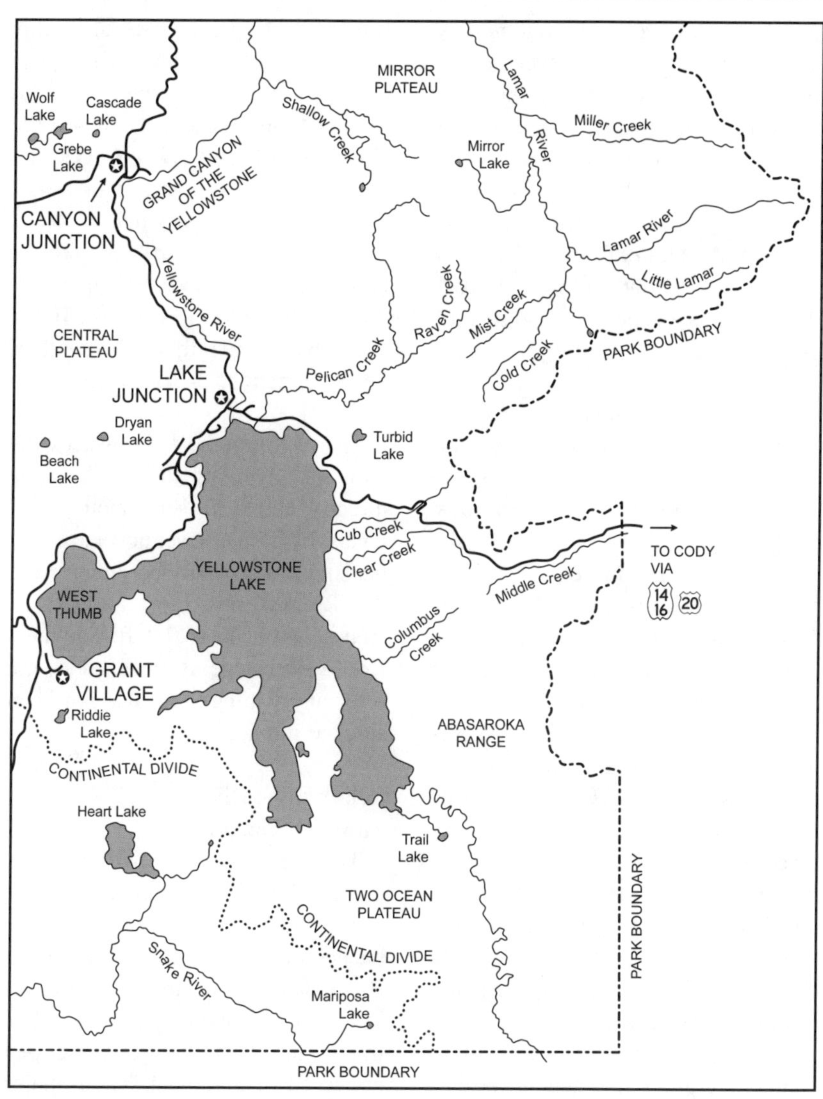

the precipitous Grand Canyon of the Yellowstone. There is spectacular fishing, but it is difficult to reach in the steep canyon. The first 3 miles of the canyon are closed and few established trails travel near the canyon. Only one spur trail leads to the water 1,200 feet below the canyon rim. Seven Mile Trail leads off the Glacial Boulder Trailhead 3.5 miles east of Canyon, down to Seven Mile Hole, 1.5 miles below. It is a steep climb back out. Fishing is for cutthroat averaging 15 inches, and is reputed to be excellent. No doubt the river's inaccessibility provides good habitat and protection for the trout in this section. Access to the lower end of the canyon is from where the road between Tower Junction and the Northeast Entrance crosses the river, the farther from the road, the better the fishing. South of the canyon is **Clear Lake** (7,850 ft; 4 ac), which is barren; and **Ribbon Lake** (7,815 ft; 4 ac), which is reached by a 2-mile trail from Artist Point, is fair for small rainbow.

Broad Creek enters the Yellowstone from the east about halfway between Canyon and Tower. Broad Creek and its tributary, **Shallow Creek**, have moderate to slow fishing for 12-inch cutthroat. Access is from the Wapiti Lake Trail near Upper Falls or by the trail up Astringent Creek near Pelican Creek (see Yellowstone Lake section). At the headwaters of Shallow Creek, **Wapiti Lake** (8,445 ft; 9 ac) is barren. Lakes at the headwaters of Board Creek, **Fern Lake** (8,255 ft; 81 ac) and **Tern Lake** (8,225 ft; 46 ac), contain no fish. **White Lake** (8,240 ft; 204 ac) contains small cutthroat. **Deep Creek, Burnt Creek, Agate Creek** (which opens July 15) and **Quartz Creek** are tributaries that enter from the east. Each of these waters are good to excellent for cutthroat to 15 inches, with the exception of Quartz Creek which does not support fish. No established trails service these creeks directly, but they can be reached from along the river or from the Specimen Ridge Trail that begins near Tower Junction. **Antelope Creek**, the most accessible water in this area, flows along the roadside south of Tower Falls. The fishing is poor in the lower parts of the creek and the upper reaches are closed to fishing. **Tower Creek** and its smaller tributary, **Carnelian Creek**, are good for small brook in the upper reaches, and below Tower Falls are rated good for small cutthroat with some to 14 inches. Tower Falls Overlook Trail, 3 miles south of Tower Junction, provides access up the creek.

The Yellowstone River leaves the Grand Canyon of the Yellowstone directly above Tower Junction and meets the Lamar River north of town, pausing momentarily before entering the Black Canyon of the Yellowstone. **Lost Lake** (6,710 ft; 4 ac) near Roosevelt Lodge at Tower, does not offer any fishing, as it has not been stocked in many years.

Yellowstone River - Tower to Gardiner

The Yellowstone River from Tower to the North Entrance at Gardiner, Montana flows through the backcountry in an area known as the Black Canyon of the Yellowstone. The Black Canyon is just as wild as the Grand Canyon area described above but less remote. Three major trails reach the Yellowstone River in the canyon. The Yellowstone River Trail beginning at the town of Gardiner, follows the Yellowstone River along its north bank all the way to Tower. Blacktail Trail begins along the Mammoth-Tower Road about 7 miles from Mammoth. Finally, Hell-

Rob Yingling/Bighorn Web Design Photo

roaring Creek Trail begins just north of Floating Island Lake, 3.3 miles west of Tower Junction. There are bridges across the Yellowstone at the bottom of Blacktail and Hellroaring Creek Trails. All trails to the river are steep, large boulders and sheer cliffs make traveling along the river impossible in many places so caution is advised. Other routes are possible, but elevation differences, between road and river, are between 700 and

1,000 feet making for tough hikes in and back out. The fishing (and the wildlife viewing) is excellent, especially during the stonefly hatch in early season. Cutthroat are the dominant species, but rainbow, brown, whitefish and brook can play a significant part in the angler's day on the river. Fish in the canyon average 12 inches, except the brook, which run much smaller. The water in this section is big and wild, with lots of boulders and swift runs.

About 4 miles downstream from Tower, the first of several tributaries enters this section of Yellowstone River. **Little Buffalo Creek** flows into the river from the north. Access to this small creek, rated good for small cutthroat, is from Hellroaring Creek Trail described previously. The Mammoth-Tower Road crosses **Lost Creek** just outside of Tower Junction and **Elk Creek** about 2 miles farther west. Both are poor to fair for small brook, and like the other tributaries, better fishing is found closer to the Yellowstone River. **Floating Island Lake** (6,585 ft; 4.5 ac) west of the Grand Loop Road is Barren. **Hellroaring Creek**, entering from the north, provides excellent fishing for 10-inch cutthroat and rainbow. Hellroaring Creek Trail crosses the Yellowstone River and meets the creek about 1 mile to the west. Much of the creek is in Montana and outside of Yellowstone N.P. **Coyote Creek**, a tributary of Hellroaring Creek, is good for 9-inch cutthroat and rainbow. About 2 miles down the Yellowstone River are **Little Cottonwood Creek** and **Cottonwood Creek** (which opens July 15), which can have cutthroat and rainbow to 14 inches. Little Cottonwood Creek is considered the better of the two. Both are accessible from the Yellowstone River Trail on the north side of the river.

Oxbow Creek, a small creek holding 9- to 11-inch brook, leaves the highway from **Phantom Lake** (6,845 ft; 5 ac), which is barren. As with the other creeks, Oxbow Creek is better in the lower reaches. **Blacktail Deer Creek**, a major tributary located about 7 miles southeast of Mammoth provides excellent fishing for brook averaging 8 inches. A trail at the highway follows the creek north to the river. **Blacktail Pond** (6,605 ft; 9 ac) is near the highway on the north side, between Mammoth Hot Springs and Tower Junction, 6 miles east of Mammoth Hot Springs. Fishing is for 12-inch brook, occasionally larger fish are caught. The pond has a special limit of 5 brook which must be under 13 inches.

Crevice Creek enters the Yellowstone River from the north about 1 mile downstream from where Blacktail Creek meets the river. The creek is fair for small brook. **Crevice Lake** (5,555 ft; 14 ac) on the north side of the Yellowstone River is barren.

The Yellowstone River from Gardiner, Montana downstream forms part of the park's northern boundary. The river here is much like the section immediately upstream from Gardiner and, like that section, receives a good deal of fishing pressure and is not rated as good by anglers as other sections within the park. Brown, rainbow, cutthroat, brook, and whitefish all are available. The average fish is around 12 inches, brown and some rainbow in this section of the river are occasionally caught to 24 inches. The highway from Gardiner gives access to the north bank outside of Yellowstone Park, therefore requiring a Montana fishing license. The south bank is within the park and is followed by Old Yellowstone Trail south to the park boundary at Reese Creek, and also requires a Montana fishing license. Three small tributaries join the Yellowstone in this section; **Landslide Creek** and **Stephens Creek** have fair fishing for small brook; **Reese Creek** has fair fishing for cutthroat/rainbow hybrids. **Cache Lake** (8,030 ft; 12 ac) at the headwaters of Reese Creek and **Rainbow Lake** (5,885 ft; 3 ac) on Landslide Creek are both barren.

Mol Heron Creek is farther west, joining the Yellowstone River outside the park. At its headwaters is **Sportsman Lake** (7,715 ft; 6 ac). The creek has small cutthroat; the lake provides excellent fishing for cutthroat to 12 inches. Access is difficult. The strenuous Sportsman Lake Trail leads to the lake from either an 11-mile hike from Specimen Creek to the west or a 13-mile hike from Glen Creek to the east.

LAMAR RIVER

The **Lamar River** joins the Yellowstone 2 miles downstream from Tower. The Lamar River and its major tributaries, Cache Creek, Soda Butte Creek and Slough Creek, are excellent fisheries. They drain the northeast quarter of the park. The Lamar River flows alongside the Northeast Entrance Road for about 7 miles, beginning about 3 miles above its confluence with the Yellowstone River. Then it bends south for nearly 30 miles to its headwaters. Cutthroat and rainbow average 12 inches, with larger fish caught. Upstream the fish get smaller, averaging 10 inches. The river can flow high well into July, so it is considered a better river for later in the season.

The **Little Lamar River** is the first tributary to join the Lamar near its headwaters. Reached by the Lamar River Trail, it is about a 14-mile hike and holds small cutthroat. **Cold Creek,** and its tributary **Mist Creek,** joins the Lamar River from the south a few miles downstream. Both creeks are fair to good for small cutthroat to 10 inches. At the headwaters of Cold Creek is **Frost Lake** (9,535 ft; 14 ac), which is barren.

As the Lamar River takes a northerly route, **Willow Creek** and **Timothy Creek** enter from the west. Both are fair for small cutthroat. On **Mirror Fork Timothy Creek**, **Mirror Lake** (8,960 ft; 14 ac) is barren. At the 8.5-mile point on the trail, **Miller Creek** joins the Lamar River and like the other creeks in the area it has small cutthroat. A trail follows the creek to its headwaters at **Canoe Lake** (9,050 ft; 2 ac), near the park boundary, which is barren. Between Miller Creek and Cache Creek, **Calfee**

Creek enters from the east and **Flint Creek** enters from the west. Both are small creeks containing small cutthroat. One of the best tributaries is **Cache Creek**, 3.3 miles in by trail. The Cache Creek Trail follows the creek for about 15 miles. Cache Creek consistently ranks high, providing excellent fishing for cutthroat averaging 10 inches, with many larger fish reportedly caught. Two small creeks, **Opal Creek** and **Chalcedony Creek**, enter the Lamar from the west before the river meets the Northeast Entrance Road. Chalcedony Creek may have a few small cutthroat, Opal Creek is too steep to support fish.

As the Northeast Entrance Road leaves the Lamar River, it follows **Soda Butte Creek** 14 miles to the park boundary. Soda Butte Creek is very good for cutthroat averaging 11 inches, with some larger, brook are found in the upper reaches of the creek outside of the park in Montana. Near the confluence with the Lamar River there are rainbow and cutthroat to 16 inches. Nine miles from the entrance, **Amphitheater Creek** enters Soda Butte Creek from the east, providing good fishing for small cutthroat for about a 0.25 upstream before the creek becomes to steep to support fish. Ten miles from the entrance, **Pebble Creek** flows into Soda Butte Creek. Pebble Creek Trail follows the creek into country of rugged beauty, where the creek has cutthroat averaging 10 inches. An unmarked trail along the highway at about 12.7 miles from the entrance leads 0.25-mile west to **Trout Lake** (6,950 ft; 9 ac). Trout Lake contains some large rainbow and a few cutthroat. The fishing is extremely slow for these temperamental lunkers to 10 pounds, but most average 16 inches. Two smaller lakes nearby, **Shrimp Lake** (7,230 ft; 2 ac) and **Buck Lake** (6,980 ft; 5 ac) are barren. Trout, Shrimp, and Buck lakes are closed to fishing until June 15, the inlet creek of Trout Lake is closed until July 15. Nearer to the confluence with the Lamar River, **Foster Lake** (6,630 ft; 10 ac) north of the road is shallow and does not have fish.

The **Lamar River** from Soda Butte Creek to the Yellowstone River is heavily fished for weary cutthroat and rainbow averaging 12 inches, with an occasional fish to 20 inches. Three minor tributaries of the Lamar River enter the river between the confluence of Soda Butte Creek and Slough Creek. **Amethyst Creek, Rose Creek, Jasper Creek**, and **Crystal Creek** are small creeks holding small cutthroat if any fish at all. **Slough Creek** is the last major tributary entering the Lamar River before it joins the Yellowstone River. A dirt road leaves the highway heading north about 6 miles east from Tower Junction; it goes 2 miles to a campground. A trail follows an old wagon road 11 miles up Slough Creek to the northern boundary of the park. The valley through which it runs is one of the most beautiful in the park. Catches average 13 inches, but trout of 20 inches are taken from

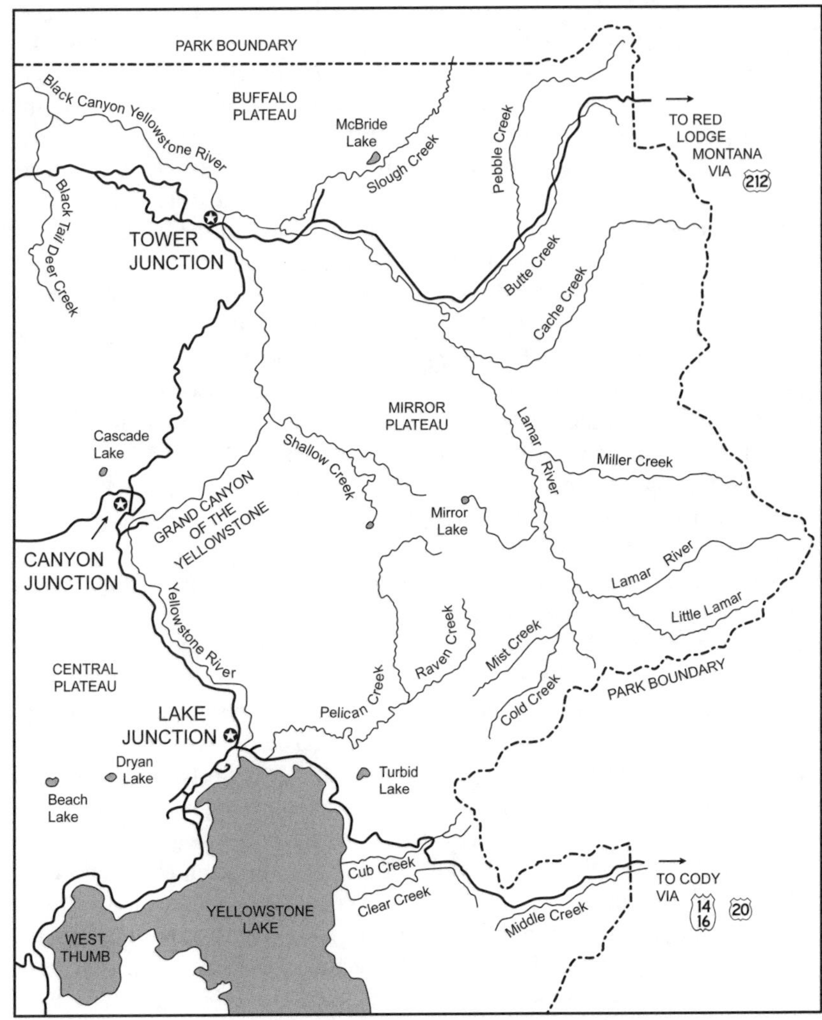

Slough Creek by experienced anglers. **Buffalo Creek**, a small tributary, enters from the north near the campground. Buffalo Creek is fair for small cutthroat inside the National Park; better fishing for rainbow is further upstream in Montana. **McBride Lake** (6,680 ft; 16 ac) is located about 3 miles up the valley. Praised for its backcountry beauty, the lake also provides very good fishing for cutthroat to 14 inches. Eight miles in, **Elk Tongue Creek** joins Slough Creek. It is good for small cutthroat. Finally, 11 miles up the valley and very near the north boundary of the park is **Cutoff Creek**, which is good for small cutthroat. Slough Creek continues into Montana for several miles outside of

Yellowstone National Park. After Slough Creek joins the Lamar River, the river flows west for about 3 miles to join the Yellowstone River at Tower Junction.

GARDNER RIVER

The most prominent tributary in this region is the **Gardner River**, which meets the Yellowstone River at Gardiner, Montana. The river heads near Electric Peak, west of Mammoth. The river meanders south through the backcountry until it meets the Mammoth-Norris Road at the Indian Creek Campground, 8.5 miles south of Mammoth. The river then flows northeast around Bunsen Peak and drops over Osprey Falls, east of the peak. The Mammoth-Tower Road crosses the Gardner River downstream, and the highway between Mammoth and the North Entrance follows the river for several miles. Access to the upper reaches of the Gardner River is by any one of several trails, although no trail follows the river directly. The lower reaches of the river are accessible by short hikes from the highways or from the Bunsen Peak Road, a one-way dirt road leaving the Mammoth-Norris Road near the Golden Gate, 4.7 miles south of Mammoth. The river is divided into two sections by Osprey Falls. Gardner River is one of the few waters in the park where children under 11 years old may fish with worms as bait.

Downstream the Gardner River contains that mixture of species common to the Yellowstone River in its lower reaches: brown, rainbow, cutthroat and brook, some large trout are available. Above the Osprey falls, the river is a brook fishery. It provides better fishing in terms of the numbers caught, but the fish are smaller.

One access to the upper Gardiner River is the Fawn Pass Trail. It leaves from near Mammoth Hot Springs and reaches the river in about 5 miles. About 0.5 mile past the river, the trail meets **Fawn Creek**, a tributary rated fair for small brook. After passing **Fawn Lake** (7,785 ft; 4 ac) the trail follows Fawn Creek to Fawn Pass, an area known for its grizzlies. Fawn Lake has brook, but is shallow and hard to fish. Fawn Lake has a special limit of 5 brook which must be under 13 inches. Another tributary, **Panther Creek** enters about 0.5 mile north of the Indian Creek campground. The Big Horn Pass Trail follows the creek upstream where there is fair fishing for small brook. Panther Creek is one of the few waters in the park where children under 12 years old may fish with worms as bait. There are no fish in the unnamed lakes seen near the pass, but there may be grizzlies around them, so be cautious.

Joffe Lake (6510 ft 1.5 ac) is at the end of a dirt road that turns off of the Mammoth-Norris Highway 1.2 miles south of Mammoth. Follow the truck route around and past the residential area and maintenance yard, then follow a dirt road 1 mile to the lake. Fishing is excellent for brook averaging 9 inches. This is a good lake for kids to fish, as kids under 12 are permitted to use worms as bait.

Indian Creek enters the Gardner River near the campground of the same name, 8.5 miles south of Mammoth. Indian Creek has good fishing for small brook. South from the campground, the highway follows **Obsidian Creek** where there is fair fishing for small brook. Indian Creek and Obsidian Creek are a few waters in the park where children under 12 years old may fish with worms as bait. Moose and elk are often seen among the willows. Above the confluence of Winter and Straight Creeks, about 11 miles south of Mammoth, Obsidian Creek becomes too small for good fishing. **Beaver Lake** (7,380 ft; 12 ac) is on the west side of the Norris-Mammoth Highway, 7.6 miles north of Norris Junction. The lake is easy to see from highway, but hard to walk to and around. The lake is shallow and does not support fish. In the area, **Lake of the Woods** (7,745 ft; 24 ac), **Obsidian Lake** (7,745 ft; 22 ac), and near the headwaters of Obsidian Creek **Twin Lakes** (7,555 ft; 5 and 12 ac), are barren.

Both **Winter Creek** and **Straight Creek** are good to excellent for 6- to 8-inch brook. A trail follows Winter Creek for about 1.5 miles before the creek turns to the west, continue south up Straight Creek to **Grizzly Lake** (7,510 ft; 138 ac), 1.5 miles farther. An alternative route is to take the Grizzly Lake Trail which leaves the highway about 1 mile south of Beaver Lake and requires a steep 2 mile hike to reach Grizzly Lake. The lake is considered excellent for brook that average 10 inches.

Trilobite Lake (8,365 ft; 7 ac) is between Mt. Holmes and Dome Mountain in the Gallatin Range. Take Winter Creek Trail to Winter Creek Patrol Cabin, which is about 6 miles, from there hike north about 3 miles on an un-maintained trail. The lake is fair for brook to 12 inches.

As the Gardner River flows north it circles around Bunsen Peak via Sheepeater Canyon. Half way through the canyon the river plummets over 100 feet down Osprey Falls, separating the upper and lower Gardner River. Above the falls expect small brook averaging 7 inches, below the falls the river offers fishing for brown, rainbow, and cutthroat all averaging 10 inches. Whitefish to 12 inches are present.

Two tributaries of the Gardner River have their confluence below Osprey Falls. **Glen Creek** joins the river north of Bunsen Peak, and has fair fishing for small brook. The Sportsman Lake Trail from Mammoth Hot Springs reaches the upper section of Glen Creek, and the Mammoth-Norris Road crosses the creek near Rustic Falls, 4.7 miles south of Mammoth. **Swan Lake** (7,275 ft; 31 ac) and several ponds on the west side of Bunsen Peak are barren. **Lava Creek** joins the Gardner River downstream from where the Mammoth-Tower Road crosses the river. The highway follows the creek for a few miles before the creek bends south into the backcountry. In its lower sections, Lava Creek has brown and rainbow, and above Undine Falls fishing is for brook. **Lupine Creek** meets Lava Creek immediately after it leaves the highway. A second tributary, **Arrow Canyon Creek** enters far upstream near the creek's headwaters. Both are good for small brook.

From Lava Creek the Gardner River tumbles through Gardner Canyon to meet the Yellowstone River. Fishing is fairly difficult for rainbow, brown, cutthroat, whitefish and some brook. Fish averaging 12 inches are common, in the fall big brown come up the river to spawn and can be over 3 pounds in size. **Slide Lake** (5,695 ft; 3 ac) and the **Mammoth Beaver Ponds** (so named for their proximity to Mammoth rather than their size) are west of the highway between Mammoth and the North Entrance. Both are barren, Slide Lake once was stocked but could not support fish.

SNAKE RIVER

The **Snake River** flows from the east past the South Entrance Station on Hwy 89-287/191 through more than 30 miles of roadless backcountry from its headwaters along the park boundary. The Snake River's headwaters lie in the Teton Wilderness and Yellowstone National Park. Two main tributaries, carrying water from three major lakes, feeds the Snake River inside Yellowstone National Park: the Heart River flows from Heart Lake and joins the Snake River in the back country; and the Lewis River, bringing water from Lewis and Shoshone Lakes, meets the Snake River near the South Entrance. Except for Lewis Lake and those portions of the Lewis River accessible from the road, fishing requires walking. Some of the water is definitely only for the physically fit, dedicated backpacker. The Snake River is accessible from the South Boundary Trail and adjoining trails. Snake River cutthroat make up a large portion of the catch but brown, lake trout, brook and whitefish are available in some sections of the river and its tributaries. Angling is fair to good for fish averaging 12 inches.

Three creeks on the Yellowstone-Teton Wilderness border in the Absaroka Mountain Range form the Snake River's starting point. They are **Fox Creek, Plateau Creek** and the Snake River itself. Pack trails from the west and south require a trip of 20 miles or more to reach these headwater creeks. Among the trails into this area are the Snake River Trail, the South Boundary Trail, and the Atlantic-Pacific Trail from the south. The headwater drainage has good fishing for cutthroat to 10 inches, most are much smaller in the higher reaches of the headwaters. The Snake River leaves the Teton Wilderness at this point and enters Yellowstone National Park.

Note: Inside the Teton Wilderness all waters are closed from November 1 to May 20. The limit on trout is 2 per day.

Near the southeast corner of the park and the headwaters of the Snake River is **Mariposa Lake** (8,950 ft;

Rob Yingling/Bighorn Web Design Photo

14 ac), a 28-mile walk by way of the South Entrance Trail. Mariposa Lake offers fair fishing for cutthroat to 14 inches. **Plateau Creek**, **Crooked Creek** and **Sickle Creek**; tributaries located downstream from Mariposa Lake along the difficult Snake River Trail (25 miles from the South Entrance), offer fair fishing for small cutthroat.

The first major tributary of the Snake River, the **Heart River**, joins the Snake River about 20 miles in. Heart River has good fishing for cutthroat to 14 inches, and an occasional brown. Lake trout, which drift down from Heart Lake, are sometimes caught. Four miles up Heart River, **Outlet Creek** and its tributary, **Surprise Creek**, are both good for small cutthroat. Three miles up Outlet Creek, **Outlet Lake** (7,780 ft; 14 ac) is fair for small cutthroat. Immediately upriver from the Outlet Creek confluence is **Heart Lake** (7,450 ft; 2142 ac). This large lake is an excellent fishery, which opens July 1. The average size fish, according to one survey, is 19 inches, but many larger cutthroat and lake trout are taken each year. Best results are had early and late in the season when the fish are in shallow water. Lake trout do not have a size or possession limit in

Rob Yingling/Bighorn Web Design Photo

Heart Lake, and all lake trout caught must be kept and not returned to the water. The park record lake trout (43 pounds) was taken from Heart Lake. Dry flies and nymphs work for rising trout. Heart Lake also contains suckers and chubs. The lake is reached by an 8-mile trail from the South Entrance Road, the trailhead is located 14.3 miles north of the South Entrance Station. The trail goes through bear country, extra caution should be taken. Near the lake, the trail crosses **Witch Creek**, one of two inlet creeks. The other, **Beaver Creek,** enters the lake on the north shore. Both are rated good for small cutthroat, with the best fishing found close to the lake.

Two miles southwest of Heart Lake on Heart Lake Trail is **Sheridan Lake** (7,380 ft; 16 ac). Along with **Basin Creek Lake** (7,390ft; 10 ac), 2 miles further, they feed **Basin Creek**, which flows into the Snake River below the Heart River confluence. The creek and lakes are good for small cutthroat.

The **Snake River** below the Heart River confluence offers good fishing for cutthroat averaging 12 inches, with a few to 18 inches. Whitefish average 12 inches, and spawning brown in the fall can reach 20 inches. Access is via the South Boundary Trail from the South Entrance. Feeding into the Snake River from the south are **Wolverine Creek** and **Coulter Creek,** which are almost completely outside of the boundaries of Yellowstone N.P. The lower reaches of the creeks are good for 11-inch cutthroat. **Harebell Creek**, a small tributary inside the park boundary, is only fair for small cutthroat.

About 6 miles from the entrance, **Red Creek** enters the Snake River from the north. Four miles in, **Forest Creek** joins the Snake River, also from the north. Both hold small cutthroat, Forest Creek is the better of the two. **Forest Lake** (7,425 ft; 7 ac) is barren.

Lewis River

The **Lewis River** enters the Snake River near the South Entrance Station. The highway follows the river for about 11 miles to a point a mile below Lewis Lake. One mile north of the entrance station, **Crawfish Creek** enters the river. Crawfish Creek is a tempting creek with good-looking water, yet is only rated poor for small cutthroat. In the lower 7 miles, the Lewis River flows through a steep-walled canyon. The canyon contains beautiful water, made even more so by its inaccessibility. Fishing for cutthroat and whitefish, averaging 12 inches, is found in the lower reaches of the canyon. Brown are catch and release below Lewis Falls, with some larger fish. From the canyon upstream to Lewis Falls, the Lewis River is a meadow stream averaging 75 feet in width. Many very small brook are in this stretch, with an occasional brown to 20 inches. This section also has good insect hatches.

From the Lewis Falls to Lewis Lake outlet, the Lewis River has varied water ranging from long riffles to

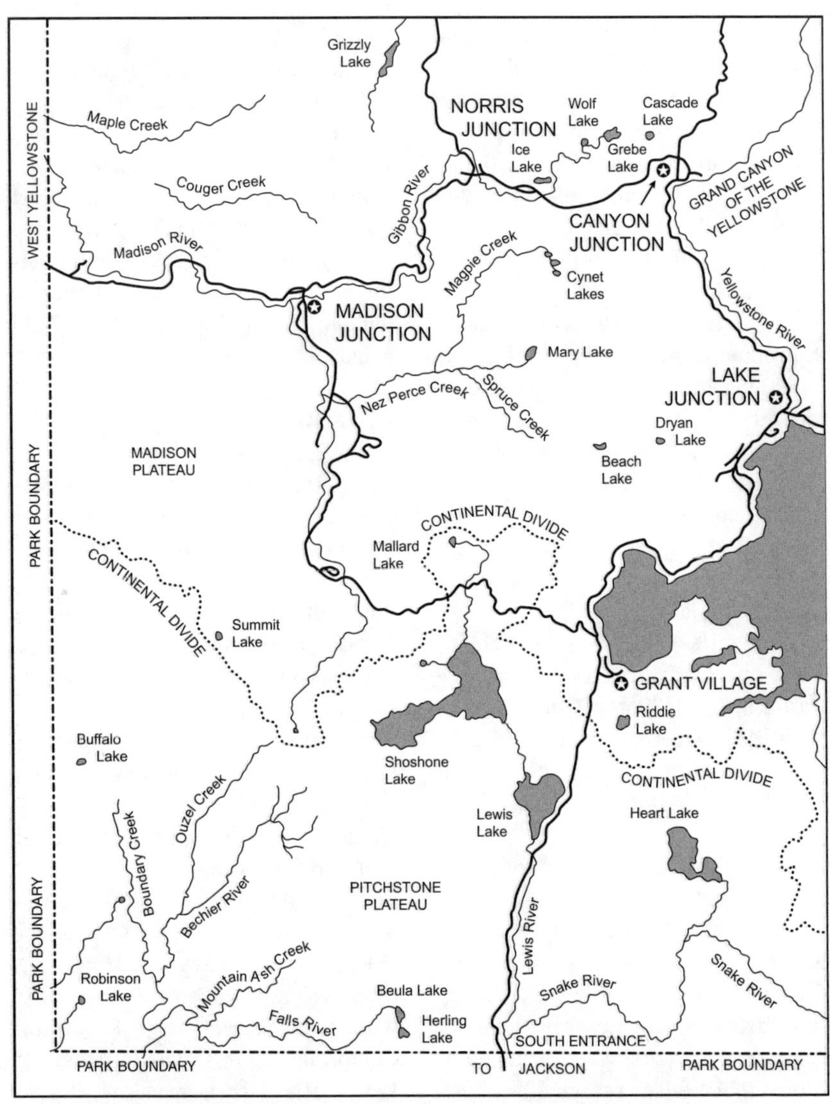

deep runs. Fishing is mostly for small brook and brown, an occasional large brown does drift down from Lewis Lake. This section holds larger brown and lake trout during the fall spawn. **Aster Creek**, a small meadow creek, enters the Lewis River immediately downstream of the highway bridge below the falls. Aster Creek is fair for small brook. At the creek headwaters is **Aster Lake** (8,130 ft; 12ac) which is barren.

Lewis Lake (7,778 ft; 2705 ac), located along the South Entrance Road, contains brown and lake trout averaging 16 inches, and some smaller brook. Lake trout over 20 pounds have been taken. Trolling is most effective except during the fall when fish are in the shallows. Motorized boats are allowed with a required boat permit. The lake is fished heavily. The ranger station, boat ramp and campground are located at the southeast corner of the lake. Brown rise to the evening caddis hatch in July and August. The lake is easily fished with chest waders, especially along the eastern shore.

At the northwest corner of Lewis Lake is its main inlet, the **Lewis-Shoshone Channel**, 4 miles of slow-moving water between Lewis Lake and the backcountry Shoshone Lake. The channel is reached by boat or by Lewis River Trail, a 2.5-mile trail that parallels the north shore. Only hand-propelled craft are allowed in the channel, where there is very good fishing for brown averaging 17 inches. Try a size 12 Adams or large caddis patterns. Fish are spooky in the clear, calm water, which is difficult to fish from the bank since wading is nearly impossible.

Shoshone Lake (7,791 ft; 8026 ac), the second largest lake in the park, is accessible by boat through the Lewis Shoshone Channel from Lewis Lake (some pulling or portaging is necessary) or 3 miles by DeLacy Creek Trail, or 5 miles on the Shoshone Lake Trail. Other longer trailheads are located along Old Faithful Road. Shoshone Lake contains large brown and lake trout with some brook to 14 inches. Fall fishing is excellent. Motorless craft are allowed, but sudden storms make boating hazardous. **Pocket Lake** (8,125 ft; 10 ac), a small lake 1-mile west of Shoshone Lake, holds small cutthroat and brook. Pocket Lake does not have a limit on brook and all brook caught must be kept and not released back to the water. There is not a defined trail to lake. **DeLacy Creek** on the north shore, **Shoshone Creek** on the west shore and **Moose Creek** on the south shore provide fair to good fishing for small brown and brook. Shoshone is the better of the three. **DeLacy Lakes** (8,540 ft; 54 ac) at the headwaters of DeLacy Creek contain no fish.

Along the South Boundary Trail directly west of the ranger station at the South Entrance is **Tanager Lake** (7,000 ft; 28.5 ac) and **South Boundary Lake** (7,390 ft; 12ac) which are both barren.

Joining the Snake River below the Lewis River confluence, **Polecat Creek** enters the Snake about 1 mile west of Flagg Ranch. Access is from Moose Falls just north of the South Entrance or along Reclamation Road. The Reclamation Road crosses the creek about 1 mile from South Entrance Road, but at that point, the creek is not within the park boundaries, Wyoming regulations apply. Hike 2 miles up the creek into Yellowstone N.P. for a 10-foot wide creek that offers fair fishing for 12-inch cutthroat and brown. Polecat Creek is closed in April and May within the park.

The Snake River leaves Yellowstone National Park near the South

Boundary Entrance. For a complete description of the Snake River and its tributaries south of Yellowstone National Park, see the Snake River chapter.

FALLS RIVER

Well to the west of the South Entrance Road of Yellowstone National Park, **Falls River** collects water from the Pitchstone Plateau. Falls River has two main tributaries, Mountain Ash Creek and the Bechler River, and is rated good for rainbow and cutthroat averaging 10 inches with the upper reaches having better fishing. The Falls River drainage is considered to be some of the most remote in the park. The river drainage is lower in elevation and wetter than other areas of the park, causing lush growth and greater variety of plant life. Browsing deer, elk and moose are common companions of anglers along the rivers and creeks. The most impressive singular feature of the Falls River drainage is the number of waterfalls, there are 21 of them, more than half the total for the entire park. Twister, Rainbow, Silver Scarf and Collonade waterfalls are on trout streams that hold some good-sized fish. Trails into the Falls River area are located along the Reclamation Road, a 45-mile dirt road paralleling, in part, the park's southern boundary. This road comes out at Marysville, on State Hwy 47, east of Ashton, Idaho.

Since nearly all the trails to the falls and other streams and lakes in the area require crossing boggy meadows and fording rivers, trips into this area are better planned for after spring run-off, usually mid to late July. If wet feet and monster

Rob Yingling/Bighorn Web Design Photo

mosquitoes don't bother you, the scenery is magnificent.

Located west of Polecat Creek in the Falls River drainage are **Beula Lake** (7,410 ft; 107 ac) and **Hering Lake** (7,420 ft; 73 ac). These lakes provide good fishing for cutthroat to 16 inches, Beula Lake is considered better fishing. Both lakes can be reached by a 2.5-mile hike on Beula Lake Trail starting from Grassy Lake Reservoir on Reclamation Road.

Proposition Creek joins Mountain Ash Creek about 2 miles downstream and is good for small cutthroat and rainbow. **Mountain Ash Creek** enters Falls River about 4 miles above Cave Falls Campground (accessible from Idaho) and is very good for cutthroat and rainbow averaging 12 inches, as is Falls River from the confluence with Mountain Ash Creek down to the campground.

Winegar Lake (6,460 ft; 23 ac), just inside of the park, on the South Boundary Trail is barren.

Bechler River

The other main tributary of the Falls River, the **Bechler River**, enters at Cave Falls from the north. Access is from Cave Falls or Bechler Ranger Station. To access the Bechler River and the southwestern corner of Yellowstone Park use the Cave Falls Road, which exits Hwy 47 a few miles east of Marysville, Idaho. The road dead-ends in the park's southwest corner. This is the best access to most of the area, from here one must walk or ride horseback. The Bechler River too, is good fishing for cutthroat and rainbow averaging 14 inches in the lower reaches. Some larger fish are found between Boundary Creek and Bechler Canyon, if you can entice them. All rainbow on the Belcher River are catch and release only. Above Bechler Canyon the fish tend to be smaller. Nearby **Lilypad Lake** (6,425 ft; 60 ac) is barren. **Boundary Creek** joins the Bechler River 3.5 miles upstream. This creek is rated good for cutthroat and rainbow to 14 inches. Another 4 miles upstream, **Ouzel Creek** flows into the Bechler River, and has fair fishing for small cutthroat and rainbow. **Ranger Lake** (6,980 ft; 58 ac) and **Lake Wyodaho** (6,810 ft; 7 ac) are barren.

After combining with the Bechler River, Falls River leaves Yellowstone National Park, flowing to the southwest along the northwest boundary of Winegar Hole Wilderness Area for 3 miles in Wyoming before exiting into Idaho.

Robinson Lake (6,495 ft; 29 ac) lies 2 miles west of Bechler River Ranger Station along the West Boundary Trail. The lake is barren, its outlet **Rock Creek**, does provide fair to good fishing for small cutthroat and rainbow, and plenty of brook. Two miles past the lake, the trail crosses **Little Robinson Creek** and then follows **Robinson Creek** north. Cutthroat and rainbow to 12 inches are found in these small creeks, as well as, small brook. **Buffalo Lake** (7,690 ft; 14 ac), 12 miles north, holds no fish.

SNAKE RIVER

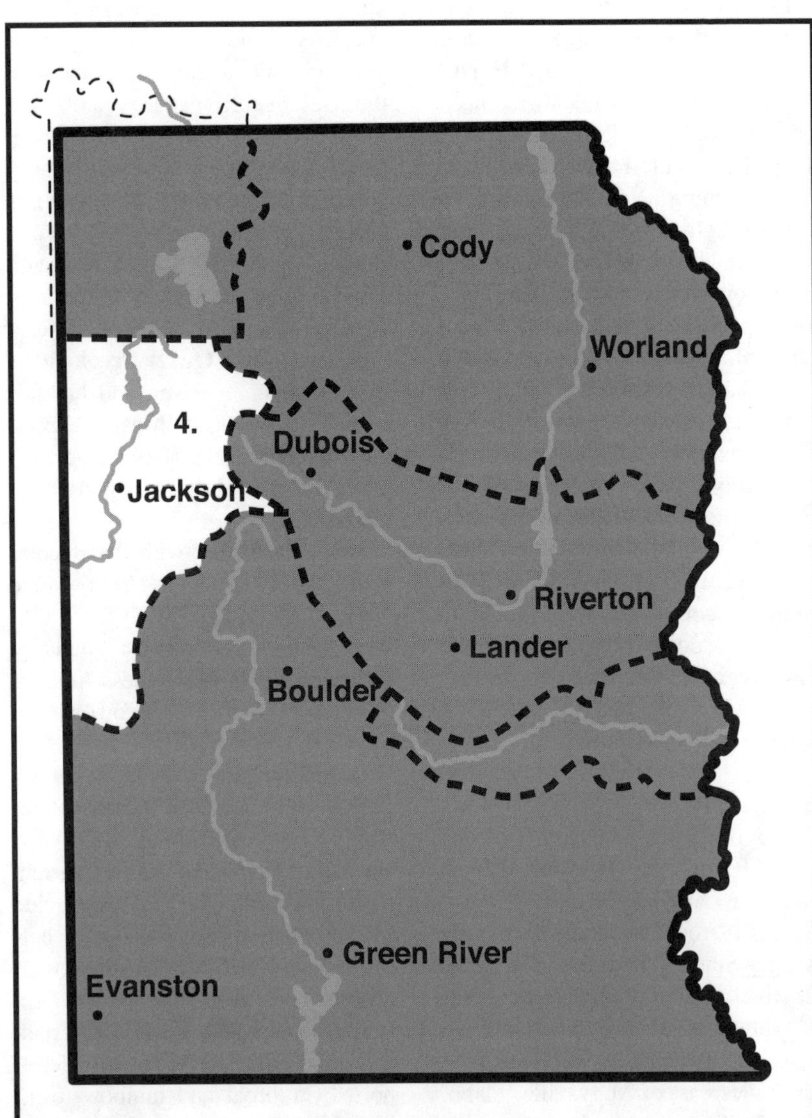

4. Snake River

SNAKE RIVER

The **Snake River** headwaters lie in the Teton Wilderness near the southeast corner of Yellowstone National Park. The river is only a trickle of a stream when it flows northwest into Yellowstone National Park, but after picking up water from the Heart and Lewis rivers and several small tributaries, the Snake River exits the park at the South Entrance looking more worthy of its world famous status. Inside Yellowstone National Park the Snake River is in very remote country, trails are the only way to reach the headwaters some 30 miles into the backcountry. After the Snake River leaves Yellowstone National Park it flows quietly through John D. Rockefeller Parkway on the way to the ever popular Jackson Lake and Teton National Park. The river is still small enough to wade at this point, fishing is for Snake River cutthroat, brown, and whitefish, although private property does limit access. Below Jackson Lake Dam the Snake River is too fast and deep to wade, besides it almost completely surrounded by private property, so most anglers employ guides to float the river. The fishing can be fabulous, anglers from around the world visit the Snake River to tempt the brown, whitefish, and native Snake River cutthroat which inhabit the river. Occasionally brook and lake trout are also caught. The Snake River flows south past such towns as Elk, Teton Village, Jackson, Moose, and Wilson, along the way the river picks up additional water from Pacific and Buffalo Fork creeks, and the Gros Ventre, Hoback, Greys, and Salt rivers. Below Hoback Junction, Highway 26 follows the river to the Idaho border where the river empties into Palisades Reservoir. Here the river is large, but more accessible to the public.

High alpine lakes and quality angling creeks are in abundance throughout the Snake River drainage in national forests and several wilderness areas. West of the Snake River Valley and the Teton Mountain Range, in the Targee National Forest, are in Winegar Hole and Jedediah Smith wilderness areas. To the east of the river are Bridger-Teton National Forest and the Teton and Gros Ventre wilderness areas.

This chapter covers the Snake River as it exits Yellowstone National Park at the South Entrance and flows south into Idaho at Palisades Reservoir. See the Yellowstone National Park chapter for a complete description of the Snake River drainage within Yellowstone National Park.

The Snake River proper from Yellowstone National Park downstream to Palisades Reservoir, is closed to trout fishing from November 1 through March 31 and closed to whitefish fishing from March 1 through March 31. The use or possession of fish, parts thereof, or fish eggs for bait is prohibited. All waters in the Teton Wilderness and Gros Ventre Wilderness are closed to fishing from November 1 through May . 1. The limit on trout is 2 fish.

The **Snake River** drainage and Teton National Park fishing seasons vary widely and the rules can be confusing. If you are unsure of any regulations please contact the Wyoming Game and Fish office in Jackson for assistance. The regulations do change often; current regulations should always be consulted.

SNAKE RIVER HEADWATERS - BELOW YELLOWSTONE NATIONAL PARK

From the Yellowstone National Park boundary the Snake River flows south through the John D. Rockefeller Memorial Parkway for about 8.5 miles on its way to Jackson Lake. The Snake River for 2 miles from the Yellowstone Park border, south to the Flagg Ranch, is paralleled by US 287. Below Flagg Ranch the Snake River swings west and then south again before making its way down to the Teton National Park Boundary. The Snake River here is small enough to wade or float for cutthroat averaging 13 inches. Large brown swim up from Jackson Lake in the fall. Many whitefish are present as well, averaging 11 inches. From the Yellowstone National Park Boundary downstream to Jackson Lake the daily limit on trout is 3 fish, only 1 can be longer than 20 inches. A Wyoming fishing license is required below Yellowstone National Park and within Grand Teton National Park; fishing is prohibited with real or artificial fish eggs; fish parts or any live minnows.

Polecat Creek enters the Snake River about 1 mile west of Flagg Ranch. Access is from Moose Falls just north of the South Entrance or along Reclamation Road. Reclamation Road crosses the creek about 1 mile from South Entrance Road, at this point, the creek is not within the Yellowstone Park boundaries. A paved road crosses the creek from Flagg Ranch, hike 2 miles up the creek into Yellowstone National Park for a 10-foot wide stream that offers fair fishing for 12-inch cutthroat and brown, Yellowstone regulations apply. Polecat Creek is closed in April and May within the park. **Glade Creek** enters the Snake River between Yellowstone National Park and Grand Teton National Park from the west for fair fishing for 10-inch cutthroat and some rainbow and brown near the Snake River. The trailhead for the creek is south from Grassy Lake Road.

JACKSON LAKE

Jackson Lake (6,770 ft; 17,800 to 25,730 ac) produced a record-setting 50-pound lake trout in 1983. The possibility of a trophy fish attracts thousands of anglers as big fish occasionally come out of the lake. The dam at the southeast end of the lake was built by the Bureau of Reclamation to provide irrigation water for Wyoming and Idaho. In addition to lake trout, Jackson Lake has fair size cutthroat, brown to 18 inches, and mountain whitefish to 15 inches. Ten-pound lake trout are not uncommon in the catch of knowledgeable anglers. Bank anglers have good luck

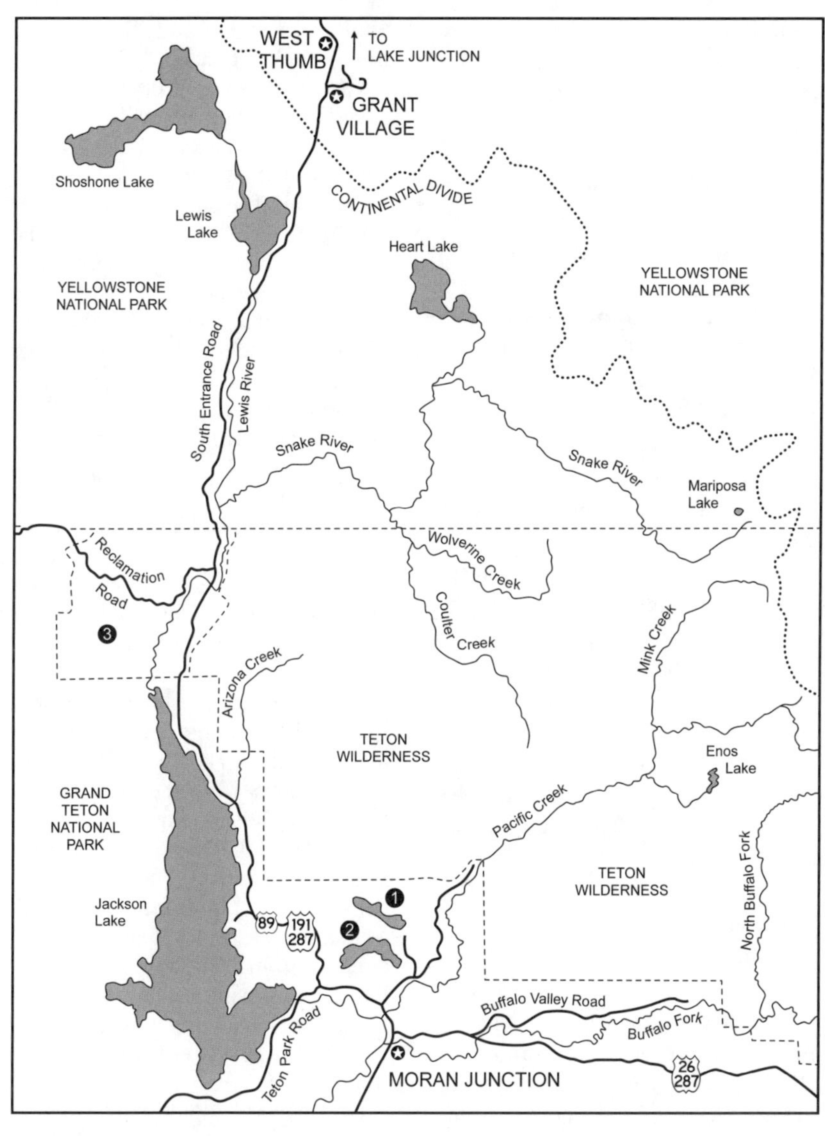

❶ Two Ocean Lake
❷ Emma Matilda Lake
❸ John D. Rockefeller Memorial Parkway

right after the ice breaks in the spring and in November. Campgrounds, fine lodgings and boat rentals are available by the lake; boat-launching facilities are at Colter Bay, Leeks Marina and Signal Mountain, all located on the east side of the lake. To get to the lake, take US 287-89 north from Moran Junction; exits are well marked. Catches here, and on Jenny and Leigh Lakes, are limited to 6 fish per day and only 1 trout can be longer than 24 inches. Jackson Lake is closed to fishing from October 1 to October 31.

Directly to the south of Jackson Lake, and best reached by trail from Leigh Lake, is **Trapper Lake** (6,880 ft; 3 ac) with fair to good fishing for cutthroat from 10 to 12 inches; and **Bearpaw Lake** (6,840 ft; 12 ac) which is fair to good for 10 to 15 inch cutthroat, and an occasional brown to 14 inches. These lakes are stocked on alternate odd years.

The high alpine lakes situated within the granitic pockets of the Teton Mountain Range in the park west of Jackson Lake are sterile - the ice stays on them much of the year and there is little food. Cutthroat were once stocked into the lakes many, many years ago, but their populations were not maintained over the last 40 to 50 years. These lakes include: **Cirque Lake** (9,600 ft; 62 ac), **Dudley Lake** (8,235 ft; 9 ac), and **Talus Lake** (9,665 ft: 19 ac).

The **Snake River,** from Jackson Lake to Hoback Junction, is roughly paralleled for about 39 miles by Highway 26. Fishing is good for cutthroat averaging 14 inches, some larger; and whitefish averaging 13 inches. The best way to fish this section is to float the river as access is limited by private property.

Snake River Fishing Regulations Below Jackson Lake

The Snake River proper for a distance of 150 feet below the downstream face of Jackson Lake Dam is closed to fishing throughout the calendar year. The Snake River proper from 150 feet below Jackson Lake dam downstream to the gauging station 1,000 feet below Jackson Lake dam the limit on trout is 3, only 1 can be over 20 inches. The Snake River proper from 1,000 feet below Jackson Lake dam (at gauging station) downstream to the Wyoming Highway 22 Bridge (Wilson Bridge) has a limit of 3 trout, only 1 can be longer than 18 inches, and all trout between 12 and 18 inches must be released. Fishing is restricted to artificial flies and lures only. The Snake River proper from the Wyoming Highway 22 Bridge (Wilson Bridge) downstream to West Table boat ramp has a limit of 3 trout, only 1 can be longer than 12 inches. The Snake River tributary streams from the Snake River Bridge at Hoback Junction, excluding the Hoback River, downstream to Palisades Reservoir are closed to fishing from November 1 through March 31. The Snake River tributary streams from Yellowstone National Park downstream to the Snake River Bridge at Hoback Junction are closed to fishing from November 1 through May 20.

A Wyoming fishing license is required within Grand Teton National Park; fishing is prohibited with real or artificial fish eggs; fish parts or any live minnows.

Grand Teton Park tributary streams below Jackson Lake Dam, excluding Buffalo Fork River, Pacific Creek,

Rob Yingling/Bighorn Web Design Photo

and Gros Ventre River have the following regulations; All tributary streams are closed to fishing from November 1 to July 31. The limit on trout is 3, only 1 can be longer than 12 inches. All tributary streams are fishing with artificial flies and lures only.

Note: All waters in the Teton Wilderness (which is to the east of Jackson Lake) are closed to fishing from November 1 through May 20. The limit on trout is 2 fish.

East of Jackson Lake

Located near Jackson Lake to the east are several lakes and ponds including: **Christian Pond** (6,825 ft; 30 ac) and **Swan Lake** (6,800 ft; 77 ac) which are closed to fishing; **Cygnet Pond** (6,830 ft; 20 ac), **Cow Lake** (6,820 ft; 17 ac), and **Heron Pond** (6,775 ft; 16 ac), which up until recently were stocked, but are no longer as they could not support fish.

Arizona Creek enters Jackson Lake on the east side of the drainage, flowing into Teton National Park from the Teton National Forest. The creek has fair fishing for cutthroat and brook. A trail following the stream also skirts **Bailey Creek** where there is fair fishing for small cutthroat. **Arizona Lake** (6,960 ft; 21ac) has fair fishing for cutthroat. **Pilgrim Creek** enters the lake farther south; it has cutthroat to 9-inches.

One mile north of Moran Junction, the marked Pacific Creek Road travels northeast 3 miles to the south end of **Two Ocean Lake** (6,905 ft; 580 ac), where there is fair fishing for 10- to 15-inch cutthroat. Fishing tends to be better in the spring and fall, evenings can be enjoyable for fly fishing for rising trout. Cutthroat are stocked yearly. From the south end of Two Ocean Lake, Emma Matilda Lake Trail goes to the west 1 mile to **Emma Matilda Lake** (6,880 ft; 890 ac) where the cutthroat population has given way to the Utah chub. No motors are allowed and no boat rental is available at either lake.

A few miles below Jackson Lake, **Pacific Creek** enters the Snake River just west of Moran Junction. The dirt Pacific Creek Road from US 287 follows the creek 7 miles to the Teton Wilderness Boundary; the Pacific Trail goes on from there. Inside the wilderness Pacific Creek is closed from November 1 to May 20 and the limit on trout is 2 fish. From the wilderness boundary downstream Pacific Creek is also closed to fishing from November 1 to May 20 and the limit on trout is 3 fish, only 1 can be longer than 12 inches. Fishing is with artificial flies and lures only. **Gravel Creek** flows into Pacific Creek 4.25 miles from the Pacific Trailhead. Gravel Creek Trail follows the creek north where there is fishing for cutthroat to 11 inches. About 4 miles from the trail is **Gravel Lake** (8,037 ft; 14 ac), which has plentiful cutthroat averaging 14 inches. Directly across from Gravel Creek and Pacific Creek confluence is a small creek to the south which drains Moss Lake. Follow the creek 3 steep miles to **Moss Lake** (8,370 ft; 8 ac), which

Rob Yingling/Bighorn Web Design Photo

has fair fishing for cutthroat 12 to 14 inches. The lake is currently being stocked every other year as no suitable spawning area is present. About 6 miles up the Pacific Creek Trail is the Enos Creek Cut-off east to Enos Lake. **Enos Lake** (7,750 ft; 190 ac) has moderate fishing for cutthroat, but shoals make shore fishing difficult; waders are recommended. The cutthroat population has been crowded over the years by a growing population of chub.

Buffalo Fork River empties into the Snake River at Moran Junction after a twisting trip west from headwaters near the Continental Divide in the Absaroka Mountains. The lower 9 miles of the river, from the Snake River to Turpin Meadows, are in Grand Teton National Park, Teton National Forest and some private lands; fishing waters are reached by foot or horseback. To get to the river's lower reaches, turn north off US 287 on the marked Buffalo Valley Ranch Road 3 miles east of Moran Junction, or turn north to Turpin Meadows at the Fourmile Meadow picnic area, halfway between Togwotee Lodge and the Blackrock Ranger Station. The Buffalo Fork River downstream of the Teton Wilderness boundary is closed to fishing from November 1 to March 31, the daily limit on trout is 3 fish with only 1 fish being larger than 12 inches. **Clear Creek**, a small tributary of the Buffalo Fork River, drains **Clear Creek Lake** (8,505 ft; 8.5 ac) several miles to the north in the wilderness. The lake has difficult fishing for small cutthroat. **Divide Lake** (8,660 ft; 4 ac), cross country 0.75 miles to the north, offers better fishing for cutthroat.

About 3 miles above Turpin Meadows, the south and north forks of the Buffalo Fork Creek unite. Above Turpin Meadows both forks are in the Teton Wilderness Area. Wilderness regulations apply. Trails follow both forks. **South Fork Buffalo Creek** provides better fish habitat for brook and cutthroat and is a favorite of outfitters; heavy run-off can effect fishing quality. Above South Fork Falls, about an 11-mile hike, fishing is mostly for cutthroat with a few rainbow present near Pendergraft Meadows. The South Buffalo Fork Trail follows the creek for 15 miles. About 8 miles upstream is the confluence with **Cub Creek**, which has brook and cutthroat for the first 2 miles and strictly brook (to 10 inches) above the junction with Trail Creek. **Morgan Lake** (9,415 ft; 2 ac) and **Mystery Lake** (9,395 ft; 5ac) are at the top of this drainage. Morgan Lake has very good fishing for small brook, Mystery Lake has cutthroat but tends to winterkill. Farther up, go north up the steep Lake Creek drainage to **Ferry Lake** (9,935 ft; 45 ac) which may harbor some golden. The lake has not been stocked in several years and has very limited spawning areas. **Blue Lakes** (9,860 to 9,960 ft; 2 to 4 ac), to the east of Ferry Lake, provide good fishing for cutthroat. The lakes are stocked on alternate odd years. A south fork in the trail will take you to the five

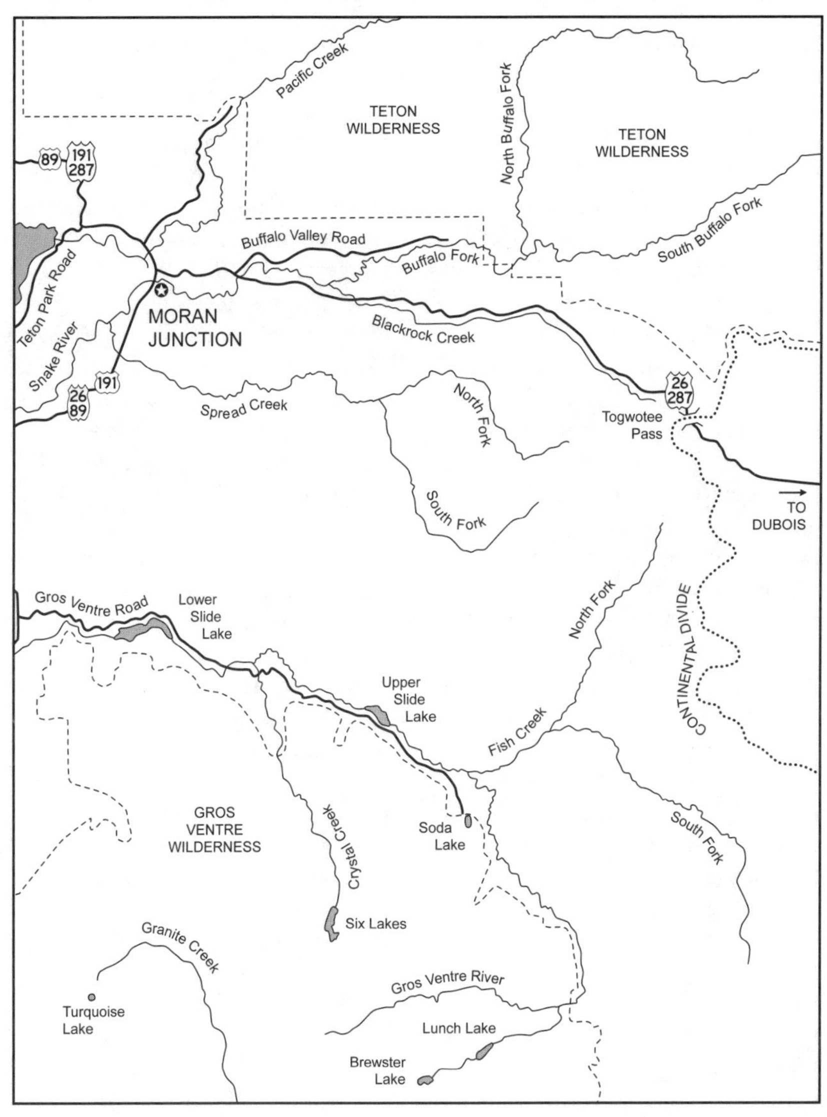

Angle Lakes (8,550 to 9,145 ft; 2 to 10 ac) which have fair to good fishing for cutthroat averaging 13 inches, with a moderate self-sustaining rainbow population in Rainbow Lake and **Johnson Creek**. The better known Angle Lakes – **Rainbow Lake, Golden Lake, Mackinaw Lake**, and **Trout Lake** - are reached by trail from Turpin Meadows to the west or Brook Lake to the south, and are heavily fished. Anglers who leave the trail to try the smaller, lesser-known lakes in the area will find an abundance of brook and cutthroat, though they tend to be small.

Two Ocean-North Buffalo Fork Trail heads north from the Turpin Meadows Trailhead. **North Buffalo Fork Creek** has some 8- to 10-inch brook and small cutthroat. **Soda Fork Creek** enters North Buffalo Fork Creek from the east about 4 miles from the trailhead. There is excellent fishing for whitefish in this stream, as well as, fair to good fishing for cutthroat averaging 10 inches and a few brook. There are also some rainbow in the upper reaches. The big meadows through which these streams flow often get nearly fished out in the fall; the steep canyons, more difficult to reach, do not. **Joy Peak Lake** (8,730 ft; 4 ac) has very good fishing for cutthroat to 10 inches. Just to the north of the headwaters of North Buffalo Creek, with no trail, is **Tri-County Lake** (10,080 ft; 14 ac). This high, rarely visited, lake has good fishing for cutthroat. The lake is stocked on alternate odd years. **Crater Lake** (9,325 ft; 74 ac) lies at the head of the Soda Fork drainage and has good fishing for wild cutthroat up to 12 inches.

Blackrock Creek flows into the Buffalo Fork Creek near the Blackrock Ranger Station after running next to US 287 from very near the top of Togwotee Pass. The creek is very good for 8- to 10-inch cutthroat, but is brushy and hard to fish. Near the stream headwaters is **Lost Lake** (9,450 ft; 14 ac) which is good for stocked cutthroat.

Spread Creek enters the Snake River from the east, 3 miles south of Moran Junction, after crossing under US 187-26-89. A dirt road (FR 30160) south from the Hatchet Campground (right below Blackrock Ranger Station) off US 287 travels 6 miles to the upper reaches of the creek. A trail leads from here up the North Fork, which has 10-inch cutthroat; the road farther along the south fork has the same kind of fishing. FR 30160 continues along **Leidy Creek** for 4 miles to **Leidy Lake** (8,720 ft; 11 ac) which has fair fishing for 10-inch cutthroat. Nearer to the Snake River, **Elk Ranch Reservoir** (6,870 ft; 102 ac) does not offer any fishing opportunities.

The two **Toppings Lakes** (lower 8,525 ft; 3 ac, upper 8,555 ft; 6 ac) lie on a small creek to the south of Spread Creek. The upper lake is barren, and the lower lake has good fishing for wild grayling. The trailhead to these lakes is on a dirt road (FR 30310) which leaves Highway 26 south of Cunningham Cabin, the last 2 miles to the lakes requires hiking on old roads to the lakes.

South of Jackson Lake

South of Jackson Lake lies Leigh Lake, String Lake, and Jenny Lake draining south into Cottonwood Creek, which later joins the Snake River. **Jenny Lake** (6,780 ft; 1200 ac) has the Teton Mountains for a backdrop, and cutthroat 12 to 16 inches and lake trout averaging 18 inches. Jenny Lake has a limit of 6

Rob Yingling/Bighorn Web Design Photo

trout per day, only one can be longer than 24 inches. Take the Teton Park Road south from Jackson Lake to reach Jenny Lake. A fee shuttle boat service provides access to the west side of the lake.

You can canoe up this chain of lakes - from Jenny Lake to String Lake to Leigh Lake - with a short portage to Leigh Lake. Motors up to 7.5 horsepower are allowed on Jenny Lake, but no motorcraft are allowed on String or Leigh lakes. Trails also connect the lakes beginning at String Lake. **String Lake** (6,880 ft; 42 ac) is a connecting lake between Jenny and Leigh lakes. The water here is shallower here than at the other lakes and has only fair fishing for cutthroat and whitefish to 14 inches. **Leigh Lake** (6,870 ft; 1200 ac) has fishing similar to Jenny Lake, but requires hiking a mile from the trailhead or a canoe trip to get there. Leigh Lake has a limit of 6 trout per day, only one can be longer than 24 inches. Leigh and Jenny Lakes are open to fishing year-round.

The Jenny Lake outlet, **Cottonwood Creek**, runs through park lands and private lands south for the 7 miles of its journey to the Snake River. It has fair to good fishing for cutthroat to 10 inches with an average stream width of 12 feet. Access is limited due to private property.

Several high mountain lakes lie to the west of these large lakes, as well as, Bradley, Taggart, and Phelps lakes. The terrain is steep and the snow stays late into the summer. Canyon Trail, Cascade Trail, Lake Solitude Trail, Valley Trail, and Amphitheater Trail provide access into the high country. These high alpine lakes are situated within the granitic pockets of the Teton Mountain Range and are mostly sterile - the ice stays on them much of the year and there is little food to support fish. Cutthroat were once stocked into the lakes many, many years ago, but their populations were not maintained over the last 40 to 50 years. These Lakes include: **Grizzly Bear Lake** (9,210 ft; 14 ac), **Mink Lake** (8,905 ft; 12 ac), **Lake Solitude** (9,035 ft; 37 ac), **Holly Lake** (9,420 ft; 7 ac), **Mica Lake** (9,560 ft 9 ac), **Lake of the Crags** (9,580 ft; 12 ac), **Ramsheild Lake** (9,510 ft; 2.5 ac), **Arrowhead Pool** (9,200 ft; 1 ac), **Laurel Lake** (7,530 ft; 3 ac), **Iceflo Lake** (10,630 ft; 23 ac), **Delta Lake** (9,045 ft; 6 ac), **Amphitheater Lake** (9,715 ft; 3 ac), **Snowdrift Lake** (10,020 ft; 52 ac), **Lake Taminah** (9,050 ft; 13 ac), **Timberline Lake** (10,320 ft; 6 ac), **Rimrock Lake** (9,910 ft; 17 ac), **Forget-me-not Lakes** (9,700 ft; 1 to 3 ac), **Indian Lake** (9,795 ft; 16 ac), **Marion Lake** (9,275 ft; 6.5 ac), and **Coyote Lake** (10,220 ft; 4 ac). Lake Solitude, Holly Lake, and Surprise Lake are rumored to harbor small populations of cutthroat. A good map or a quality guide service is recommended when planning a trip to any of these lakes.

Two miles west of Cottonwood Creek via marked trails are **Bradley Lake** (7,020 ft; 67 ac) and **Taggart Lake** (6,905 ft; 115 ac) with fair fishing for cutthroat, whitefish and brook. Brook are prevalent in Taggart Lake. Use of motorized watercraft is prohibited on Taggart Lake.

To the west of the Snake River and Moose Junction, **Phelps Lake** (6,625 ft; 451 ac) is located off the Moose-Wilson Road about 4 miles south of the town of Moose. From Moose- Wilson Road, follow Death Canyon Trailhead Road to the Death Canyon Trailhead, the lake is about 2 miles to the west. There is a road access to the lake but it is private. The lake has good fishing for cutthroat averaging 14 inches and lake trout.

GROS VENTRE RIVER

The **Gros Ventre River** enters the Snake River about 9 miles north of Jackson, crossing under US 187-26-89 from the east. The Gros Ventre River drainage upstream from the Snake River is closed November 1 to May 20. A paved road follows the river to Upper Slide Lake; there are good gravel roads for another 35 miles and trails beyond that. The Gros Ventre River has cutthroat averaging 12 inches, and is best in July and August. A few rainbow are found in the lower reaches of the river around the town of Kelly. **Lower Slide Lake** (6,910 ft; 575 ac), which was formed by a landslide across Gros Ventre Canyon in 1925, is 12 miles by good road from the highway. It has cutthroat averaging 12 inches, as well as, lake trout. Motors are allowed, and there are launching facilities but no boat rental. Two campgrounds are located within 3 miles upstream of the lake. **Note: All waters in the Gros Ventre Wilderness Area (which is south of the Gros Ventre River) are closed from November 1 to May 20. The limit for trout is 2 fish.**

Grizzly Lake (7,180 ft; 5ac) is 1.5 miles by trail from the upper end of Lower Slide Lake, and is stocked with small cutthroat.

Blue Miner Lake (9,400 ft; 26 ac) is barren, golden were stocked in the 1960's but did not survive.

Crystal Creek enters the Gros Ventre River 4 miles above Lower Slide Lake; a road follows the creek for 2 miles and then becomes a trail. The creek has small cutthroat and whitefish. Just above the Crystal Creek Campground, **Slate Creek** enters the Gros Ventre River from the north, offering fishing for small cutthroat. **Jagg Creek** comes in from the southwest getting water from **The Six Lakes** (9,270 to 9,320 ft; 2 to 85 ac), which are inside the Gros Ventre Wilderness. These lakes do not support fish, as even the largest of these lakes, **Dry Basin Lake**, runs low on water by the end of summer. One of the lakes, **Triangle Lake**, is reported to have some brook if they have not winterkilled.

Three miles up the Gros Ventre Road from Crystal Creek is **Upper Slide Lake** (7,275 ft; 75 ac). The lake first filled with sediment, then was bypassed by the Gros Ventre River, leaving it unable to support any fish. The lake is now managed as a swan habitat. **Cottonwood Creek** and **Fish Creek** enter the river from the north about 4 miles above Upper Slide Lake. Four wheel drive and

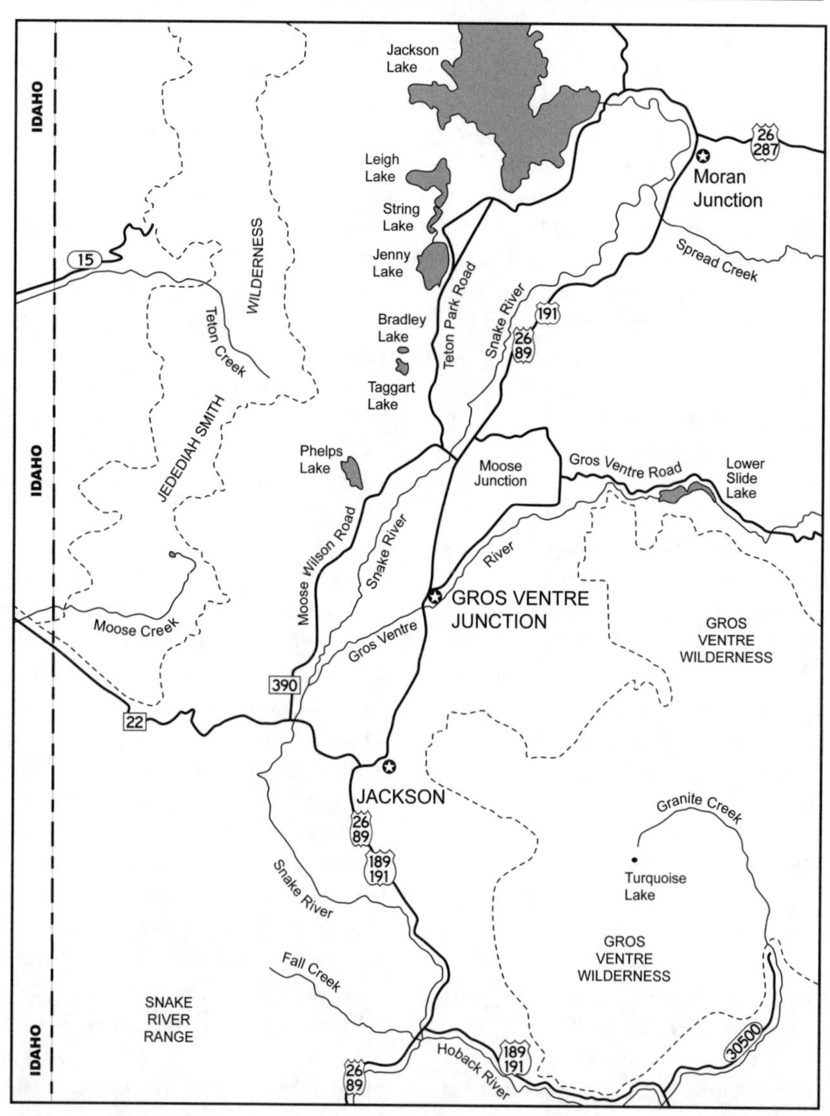

hiking trails provide access, with fair to good fishing for cutthroat averaging 10 inches.

At the headwaters of **South Fork Fish Creek** are the numerous **Fish Creek Lakes** (above 9,000 ft; 4 to 21 ac) with good fishing for cutthroat and brook averaging 10 inches. The best way to access these lakes is from Union Pass Road which connects the town of Dubois and the Upper Green River drainage. There are 4 wheel drive roads, foot trails, and horse trails from the west side of the Continental Divide near the summit of Union Pass. From the east of the summit of Union Pass a trail south leads to a group of lakes known as **Seven Lakes; Granite Lake** (10,215 ft; 44 ac), **Deep Lake** (9,990 ft; 23 ac), **Dollar Lake** (9,915 ft; 9 ac), **Horseshoe Lake** (9,855 ft; 43 ac), **Abosko Lake** (9,830 ft; 7 ac), **Grass Lake** (9,810 ft; 7 ac), and **Flat Lake** (10,100 ft; 8 ac) offer very good fishing for small cutthroat and brook.

To the north of Fish Creek Lakes and Seven Lakes is **Lake of the Woods** (9,245 ft; 89 ac). The lake is located just to the west of the summit of Union Pass, and offers fishing for cutthroat averaging 10 inches and grayling. Use of gas engines is prohibited.

Above Upper Slide Lake, 5.5-miles south off of Gros Ventre Road, is **Soda Lake** (7,800 ft; 55 ac) which is outside of Gros Ventre Wilderness. Soda Lake is managed as a trophy fishery for cutthroat up to 5 pounds. The lake is closed to fishing from November 1 to May 20. Fishing is with artificial flies and lures only. The daily limit on cutthroat is 1 fish over 20 inches, all cutthroat less than 20 inches must be released.

Inside Gros Ventre Wilderness near the headwaters of the Gros Ventre River are several lakes. **Chateau Lake** (8,820 ft; 7ac) has good fishing for brook. The two **Farney Lakes** (9,770 ft; 4.5 and 6 ac) are shallow and do not have fish. **Lunch Lake** (9,200 ft; 60 ac) and **Brewster Lake** (9,725 ft; 66 ac) are on the upper reaches of Dry Fork. Brewster Lake is stocked with small Snake River cutthroat. Lunch Lake has an occasional cutthroat, which most likely has drifted down from Brewster Lake.

JACKSON AREA

A second **Fish Creek**, which joins the Snake River 4 miles south of the town of Wilson, offers 6 miles of fishing north and south of Wilson, but is on private lands where permission to fish is required. The stream has cutthroat averaging 12 inches and some brook.

Flat Creek flows through the town of Jackson and enters the Snake River 8 miles to the south. **Elk Park Pond** (6,210 ft; 8 ac) and Flat Creek, from the west boundary of the National Elk Refuge to the US Highway 26/89/191 Bridge on West Broadway, are closed to fishing from November 1 to March 31. Fishing is prohibited for anyone 14 years old and older. Flat Creek from the Old Crawford Bridge site downstream to the refuge boundary fence (US highway 26/89/191) is closed throughout the calendar year. In its journey on the National Elk Refuge between Mcbride Bridge to the Old Crawford Bridge site the creek is closed to fishing from November 1 to July 31. Fishing is with artificial flies and lures only. The limit for cutthroat is 1 fish, all cutthroat less than 20 inches must be released.

Above the National Elk Refuge Flat Creek is open to the public and

is 4 wheel drive accessible for 3 miles. A trail continues up the drainage. This stream is good for cutthroat up to 12 inches and small brook. Vehicle traffic stops at the entrance to a private ranch, which adjoins **Flat Creek Lake** (7,460 ft; 55 ac). You can hike the 1.5 miles around the ranch to the lake, which has moderate fishing for cutthroat averaging 11 inches and small brook.

The lower part of Flat Creek in the South Park Elk Feeding Ground off US 187 is open to the public. The rest requires access permission from private landowners.

Nowlin Creek, a small creek to the south of Flat Creek, has limited fishing for cutthroat. Nowlin Creek above "closed area" signs is closed to fishing. On the National Elk refuge from the "closed area" signs downstream to the confluence with Flat Creek is closed to fishing from November 1 to July 31. The limit on cutthroat is 1 fish; all cutthroat over 20 inches must be released. This area is fishing with flies and lures only.

Goodwin Lake (9,500 ft, 10.5 ac), inside Gros Ventre Wilderness, has fair fishing for small cutthroat.

SNAKE RIVER BELOW JACKSON

From the Grand Teton Park downstream to the South Park Elk Feeding Ground, the **Snake River** is about 150-175 feet wide, much of it flowing through private land. There is a lot of floating and fishing pressure on this river. There is a limited public access area available along the flood control dikes 6 miles south of US 22 Bridge east of the town of Wilson. From the South Park Feeding Ground to Palisades Reservoir, the Snake River is on National Forest lands and open to the public. Numerous campgrounds and boat ramps are located long the river which is followed by Highways 26/89 to Palisades Reservoir. There are many rafters in this section and the river is large. The fishing is fair to good for cutthroat averaging 12 inches, some larger. The Snake River proper from the Wyoming Highway 22 Bridge (Wilson Bridge) downstream to West Table Boat Ramp has a limit of 3 trout, only 1 can be longer than 12 inches. The Snake River tributary streams from the Snake River Bridge at Hoback Junction, excluding Hoback River, downstream to Palisades Reservoir are closed to fishing from November 1 through March 31. The Snake River tributary streams from Yellowstone National Park downstream to the Snake River Bridge at Hoback Junction are closed to fishing from November 1 through May 20.

HOBECK RIVER

The **Hoback River** flows from the south into the Snake River 14 miles below the town of Jackson. It drains the west side of the Gros Ventre Mountains. US 187 runs alongside the river for 30 miles south from Hoback Junction. The river has long riffles and deep pools with fair fishing for cutthroat averaging 10 inches and whitefish to 12 inches. Winter

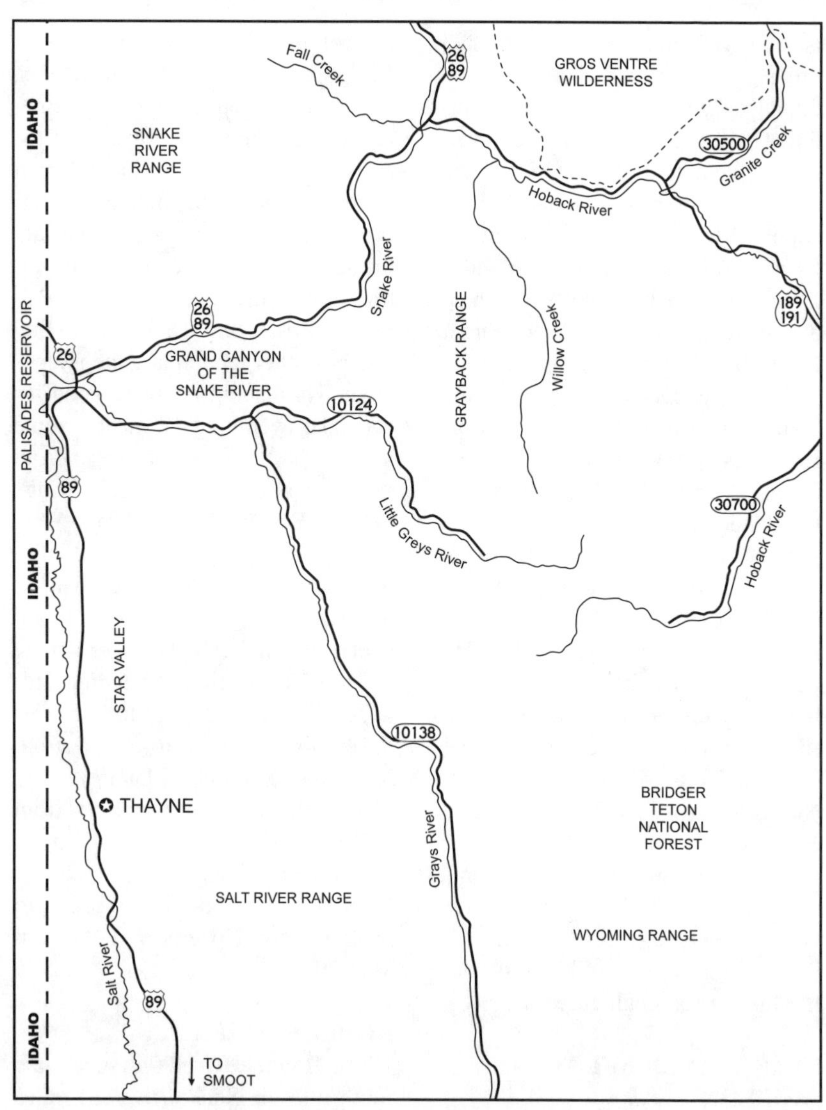

habitat is limited, and lower portions are on private property. There are two campgrounds off the road upriver from the Snake River, 7 and 12 miles from Hoback Junction. **Granite Creek**, the largest tributary, is 12 miles above Hoback Junction. A good gravel road (FR 30500) runs 9 miles along the stream to a campground and hot spring-fed swimming pool. The stream is heavily fished and has only fair fishing for cutthroat stocked to about 10 inches, and some possible small whitefish. Both the

Hoback River and Granite Creek fisheries are stocked, but are largely restricted by severe winter conditions and lack of suitable habitat. **Box Lake** (8,680 ft; 8 ac) is barren, it was stocked in the mid 1960's with golden but could not support fish. **Turquoise Lake** (9,450 ft; 14 ac) is 10 miles beyond the Granite Creek campground by trail. It has a self-sustaining cutthroat population, with fish to 12 inches.

Farther upriver, **Cliff Creek, Dell Creek, Jack Creek** and **Fisherman Creek** are marked at the highway and have dirt roads that follow them. They have small cutthroat, but fishing is only fair.

Fall Creek enters the Snake River less than a mile below Hoback Junction from the west. Ranging in width from 15 to 20 feet, it offers 6 miles of fishing for small cutthroat. You can reach it by dirt road (Wilson/Fall Creek Rd) from the town of Wilson south or go north on FR 3100 that leaves the highway 1-mile below Astoria Hot Springs. There is some posted land and private land along the creek.

Bailey Creek enters the Snake River from the south as the river changes its southern coarse to head west into the Grand Canyon of the Snake River. The creek is small offering fishing for small cutthroat. A trail follows the creek 3.75 miles to **Bailey Lake** (6,520 ft; 36 ac) which has good fishing for cutthroat to 12 inches, and brook in the 8 to 10 inch range.

GREYS RIVER

The **Greys River** splits the Wyoming Mountain Range from the Salt River Mountain Range and empties into the Palisades Reservoir near Alpine Junction on US 26-89. A gravel road (Greys River Road) follows the river for its full 55 miles. Near Alpine Junction the fishing is only poor to fair for small cutthroat. Whitefish average 10 inches. The stream can be waded above the juncture with the **Little Greys River**, 9 miles from Palisades. Greys River and Little Greys River have 10- to 16-inch cutthroat and are especially good for the experienced fly fisherman. Catch-and-release fishing is encouraged. Slot limit regulations have been imposed on the Greys River. From the Murphey Creek Bridge upstream to Corral Creek the limit for cutthroat is 2 fish per day; only 1 may exceed 16 inches. All cutthroat between 11 to 16 inches must be released immediately. Fishing is with artificial flies and lures only.

Fawn Creek, a half mile above Murphy Creek Campground, drains **Stump Lake** (6,690 ft; 5 ac). The lake currently supports a small population of rainbow, cutthroat will most likely be introduced into the lake in the near future. A short hike is required to reach the lake. **North Three Forks Creek,** a half mile above Forest Park campground, drains **Lake Bastow** (8,095 ft; 16 ac) which has fair fishing for wild cutthroat. Above Broad Canyon **Crow Creek** drains **Crow Creek Lakes** (9,205 and 9,440 ft; 3 and 10 ac). The

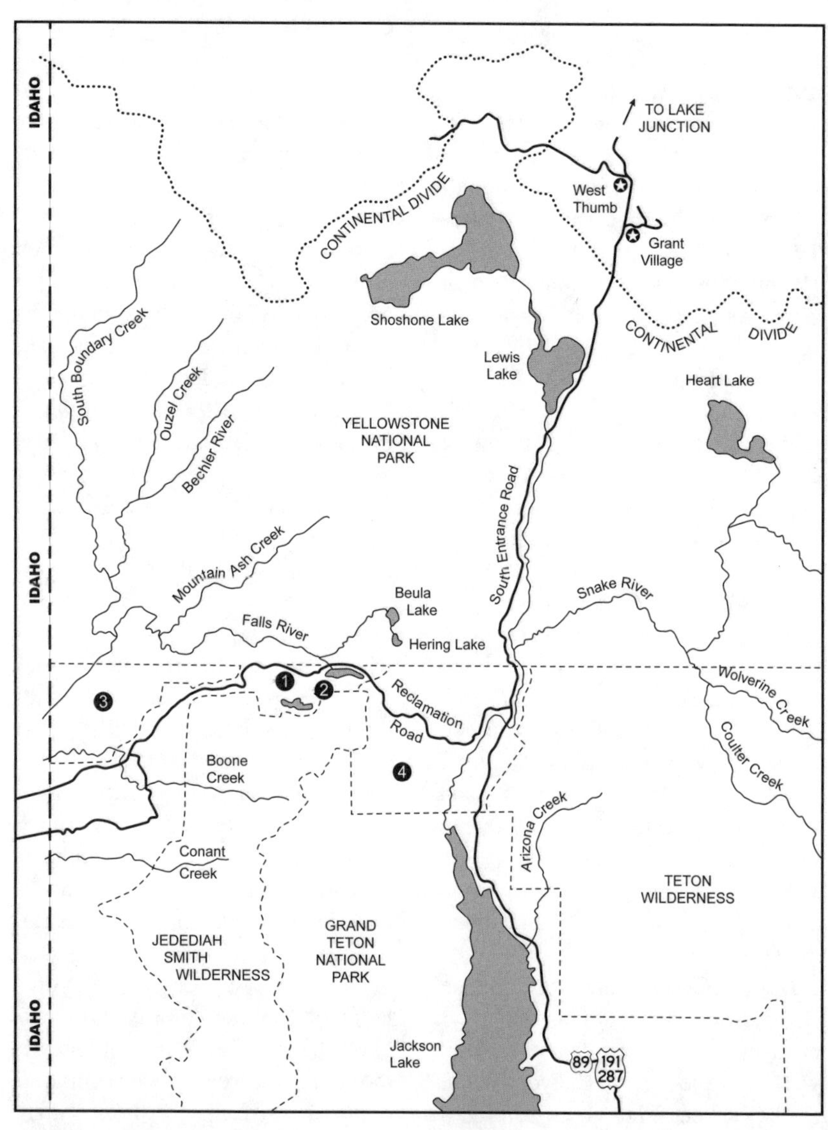

1. Lake of the Woods
2. Grassy Lake
3. Winegar Hole Wilderness
4. John D. Rockefeller Memorial Parkway

upper lake is barren, and the lower lake may have some wild cutthroat. **Corral Creek** enters Greys River from the west at Corral Creek Guard Station. At the headwaters of the creek 6.75 miles by steep trail is **Corral Creek Lake** (9,530 ft; 17 ac) with excellent fishing for cutthroat. The lake is stocked with cutthroat every other year.

SALT RIVER

The **Salt River** meanders through the rich bottomlands of the Star Valley and joins the Snake River drainage at Palisades Reservoir, which it enters from the south. US 89 runs along this stream from the reservoir to the south end of the Star Valley, which has been dubbed the "Little Switzerland" of Wyoming due to its mountainous beauty and dairy industry. The catch is for cutthroat, brown, rainbow, some brook. Whitefish are found in the lower reaches. The Salt River drainage upstream from the Upper Narrows Bridge (Wyoming Highway 238) is closed to trout fishing from November 1 through December 31. The Salt River from U.S. Highway 89 Bridge at the Silverstream Lodge downstream to Thayne Lane (County Road 125) has a limit of 4 trout per day; only 1 can be longer than 18 inches; all trout from 11 to 18 inches must be released, fishing is permitted by the use of artificial flies and lures only.

The river has excellent fishing after spring run-off for cutthroat and brown; and some brook, rainbow and whitefish. Upstream from Afton, the fish population is entirely cutthroat. Trophy brown can be caught in the fall using large streamers and sunken lines.

The Salt River downstream from the Upper Narrows Bridge on Hwy 238 near Afton is open all year. In the fall and winter the big brown from the lower reaches of the river come up the Salt River to spawn. They run 3 to 4 pounds and can get as large as 6 pounds.

Willow Creek enters the Salt River from the east between the towns of Thayne and Afton. Five miles of dirt road follow the creek, with a parking area at the end. There are brook, cutthroat and brown in this stream and its tributaries. There is much private land so get permission before crossing or fishing.

Cottonwood Lake (7,460 ft; 28 ac) lies 8 miles east of Smoot. A good gravel road (FR 10208) from US 89 runs 7 miles to the lake. Motors are allowed and there is a campground, but no boat rental. Cottonwood Lake has cutthroat and brook to 10 inches.

At the Salt River headwaters, overshadowed by Mt. Wagner, is **Wagner Lake** (9,815 ft; 6 ac) which is shallow and barren.

Palisades Reservoir (5,615 ft; 700 acres when full) is a BuRec (Bureau of Reclamation) reservoir that fluctuates as it serves irrigation needs in Idaho. The reservoir has maintained low levels of water (minimum pool) over the past few years due to drought conditions. Angling at the reservoir is primarily for cutthroat from 10 to 12 inches, which are stocked annually. Lake trout to 5 pounds are occasionally caught. Fishing is good from the shore at the mouths of the Snake, Greys and Salt rivers. Trolling is best in midsummer and fall, when sufficient water is held. There is no fishing reciprocity so a Wyoming fishing license only allows fishing in the Wyoming portion of the reservoir.

IDAHO BORDER WATERS

Note: All waters in the Jedediah Smith and Winegar Hole wilderness areas; and all waters on the west slope of the Teton and Snake River Mountain Ranges (excluding Grassy Lake Reservoir) are closed to fishing from November 1 to March 31. The limit for trout is 2 fish per day.

To the south of Yellowstone National Park, and to the west of the South Entrance to the park, Reclamation Road provides access to Cascade Creek and several lakes. Cascade Creek drains several lakes before flowing northeast into Falls River inside of Yellowstone National Park. **Grassy Lake Reservoir** (7,211 ft; 290 ac) has fair to good fishing for cutthroat from 13 to 17 inches and lake trout from 15 to 24 inches and occasionally to 15 pounds. Fishing for lake trout is best along the north shore early in the summer when the ice first breaks. Two-mile southwest of Grassy Lake is **Lake of the Woods** (7,375 ft; 175 ac), with fair fishing for rainbow averaging 10 to 15 inches. Access is from Camp Loll Road to the west end of the lake, which is open from April 1 to October 31. Also on the Cascade Creek drainage, below Lake of the Woods, is **Tillery Lake** (7,300 ft; 11ac), which is actually a water diversion dam, containing small rainbow. Cascade Creek is good for cutthroat averaging 9 inches.

To the northwest of Reclamation Road on the border of Yellowstone National Park and in the Winegar Hole Wilderness is **Fish Lake** (6,460 ft; 17 ac). The lake is a 0.5 mile hike from the end of the rough (4 wheel drive) Fish Lake Road. Fishing is good for small brook, cutthroat have been stocked to re-establish the native species. **Junco Lake** (6,440 ft; 9 ac) to the west is barren. Further to the west **Falls River** leaves Yellowstone National Park, northwest of Winegar Hole Wilderness Area. The river flows for 3 miles in Wyoming before exiting the state into Idaho. Fishing is fair for rainbow and cutthroat averaging 12 inches.

South of Falls River, down to Highway 22, numerous streams drain the western side of Jedediah Smith Wilderness. With the exception of waters around the Falls River and Reclamation Road these waters are only accessible from roads and trails coming in from Idaho. South of Falls River, and accessible from Idaho via Steele Lake Road and trail, is **Widgit Lake** (6,350 ft; 22 ac) which is barren.

Boone Creek, flowing from the west, drains the northwestern portion of Jedediah Smith Wilderness. Boone Creek has good fishing for small brook. The creek is crossed by Reclamation Road. Where the road crosses **North Boone Creek,** a road leading to the north accesses the barren **Loon Lake** (6,455 ft; 24 ac) and Fish and Junco lakes. Further down stream where the road crosses **Middle Boone Creek** is **Moose Lake** (6,440 ft; 17 ac). Moose Lake is not stocked but occasionally has a few nice sized brook which drift in from Boone Creek, otherwise the lake tends to winterkill. From here Boone Creek and Reclamation Road head west and go into Idaho passing by **Indian Lake** (6,420 ft; 100 ac), which is shallow and only supports lily pads. Neither **Bergman Reservoir** (6,385 ft; 24 ac) or **Ernest Lake** (6,545 ft; 12 ac) offer any fishing opportunities.

Conant Creek which flows west out of the wilderness and into Idaho, has good fishing for cutthroat. **Hidden Lake** (7,225 ft; 16 ac), also inside Jedediah Smith Wilderness, offers good fishing for stocked cutthroat.

Further south is **Bitch Creek, Jackpine Creek, Badger Creek, Leigh Creek, Teton Creek, Darby Creek, and Fox Creek** offering fishing for small cutthroat.

To the north of SR 22, and accessible from Idaho, is **Moose Creek** which drains **Moose Lake** (9,300 ft; 7.5 ac) and the lower south portion of the Jedediah Smith Wilderness. A 7.5-mile hike and a 2,500 ft climb in elevation is required to reach the lake which has excellent fishing for stocked cutthroat.

GREEN RIVER

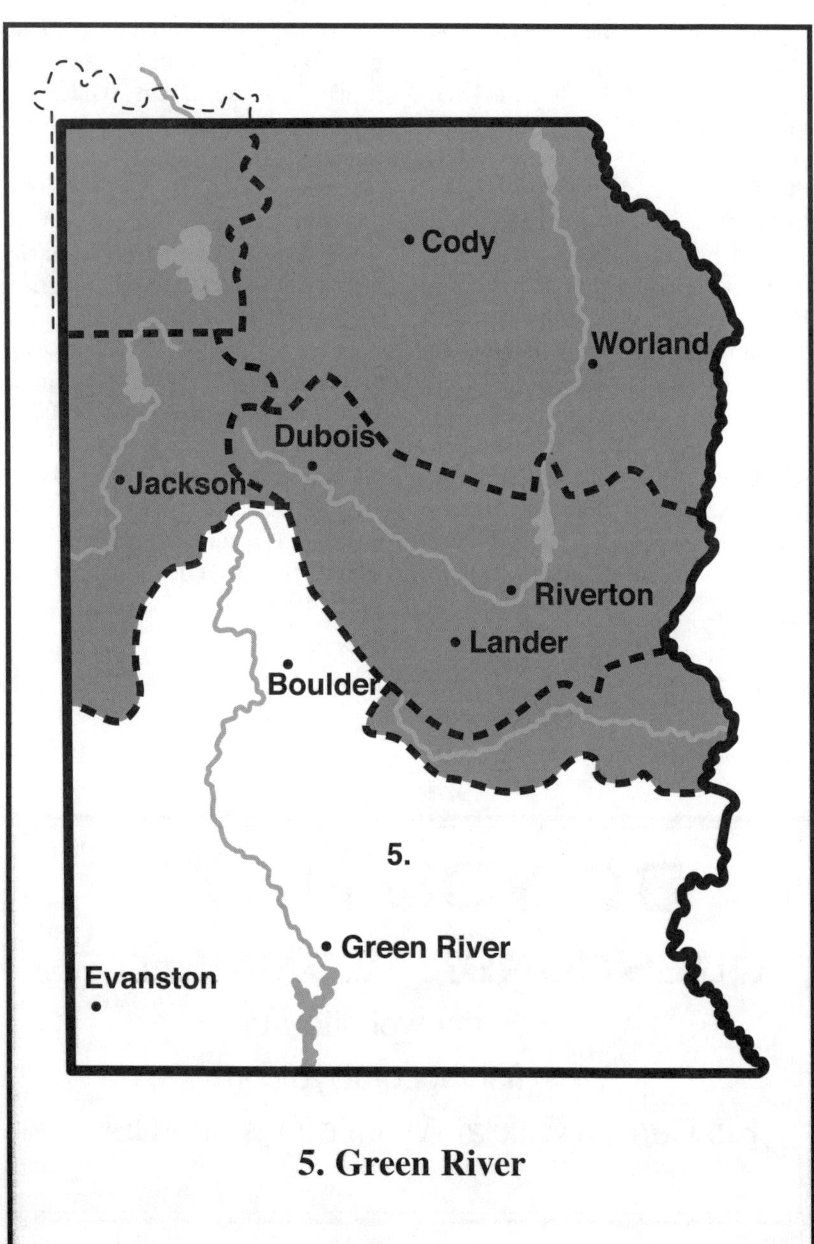

5. Green River

GREEN RIVER

The **Green River** headwaters begin high up in the Bridger Wilderness on the west side of the Wind River Mountain Range. The Bridger Wilderness, like the Fitzpatrick and Popo Agie Wilderness Areas on the east slope of the Wind River Mountains, has a plethora of alpine lakes providing a wealth of angling opportunities for golden, cutthroat, rainbow, brown, grayling, brook, and lake trout. A guide or outfitter is a good idea if you are not familiar with the area. The weather here can be temperamental, inclimate weather can appear out of nowhere. There are many unnamed lakes and shallow ponds, referred to as tarns, that appear on maps of this area. A guide or outfitter can steer you clear of some of the barren mountain waters that might look inviting on a map. In addition, many trails are often poorly marked or nonexistent. Topographic maps are an absolute must for the backcountry angler.

There are at least seven approaches to the Bridger Wilderness. Trailheads at Green River Lakes, New Fork Lakes, Spring Creek Park (Willow Lake), Elkhart Park, Boulder Lake, Scab Creek, and Big Sandy provide access into the countless lakes and streams in the Bridger Wilderness Area, as well as, to the north/south Highline, Lowline, and Fremont trails. The trailhead at Lower Green River Lake is the northernmost entry, from this trailhead the Highline Trail stretches almost 75 miles to the south. The Bridger Wilderness receives heavy pressure from backpackers, campers, hikers, anglers, and rock and mountain climbers.

The Green River from the forest boundary north of the town of Cora to Fontenelle Reservoir flows through almost exclusively private property, some BLM and state lands exist, using a quality guide service to float the river is highly recommended. After the Green and East Fork rivers combine south of the town of Boulder, the Green River flows southwest from the mountain lakes and glaciers of the Wind River Range, then south through high desert to the Utah border, a trip of almost 200 miles. Along the way the Green River fills Fontenelle Reservoir south of the town of La Barge. Below Fontenelle Reservoir the Green River flows through Seedskadee National Wildlife Reserve, and from there through a good share of public lands on the way to the Utah/Wyoming border and the infamous Flaming Gorge Reservoir. Several fine tributaries, with quality fishing opportunities, enter the Green River between Fontenelle Reservoir and Utah border, such as; Big Sandy, Hams Fork, Blacks Fork, and Henrys Fork rivers which drain much of the southwest corner of the state.

In Wyoming, the northern flowing Bear River makes a brief appearance on the western border with Utah and Idaho before making its long looping trip back down south to flow into the Great Salt Lake west of Brigham City, Utah.

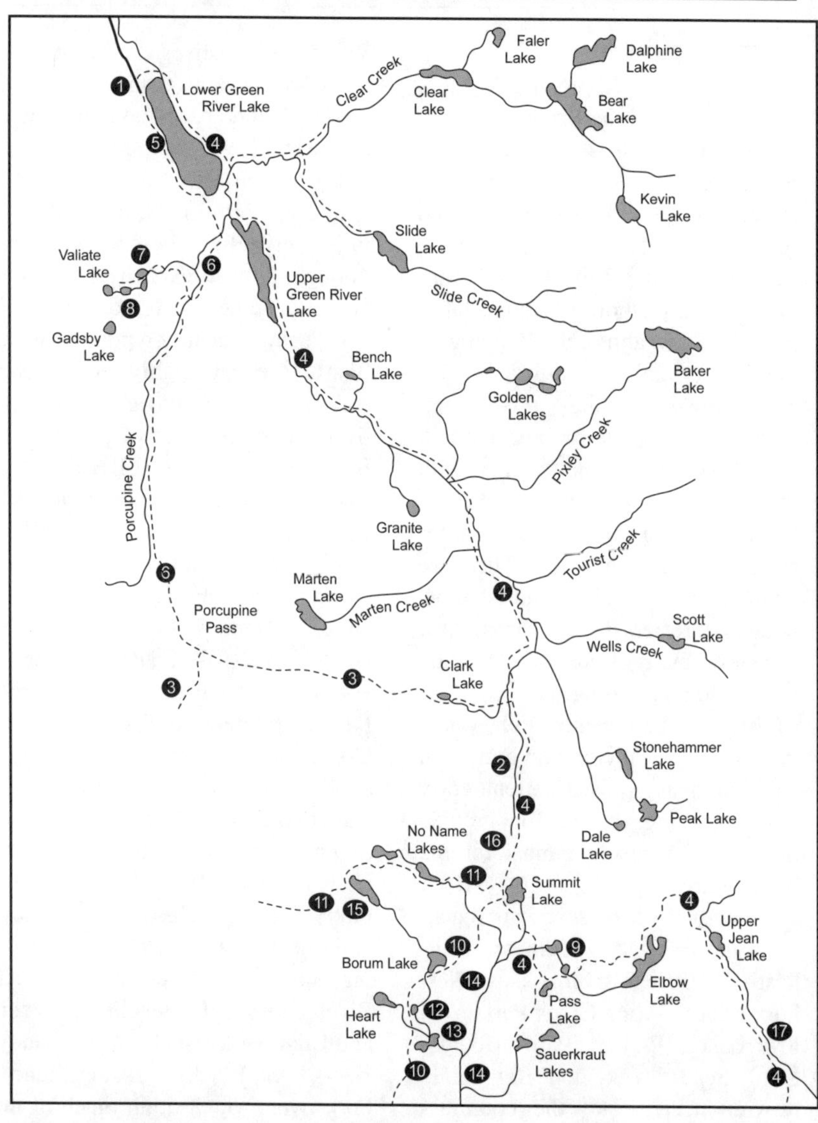

1 Highline Trailhead
2 Trail Creek
3 New Fork Trail
4 Highline Trail
5 Lakeside Trail
6 Porcupine Trail
7 Twin Lakes
8 Shirley Lake
9 Twin Lakes
10 Pine Creek Canyon Trail
11 Doubletop Mountain Trail
12 Gottfried Lake
13 Neil Lake
14 Pine Creek
15 Cutthroat Lake
16 Green River Pass
17 Fremont Creek

Additionally, the Little Snake River drainage near the towns of Baggs and Savery, on the Colorado border, drains a small southern portion of the state before making its way through Colorado to meet up with the Yampa River east of Dinosaur National Monument.
Note: The Wyoming Fishing Regulations that allow for an additional limit of 10 brook trout does not apply to the entire Green River drainage.

GREEN RIVER HEADWATERS

To get to the headwaters of the Green River, drive 4 miles west of Pinedale on US 191; turn north on Hwy 352 and drive about 25 miles on paved road to the forest boundary, followed by another 18 miles of dirt road, to the lower end of the **Green River Lakes,** and several trails into the surrounding wilderness area. **Lower Green River Lake** (7,961 ft; 453 ac) lies on the edge of the Bridger Wilderness. The lake has rainbow from 10 to 16 inches, some larger, and lake trout as large as 10 pounds. Whitefish and brook are also present. Lower Green River Lake is a popular ice fishing lake. To the south is **Upper Green River Lake** (7,965 ft; 135 ac) with cutthroat and rainbow to 15 inches. There are an occasional brook to 10 inches, plus lake trout. Green River Lakes (upper and lower lakes) have a limit on trout, salmon and grayling of 6 fish, only 1 trout can be longer than 20 inches. All lake trout between 16 and 26 inches must be released.

The Highline Trailhead (8,050 feet) leaves from the lower lake and provides access to the Upper Green River Lake and the upper reaches of the Green River in the Bridger Wilderness. The Green River above Upper Green River Lake to the headwaters is fair for small brook, cutthroat, and an occasional rainbow, most fish are 8 inches or smaller.

About 2 miles above from Lower Green River Lake to the northeast is **Bench Lake** (9,192 ft; 1 ac) which is barren.

About 4 miles up the Green River on the Highline Trail, a small stream enters from the southwest, draining **Granite Lake** (9,247 ft; 15 ac). Granite Lake has good fishing for brook to 10 inches and some cutthroat. Another mile up the trail, **Elbow Creek** enters from the east, draining the three **Golden Lakes** (10,940 to 11,100 ft; 6 to 13 ac). These lakes have fair fishing for golden up to 12 inches. These drainages do not have maintained trails. Above Elbow Creek less then 0.25 miles **Pixley Creek** enters from the east and heads at the barren **Baker Lake** (11,670 ft; 102 ac).

Another mile along the Highline Trail, **Marten Creek** enters the river from the west. It heads at **Marten Lake** (10,925 ft; 47 ac), which is good to very good for 10-inch brook. Wells Creek enters from the east after draining **Scott Lake** (10,530 ft; 27 ac), which is barren.

Two miles upstream from the confluence of Marten Creek and the Green River, the Highline Trail bends southwest, following **Trail**

Rob Yingling/Bighorn Web Design Photo

Creek. A mile along Trail Creek, the New Fork Trail comes in from the west. Take the New Fork Trail west up the **Clark Creek** drainage to **Clark Lake** (10,265 ft; 4 ac) for small rainbow. Trail and Clark creeks are rated fair for small rainbow and brook.

About 1.5 miles up the trailless banks of the Green River above Trail Creek, an unnamed creek enters from the east. Half a mile up this creek is **Stonehammer Lake** (10,260 ft; 17 ac), which has fair fishing for golden averaging 10 inches. No marked trail. Another 0.5 mile up the drainage is **Peak Lake** (10,515 ft; 32 ac) with small, healthy golden. Over a small saddle to the west is **Dale Lake** (10,704 ft; 5 ac) which does not contain fish.

The upper portion the Green River drainage is an area that is accessible from the Green River Lakes but also by the New Forks Trail from New Fork Lakes. The New Fork trailhead is about 15 miles west of the Green River's upper reaches and follows along the New Fork River. The trail enters this drainage just west of Clark Lake. The Highline Trail continues along Trail Creek over Green River Pass to Summit Lake and the Pine Creek drainage, which is discussed later in the chapter.

CLEAR CREEK

Between Lower and Upper Green River Lakes on the Highline Trail, **Clear Creek** runs into the Green River from the east. Clear Creek Trail follows the creek 3 miles to Clear Creek Natural Bridge, another 3 miles up the drainage is **Clear Lake** (8,855 ft; 53 ac), with golden to 13 inches. **Faler Lake** (10,185 ft; 13 ac) with 10 to 12 inch golden, with a few larger possible, is a long rough 1 mile climb northeast of Clear Lake. Two miles east from Clear Lake is **Bear Lake** (10,540 ft; 107 ac) with good fishing for rainbow to 12 inches. Less than 0.5 mile north of Bear Lake is **Daphne Lake** (11,202 ft; 80 ac) with decent rainbow. **Kevin Lake** (11,295 ft; 42 ac) is barren. About 1 mile above the Highline Trail, Clear Creek is joined by **Slide Creek**, which drains **Slide Lake** (9,490 ft; 75 ac). Slide Lake is a tough 3 mile hike up Slide Lake Trail from Clear Creek Trail. Fishing is rated fair for brook to 10 inches in Slide Lake, Slide Creek has small brook and rainbow.

Flowing from the west into the Green River between Upper and Lower Green River lakes is **Porcupine Creek**. From the Green Lakes Trailhead follow the Lakeside Trail around the west side of Lower Green River Lake for 3 miles to the Porcupine Trail, follow this steep trail 1.5 miles to the southwest up Porcupine Creek. A trail leaves the main trail to the north to several small lakes with fair cutthroat fishing. They include; **Twin Lakes** (9,820 ft; 4and 6 ac), **Shirley Lake** (10,195 ft; 4 ac), **Valiate Lake** (10,075 ft; 4 ac) and **Gadsby Lake** (10,255 ft; 10 ac), all within a 1 mile radius. The Porcupine Trail continues along Porcupine Creek and over Porcupine Pass into

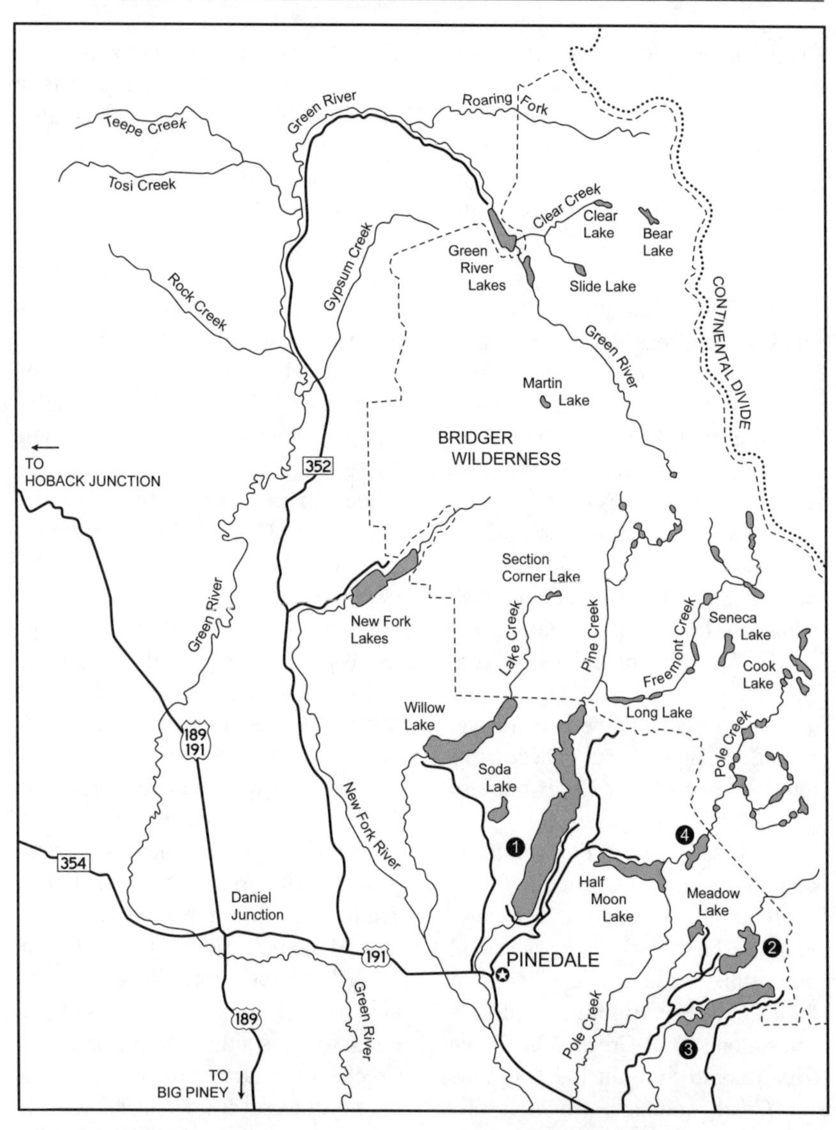

1 Fremont Lake
2 Burnt Lake
3 Boulder Lake
4 Fayette Lake

the New Fork River drainage.

Below Green River Lakes, fourteen miles from the forest boundary, **Roaring Fork Creek** drains into the Green River from the northeast. The creek offers good fishing for brook and cutthroat. A 4 wheel drive road (FR 146—closed within the Bridger Wilderness) follows it much of the way. It is about 15 miles to the headwaters where **Native Lake** (9,925 ft; 14 ac) is located. The lake is good for golden, rainbow and rainbow/golden crosses to 10 inches, with some larger. Still higher in the Roaring Fork Creek drainage are **Crescent Lake** (10,730 ft; 13 ac) and **Upper Crescent Lake** (10,770 ft; 6 ac) with plentiful small cutthroat, with an occasional larger fish.

Wagon Creek comes in from the north at a curve in the river known as, "The Big Bend". **Mosquito Lake** (8,885 ft; 85 ac), near the headwaters, and the creek has small brook.

Three miles northwest of the Kendall Bridge on a good gravel road (FR 156) is **Tosi Creek**, which can be followed west on a rough road (FR 015). Private land 2-3 miles above FR 156 will require landowner permission to cross. Fishing is fair for cutthroat and brook to 12 inches. A tributary to Tosi, joining it 3 miles west of the Green River, is **Tepee Creek** (off FR 257), which is fair for brook to 10 inches and an occasional cutthroat.

Cross the bridge over the Green River at Whiskey Grove Campground to the west side of the river and travel south on a dirt road (FR 10132) 2.5 miles to **Rock Creek**, which joins the Green River at the forest border. Follow this 10- to 15-foot wide stream for several miles by 4 wheel drive road (the road is blocked by avalanche about 3 miles up the creek) and farther by trail, for fair fishing for brook and cutthroat and at the lower end for brown and rainbow to 12 inches.

Also very near the forest border is a 4 wheel drive road (FR 102) leading east along **Gypsum Creek**. This 10- to 15-foot wide creek provides 8 miles of fishing for cutthroat and brook. It heads at **Big Sheep Mountain Lake** (10,007 ft; 6 ac), which has small cutthroat.

There are 2 miles of the Green River between Whiskey Grove Campground and the Forest Service boundary downstream open to public fishing, the Green River itself offers good fishing for rainbows, brook and whitefish averaging 12 inches from Kendall Warm Springs downstream to the forest boundary. **Kendall Warm Springs** and **Kendall Warm Springs Creek** are closed to fishing to protect the Kendall Dance. From the forest boundary south there are 17.3 miles of private land to the beginning of the Warren Bridge Easement, the next area open to public fishing. The Green River, from the confluence with Kendall Warm Springs downstream to the uppermost boundary of the Warren Bridge access area, the limit for trout is 2 fish, only 1 can be longer than 20 inches. All trout between 10 and 20 inches must be released. Fishing with artificial flies and lures only.

From the forest boundary south of Whiskey Grove Campground, the Green River flows over 50 miles down to Fontenelle Reservoir, mostly through private land. Floating the river is almost the only method of accessing the river. Floating is through private lands, crossing or landing on private property is trespassing; for this reason, those not familiar with the river should enlist the help of a guide and a good set of BLM maps.

Warren Bridge Fishing Easement (9.5 miles north of Daniel Junction on Highway 189/191) provides about 10 miles of heavily used public fishing and float launching. **Daniel Fishing Easement** (access from Pape Road 3.5 miles from Daniel Junction on Highway 189/191) offers about 6 miles of heavily used fishing public fishing. Fishing in both, overused easements, is for rainbow and brown averaging 10 inches, occasionally larger fish to 4 pounds are caught.

A popular floating area starts at the Warren Bridge and runs downstream toward the town of Daniel on Hwy 191. There are two access points between the Warren Bridge and Daniel Junction; one is west of Daniel Junction, the other is near the Daniel Fish hatchery. Below Daniel, there is a pull-out at Trappers Point and another between there and the Green River's confluence with the New Fork River, a stretch of more than 20 miles. This is a long float. You will need maps and/or help from the Wyoming Game and Fish Department, BLM officials or a guide to locate pull-outs. This area has rainbows, cutthroat, brown and whitefish averaging 13 inches, occasionally larger fish to 6 pounds are caught. From the lower boundary of the Blackmon McLaughlin Public Fishing Easement (Forty Rod Public Fishing Area) downstream to the Swain's (Wood's) Bridge on Road 23-179 the limit on trout is 2 fish, only 1 trout can be longer than 20 inches. All trout between 10 and 20 inches must be released. Fishing is with artificial flies and lures only.

The Green River from Swains's (Wood's) Bridge Road 23-179, downstream to Fontenelle Reservoir the limit on trout, salmon and grayling is 6 fish; only 1 trout can be longer than 20 inches, and only 3 can be a trout. This water is deep, fairly fast and has numerous holes, but the fishing is not as good as upstream. Rainbow and brown up to 14 inches are caught. Be careful and do not trespass on private land; most anglers who float this section of the Green River employ the assistance of a qualified outfitter or guide. There are a couple of public access points on the Green River, below the confluence with the East Fork River. One is 5 miles northeast of the town of Big Piney and another along Hwy 189 south of the town of LaBarge. Watch for signs indicating public access.

Note: Private property is just that, private. No matter how good private land and water look for fishing or landing, do not trespass. Many public

Rob Yingling/Bighorn Web Design Photo

Rob Yingling/Bighorn Web Design Photo

places with great fishing opportunities abound around the state so please stay off land belonging to others.

NEW FORK RIVER

The **New Fork River** flows west out of the mountains about 10 miles north of the town of Cora. The two **New Fork Lakes** (7,820 ft; combined size 1250 ac), combined as they are actually connected by a channel, lie outside the wilderness area and have a boat launching site with parking area and two campgrounds. With depths as great as 200 feet, the lakes have lake trout to 30 inches and up to 20 pounds, plus brook and kokanee salmon to 12 inches. Fishing is fair for rainbow in the 10 to 15 inch range. New Fork Lakes are easily reached by driving 6 miles west on US 191 from Pinedale to paved SR 352, follow this road north 14.5 miles to New Fork Road, and 2.5 more miles to the lakes. The river above New Forks Lakes has fair fishing for cutthroat to 10 inches and small brook in the upper reaches. Above the lakes the New Fork River is closed to fishing September 1 through April 30.

On the north side of the lakes, near the Narrows Campground, is the New Forks Trailhead (7,900 feet). The New Fork Trail roughly follows the New Fork River for seven miles to New Fork Park. From New Fork Park, New Fork Trail continues north and then east for 8 miles to Clark Lake in the Upper Green River drainage. To the southeast of New Fork Park, Palmer Lake Trail follows **Reynolds Creek** over a high divide to Palmer Lake on the Lake Creek drainage. To the east of Palmer Lake Trail lie a group of lakes called **Hidden Lakes** (10,720 to 10,900 ft; 12 to 13 ac) with good to very good fishing for brook to 10 inches. The lakes are difficult to reach and require a steep uphill cross country hike without a trail. Other unnamed and remote ponds and lakes in this area offer fair fishing for golden to 12 inches, many of the ponds are barren so a guide is recommended to show you which lakes support fish.

The New Fork River flows out of Bridger National Forest, just below New Fork Lakes, and turns south for more than 30 miles to its confluence with the East Fork River. It then turns west another 20 miles to merge with the Green River just east of the town of Big Piney. Above the town of Pinedale the river is mostly private with a mixture of private and public land below.

West of the town of Pinedale **Duck Creek** flows from the northwest into the New Fork River, Hwy 191 parallels the lower reaches of the creek where there are 3 walk-in access areas. Fishing is for wary brown averaging 12 inches, with larger brown averaging 15 inches in the fall. Below the town of Pinedale the New Forks River, from the Mesa Road Bridge downstream to the uppermost boundary of the Boulder Bridge Easement, has a limit for trout, salmon, and grayling of 6 fish; only 2 can be trout, and all trout between 10 and 20 inches must be released. Fish-

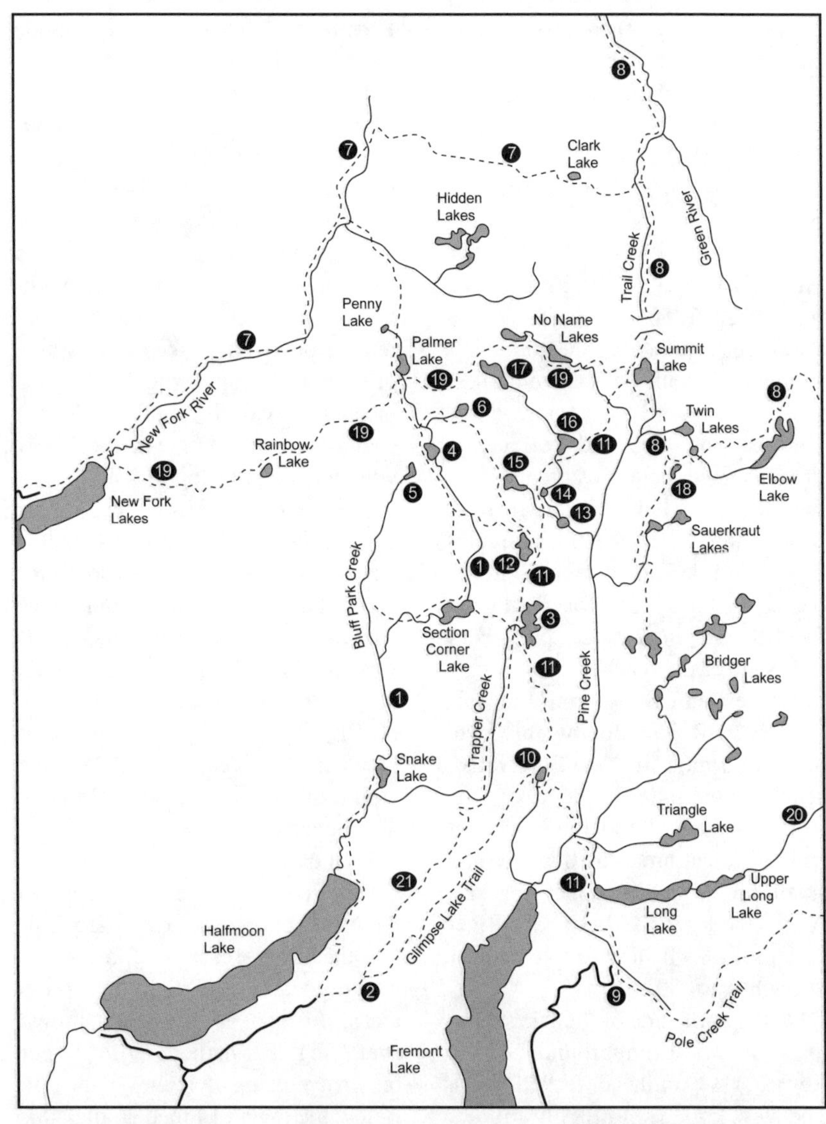

1. Lake Creek
2. Spring Creek Park Trailhead
3. Trapper Lake
4. Round Lake
5. Lost Camp Lake
6. Dean Lake
7. New Fork Trail
8. Highline Trail
9. Elkhart Park Trailhead
10. Glimpse Lake
11. Pine Creek Canyon Trail
12. Trail Lake
13. Neil Lake
14. Gottfried Lake
15. Heart Lake
16. Borum Lake
17. Cutthroat Lake
18. Pass Lake
19. Doubletop Mountain Trail
20. Fremont Creek
21. Trapper Creek Trail

ing is with artificial flies and lures only. Below the upper most boundary of the Boulder Bridge Easement to the Green River the limit for trout, salmon, and grayling is 6 fish. Only 3 can be trout, and only 1 trout, salmon or grayling can be over 20 inches.

The New Fork River, like the Green River, is a popular river to float in its lower reaches. The fishery here leans more toward browns than rainbows, and some brook. The trout average 12-14 inches, but there are some 4 pound browns taken. Small hairwings and dry flies are successful.

North of the junction with the East Fork River, the New Fork River is surrounded mostly by private land. Floaters often put their craft in at the town of Boulder, pull out on the BLM lands below the New Fork and East Fork rivers confluence. Careful attention to land ownership - or better still, a guide - is important. Floaters also pull out at the Big Piney cutoff. Like the Green River, New Forks River receives a great deal of fishing pressure.

WILLOW CREEK

The headwaters of **Willow Creek** are inside the wilderness about 3 miles from the Willow Creek Guard Station at **Rainbow Lake** (10,190 ft; 8 ac), which has good fishing for rainbow and some brook. Below the forest and wilderness boundaries Willow Creek flows through private property to the New Fork River.

Several miles south, outside of the wilderness, is **Willow Lake** (7,745 ft; 1805 ac), about 14 miles north of Pinedale on Willow Lake Road. There are campgrounds on this big lake and a concrete boat ramp for smaller trailered boats. Willow Lake has lake trout 4 to 8 pounds, rainbow from 10 to 18 inches, and brook that average 8 inches. Kokanee are also present. Lakes and streams above Willow Lake are in Bridger Wilderness.

On the south side of the Willow Lake is Spring Creek Park Trailhead (8,225 feet). From the northwest of the trailhead, a trail skirts the southeast side of Willow Lake and follows **Lake Creek** 1.5 miles above Willow Lake to **Snake Lake** (7,795 ft; 18 ac) which has small brook. The rest of the lakes on the Lake Creek drainage are easier reached from Trapper Creek Trail which leaves out of the Spring Creek Park Trailhead. Follow Trappers Creek Trail from Spring Creek Park Trailhead for 7 miles to **Trapper Lake** (9,682 ft; 58 ac) with good fishing for cutthroat to 12 inches. The Pine Creek Canyon Trail continues northeast from Trapper Lake to Trail Lake on the Pine Creek drainage. A mile northwest of Trapper Lake, on Section Corner Trail, is **Section Corner Lake** (9,245 ft; 56 ac). The lake has brook and grayling to 9 inches and some brown to 15 inches. The Palmer Lake Trail from the north side of the lake follows Lake Creek 1 mile to **Coyote Lake** (9,678 ft; 10 ac) which has grayling. Two and a half miles north of Section Corner Lake, on the Palmer Lake Trail, is **Round Lake** (9,952 ft; 22 ac) with brook to 11 inches. Over

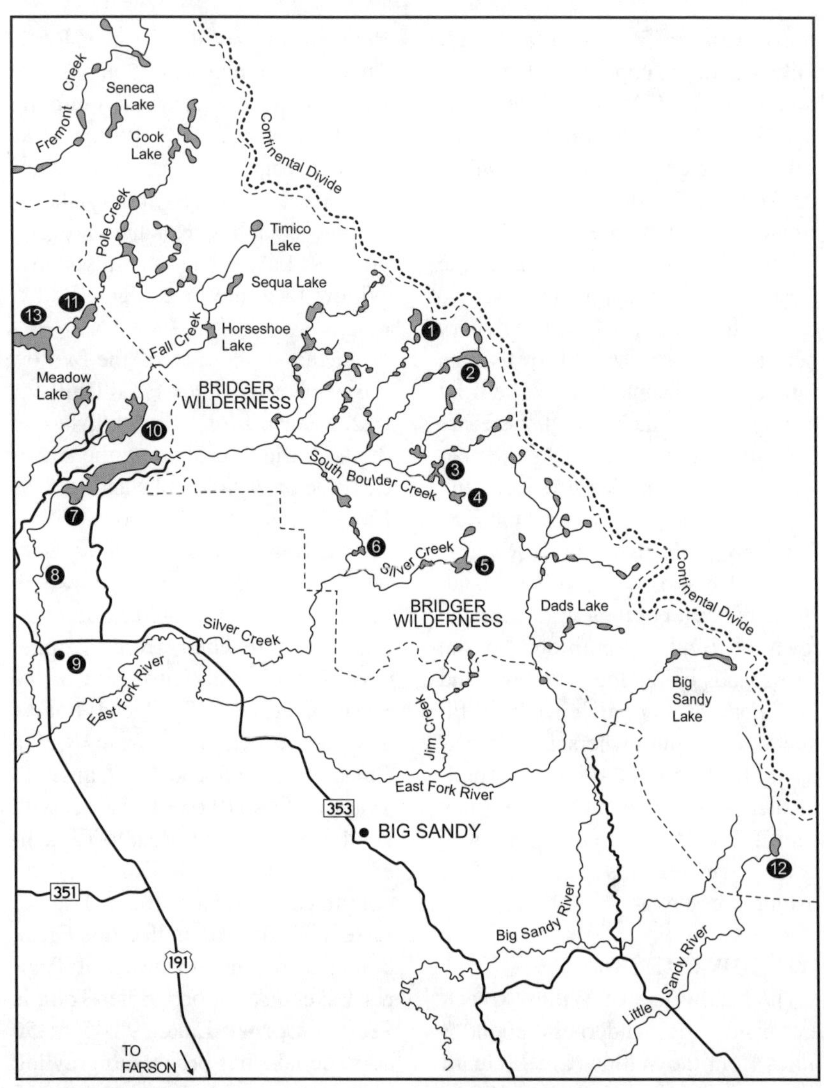

1 Halls Lake
2 Middle Fork Lake
3 Raid Lake
4 Cross Lake
5 Silver Lake
6 Star Lake
7 Boulder Lake
8 Boulder Creek
9 Boulder
10 Burnt Lake
11 Fayette Lake
12 Little Sandy Lake
13 Halfmoon Lake

a low saddle 0.25 miles to the southwest, on **Bluff Park Creek,** is **Lost Camp Lake** (9,812 ft; 12 ac) where there is good fishing for brook to 12 inches. Just above Round Lake, a trail forks east to **Dean Lake** (10,165 ft; 13 ac) with small brook. Continuing north 1.25 mile above Round Lake on Palmer Lake Trail is **Palmer Lake** (10,165 ft; 19 ac), with good fishing for brook to 10 inches. From Palmer Lake the Doubletop Mountain Trail heads east into the Pine Creek drainage and Summit Lake. **Penny Lake** (10,376 ft; 3 ac) is 0.5 miles above Palmer Lake at the headwaters of the drainage has good fishing for brook to 10 inches. Above Penny Lake the Palmer Lake Trail continues north over a high divide and into the New Fork River drainage.

Soda Lake (7,546 ft; 312 ac) lies about 7 miles north of Pinedale by Willow Lake Road, which starts out paved but turns to gravel. Brook average 10 to 14 inches, and the brown fishing is good for fish 2 to 3 pounds, most average 15 inches. Boats with motors are allowed, with the exception of May 10 to May 31. The best fishing here is just after the ice-off in the spring. The lake is closed from October 1 through May 9. Soda lake is 7 miles north of Pinedale via Willow Lake Road. A 4 wheel drive road continues to **Little Soda Lake** (7,605 ft: 54 ac) which may have some rainbow to 16 inches when the lake does not winterkill.

PINE CREEK

The next drainage to the south is **Pine Creek**, which empties dozens of high mountain lakes and delivers their waters to **Fremont Lake** (7,420 ft; 4750 ac), which is a popular lake that receives heavy fishing pressure. It has depths to 600 feet, so lake trout as big as 20 pounds and brown to 8 pounds are occasionally taken. Small rainbow and kokanee salmon to 12 inches are also in the lake. The lake is located 3 miles north of Pinedale by paved Fremont Lake Road. There are boat ramps and campgrounds on the east and north sides. Anglers troll from boats for the bigger fish and spin-cast for rainbow from the shore. Large numbers of anglers ice fish here in the winter months.

At the northeastern end of Fremont Lake is the very popular Elkhart Park Trailhead (9,250 feet) on the Bridger Wilderness boundary. Elkhart Park Trailhead provides access to numerous lakes, trails, and streams in the Bridger Wilderness. This trailhead is very busy throughout the summer, expect a lot of company.

Four miles northeast of Elkhart Park Trailhead up some steep switchbacks on Pine Creek Canyon Trail is **Glimpse Lake** (9,373 ft; 11 ac), with good fishing for small brook. Glimpse Lake Trail, from the Spring Creek Park Trailhead, is not as steep but is a 6 mile hike.

Pine Creek drains several high lake before flowing south through a narrow and steep canyon and into Fremont Lake. The creek has cutthroat and brook, but the steep canyon

Rob Yingling/Bighorn Web Design Photo

makes fishing very difficult. From the Elkhart Park Trailhead, after 4 miles Pine Creek Canyon Trail passes by Glimpse Lake and then loosely follows the western rim of the canyon for 2.25 miles to Trapper Lake on the Willow Creek Drainage. A more recommend, but longer route, is from Spring Creek Park to Glimpse Lake. At Glimpse Lake, Pine Creek Canyon Trail and Glimpse Lake Trail meet, Pine Creek Canyon Trail continues on north to Trapper Lake. At Trapper Lake, Pine Creek Canyon Trail continues north 1 mile to **Trail Lake** (9,753 ft; 20 ac) with grayling to 10 inches. To the northeast **Neil Lake** (9,730 ft; 9 ac) has very good fishing for cutthroat and rainbow to 14 inches. Another 0.5-mile north is **Gottfried Lake** (9,800 ft; 3 ac) with cutthroat and rainbow of the same size. A short distance to the west is **Heart Lake** (10,014 ft; 23 ac) with rainbow to 14 inches. To the northeast above Gottfried Lake 1 mile on the Pine Creek Canyon Trail is **Borum Lake** (10,145 ft; 29 ac) with cutthroat to 13 inches. Northwest cross-country from Borum Lake 1.5 miles is **Cutthroat Lake** (10,595 ft; 23 ac) with cutthroat to 12 inches. Half a mile northeast of Cutthroat Lake are the **No Name Lakes** (10,600 ft; 18-23 ac) with good to very good fishing for cutthroat up to 14 inches. Two miles east of No Name Lakes is **Summit Lake** (10,324 ft; 37 ac) with cutthroat to 14 inches. The Pine Creek Canyon Trail travels 1.5 miles northeast from Borum Lake to hook up with the Highline Trail at Summit Lake. From Summit Lake a maintained Doubletop Mountain Trail cuts back west to provide trail access to the No Name Lakes, Cutthroat Lake, and on to Palmer Lake in the Willow Creek drainage.

From Summit Lake the Highline Trail travels north into the Upper Green River drainage; and south to Elbow Lake, and then on to the Fremont Creek drainage to the south. Follow the Highline Trail south 1.25 miles from Summit Lake to an unmaintained trial, which passes **Pass Lake** (10,450 ft; 10 ac), and heads over Gunsight Pass. Pass Lake has fair fishing for small cutthroat. One mile to the south of the pass are the three **Sauerkraut Lakes** (10,200 ft; 4-16 ac). These lakes drain into Pine Creek from the east and have good fishing for cutthroat.

The Highline Trail heads east along **Elbow Creek**, a main tributary of Pine Creek, passing the two **Twin Lakes** (10,345 and 10,340 ft; 4 and 11 ac). These lakes have good fishing for cutthroat, golden and cutthroat/golden crosses. On Elbow Creek, 2 miles east of Pine Creek, on the Highline Trail is **Elbow Lake** (10,777 ft; 80 ac) offering good fishing for golden to 15 inches. Several other unnamed lakes are the Elbow Lake area, but do not support fish. The Highline Trail continues south over a high pass and into the Fremont Creek drainage.

At the northern tip of Fremont Lake, Pine Creek is joined from the east by **Bridger Creek**, a fast stream with 8- to 14-inch brook, cutthroat and rainbow. The **Bridger Lakes,** with no trail, lie about 4 miles northeast of Fremont Lake at elevations ranging from 10,100 to 10,500 feet. There are a half-dozen lakes ranging in size from 4 to 36 acres. The highest of these lakes have brook to 10 inches and excellent fishing; the lower lakes have excellent fishing for golden to 12 inches.

Two miles east of the confluence of Bridger Creek and Pine Creek, by a very difficult climb without a trail, is **Triangle Lake** (8,895 ft; 55 ac) with excellent fishing for golden 8-10 inches.

FREMONT CREEK

Fremont Creek, which joins Pine Creek directly above Fremont Lake, flows in from the southeast after draining a large portion of the high lakes in the Bridger Wilderness. **Long Lake** (7,878 ft; 138 ac), 2 miles from the Elkhart Park Trailhead, has fair fishing for cutthroat, brook and rainbow. Above Long Lake, Fremont Creek flows through a very steep and narrow canyon with no trail and difficult access. **Upper Long Lake** (7,945 ft; 39 ac), which requires a difficult hike, also has fair fishing for cutthroat, brook, and rainbow. One mile above the Upper Long Lake is **Suicide Lake** (8,795 ft; 12ac) with some rainbow and brook. Two tough miles above Upper Long Lake is **Gorge Lake** (8,870 ft; 60 ac), which is also difficult to access, with rainbow and brook around 10 inches. Two miles north of Gorge is **Lost Lake**, (9,755 ft; 52 ac) which is rated good for brook and rainbow 10-12 inches. Lost Lake Trail north from Seneca Lake Trail provides easier access to the lake. **Miner Lake** (10,510 ft; 7.5 ac) is barren.

At Elkhart Park Trailhead, Pole Creek Trail heads east providing access to Seneca Lake Trail and from there several lakes higher up in the Fremont Creek drainage; and access to the Pole Creek and Sweeney Creek drainages.

Five miles east of the Elkhart Park Trailhead, the Pole Creek Trail meets the Seneca Lake Trail, which is a good approach to the upper Fremont Creek drainage. Seneca Lake Trail goes north passing **Eklund Lake** (10,255 ft; 8 ac) and **Barbara Lake** (10,200 ft; 4 ac). Ekland Lake has rainbow to 12 inches and Barbara Lake has small rainbow. **Hobbs Lake** (10,075 ft; 20 ac) is 1.25 mile above Pole Creek Trail on Seneca Lake Trail and has good fishing for rainbow to 10 inches. North of Hobbs Lake 2 miles is **Seneca Lake** (10,270 ft; 159 ac) with good fishing for rainbow to 14 inches. Lost Lake Trail leaves the north side of Seneca Lake and travels north 1.75 to Lost Lake before looping back east to meet the Highline Trail just north of "the Big Slide" waterfall. Northeast of Seneca Lake 0.5 miles is **Little Seneca Lake** (10,350 ft; 11 ac) with small rainbow. Another 1.5 miles northeast is **Island Lake** (10,346 ft; 118 ac) with good to very good fishing for rainbow, cutthroat and golden. This lake can be circled on the

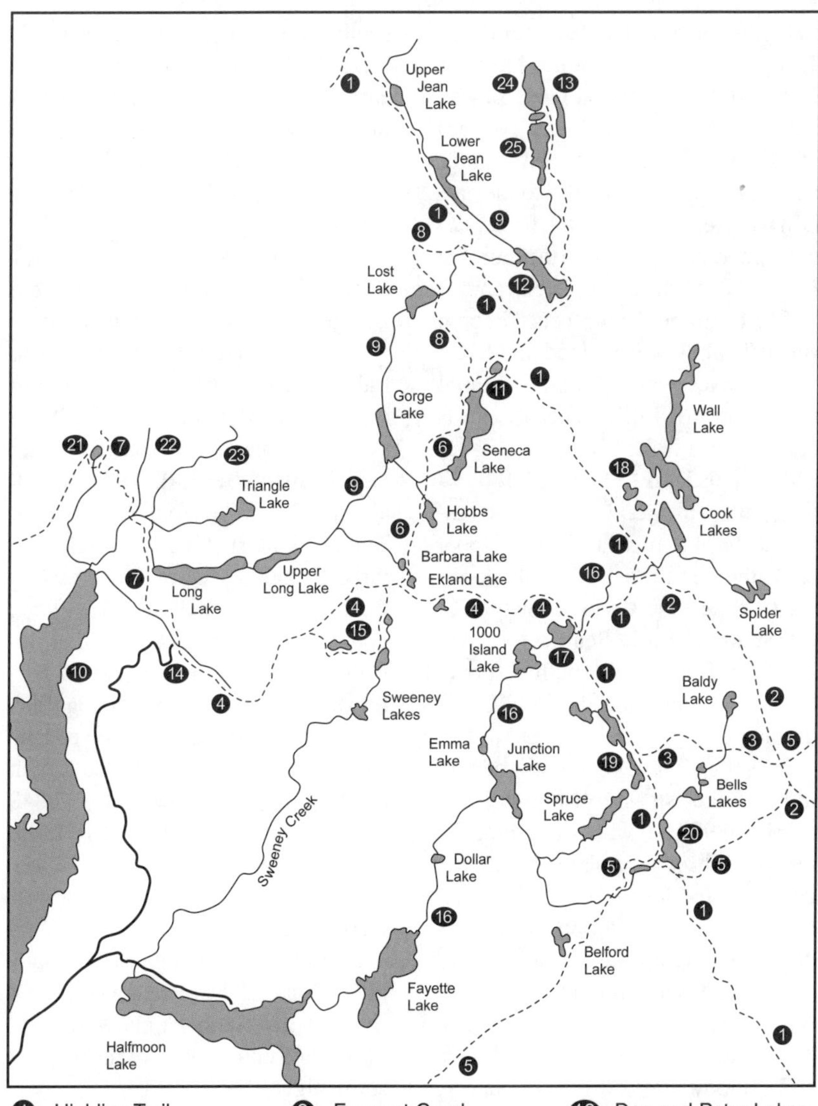

1 Highline Trail
2 Fremont Trail
3 Bell Lakes Trail
4 Pole Creek Trail
5 Timico Lake Trail
6 Seneca Lake Trail
7 Pine Creek Canyon Trail
8 Lost Lake Trail
9 Fremont Creek
10 Fremont Lake
11 Little Seneca Lake
12 Island Lake
13 Mistake Lake
14 Elkhart Park Trailhead
15 Miller Lake
16 Pole Creek
17 Pole Creek Lake
18 Don and Peter Lakes
19 Chain Lake
20 Barnes Lake
21 Glimpse Lake
22 Pine Creek
23 Bridger Creek
24 Upper Titcomb Lake
25 Lower Titcomb Lake

east side; then up the Titcomb Basin Trail, it is 2 miles to **Upper Titcomb Lake** (10,598 ft; 106 ac) and **Lower Titcomb Lake** (10,575 ft; 106 ac) where there is good fishing for golden up to 12 inches. Nearby to the east is **Mistake Lake** (10,782 ft; 23 ac) with good-size golden. **Summer Ice Lake** (11,160 ft; 26 ac) is barren.

The Highline Trail meets Titcomb Basin Trail between Island and Little Seneca lakes. On the Highline Trail 4 miles north of Little Seneca Lake is **Lower Jean Lake** (10,651 ft; 57 ac) and **Upper Jean Lake** (10,799 ft; 17 ac), both with good fishing for cutthroat to 14 inches. From Upper Jean, the Highline Trail leads northwest to the Pine Creek drainage. To the South of Little Seneca Lake the Highline Trail travels southwest over Lester Pass and into the Pole Creek drainage.

Less than 2 miles southeast of Fremont Lake sits **Halfmoon Lake** (7,610 ft; 900 ac) with fair fishing for rainbow, brown, kokanee salmon, grayling, and lake trout. With depths to 282 feet Halfmoon Lake has developed a fair lake trout fishery with lake trout primarily in the 15-inch range, but some are larger. There are some rarely caught brown and rainbow up to 6 pounds lurking in these depths. The limit for salmon, trout, and grayling is 6 fish, of those only 1 trout may be over 20 inches, and only 2 can be lake trout. There are a couple of campgrounds and an adequate boat ramp at the lake. Take paved Fremont Lake Road north from the town of Pinedale to the south end of Fremont Lake, then follow FR 134 four miles north and turn east to Halfmoon Lake. **Little Halfmoon Lake** (7,580 ft; 57 ac) is just to the south of the larger lake. Fishing is fair for brown and rainbow averaging 10 inches.

Above Halfmoon Lake, **Sweeney Creek** drains several lakes on the Bridger Wilderness boundary; Sweeney Creek Trail from Halfmoon Lake provides access, better access is from the Elkhart Park Trailhead south on Pole Creek Trail to Miller Lake Trail. **Miller Lake** (9,865 ft; 19 ac), a 4 mile hike from Elkhart Park Trailhead, has fishing for brook. The three **Sweeney Lakes** (lower 9,695 ft; 17 ac, middle 9,890 ft; 17 ac, upper 10,070 ft; 8 ac) are a mile from Miller Lake. The upper lake is barren, the middle lake has some golden and a few brook, and the lower lake has mostly cutthroat and brook, with a few golden. **Grouse Lake** (7,840 ft; 6 ac) and **Mud Lake** (7,510 ft; 28 ac) are barren.

POLE CREEK

Up Pole Creek 1-mile east of Halfmoon Lake is **Fayette Lake** (7,960 ft; 300 ac) with rainbow, brook, brown and cutthroat to 14 inches, and some bigger.

A number of lakes on the Pole Creek drainage directly above Fayette Lake do not have established trails, but do offer good fishing opportunities. About 1.25 miles up the drainage is **Dollar Lake** (8,545 ft; 14 ac) which has brook and rainbow that average 10 inches. **Junction**

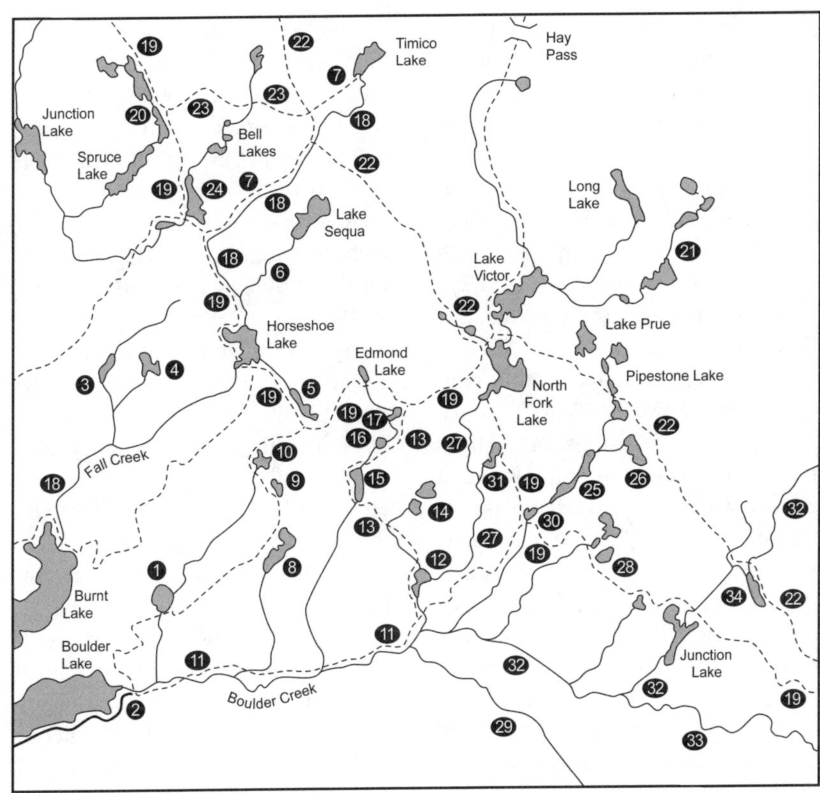

1 Blueberry Lake (Ruff Lake)
2 Boulder Lake Trail-head
3 Suprise Lake
4 Hidden Lake
5 Lake George
6 Little Fall Creek
7 Timico Lake Trail
8 Lovatt Lake
9 Cross Lake
10 Coyote Lake
11 Boulder Canyon Trail
12 Lake Ethel
13 Lake Ethel Trail
14 Norman Lakes
15 Christine Lake
16 Perry Lake
17 Macs Lake
18 Fall Creek
19 Highline Trail
20 Chain Lakes
21 Europe Creek
22 Fremont Trail
23 Bell Lakes Trail
24 Barnes Lake
25 Lake Isabella
26 Howard Lake
27 North Fork Boulder Creek
28 Firehole Lakes
29 Divide Creek
30 Lake Vera
31 Lake Winona
32 Middle Fork Boulder Creek
33 South Fork Boulder Creek
34 Sandpoint Lake

Lake (9,048 ft; 100 ac), 1.5 miles northeast of Dollar Lake, has good fishing for rainbow, brook, cutthroat and cutthroat/rainbow crosses to 15 inches. South of Junction Lake up **Spruce Creek** is **Sturrey Lake**

(9,155 ft; 24 ac) with good brook fishing, and some rainbow; **Emma Lake** (9,053 ft; 6 ac), a short distance north of Junction, has rainbow, cutthroat and brook.

Numerous lakes lie on the extensive Pole Creek drainage above Junction Lake. Several ways to reach these lakes are available, consulting a good set of maps is recommended. Pole Creek Trail from the Elkhart Park Trailhead from the north is covered here, however, Timico Lake Trail from Meadow Lake, the Highline Trail coming in from Fremont Creek drainage over Lester Pass, or the Highline Trail coming in from the Fall Creek drainage to the south also provide access to the drainage.

From the Elkhart Park Trailhead take the Pole Creek Trail east 9 miles to **Pole Creek Lake** (9,731 ft; 52 ac), which has good fishing for brook and cutthroat; to the southwest of Pole Creek Lake 0.25 miles is **1000 Island Lake** (9,580 ft; 70 ac) with the same fishing, plus lake trout to 4 pounds. At Pole Creek Lake, Pole Creek Trail ends at the Highline Trail. The Highline Trail from this point provides access to the higher lakes and trails on Pole Creek to the north; and to the southeast the trail provides access to the Spruce Creek and other tributaries of Pole Creek. To the northeast 1.75 miles the Highline Trail meets with the Cook Lakes Trail and Fremont Trail, before heading northwest to Lester Pass. From this junction follow Cook Lake Trail 0.25 miles to **Lower Cook Lake** (10,143 ft; 82 ac) which has excellent fishing for small brook. Another 0.25 mile north is **Upper Cook Lake** (10,170 ft; 163 ac) with very good fishing for brook 8 to 10 inches, and still farther to the north is **Wall Lake** (10,450 ft; 105 ac). Wall Lake has fishing for golden between 8 and 10 inches. Southwest of Upper Cook Lake 0.5 mile is **Don Lake** (10,220 ft; 19 ac) with lake trout, golden and brook; nearby **Peter Lake** (10,175 ft; 32 ac) has similar fishing. **Spider Lake** (10,495 ft; 53 ac), to the south, has fair fishing for small cutthroat.

From Pole Creek Lake, follow the Highline Trail south 1.25 miles to the three **Chain Lakes** (9,800 ft; 21-67 ac) with rainbow, cutthroat and crosses to 14 inches. An unnamed trail from the lower lake goes 0.25 miles to **Spruce Lake** (9,797 ft; 98 ac) with good fishing for rainbow and cutthroat around 14 inches. Below Spruce Lake, **Baldy Creek** flows into Sturrey Lake from **Barnes Lake** (9,747 ft; 66 ac), which is 0.5 mile south of Chain Lakes on the Highline Trail and has cutthroat to 14 inches. Above Barnes is **Bell Lake** (10,010 ft; 15 ac) with good fishing for cutthroat to 12 inches. At the top of this drainage is **Baldy Lake** (10,350 ft; 30 ac) with cutthroat to 14 inches.

Flowing into Pole Creek from the south, just above Fayette Lake, is a creek from **Trophy Lake** (9,430 ft; 22 ac) which has fishing for brook from 10 to 13 inches, and **Belford Lake** (9,550 ft; 28 ac) with good fishing for brook to 13 inches. There is not a trail to these lakes.

Rob Yingling/Bighorn Web Design Photo

FALL CREEK

The next drainage to the south is **Fall Creek**, which flows down from the higher elevations into **Burnt Lake** (7,923 ft; 1000 ac), which produced a 23-pound rainbow in 1969 - the state record. Outside the Bridger Wilderness, this lake has rainbows averaging 13 inches, small brook, and lake trout to 3 pounds. North of the town of Boulder about a mile is Burnt Lake Road to the northeast, the lake is 11 miles by dirt road. Burnt Lake is closed from November 15 to April 30. Fall Creek, from Burnt Lake downstream 500 yards, is closed to fishing from May 1 through June 30.

Up Fall Creek, without a trail, is **Surprise Lake** (8,930 ft; 26 ac) with a small population of golden, and **Hidden Lake** (9,455 ft; 30 ac) which is barren. **Surprise Creek** drainage (including Surprise Lake) is closed to fishing from November 1 through July 31.

Burnt Lake Trail from the east side of Burnt Lake leads 6 miles north to the Highline Trail at **Horseshoe Lake** (9,457 ft; 100 ac), where fishing is for small brook. A mile to the south on the Highline Trail is **Lake George** (9,679 ft; 16 ac) with excellent fishing for brook 8-10 inches. Two miles to the northeast of Horseshoe Lake, on **Little Fall Creek,** is **Lake Sequa** (9,940 ft; 106 ac). Lake Sequa has excellent fishing for small brook. Above Horseshoe Lake the Highline Trail follows Fall Creek for a short distance before meeting the Timico Lake Trail. The Highline Trail continues northwest into the Pole Creek drainage, Timico Lake Trail follows Fall Creek northeast to **Timico Lake** (10,505 ft; 72 ac). The lake has good fishing for brook to 12 inches. Another route to the lake is to follow the Timico Lake Trail from its beginning at Meadow Lake. This hike requires a steep 11 mile hike. At the top of the drainage, around 10,200 feet, are the three **Fall Creek Lakes**, with small brook.

Meadow Lake (9,500 ft; 109 ac) is 0.5-mile northwest of Burnt Lake on **Meadow Creek**, with excellent fishing on flies and lures for large grayling 12 to 14 inches. There is a dirt boat ramp area, and shore fishing is difficult. A boat or float tube is a good way to fish here. Meadow Lake is closed to fishing November 15 through April 30. Part of the eastern portion of the lake and all of Meadow Creek is closed April 1 to June 30. North of the town of Boulder about a mile is Burnt Lake Road to the northeast, Meadow Lake is near the end of this dirt road 12 miles, just north of Burnt Lake.

BOULDER CREEK

A mile south of Burnt Lake is **Boulder Lake** (7,300 ft; 1200 ac), 7 miles north of Boulder via Burnt Lake Road. The fish in this lake include rainbow averaging 10-15 inches, kokanee, and some larger lake trout. Campsites and Boulder Lake Trailhead lie at the east end of the lake. Access to the southeast side of the lake is via SR 353 east of Boulder to Boulder Lake Road. From

Boulder Lake to North Boulder Creek (about 5 miles), Boulder Creek is closed to fishing from April 1 to June 30.

Boulder Creek is a rapid flowing stream with good fishing for rainbow and brook. The numerous high lakes and streams in the drainage are contained within the Bridger Wilderness, and offer a superb backcountry experience. Major tributaries of Boulder Creek are; North Fork Boulder Creek, Pipestone Creek, Middle Fork Boulder Creek, South Fork Boulder Creek, and Divide Creek from the southwest. From the Boulder Lake Trailhead (7,300 feet), Boulder Canyon Trail provides the best access into Boulder, North Boulder, Pipestone, and Middle Boulder creeks. The Scab Creek Trailhead to the south is best for hiking into South Boulder Creek and Divide Creek drainages. Several miles to the east both trailheads eventually reach the Highline Trail, which travels in a north/south direction providing access into numerous lakes and creeks in this drainage. Quality maps or a good guide service is recommended.

Boulder Canyon Trail follows Boulder Creek east into the Bridger Wilderness from the east side of Boulder Lake. Within 0.5 mile, Ruff Lake Trail heads north for 2 miles to **Ruff Lake (Blueberry Lake)** (8,476 ft; 55 ac) with good fishing for brook, grayling, and some cutthroat. Two miles northeast of Ruff Lake is **Lovatt Lake** (9,456 ft; 70 ac) with good fishing for brook averaging 12 inches. Half a mile farther north is **Cross Lake** (9,550 ft; 13 ac) with brook and grayling; a short distance farther is **Coyote Lake** (9,515 ft; 23 ac) with grayling 8-12 inches.

Boulder Canyon Trail follows Boulder Creek for about 6 miles east to **Lake Ethel** (8,660 ft; 27 ac). The lake has cutthroat that average 12 inches. The Lake Ethel Trail begins at the lake with forks to the north and east. On Lake Ethel Trail 1.25 miles to the north are the two **Norman Lakes** (lower 9,385 ft; 17 ac, upper 9,390 ft; 25 ac), with golden to 12 inches. Lake Ethel Trail continues into the Macs Creek drainage to the northwest, and to **Christine Lake** (9,255 ft; 27 ac) with small brook. Another 0.25 miles further is **Perry Lake** (9,410 ft; 7.5 ac) with small brook.

Half a mile further northeast lies **Macs Lake** (9,382 ft; 9 ac) with excellent fishing for small brook. The nearby **Edmond Lake** (9,965 ft; 5 ac) is barren. At Macs Lake the Lake Ethel Trail ends at the Highline Trail. From Macs Lake the Highline Trail continues to the northeast another 2 miles to North Fork Boulder Creek and **North Fork Lake** (9,754 ft; 163 ac), with good fishing for cutthroat averaging 12 inches and sometimes larger. **Valley Lake** (10,149 ft; 45 ac) and **Medina Lake** (10,0060 ft; 12 ac) are both within a mile of North Fork Lake, Valley Lake is fair for cutthroat and Medina Lake is barren. Northwest half mile is **August Lake** (9,856 ft; 6 ac) and another half mile to **Rambaud Lake**

(10,070 ft; 6 ac). August Lake has fair fishing for cutthroat to 13 inches, Rambaud Lake does not support fish. North of North Fork Lake on the **North Fork Boulder Creek** is **Lake Victor** (9,834 ft; 139 ac) with cutthroat up to 16 inches. The North Fork Trail from Lake Victor north goes over Hay Pass and into the Wind River drainage. Several more miles up the North Fork Boulder Creek is **Barber Lake** (10,322 ft; 25 ac) with cutthroat. At the headwater of the creek is **Glacier Lake** (10,550 ft; 29 ac), which is fair for small cutthroat. Also draining into Lake Victor is **Long Lake** (10,683 ft; 55 ac) and the unnamed lakes up **Europe Creek**, all of which have cutthroat. The creeks as well as the lakes in this area have good fishing for cutthroat.

From North Fork Lake the Highline Trail travels south into the Pipestone Creek drainage, and to the west to Horseshoe Lake in the Fall Creek Drainage. Below North Fork Lake 0.75 miles to the south along the Highline Trail is **Lake Winona** (9,688 ft; 26 ac), with good to very good fishing for cutthroat to 16 inches. Other lakes in the area are barren. From above North Fork Lake the Fremont Trail travels east to the Pipestone Lakes, and west to Hat Pass and the upper reaches of the Fall Creek drainage.

From Lake Ethel, Lake Ethel Trail loosely follows **Pipestone Creek** northeast 3.5 miles to **Lake Vera** (9,625 ft; 8 ac). The lake has fair fishing for cutthroat to 14 inches. A trail goes southeast from the lower end of this lake 1-mile to **Lake Isabella** (9,719 ft; 51 ac), a narrow lake with very good cutthroat fishing. Above Lake Isabella are the **Pipestone Lakes** (10,125 ft; 9-21 ac) with good fishing for cutthroat to 13 inches. Northeast of Lake Isabella at the headwaters of Pipestone Creek is **Lake Prue** (10,155 ft; 43 ac) with good fishing for 10 to 14 inch cutthroat. A half-mile northeast of Isabella is **Howard Lake** (10,013 ft; 45 ac) with good to very good fishing for 15-inch cutthroat. The three **Firehole Lakes**; **Lake Susan** (9,620 ft; 27 ac), **Wilderness Lake** (9,630 ft; 30 ac), and one unnamed lake drain into Pipestone Creek. Firehole Lakes are on the Highline Trail 1.25 miles east of Vera Lake. All three lakes have good fishing for cutthroat to 12 inches.

MIDDLE FORK BOULDER CREEK

The **Middle Fork Boulder Creek** has an abundance of lakes that contain primarily brook. Hike 3 miles southeast from Lake Vera on the Highline Trail, past the Firehole Lakes to **Full Moon Lake** (9,580 ft; 15 ac), which does not contain fish. **Junction Lake** (9,575 ft; 79 ac) is 0.5 miles further and has good fishing for brook 10 inches, with some larger. **Halls Creek** drainage has numerous small ponds and lakes that are barren, a few of the deeper lakes have small brook. Near the headwaters of the creek is **Halls Lake** (10,602 ft; 206 ac) which has excellent fishing for small brook, above

Halls Lake is **Howe Lake** (10,655 ft; 51 ac) with more of the same. A mile northeast of Junction Lake on the Middle Fork Trail is **Sandpoint Lake** (9,810 ft; 32 ac) with excellent fishing for small brook.

Several trails criss-cross the area around Sandpoint Lake. Fremont Trail heads northwest into the Pipestone drainage, and southeast 0.25 miles to **Bob's Lake** (9,875 ft; 20 ac) with very good fishing for small brook. Continuing past Bob's Lake the Fremont Trail continues into the Dream Creek drainage. Middle Fork Trail, from Sandpoint Lake, leads 3.5 miles northeast to **Middle Fork Lake** (10,252 ft; 257 ac) where there is excellent fishing for small brook. **Lee Lake** (10,305 ft; 87 ac) and **Bewmark Lake** (10,760 ft; 59 ac) are within a quarter mile of the lake are both barren. Several smaller unnamed lakes lie below Middle Fork Lake on the Middle Fork Boulder drainage; small brook are predominant in them.

South of Bob's Lake 0.75 miles on the Fremont Trail is the **Dream Creek** drainage, which joins the **South Fork Boulder Creek** below Dream Lake. **Dream Lake** (9,842 ft; 63 ac) has good fishing for brook and cutthroat averaging 9 inches. Rainbow Lake Trail leaves the northeast end of the lake and travels north 2 miles to **Rainbow Lake** (10,341 ft; 76 ac), which has excellent fishing for rainbows to 16 inches. Also in this drainage, just south of Rainbow Lake, is **Sunrise Lake** (10,380 ft; 28 ac) with cutthroat up to 14 inches.

DIVIDE CREEK/SOUTH FORK BOULDER CREEK

South Fork Boulder Creek, while it can be accessed from the Highline Trail from the north, is easier reached from the Scab Creek Trailhead. Scab Creek Trailhead (8,195 feet) is located east of the town of Boulder off SR 353. From Boulder drive east 6.5 miles to CR 123 (Scab Creek Road), take this rough, but passable road 8.25 miles to the trailhead.

Scab Creek Trail parallels **Scab Creek** for about 2 miles to the Bridger Wilderness boundary and the numerous shallow **Toboggan Lakes** (9,300 to 9,535 ft; 6 to 12 ac). Most of the ponds are barren, a few near Divide Lake may have small brook. **Scab Creek** does not offer much in the way of fishing opportunities, as it receives its water supply from a connecting ditch from Divide Lake. The trail continues another 4 miles to Little Divide Lake on the Divide Creek drainage. **Little Divide Lake** (9,603 ft; 14 ac) is excellent for small brook. **Divide Lake** (9,668 ft; 134 ac), 500 feet above Little Divide Lake and at the top of the drainage, has good fishing for rainbow to 14 inches, and small brook. To the northwest of Little Divide Lake 0.5 miles on Divide Creek, without a trail, is **Pine Island Lake** (9,478 ft; 10 ac) and another 0.25 mile to **Three Elk Lake** (9,320 ft; 4 ac). Both lakes offer good fishing for small rainbow and cutthroat. Below Three Elks Lake **Divide Creek** enters **Boulder Creek** 5 miles east of the Boulder Lake Trailhead, however there is not a trail up the

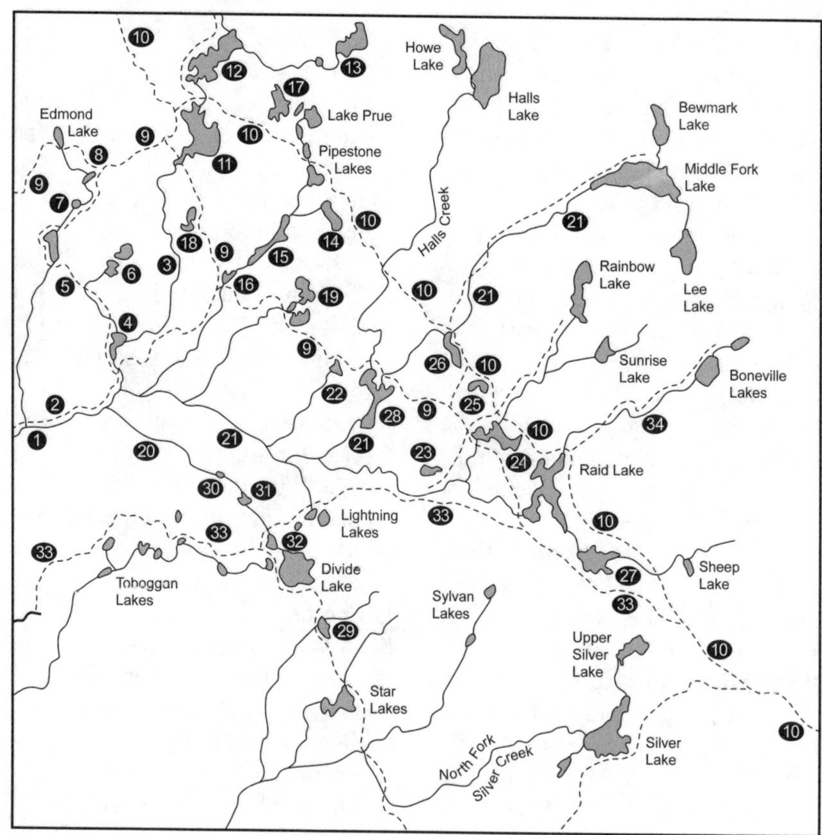

1 Boulder Creek
2 Boulder Canyon Trail
3 N. Fork Boulder Creek
Lake Ethel
5 Lake Ethel Trail
6 Norman Lakes
7 Perry Lake
8 Macs Lake
9 Highline Trail
10 Fremont Trail
11 N. Fork Lake
12 Lake Victor
13 Europe Creek
14 Howard Lake
15 Lake Isabella
16 Lake Vera
17 Valley Lake
18 Lake Winona
19 Firehole Lakes
20 Divide Creek
21 Middle Boulder Creek
22 Full Moon Lake
23 Crescent Lake
24 Dream Lake
25 Bob's Lake
26 Sandpoint Lake
27 Cross Lake
28 Junction Lake
29 Monroe Lake
30 Three Elk Lake
31 Pine Island Lake
32 Little Divide Lake
33 Scab Creek Trail
34 S. Fork Boulder Creek

creek. Monroe Lake and the Silver Creek drainage lie 0.5 miles to the south of Divide Lake.

From Little Divide Lake the Scab Trail travels east 0.5 miles over a low divide to the three **Lightning Lakes** (9,730 to 9,775 ft; 3 to 11 ac), which are good for small brook. From these lakes the Scab Creek Trail drops 1.5 miles into the South Boulder Creek drainage. Scab Creek Trail follows South Boulder Creek upstream, 0.5 mile east and just to the north is **Crescent Lake** (9,751 ft; 16 ac) with excellent fishing for small brook. The Scab Creek Trail continues 2.75 miles to **Cross Lake** (10,087 ft; 83 ac), which offers excellent fishing for brook to 10 inches and small lake trout. **Sheep Lake** (10,335 ft; 8 ac), 0.75 miles above Cross Lake, has small brook. East of Crescent Lake, Dream Lake Trail makes its way to the northeast providing access to Dream Lake and numerous lakes to the north via the Highline and Fremont trails previously discussed.

To the southeast of Dream Lake less than 0.25 miles is **Raid Lake** (9,946 ft; 131 ac), with excellent fishing for small brook, and lake trout up to 4 pounds. Northeast of Raid Lake on the South Boulder Creek drainage, about 2 miles with no established trails, is **Jim Harrower Lake** (10,521 ft; 16 ac). The lake has fair fishing for small golden. **Bonneville Lake** (10,825 ft; 51 ac) is a mile upstream and has mostly brook, with some golden.

SILVER CREEK

The next drainage to the south is Silver Creek, a northern tributary to the East Fork River. This drainage lies to the south of the South Boulder Creek drainage and southeast of Divide Lake (on the Divide Creek drainage). Trails in the drainage are not maintained, a good map or guide is highly recommended for traveling in this area. Access to the drainage is via Scab Creek Trail to Divide Lake. South of Divide Lake 0.5 miles on the Lowline Trail is **Monroe Lake** (9,570 ft; 20 ac), which has brook to 12 inches and some cutthroat. To the east a half-mile from Monroe Lake, on the Lowline Trail, are the two **Knob Lakes** (9,880 and 9,900 ft; 5 and 13 ac) which are barren. Nearby to the east is **Moose Lake** (9,790 ft; 12 ac) that is also barren. Along the Lowline Trail south from Monroe Lake, less than 1 mile, is barren **Star Lake** (9,507 ft; 49 ac). Continue on the Lowline Trail south 3 miles to pick up the Sylvan Lakes Trail, follow trail 3 miles north to **Lower Sylvan Lake** (9,825 ft; 9 ac), and a mile further to **Upper Sylvan Lake** (10,000 ft; 10 ac), where there is good fishing for brook. South Fork Boulder Creek and Raid Lake are a mile further (discussed in the South Boulder Creek section of this chapter). **Warbonnet Lake** (10,195 ft; 10 ac) lays cross country to the east of Upper Sylvan Lake. No trail. This remote lake is good for rainbow and brook. **Lower Silver Lake** (9,928 ft;

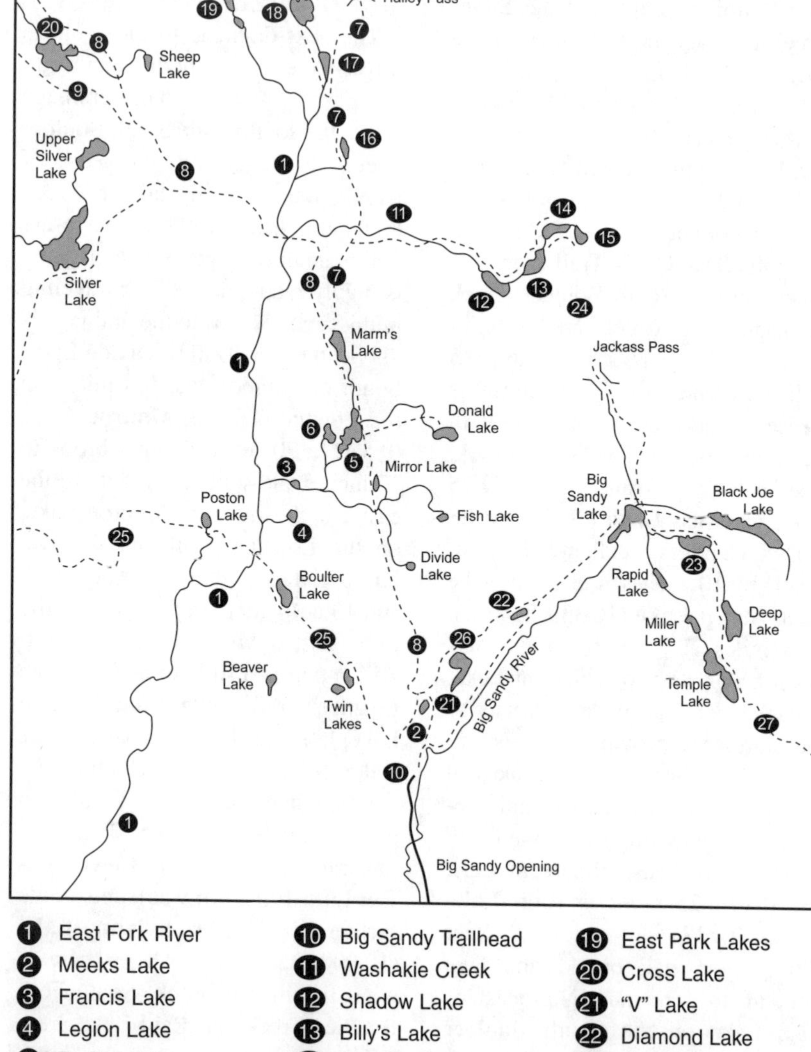

1 East Fork River
2 Meeks Lake
3 Francis Lake
4 Legion Lake
5 Dad's Lake
6 Little Dad's Lake
7 Hailey Pass Trail
8 Fremont Trail
9 Scab Creek Trail
10 Big Sandy Trailhead
11 Washakie Creek
12 Shadow Lake
13 Billy's Lake
14 Barren Lake
15 Texas Lake
16 Skull Lake
17 Maes Lake
18 Pyramid Lake
19 East Park Lakes
20 Cross Lake
21 "V" Lake
22 Diamond Lake
23 Clear Lake
24 Cirque of the Towers
25 Lowline Trail
26 Diamond Lake Trail
27 Little Sandy Trail

171 ac) and **Upper Silver Lake** (9,967 ft; 66 ac) both with good to very good fishing for brook to 12 inches, are at the headwaters of Silver Creek.

To the south of Lower Silver Lake, over a low divide and past barren **Jessie Lake** (9,842 ft; 20 ac), on South Fork Silver Creek is **Wolf Lake** (9,580 ft; 39 ac). Wolf Lake has rainbow and brook, some large ones in the 13 to 15 inch range. To the south a little over a half mile on the **Cottonwood Creek** drainage is **Cottonwood Lake** (9,545 ft; 18 ac) with some rainbow. No trail. Further to the south on Pocket Creek is **Pocket Creek Lake** (9,215 ft; 6 ac), which is barren. **Jim Lake** (9,747 ft; 24ac) on **Jim Creek** is also barren.

EAST FORK RIVER (VIA BIG SANDY TRAILHEAD)

Moving south, the next major drainage is the **East Fork River**, which flows south and then west out of the national forest and across a patchwork of private and public land before joining the New Fork River; 4 miles south of the town of Boulder, just west of US 191. The East Fork River has brown and rainbow in the 8- to 15-inch range; here, as elsewhere, respect the private ownership along the river. A signed rough dirt road 2 miles north of the town of Big Sandy provides access to the river on BLM lands. Another area open to the public, at the Boulder Fish Hatchery, is 2.5 miles south of the town of Boulder, and then 1.5 miles east on Boulder Rearing Station Road. Rainbow, brown and whitefish average 11 inches in both access areas, brook average 7 inches.

Lakes in the upper East Fork River drainage are in the Bridger Wilderness and are reached by way of the Big Sandy Trailhead (9,075 feet). Access to the upper reaches of the East Fork River is via the Big Sandy Entrance and Big Sandy Campground which is accessible from Boulder by going about 20 miles east and south on Hwy 353 to Big Sandy Village. The Trailhead is another 8 miles south and 14 miles northeast on the extremely rough Big Sandy Road. The trailhead is well used, expect plenty of company in the backcountry. The Big Sandy Trailhead provides access to the East Fork River and Big Sandy River drainages.

Within a half mile of the campground are **Johnson Lake** (9,068 ft; 9 ac) and **Mud Lake** (9,070 ft; 10 ac). Johnson Lake has a few grayling and Mud Lake has some brown and brook to 13 inches.

To reach the lakes on headwaters of the East Fork River, follow the Fremont Trail past Meeks Lake (which is actually on a tributary of the Big Sandy River) to the East Fork River. To reach the Fremont Trail, leave the Big Sandy Trailhead and travel north 0.5 miles to **Meeks Lake** (9,303 ft; 11 ac). Meeks Lake has small brook to 8 inches. The trail splits at Meeks Lake, the northeast fork is the "V" Lake Trail, the fork to the north is the Fremont Trail, and on the southwest side of the lake is the

Lowline Trail.

The Lowline Trail leaves from the west side of Meeks Lake, travels south briefly then swinging to the northwest for 1.75 miles to **Twin Lakes** (9,540 ft; 10 ac each), which are barren. The trail continues 1.25 miles northwest to **Boulter Lake** (9,225 ft; 31 ac) with good fishing for 12-inch cutthroat and brook. A half-mile to the south is **Beaver Lake** (9,361 ft; 10 ac) which is barren. The Lowline Trail continues 1.5 miles to the northwest of Boulter Lake, and after crossing the East Fork River at Poston Meadows, reaches **Poston Lake** (9,350 ft; 13 ac), which has small brook. From Poston Lake the Lowline Trail continues west into the Silver Creek drainage.

Follow the Fremont Trail 2.75 miles north from Meeks Lake over a low divide to Fish Creek Park. The trail passes near **Divide Lake** (9,965 ft; 7 ac) with small brook, and **Mirror Lake** (9,830 ft; 5 ac) with small rainbow and brook. **Fish Lake** (10,105 ft; 6 ac), a 0.5 mile to the east contains small brook. **Legion Lake** (9,470 ft; 6 ac) and **Francis Lake** (9,515 ft; 4 ac) are 1 mile cross-country west of Fish Creek Park. Both lakes are good for small brook and cutthroat. Continue on Fremont Trail 0.5 miles past Mirror Lake to **Dad's Lake** (9,740 ft; 53 ac) and **Little Dad's Lake** (9,745 ft; 12 ac) with brook and cutthroat averaging 10 inches. A mile east of Dad's Lake is **Donald Lake** (10,153 ft; 25 ac) with cutthroat to 12 inches. North of Dad's Lake 1.25 miles is **Marm's Lake** (9,880 ft; 33 ac) with good fishing for 12- to 14-inch brook. Above the lake Fremont Trail continues to the northwest, across the East Fork River and into the Silver Creek and South Boulder Creek drainages to the west. From the north end of Marm's Lake the Hailey Pass Trail goes north to provide access to several lakes with good fishing opportunities. Two miles up the trail is **Washakie Creek,** entering the East Fork River from the east. Shadow Lake Trail follows the creek east 2 miles to **Shadow Lake** (10,338 ft; 44 ac), which has small brook; still higher on Washakie Creek 0.25 mile is **Billy's Lake** (10,717 ft; 22 ac). Billy's Lake has good fishing for small brook, as does **Barren Lake** (10,725 ft; 27 ac) a half mile further. Barren Lake also has a few brown. At the top of the drainage, **Texas Lake** (10,740 ft; 14 ac) is barren.

Hailey Pass Trail continues past Washakie Creek, after 1 mile the Washakie Pass Trail leaves to the east and goes over Washakie Pass into the South Fork Little Wind River drainage. After 0.25 mile more the trail comes to **Skull Lake** (10,280 ft; 14 ac), good for brook to 10 inches. Hike 0.75 miles above Skull Lake to **Maes Lake** (10,343 ft; 26 ac), which fair fishing for rainbow, brook and lake trout. Occasionally a golden will drift down from Pyramid Lake. At the lake Hailey Pass Trail goes to the northeast over the Continental Divide and into the South Fork Little Wind River Drainage. Near the top of the drainage, 1 mile past Maes Lake, is **Pyramid Lake** (10,570 ft; 55 ac) with temperamental golden from 12 to 18 inches. At the headwaters of East Fork River, cross-country to the west of Pyramid Lake, are the three **East Fork Lakes** (10,305 to 10,564 ft; 8 to 40 ac), which have golden, and brook in the lower lakes.

BIG SANDY RIVER

The **Big Sandy River** at the southern end of the Wind River Mountains collects waters from the high peaks and dumps them some 60 miles to the south in turbid and unattractive Big Sandy Reservoir.

Before it leaves the mountains, the Big Sandy River drains some good fishing lakes. This area receives heavy fishing pressure. Lakes in the drainage are in the Bridger Wilderness and are reached by way of the Big Sandy Trailhead. The trailhead to the Big Sandy River is via the Big Sandy Entrance and Big Sandy Campground which is accessible from Boulder by going about 20 miles east and south on Hwy 353 to Big Sandy Village. The Trailhead is another 8 miles south and 14 miles northeast on the extremely rough Big Sandy Road. The Big sandy Trailhead (9,075 feet) is well used by anglers, hikers and backpackers, and mountain climbers, so expect plenty of company in the backcountry. The Big Sandy Trailhead provides access to the Big Sandy River and East Fork River drainages.

Meeks Lake (9,303 ft; 11 ac) is close to the trailhead, and therefore is more heavily fished for small brook. From the Big Sandy Trailhead hike north 0.5 miles to the Meeks Lake Trail, the lake is 0.5 miles to the north. From the northern side of the lake Diamond Lake Trail goes to the northeast 0.5 miles to **"V" Lake** (9,420 ft; 42 ac), which is heavily fished for rainbow around 11 inches, occasionally rainbow to 15 inches are caught. Continue on the trail 1.75 miles to **Diamond Lake** (9,450 ft; 12 ac), which is rated poor for cutthroat 12-14 inches. Diamond Lake is also easily reached from hiking 3.5 miles along the Big Sandy Trail.

From the Big Sandy Trailhead, it is an easy 3.5 mile hike northeast along the Big Sandy River to Diamond Lake and a 5-mile trek to **Big Sandy Lake** (9,690 ft; 57 ac), not to be confused with the Big Sandy Reservoir. Big Sandy Lake has excellent fishing for small brook and some cutthroat. There is heavy backpacking, angling, and camping traffic in the area.

To the east 0.75 miles, on the Big Sandy River, is **Clear Lake** (10,012 ft; 44 ac) with good to very good fishing for small brook. Upstream from Clear Lake 0.75 miles south is **Deep Lake** (10,526 ft; 62 ac), which has good fishing for brook to 10 inches. To the north of Clear Lake on the Black Joe Trail is **Black Joe Lake** (10,550 ft; 76 ac) with cutthroat from 10 to 14 inches. The area around these lakes receives heavy use; Haystack Mountain and Temple Peaks lie to the east of the lakes.

To the north of Big Sandy Lake is the North Creek drainage. A very steep trail follows the creek to the headwaters and Jackass Pass; over the pass is "Crique of the Towers", a very popular rock climbing destination. On the North Creek drainage is **North Lake** (10,098 ft; 9 ac) and **Arrowhead Lake** (10,465 ft; 5.5 ac) which both have small brook.

By trail up Rapid Creek, **Rapid Lake** (10,292 ft; 11 ac), **Miller Lake** (10,591 ft; 9 ac), and **Temple Lake** (10,653 ft; 78 ac) have small brook. Little Sandy Trail continues past Temple Lake into the Little Sandy Drainage.

At the southernmost end of the western slope of the Wind River Mountains, **Little Sandy Creek** drains **Little Sandy Lake** (9,479 ft; 94 ac) which has small cutthroat and brook. **Sheet Lake** (9,340 ft; 28 ac) and **Frozen Lakes** (11,370 to 11,495 ft; 18 to 27 ac) are barren.

BIG SANDY RESERVOIR

Big Sandy Reservoir (6,500 ft; 3000 ac, when full) and State Recreation Area, is located 9 miles northeast of the town of Farson on Highway 191, east on Big Sandy Reservoir Road. The reservoir has a boat launching area on the west shore; fishing is fair with trolled lures for large brown. Rainbow can reach good sizes. There are some cutthroat, brook, whitefish, channel catfish and an abundance of suckers and wind. **Eden Reservoir** (6,715 ft; 886 ac), to the south east of Big Sandy Reservoir, is an overflow irrigation reservoir connected by canal. Fishing is poor to fair for rainbow to 12 inches in this treeless high desert reservoir. Larger brown are occasionally caught, as are catfish.

The Big Sandy and Little Sandy Creeks converge at the town of Farson and then flow more than 30 miles southwest through high desert with poor fishing to enter the Green River in the badlands of Seedskadee National Wildlife Refuge. Public fishing access points are above and below the town of Farson along SR 28, watch for signs indicating public access. Fishing is for rainbow, brown, and cutthroat. **Bone Draw** southwest of Farson on SR 28 is closed to fishing.

WESTERN STREAMS

While most of the fishing around the Green River happens in the Wind River Range and Bridger Wilderness on the eastern side of the drainage, waters flowing from the Wyoming Range to west do offer some great fishing opportunities.

Beaver Creek, Horse Creek, Lead Creek, and **Cottonwood Creek,** have fair fishing for cutthroat and an occasional brook. Lower reaches are on private property; upper reaches are in the National Forest. The creeks are reached by county and forest service roads west of US 189 between the towns of Daniel and Big Piney. South Cottonwood Creek (excluding Soda Lakes), North Cottonwood Creek (including **Maki Creek**), North Horse Creek, South Horse Creek, and Lead Creek drainages above the National Forest boundary are catch and release for all

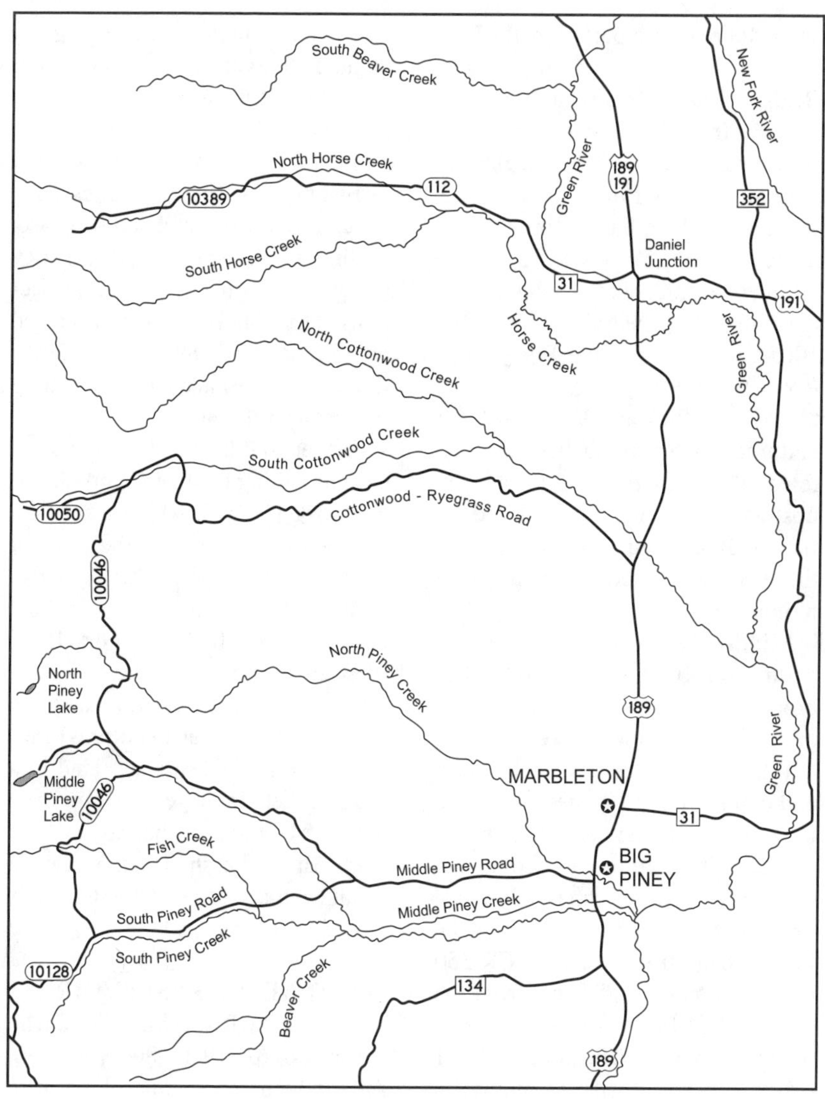

cutthroat, and fishing with artificial flies and lures only. Located on **South Cottonwood Creek** inside the national forest is **Soda Lakes** (8,295 ft; 4 to 10 ac) which have good fishing for brook to 12 inches.

North Piney Creek, **Middle Piney Creek** and **South Piney Creek** enter the Green River from the west near the town of Big Piney.

They drain a large portion part of the eastern Wyoming Mountains in Bridger-Teton National Forest. **North Piney Creek** has fair fishing for brook and cutthroat to 12 inches. It drains **North Piney Lake** (8,685 ft; 32 ac), which has cutthroat to 14 inches and some brook to 12 inches. A steep 4-mile hike is required to reach the lake. The trailhead is on FR 10054 just past Middle Piney Lake Road. North Piney Lake is restricted to artificial flies and lures only. All cutthroat under 10 inches must be released. North Piney Lake and its upstream tributaries are closed to fishing June 1 through July 15 and the lake is closed to boats with motors.

Middle Piney Creek ranges in width from 10 to 20 feet and has fair brook fishing for 8- to 10-inch fish. It drains **Middle Piney Lake** (8,820 ft; 150 ac), which has, brook, kokanee and cutthroat to 12 inches, and some larger rainbow, and lake trout up to 4 pounds. The limit on trout and salmon is 6 fish of which only 2 can be lake trout, and only 1 may be longer than 20 inches. Take CR 350 (Middle Piney Road) west from the town of Big Piney for 10 miles, the road gets rough and becomes CR 111 (Middle Piney Road). Continue on this road 10 miles to FR 10024 (Middle Piney Lake Road), and south for 3 miles to the lake. There are campsites near the lake. Just beyond the forest boundary on CR 111, a road (FR 10046) forks to the south; it goes 9 miles to **South Piney Creek**, which has fair fishing for rainbow, brook and cutthroat averaging 10 inches. **Beaver Creek** and **Fish Creek** are tributaries of the South Fork Piney Creek with cutthroat to 10 inches. Both creeks are restricted to fishing with flies and lures only, all cutthroat are catch and release. Further to the south is **Dry Piney Creek**, which has the same restrictions. Dry Piney Creek is accessed off of Highway 189 via Dry Piney Road to the west and has poor fishing for small cutthroat.

Farther south, **La Barge Creek** has fair fishing for 10-inch brook and cutthroat. CR 315, which leaves US 189 two miles south of the town of La Barge, follows the creek northwest over a natural divide to the headwaters of the Greys Fork River (described in Snake River Chapter). Stretches of the creek near the town of La Barge and outside of the forest boundary are on private land. La Barge Creek drainage upstream from the BLM boundary has a limit for cutthroat of 1 fish. **Rock Creek,** a small tributary of La Barge Creek, is closed to fishing.

FONTENELLE RESERVOIR

The Green River fills **Fontenelle Reservoir** (6,519 ft; 8000 ac when full), which is 20 miles long with depths to 100 feet and about 8000 acres when full. The reservoir is 35 miles northeast of the town of Kemmerer on Highway 189. The reservoir offers good fishing for large brown in the fall during spawning season, brown to 5 pounds are occasionally caught. Rainbow average 13

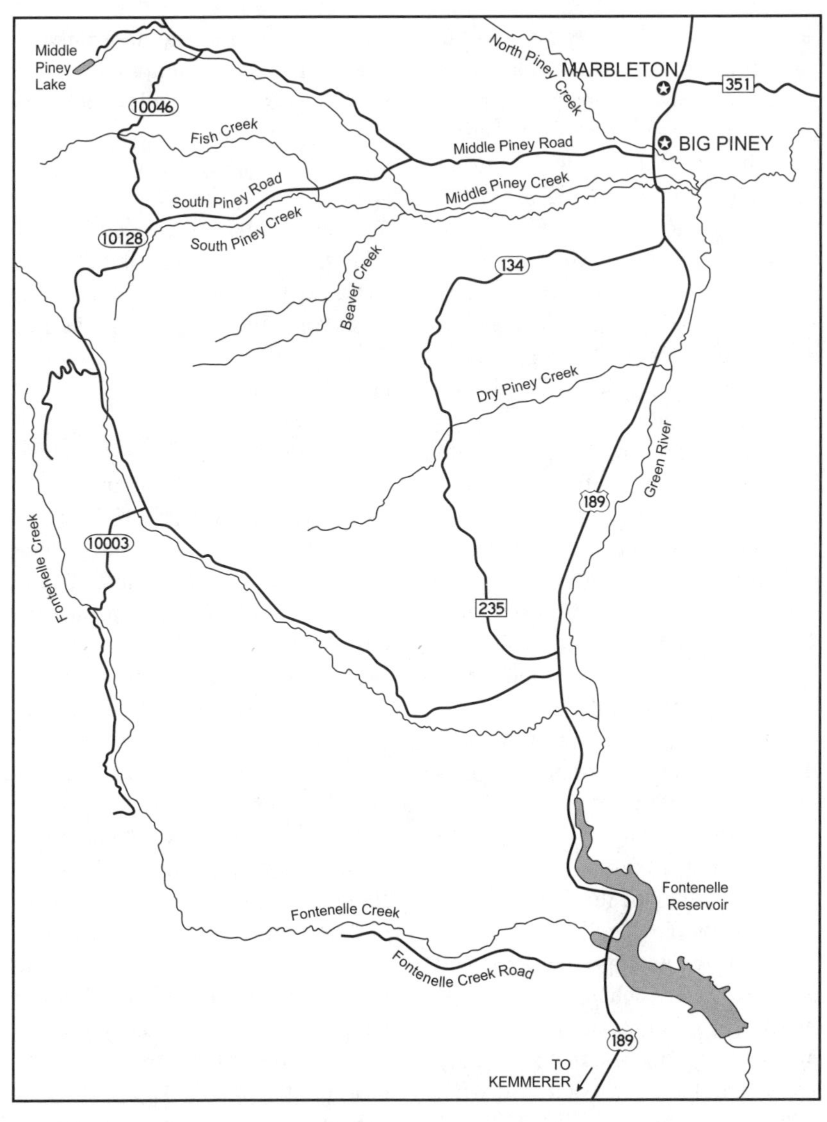

inches, but can run 1 to 3 pounds. Some kokanee are available. Boat anglers have the best success trolling with pop gear and worms, rapallas, crocodiles and bait such as cheese, nightcrawlers and flatfish lures. Fishing is better in the spring and fall, as the summer months tend to be to warm at this large lowland reservoir. There are campgrounds and a boat launch area on the west side of Fontenelle Reservoir, but because of drawdowns in the spring and fall the launching site may be difficult to use. Ice fishing in the winter occasionally produces a brown up to 10 pounds and rainbows to 4 pounds. Lake trout and kokanee are caught occasionally. The Green River from Fontenelle Dam downstream approximately one (1) mile to the U.S. Geological Survey gauge station (cable crossing) at the Weeping Rocks Campground is closed to fishing from October 7 through November 7.

Fontenelle Creek runs into Fontenelle Reservoir from the west, Fontenelle Creek Road (CR 314) runs along the creek's lower stretch where there is fair angling for brook and rainbow in the 10-inch range. Take CR 306 north of Kemmerer to reach the upper reaches of the creek, where the fishing in the national forest is better for brook and cutthroat in the 12 inch range. **Fontenelle Lakes** (8,950 to 9,450 ft; 2 to 5 ac) are at the top of the drainage offering good fishing for small brook.

The 75 miles of the lower **Green River** below Fontenelle Reservoir is no match for its upper portions, and is an extremely delicate fishery, primarily for rainbow and brown averaging 14 to 16 inches. In the past, dry fly fishing has been good in the fall with browns as large as 10 - 15 pounds caught above the Big Sandy juncture. From the Sweetwater County Road 8 Bridge, 4.5 miles below Fontenelle Dam, downstream to the Big Sandy River the limit on trout is 1 fish. All trout less than 20 inches must be released. Fishing is with artificial flies and lures only.

Kokanee from Flaming Gorge run the Green River annually from September 1 to November 30 as far upriver as Fontenelle Dam. The peak spawning run lasts for the month of October and the fish average 15 to 20 inches. Whitefish averaging 12 inches are plentiful. Below the Fontenelle Reservoir, **Flume Creek** flows into the Green River from the west and is closed to fishing.

Access to the lower Green River is not as limited as the river above Fontenelle Reservoir, the river flows mostly through Bureau of Reclamation, US Fish and Wildlife Service, Seedskadee National Wildlife Refuge, and BLM lands. Good maps are recommend for those not using a guide to float this section of the river, as plenty of private property still does exist along this portion of the river.

HAMS FORK RIVER

The **Hams Fork River** comes out of the southern end of the Wyoming Range and flows south through the coal-mining town of Kemmerer before turning east to join Blacks Fork and to empty into Flaming Gorge Reservoir. State Hwy 233 follows the stream north from Kemmerer to the forest boundary, and Forest Service roads continue along the stream for several miles more. Cutthroat and small brook are found on Hams Fork River in the Bridger-Teton National Forest. Below Viva Naughton Reservoir and Kemmerer City Reservoir there is fair fishing in the stream for rainbow averaging 11

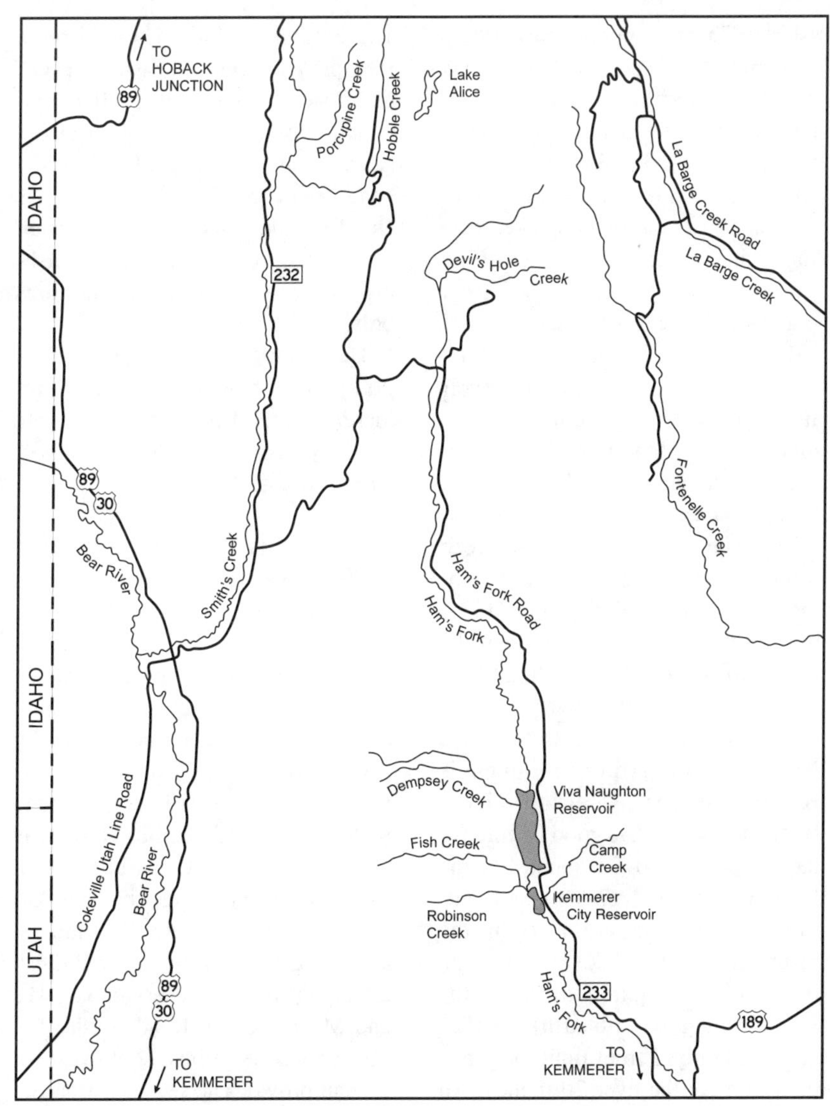

inches. Between Kemmerer Reservoir and Viva Naughton Reservoir a stretch of about a mile, no fishing is allowed from April 1 to June 30. **Viva Naughton Reservoir** (7,240 ft; 1350 ac), 16 miles north of Kemmerer, is a Utah Power and Light reservoir. It has boat launching facilities and a campground, both of which charge fees. There is no charge for fishing. There is public parking by the dam (the dam is closed to fishing) and at the upper end of the reservoir. This is primarily a rainbow fishery with catches averaging 16 inches. There are a few brown and big whitefish, as well as some splake, cutthroat and brook. Shoreline fishing produces decent catches, but most anglers troll using lures and worms. This is also a popular ice fishing spot. All tributaries of the reservoir are closed to fishing from April 1 to June 30, as is the Hams Fork River upstream about 1.75 miles to Corral Creek.

The Hams Fork River, between Viva Naughton Reservoir and Kremmerer City Reservoir, has a limit of 2 trout, of which only one can be longer than 20 inches, artificial flies and lures only. All brown 13 to 20 inches must be released. Below Viva Naughton Reservoir 1.5 miles is **Kemmerer City Reservoir** (7,145 ft; 186 ac) which has good fishing for large rainbow to 21 inches, some large brown, and some small cutthroat. Whitefish are also in the reservoir. A short hike of less than 0.5 miles is required to reach the lake. Fishing is with artificial flies and lures only, 2 trout limit, only one of which can be over 20 inches. All trout 13 to 20 inches must be released. Boats are allowed without motors.

Several of the tributary streams of Kremmerer City Reservoir, Hams River, and Viva Naughton Reservoir have restrictions to protect the cutthroat during spawning season. These waters include: **Camp Creek**, **Dempsey Creek**, **Fish Creek**, **Robinson Creek**, and **Trail Creek** which are closed to fishing from April 1 through June 30. Near the headwaters of the Hams Fork is **Devil's Hole Creek** which is catch and release for all cutthroat, and fishing is by artificial flies and lures only.

The lower reaches of the Hams Fork River below the town of Kemmerer mostly flow through private property, fishing is fair for rainbow and browns to 16 inches.

BLACKS FORK

Blacks Fork, which drains a portion of Utah's Uinta Mountain Range, flows north from Meek's Cabin Reservoir on the Utah-Wyoming border through Lyman, eventually turns east and, joined by Hams Fork, loops south into the northern end of Flaming Gorge Reservoir. **Meek's Cabin Reservoir** (8,566 ft; 585 ac when full) fluctuates with irrigation use but has fair fishing for cutthroat up to 13 inches, averaging 8 to 10 inches. Whitefish are plentiful in the reservoir. CR 410 and Meek's Cabin Road south of I-80—about 28 miles southwest of Lyman provides access the reservoir. Two public fishing areas are 3 and 4 miles below the reservoir on Blacks Fork, which is about 40 feet in width and rated fair for 8- to 12-inch brook, cutthroat and rainbow, with an occasional large brown taken between Lyman and Fort Bridger. Much of this vicinity is private land, requiring

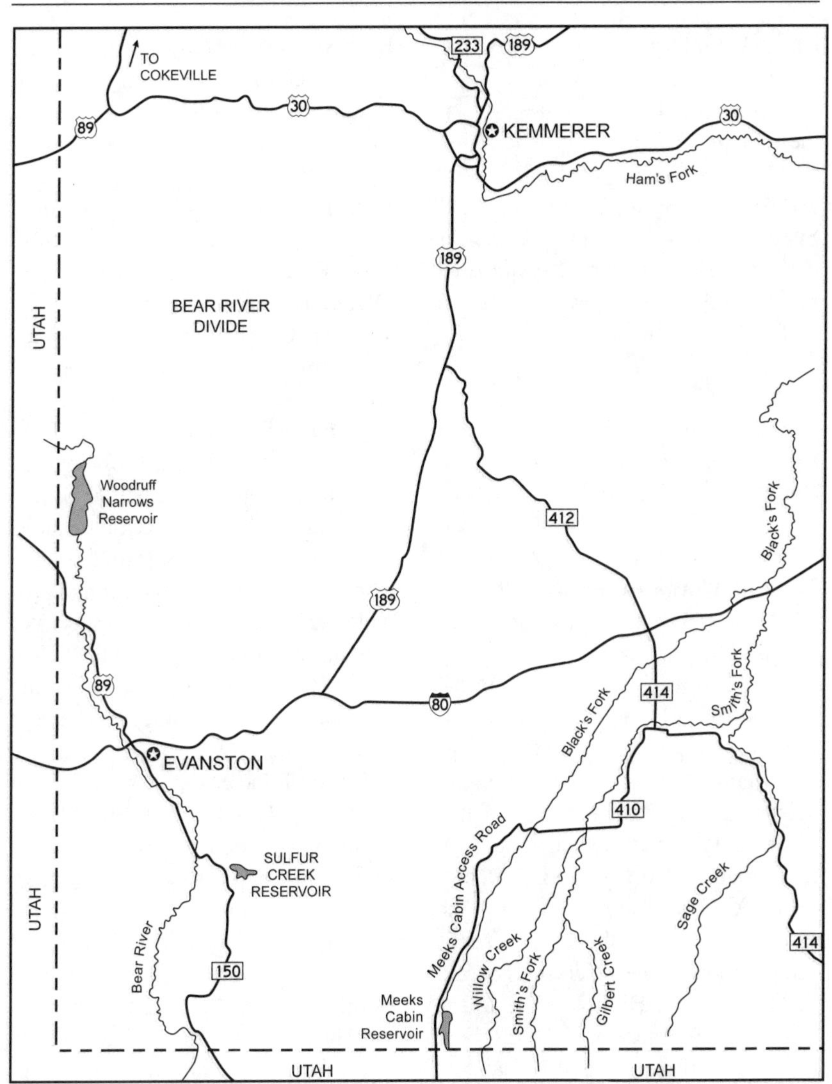

landowner's permission to fish.

Smiths Fork directly to the east of Henry Fork drains the middle portion of Utah's High Uinta Mountain Range, in Wyoming, fishing is best in the Wasatch National Forest for small cutthroat and brook. From the national forest boundary upstream, **Gilbert Creek** drainage and **Sage Creek** drainage have regulations in place to protect the cutthroat trout. All cutthroat are catch and release, and fishing is by artificial flies and lures only. **Willow Creek** from the

BLM boundary upstream has the same restrictions.

Henrys Fork also comes out of the Uinta Mountains in Utah just north of the Wyoming-Utah border and flows east to Flaming Gorge. State Hwy 414 runs near it much of the way. Henrys Fork River offers fair fishing for rainbow, brown and cutthroat to 12 inches.

FLAMING GORGE RESERVOIR

After draining the Wind River Range and meandering through the southwestern badlands, the Green River will have traveled almost 200 miles as it leaves Wyoming via **Flaming Gorge Reservoir** (6,053 ft; 42,000 ac). The area was named for its red canyon walls in 1869 by Major John Wesley Powell. With the completion of the dam in 1964, Flaming Gorge Reservoir was created. Flaming Gorge has beautiful scenery and a lot of the kind of trophy fishing that attracts anglers from afar. Flaming Gorge National Recreation Area is administered by the Forest Service. There are roads around most of the reservoir, SR 530 to the west and Highway 191 to the east provides access. Several boat ramps and marinas are also available on the east and west sides of the reservoir.

Flaming Gorge has abundant rainbow and brown, averaging 16 to 18 inches, but anglers are increasingly attracted by the lake trout and kokanee. Kokanee sometimes weigh in at more than 3 pounds, although most average 18 inches. Boat anglers have best success catching lake trout. Anglers coming to Flaming Gorge in search of lake trout benefit from a good fish finder and heavy-duty deep-water fishing gear, as the water is deep and the fish at times are difficult to locate. Lake trout averaging 20 pounds are possible. The Wyoming record for lake trout in Flaming Gorge is 50 pounds. Flaming Gorge Reservoir is not only a trout fishery, smallmouth bass and catfish are also in the reservoir. Bass fishing in the Lowell Canyon area and areas near the pipeline at the lower narrows are popular bass sites. Channel catfish are found at the northern end of the reservoir and provide bank fishing during warm water conditions, June - September. Catfish up to 20 pounds are found above the confluence of the Blacks Fork and Green River arms.

To reach the east side of the reservoir, take Hwy 191 south from I-80, 4 miles west of Rock Springs. Boat ramps, on the east side of the reservoir, are available at Fire Canyon and Upper Marsh Creek. The west side of Flaming Gorge is reached by turning south from I-80 west of Green River on Hwy 530. It runs along the west side of the reservoir. There are campgrounds and boat ramps about 22 miles from Green River at Buckboard Crossing and a boat ramp at Squaw Hollow, another 10 miles south. There is a commercial marina at Buckboard Crossing.

Since Flaming Gorge Reservoir saddles the Wyoming/Utah border either a Wyoming or Utah fishing

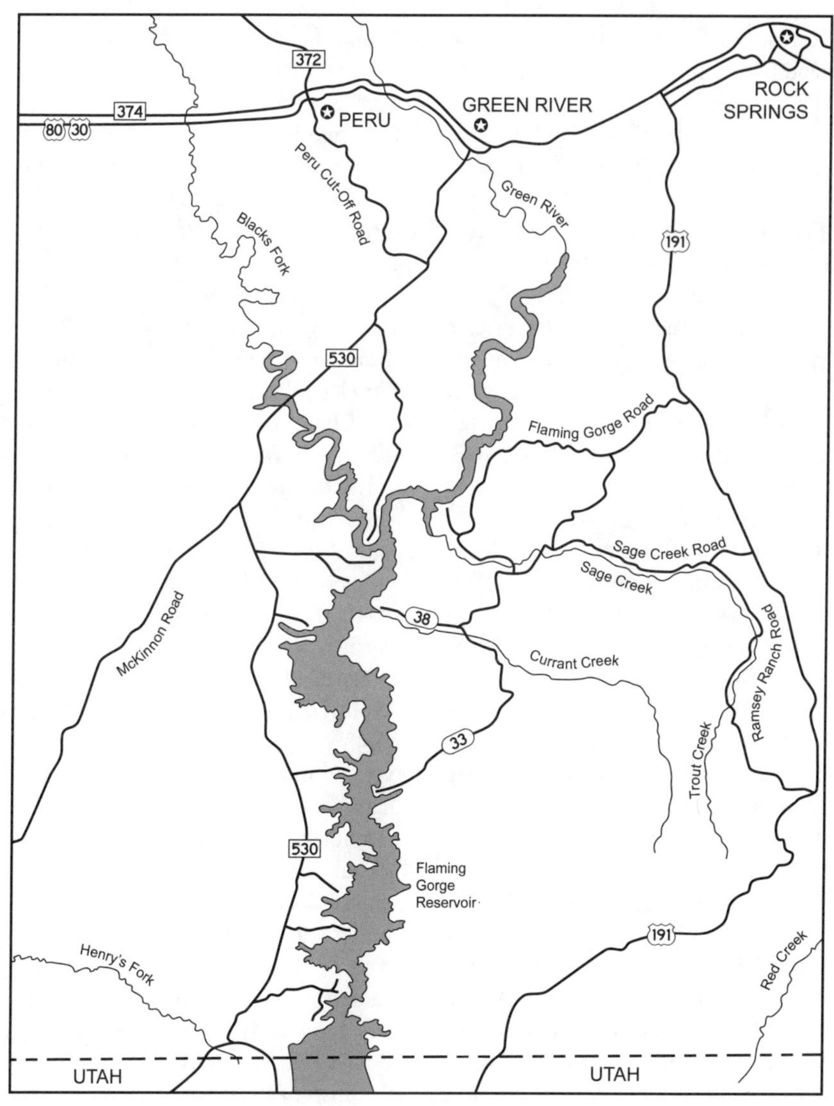

license is required at Flaming Gorge. To fish in the other state's waters, a reciprocal fishing stamp from that state is necessary. In Wyoming Flaming Gorge Reservoir has a limit of 6 trout or salmon; of these only 3 may be salmon and/or only 4 can be lake trout, only one of which maybe over 28 inches. Kokanee Salmon are catch and release October 1 to November

7. Possession of, or use of gaffs to land fish, is prohibited. Utah has similar regulations on trout and salmon please check regulations before fishing on the Utah side of the border.

Current Creek flows into the Flaming Gorge Reservoir from the east. Flaming Gorge Road provides access to the lower reaches of the creek, which are mostly on private property. The upper reaches are on public lands and offer fair fishing for small cutthroat. Fishing is restricted to catch and release on all cutthroat, artificial flies and lures only. Current Creek is closed to fishing from April 1 to June 30. **Trout Creek** drainage to the north, upstream from Sage Creek, has the same restrictions.

Further to the east of Flaming Gorge Reservoir and Highway 191 on the Wyoming/Utah border is Red Creek, which flows west before turning south into Utah. **Red Creek** upstream from the confluence of **Little Red Creek** is closed to fishing.

BORDER WATERS - UTAH

West of the Green River lies the **Bear River**. Fishing is good for cutthroat and some large brown. Access to the river is very limit, private property limits public access. Bear River from the upper boundary of the Bear River State Park downstream to the northern boundary of the Evanston City Limits (Simms Lane) has a limit of 2 trout, only 1 can be longer than 20 inches.

West of the town of Kemmerer, near Cokeville on US 30, several tributaries of Bear River have good fishing for brook and cutthroat averaging 8 inches; cutthroat and brown averaging 14 inches in the Smiths Fork and West Smiths Fork rivers. In the **Smiths Fork Bear River** drainage (including **Porcupine Creek**), **West Fork Smiths Fork** drainage (including **Archie Creek**), **Hobble Creek** drainage (including Lake Alice), and **Thomas Fork** drainage (including **Raymond Creek**), all cutthroat under 10 inches must be returned to the water. Fishing is with flies and lures only.

Lake Alice (7,740 ft; 246 ac) has good fishing for cutthroat. TR 025 leads from FR 10070 to the east 1.75 miles to the lake. Lake Alice and all tributaries upstream are closed from April 1 through June 30.

North of the town of Evanston is **Woodruff Narrows Reservoir** (6,439 ft; 2000 ac), a private reservoir with public access allowed. The reservoir has brown, cutthroat and rainbow to 20 inches with an occasional 5-pounder being hooked, but most fish are smaller. The reservoir is subject to drawdown, affecting the size of fish caught. There are no camping facilities. Fishing is poor in late summer. The reservoir is on the Bear River, about 10 miles north of the town of Evanston via Hwy 89 and US 30.

To the east of the town of Evenston are **Crompton Reservoir** (6,750 ft; 101 ac) and **Painter Reservoir** (6,945 ft; 23 ac), which are both private.

Sulphur Creek Reservoir (7,172 ft; 209 ac), 11 miles south of

Evanston on Hwy 150, and 1 mile east on signed road to reservoir. The reservoir offers good fishing for rainbow, brown and cutthroat up to 18 inches. A boat ramp is available on the south side of the reservoir. **Sulphur Creek** above the reservoir is closed to fishing from April 1 through June 30.

BORDER WATERS - COLORADO

The **Little Snake River** flows from Colorado into Wyoming and back again several times along the Wyoming/Colorado border before making its way down to the Yampa River in Colorado. The limit for the Little Snake River proper in Wyoming is 6 fish, only 1 may be a cutthroat. The Little Snake River headwaters lie in Colorado, except the **North Fork Little Snake River** and **Roaring Fork Little Snake River** whose waters start in Huston Park Wilderness near the Continental Divide. The upper reaches of these creeks offer some fishing for cutthroat and small brook. The North Fork Little Snake River drainage from FR 809.1b down to the Colorado State Line has a limit of 6 fish, only 1 may be a cutthroat. The North Fork Little Snake River above FR 809.1b is closed to fishing. The Roaring Fork, from the Huston Park Wilderness Area boundary to the Colorado State Line has a limit of 6 fish, only 1 can be a cutthroat. Inside the wilderness area the Roaring Fork Little Snake River is closed to fishing.

Tributaries entering the Little Snake from the north tend to be small, dry and offer very little fishing opportunities. **Muddy Creek** and **Savery Creek** offer marginal fishing for small cutthroat and brook, and some stocked rainbow. Private property limits angler access to most of the lower reaches of the creeks. The limit for trout on both creeks is 6 fish, only 1 may be a cutthroat. The upper reaches of **Battle Creek** are in the Medicine Bow National Forest and Huston Wilderness, with fair fishing for brook and cutthroat, and some stocked rainbow. **Battle Lake** (9,233 ft; 19 ac), to the south of SR 70 near the old mining town of Rambler, has fair fishing for cutthroat and small brook. The lake is 1 miles south of the road, hike down to lake on old mining roads. Battle Creek drainage upstream from the Little Snake River has a limit of 6 trout, only 1 can be a cutthroat.

SWEETWATER RIVER

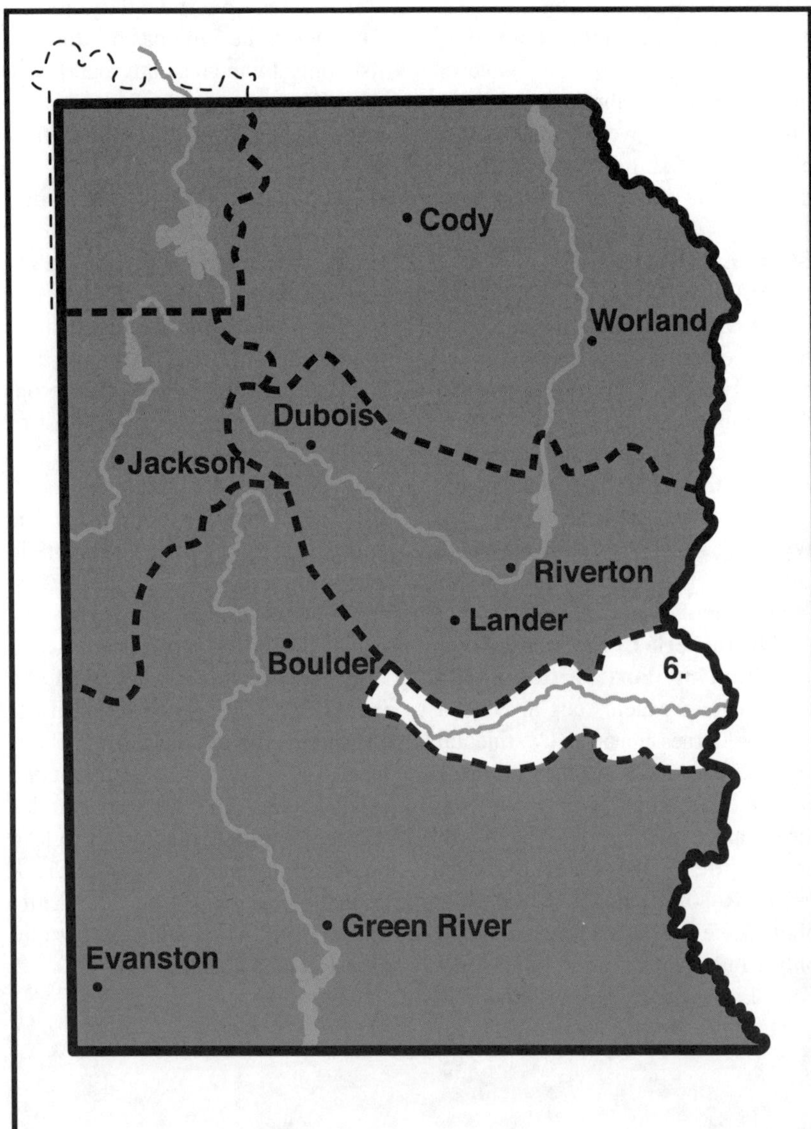

6. Sweetwater River

SWEETWATER RIVER

The **Sweetwater River** drains the southern end of the Wind River Mountains, then flows east to Pathfinder Reservoir and the North Platte River drainage. The Wind River Mountains produce so many prolific angling opportunities that some, like the Sweetwater River, are almost overlooked.

Portions of its upper reaches, where the river drops out of the Bridger Wilderness at the southern end of the Wind River Range, attract serious fly anglers, especially in the spring and fall. The river journeys more than 100 miles through a mixture of private property, BLM and state lands to Pathfinder Reservoir. The Oregon and Mormon trails of the 1840's and later follow much of its length and offer a historic touch to the river.

Game fish are not abundant in the Sweetwater River, partly because it runs low in the late summer and the water becomes too warm in its lower reaches. The best fishing that the Sweetwater River and its tributaries have to offer - from brown, rainbow, brook and cutthroat - lies above Hwy 287 between Sweetwater Station and Muddy Gap Junction.

SWEETWATER RIVER HEADWATERS

About an hour's drive south of Lander, at South Pass, SR 28 crosses the Sweetwater River less than 2 miles from the Continental Divide. Just beyond the river the highway intersects the Lander Cutoff, a well-maintained gravel road that follows the river northwest. This road (CR 23-132) parallels first the river and then one of its tributaries, **Lander Creek**. Lander Creek has fair fishing for small brook.

The headwaters of the Sweetwater River lie in the Bridger Wilderness, at the extreme southern end of the Wind River Mountain Range. To reach the headwaters follow the Sweetwater Gap Trail from the Sweetwater Trailhead (8,900 ft). From SR 28 take the Lander Cutoff Road northwest to Sweetwater Road, the trailhead is several miles to the north along this rough road, the last few miles to the trailhead are passable by 4 wheel-drive vehicles only. The Sweetwater Gap Trail follows the river, which is only a small stream at this point, to Sweetwater Gap. Sweetwater Gap Trail continues over the pass (10,325) to the Middle Fork Popo Agie River, Popo Agie Wilderness, and Tayo Park. At the Sweetwater Trailhead, a faint and hard to follow Little Sandy Trail heads cross-country northwest 3.5 miles to Little Sandy Lake and the Little Sandy River drainage.

The alpine lakes that feed into the Sweetwater River are, for the most part, barren because of high altitude and shallow water. Two lakes near the rivers headwaters, **Blucher Lake** (9,350 ft; 6 ac) and **Needles Lake** (9,022 ft; 9 ac) in the Bridger Wilderness, have small brook. Trails are poorly marked, so good maps are essential. Needles Lake is reached by the Sweetwater Gap Trail. Local

Rob Yingling/Bighorn Web Design Photo

inquiry is recommended because most maps (other than USGS topographic) are vague.

Blucher Creek, **Little Sweetwater Creek** and **Jack Creek**, all of which feed into the upper Sweetwater River drainage from Forest Service land above SR 28, have small brook and are accessible to the wilderness border by 4 wheel drive roads, and from there by foot. The upper reaches of the Sweetwater River, as well as, **East Fork Sweetwater River** (also above the highway) have brown, brook and stocked rainbow to 12 inches.

After the Sweetwater River runs under the highway, it crosses a mixture of private, BLM and state lands in the high desert, draining the old gold mining region of South Pass. From the many dirt roads that etch this barren landscape, the river appears like a meandering oasis, winding along and lined by low brush and a few trees. The river bottom gives refuge to antelope, waterfowl and moose. You will need maps and a careful eye for property markers to distinguish public and private land along this part of the river. Don't expect great numbers of fish, but there are a few large brown and rainbow.

Willow Creek, which empties into the Sweetwater from the north near Atlantic City, has brook and cutthroat. Most of the creek is on private property, some Walk-In Access is accessible by dirt roads southwest of the town of Atlantic City. **Rock Creek**, much of it located on private land below Atlantic City, has brook, brown and rainbow - some of good size. A higher section of Rock Creek can be reached above Hwy 28 by taking the Louis Lake "Loop" Road running north from the highway near Atlantic City. **Rock Creek Reservoir** (8,345 ft; 80 ac) has rainbow to 12 inches, access is on FR 310 (4 wheel-drive). Rock Creek Reservoir is closed to fishing from November 1 through May 31 and the use of gas motors is prohibited. **Big Atlantic Gulch**, also on BLM land near Atlantic City, offers 2.7 miles of access to anglers, and is heavily fished for cutthroat and brook. In the area, **Diamond Springs Reservoir**, is no longer a viable fishing reservoir due to lack of water.

LOWER SWEETWATER RIVER

Southeast of Atlantic City the **Sweetwater River** flows for several miles through private land. East of the Phelps Dodge Bridge the river flows through the steep Sweetwater Canyon, which is on BLM land. Check BLM land ownership maps before crossing lands into the canyon. A mile northwest of Sweetwater Junction is **Carmondy Lake** (6,605 ft; 85 ac), a shallow lake with fishing for stocked rainbow. Access to the lake is off of Highway 287 on a marked gravel BLM road. Between Sweetwater Station and Muddy Gap Junction the Sweetwater River flows east and is paralleled by Highway 287. To the north of the highway, east and west of Jeffrey City, are 7 Wyoming Game and Fish Depart-

Rob Yingling/Bighorn Web Design Photo

ment Walk-In-Lease areas. Brown and rainbow up to 16 inches are present.

South of Jeffrey City 14 miles is **Jensen Reservoir** (7,290 ft; 7 ac), which has good fishing for stocked rainbow. From Jeffrey City, take Crooks Road south 8.25 miles to a fork in the road, take the left or straight dirt road for 5.75 miles. The reservoir will be visible on the south side of the road, watch for signs indicating public access as the reservoir is a Wyoming Game and Fish Department Walk-In-Lease area. Leave vehicle in one of two parking areas and hike 0.25 mile to reservoir.

About 12 miles east of Jeffrey City Highway 287 turns southeast to Muddy Junction as the Sweetwater River, where there is more private than public land, continues east to Pathfinder Reservoir. There are brown and rainbow trout up to 16 inches, and there is not much fishing pressure, but reaching the river can be difficult. Be sure to check with landowners before crossing private land. There are also carp and suckers in this part of the river. The Sweetwater River ends its journey at Pathfinder Reservoir, 45 miles southwest of Casper.

In the Great Divide Basin, to the south of Sweetwater River and just to the west of Highway 287, is **Lost Soldier Lake** (6,575 ft; 31 ac). Fishing is fair for rainbow; most average 12 inches, but some larger are occasionally caught. Brook are also present, most are small. The limit for trout is 3 fish, only one can be longer than 15 inches. Nearby **A & M Reservoir** no longer has water, or fish.

To the south of the river along SR 220, to the northeast of Muddy Creek Junction and Highway 287, are the two **Bucklin Reservoirs**. **Bucklin Reservoir #1** (6,165 ft; 27 ac) is stocked with small rainbow and **Bucklin Reservoir #2** (6,165 ft; 36 ac) has small yellow perch.

NORTH PLATTE RIVER

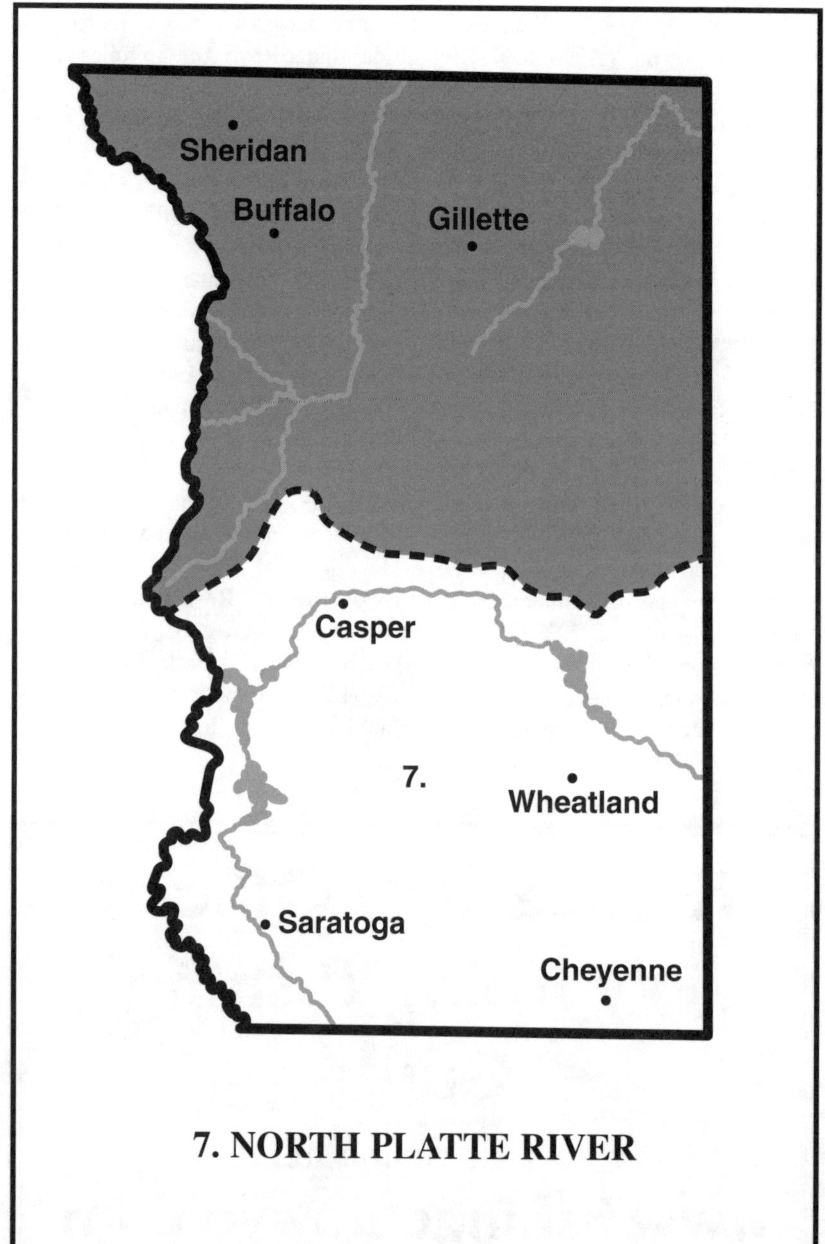

7. NORTH PLATTE RIVER

NORTH PLATTE RIVER

The **North Platte River** offers a variety of fishing experiences, ranging from the cold, swift creek and the meandering river to pristine lakes and reservoirs. The North Platte flows north out of Colorado, through picturesque Medicine Bow National Forest; fills six reservoirs, including Seminoe, Kortes, Pathfinder, Alcova, Glendo and Guernsey; heads east through Casper and finally exits the state near the town of Torrington. The North Platte River collects water from three major tributaries including: the Encampment, Medicine Bow, and Laramie rivers; the North Platte River collects water from the North Platte River, Savage Run, Huston Park, and Encampment Wilderness Areas; and offers plenty of fishing opportunities in lakes and streams located in the Medicine Bow, Sierra Madre, Wind River (by way of the Sweetwater drainage), and Laramie Mountain ranges.

Brown and rainbow predominate in the river itself and range from 14 to 16 inches on average, walleye which swim up from Seminoe Reservoir are also present. The North Platte's tributaries and surrounding bodies of water below Seminoe Reservoir hold the aforementioned fish, as well as brook and cutthroat. Much of the first 90 miles of the North Platte River in Wyoming is inaccessible by vehicle, therefore hiking, horses, or floating the river is necessary. The North Platte River throughout its flow through Wyoming is almost completely surrounded by private property, so many anglers float the river. If you decide to float the river a quality guide service is recommended. Most of the river is surrounded by private property in which crossing, wading or landing boats requires landowner permission to avoid trespassing.

Note: Inside the boundaries of the Medicine Bow National Forest boats with internal combustion (gas) motors are prohibited in all lakes with the exception of Sand Lake, Turpin Reservoir, Lake Owen, Rob Roy Reservoir, and Hog Park Reservoir.

NORTH PLATTE RIVER – COLORADO BORDER TO GREY REEF RESERVOIR

The headwaters of the North Platte, Encampment, and Laramie rivers are several miles to the south in Colorado. The North Platte River gathers water from high up in the Never Summer, Medicine Bow, Madre Park, and Rabbit Ears mountain ranges then flows through an area known in Colorado as North Park before crossing the Wyoming/Colorado state border 26.5 miles southeast of the town of Riverside. For a complete description of the North Platte River headwaters in Colorado refer to *Kip Carey's Official Colorado Fishing Guide*.

From the Colorado border, the North Platte runs within Medicine Bow National Forest and the Platte River Wilderness for about 17 miles. A float map is available from the Laramie Office of the Wyoming

Rob Yingling/Bighorn Web Design Photo

Game and Fish Department (307-745-4046), which details public easements for the North Platte River from the Wyoming/Colorado State line to Seminoe Reservoir including private land, parking areas, access roads, public access points and other useful information (there is a $9 fee for the map). The river first flows through the Platte River Wilderness, then through private land for the remaining distance to Seminoe Reservoir. The following text details the major accesses and highlights of the river, if you decide to float the river a quality guide service is recommended. Most of the river is surrounded by private property in which crossing, wading or landing boats requires landowner permission to avoid trespassing.

The **North Platte River** as it enters the state of Wyoming is in the Platte River Wilderness Area for about 17 miles. Four wheel drive roads head east from the western branch of Hwy 230 (that is before the highway dips down into Colorado and returns to Wyoming to the east) to trails that lead to the river below the Colorado State Line. Forestry or topo maps are essential. About 4 miles downstream, at Six Mile Campground, FR 492 provides access to the river and the Platte River Trail. The Platte River Trail is an 8.5-mile foot trail through the Platte River Wilderness from Six Mile Gap downstream to Pickaroon Campground.

Pickaroon Campground and Pickaroon Access Area can only be accessed from the east. From the town of Keystone follow FR 543, 511 and 512 to the east side of the river, north of Douglas Creek. There is heavy floater pressure in this area. Further down the river, 17.5 miles, is Bennett Peak Access which has BLM campgrounds, a mile of fishing on public land and boat launching sites. French Creek Road (CR 660) provides access from Highway 230 about 4 miles southeast of the town of Riverside. Follow French Creek Road across the river and drive 3 miles farther east to a gravel road (BLM 3404), from there it is approximately 6.5 miles north to the Bennett Peak Access Area. The main North Platte River is excellent for fly-fishing, particularly during the fall. Prime spincast fishing with lures such as Panther Martins is found during the months of June and July. Those fishing with spinning gear should wait at least until late June because the river is usually pretty roily with run-off until then. Fishing, however, can be excellent in April and May, prior to run-off. Brown and rainbow in the river average 12-14 inches, with some larger. The North Platte River, from Colorado-Wyoming State Line downstream to the Saratoga Inn Bridge, the limit for trout is 6 fish, only one 1 trout can be longer than 16 inches. All trout between 10 and 16 inches must be released. Fishing is with artificial flies and lures only.

Douglas Creek flows northwest out of the Snowy Range, joining the North Platte River 8 miles downstream from Six Mile Gap. There is camping near its confluence with the North Platte River at the Pikepole and Pickaroon Campgrounds. The creek provides good fishing for brown, brook and rainbow averaging 10 inches. Lower reaches are in Platte River Wilderness; upper reaches are accessible from the east and are in Medicine Bow National Forest. Douglas Creek Road follows the upper reaches of the creek below Rob Roy Reservoir. Three tributaries of Douglas Creek, **Pelton Creek, Lake Creek** and **Muddy Creek**, offer fair fishing for brown and brook. Muddy Creek is accessible from the town of Albany on FR 500, FR 542 and FR 553 (4 wheel drive), which parallels the creek. Pelton Creek and Lake Creek can be approached from the south on FR 898. There are two campgrounds near Pelton Creek.

High up in the Douglas Creek drainage is **Rob Roy Reservoir** (9,420 ft; 375 ac) with fair to good fishing for small brook, rainbow to 12 inches, and an occasional brown. The reservoir is reached from the east via FR 500 from the town of Albany or from the south via Hwy 230, then FR 512 and FR 543. From the west the reservoir is about 20 miles east of French Creek Campground on the French Creek Road. Boats with gas motors are allowed, a boat ramp and campground are present.

Cottonwood Creek, Savage Run Creek, and most of **North Mullen Creek** and **South Mullen Creek** are in the Savage Run Wilderness. These creeks drain the western side of the Snowy Range, they tend to be brushy and have only fair fishing for small brook. Much of the creeks are in the Savage Run Wilderness, the upper reaches of North and South Mullen creeks are in the national forest.

Big Creek, which originates in Colorado, enters the North Platte River from the southwest about 1.5 miles downstream from the Mullen Creek juncture. Hwy 230 crosses the creek about 8 miles from the Colorado-Wyoming border and about 6 miles south of its confluence with the North Platte River. There is 1 mile of public fishing downstream from this point, marked by a public fishing access sign and small parking lot; upstream, the Big Creek runs mostly on private land for 3 miles to Medicine Bow National Forest where the creek is on public lands. The lower reaches of the creek are 15-20 feet wide and have good fishing for brook, rainbow and brown to 12 inches.

About 12 miles west of Snowy Range Pass, **North Fork Barrett Creek** parallels Hwy 130 and has small brook.

French Creek, reached by CR 660, flows west out of the Snowy Range and joins the North Platte 14 miles east of the town of Encampment. Brook and rainbow average 10 inches and, in the lower reaches, brown average 12-14 inches in the fall. French Creek Campground is on the edge of the national forest. A mile east of North Fork Barrett

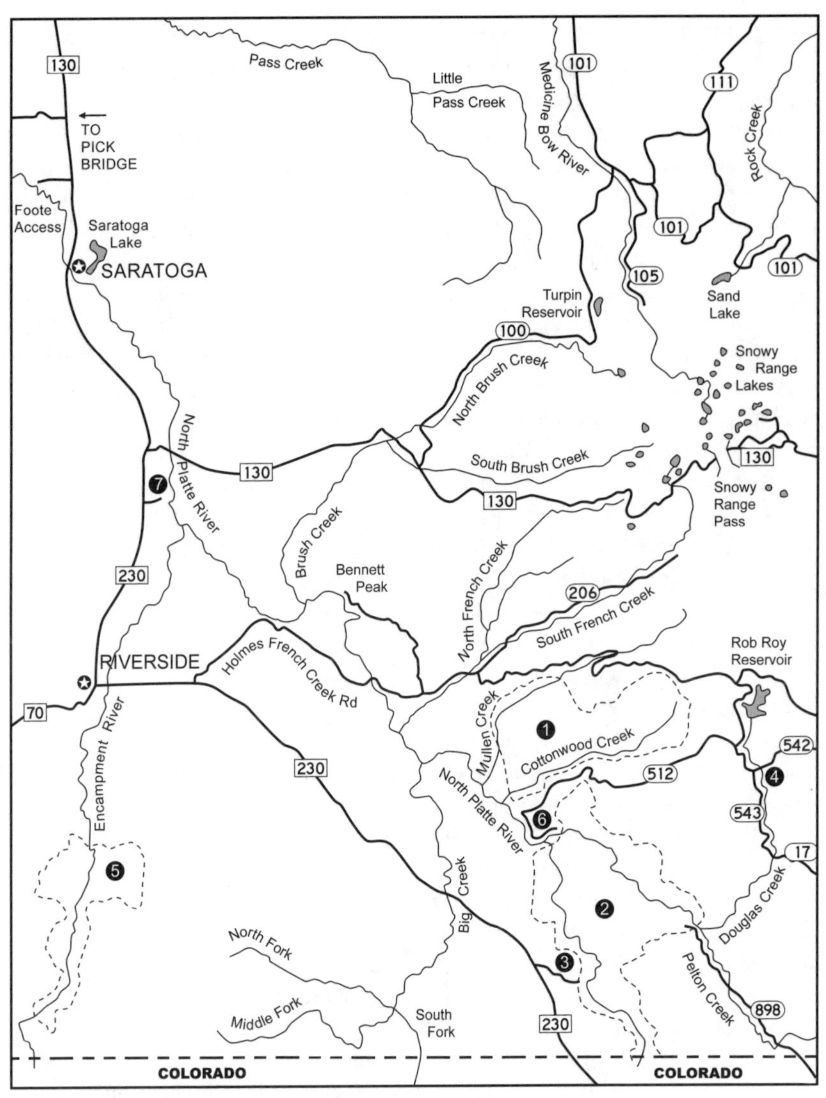

1. Savage Run Wilderness
2. Platte River Wilderness
3. Six Mile Gap
4. Keystone
5. Encampment Wilderness
6. Pickaroon
7. Treasure Island

Creek, FR 227 leaves the highway and heads south. **North French Creek** parallels this stretch of road and, when not too high, is fair for brook. Several of the Snowy Mountain Range Lakes are on this drainage, see the Snowy Range Lakes section in this chapter for complete descriptions.

Encampment River

Another fine tributary that flows into the upper North Platte River from the southwest is the **Encampment River**, which enters Wyoming from Colorado and flows 25 miles to the North Platte River. For a complete description of the Encampment River headwaters in Colorado refer to *Kip Carey's Official Colorado Fishing Guide*. The lower reaches of the river run on private land, limiting public access. There is, however, a public access area just south of the town of Encampment. The Encampment River, from Highway 230 at the town of Riverside, downstream to the North Platte River has a limit of 6 fish, only 1 can be larger than 16 inches. All trout between 10 and 16 inches must be released; fishing is with flies and lures only. Above the town of Encampment the Encampment River Trail follows the river upstream across state and public lands into the Medicine Bow National Forest and Encampment River Wilderness, where there are 12 miles of good fishing for brook, brown and rainbow that average 12 inches. To reach the trailhead follow CR 353 and CR 3407 southwest of the town of Encampment, the trail ends near Hog Park Reservoir and FR 496. **Hog Park Reservoir** (8,530 ft; 164 ac) is a good fishery about 2 miles north of the Colorado border within the national forest, and is easily accessible from Encampment and Riverside. Head west on Hwy 70 out of Encampment about 6 miles then turn south onto FR 550. FR 550 is a well-maintained gravel road that runs about 17 miles through magnificent scenery between the Encampment River and Huston Park wilderness areas to the reservoir. Boats with motors (gas) are allowed on the reservoir, and camping is permitted within the national forest at several campsites. A boat ramp is present. Besides rainbow that average 14 inches, the reservoir has good fishing for small brook. The ice usually leaves this water around the first of June, about this time many of the rainbow in the reservoir begin spawning in **Robinson Creek** and **Hog Park Creek,** and this means excellent fishing for 12 to 16 inch fish at the inlets and further upstream in these tributaries. Hog Park Creek below the reservoir offers good fishing for brook, and later in the fall, some brown. FR 550 splits as it nears the dam, FR 496 continues south, crosses Hog Park Creek and heads toward the Colorado border. After the road crosses the Colorado border it doubles back along the Encampment River.

Rob Yingling/Bighorn Web Design Photo

Cottonwood Creek to Seminoe Reservoir

When the North Platte River rolls out of the Medicine Bow National Forest and the Platte River Wilderness near its juncture with **Cottonwood Creek**, it runs primarily on private lands to Saratoga. Landowners, many of whom run fishing clubs and dude ranches, are very protective of their stretches of the river. A little over 9 miles upstream from Saratoga, just south of the junction of Hwys 130 and 230, the Treasure Island Public Fishing and Hunting Area opens over a mile of the river to bank anglers. Treasure Island is an 11.8 mile float from Bennett Peak access upstream. There is a campground and a launching area for floaters, who float the 12 miles down to Saratoga. Fishing is for rainbow and brown averaging 12 inches. Remember: The North Platte River from Colorado-Wyoming State Line downstream to the Saratoga Inn Bridge the limit for trout is 6 fish, only one 1 trout can be longer than 16 inches. All trout between 10 and 16 inches must be released. Fishing is with artificial flies and lures only.

Cow Creek enters the North Platte River from the west near the town of Days. Almost the entire length of the creek flows through private property, only the very high headwaters are in the national forest where there is poor fishing for small brook. Near the headwaters is **Cow Creek Reservoir** (8,822 ft; 9 ac) which is private; and higher up **Silver Lake** (9,180 ft; 16 ac), which is reach by hiking about 2.25 miles on old roads along the Continental Divide to the north from SR 70 at the town of Battle. Silver Lake has fishing for brook to 11 inches.

Spring Creek enters the North Platte from the southwest on the southern outskirts of Saratoga. Most of its lower portions are on private lands where permission to fish is necessary. Fishing is fair to good in the upper reaches along **North Fork Spring Creek** and **South Fork Spring Creek** in Medicine Bow National Forest for brook to 10 inches. However, only the creeks extreme upper reaches are on public land; the rest is private property. The South Fork of Spring Creek heads toward **South Spring Creek Lake** (9,022 ft; 12 ac), at the foot of Bridger Peak, which is private. The creek has brook, and can be reached by trail from the Jack Creek Campground, 8 miles to the northwest. Better fishing might be found on **North Spring Creek Lake** (9,842 ft; 20 ac), 6 miles southwest of the Jack Creek Campground, which has plenty of brook to 10 inches.

Saratoga Lake (6,790 ft; 276 ac), at the northeast edge of town off Hwy 130, boasts 12- to 18-inch rainbow. A boat ramp is available and campgrounds are located nearby. Saratoga Lake is a popular location in both summer and winter.

There are camping and Platte River put-in/pull-out sites off Hwy 130 north of the town of Saratoga.

Jack Creek heads toward Bridger Peak and runs north 10 miles before swinging northeast to join the North Platte River from the west, 3 miles north of Saratoga. It offers fair fishing for small brown and brook but is mostly on private property, therefore, permission from the landowners must be sought. Its headwaters can be reached by taking CR 500 west from Saratoga to Jack Creek Road that swings southwest along Jack Creek to the forest boundary. Jack Creek Campground is about 27 miles southwest of Saratoga.

To access to the North Platte River north of Saratoga go about 4 miles to the Foote Recreation Area turnoff, then about 2 miles to the river on Foote Road (the float from Saratoga to Foote is 6.3 miles). Floaters at Foote leave another vehicle about 2.5 miles downstream at Pick Bridge and float the river. The 4.5-mile trip can last from 2 to 4 hours, depending on the flow of the river. Pick Bridge is located in the Sanger Access 6 miles north of the town of Saratoga. Take Highway 130 north to Pick Bridge Road, and 4 miles west to the river. The fishing is good for brown and rainbow averaging 12 inches; fishing improves as the season progresses. Floaters put in at Pick Bridge and work the river down to the Old Frazier Place Easement about 4.5 miles downstream. The fishing is better earlier in the year, as the river runs low later in the summer making floating more difficult. The North Platte River from Pick Bridge (County Road 508) downstream approximately 5 miles to the downstream end of the Old Frazier Place Public Fishing Area the limit for trout is 6 fish; only 1 trout can be longer than 20 inches and, all trout between 10 and 20 inches must be released. Fishing is with artificial flies and lures only.

From The Old Frazier Place the North Platte River slowly meanders its way north with no public access for 18.5 miles, which is Eagles Nest Access Area located off of FR 347. The river here is more broad and slower, making floating more difficult later in the year and not providing the same fishing quality as upstream. Trout, large ones, are still caught along with walleye averaging 12 inches coming up from Seminoe Reservoir. The next access point for floaters is at I-80, 10.4 miles downstream.

Sage Creek meets the North Platte River halfway between the Old Frazier Place Easement and Eagles Nest Access Area, and like Jack Creek to the south, flows through private property and offers little fishing for small brown and brook. **Little Sage Creek** to the north offers little fishing opportunities, except for **Teton Reservoir** (7,020 ft; 61 ac) which is located about 13 miles south of Rawlins on Hwy 71. A campground is available, and boats are allowed. Fishing is for stocked brown and rainbow up to 12 inches. Other reservoirs in the vicinity are private. **Rim Lake** (7,175 ft; 18 ac) is located 8 miles north of Teton Reservoir on Hwy 71 toward Rawlins, watch for signed gravel road that goes 2 miles west to the lake. Rim Lake is a shal-

Rob Yingling/Bighorn Web Design Photo

low reservoir stocked with rainbow to 12 inches. Camping is available.

Pass Creek quietly joins the North Platte River upstream of I-80. It meanders northwest out of the Snowy Range to its juncture with the North Platte River. The creeks lower reaches are mostly dewatered and are on private land, where permission to fish is necessary. Take Pass Creek Road (CR 404) off Hwy 130 about 11 miles north of Saratoga, or, to reach Pass Creek's uppers stretches in Medicine Bow National Forest, take CR 504 east of the town of Saratoga to the forest boundary and proceed from there on rough Forest Service roads. The creek offers fair to good fishing for 8- to 10-inch brook in beaver ponds; there are brown and rainbow from 10-12 inches in its lower reaches.

The North Platte River runs under I-80 about 2 miles south of Fort Steele (an historic monument), 14 miles east of the town of Rawlins. The river is open to anglers on the Rochelle Access for 11 miles south of Fort Steel, with paved roads, gravel roads and trails to various reaches of the river. No overnight camping is allowed. Rainbow averaging 12 inches are common in this area; larger fish especially brown are caught in the fall. Cutthroat are also present, as well as, walleye that swim up the river from Seminoe Reservoir.

Seminoe Reservoir

Although not the most aesthetic part of the state, the North Platte River between I-80 and Casper holds some of the most productive water in the state - and some of the most heavily fished. The river flows north from Fort Steele, filling Seminoe and Kortes reservoirs; then winds its way through the ever-popular "Miracle Mile;" through Pathfinder and Alcova reservoirs and eventually loops toward Casper.

Seminoe State Park and **Seminoe Reservoir** (6,365 ft; 20,000 ac when full) is about 20 miles long, comprising about 20,000 surface acres when full. The water level fluctuates frequently and the fishing can be poor when there are big drawdowns due to irrigation demands from Nebraska. The wind, too, can be unforgiving but bays on the reservoir offer some protection for boaters. The reservoir is primarily a walleye and rainbow fishery, with some cutthroat and brown. The brown in Seminoe Reservoir tend to be larger, to 20 inches, than the rainbow, but are more difficult to catch. Look for better brown fishing in the fall. Rainbow average 15 inches, with some to 18 inches. Cutthroat are few in numbers and average 14 inches. Angling for walleye is best from a boat, and average 14 inches, and some to 11 pounds. Beginning in 2002, the limit for walleye is the same as the statewide limit, which is 6 fish. There are boat ramps and campgrounds on the west side of Seminoe Reservoir, with several miles of shoreline open to public use. The Medicine Bow River Arm also has a boat ramp. Seminoe Reservoir is reached by driving north on CR 351 from the town of Sinclair. It can also be approached from the north by driving southwest from Casper to the town of Alcova on Hwy 220, then taking the Kortes Road (CR 291) south to Kortes Dam, and from there south on Seminoe Road. It may also be accessed from the town of Medicine Bow via Hwys 487, 77 and CR 102.

Medicine Bow River

The **Medicine Bow River** and the **Little Medicine Bow River** join northeast of the town of Medicine Bow and flow into the Medicine Bow Arm of Seminoe Reservoir. The rivers have fair fishing for 10-inch brown and rainbow, with larger fish nearer to Seminoe Reservoir. Much of the flow is on private land, where permission is required. The Medicine Bow River drains the northern end of the Snowy Mountain Range, and headwater streams have good populations of brook in several hundred beaver ponds. County Road 101, south from Elk Mountain on I-80, follows the Medicine Bow River onto Forest Service land.

Fishing is limited on the Little Medicine Bow River due to private land holdings. **Shirley Basin Reservoir** (7,020 ft; 14 ac) has fair fishing for stocked rainbow around 12 inches. To reach the reservoir from the town of Medicine Bow, follow SR 487 north for 22 miles, and SR 77 to the northwest for 6 miles to signed access to reservoir. The northeast side of **Walker Jenkins Lake** (6,910 ft; 54 ac) and several miles of the Little Medicine Bow River have been leased as part of the Wyoming Game and Fish Walk-in Area Program. Fishing is good for rainbow to 10 inches in both the lake and the river. Walker Jenkins Lake is 34 miles north of the town of Medicine Bow via SR 487, and 3.5 miles east on CR 2 (Shirley Ridge Road) to the lake and parking area.

South of the town of Medicine Bow, **East Allen Lake** (6,539 ft; 160 ac) off Medicine Bow- Mcfadden Road (CR 1), has rainbow and cutthroat averaging 14 inches. Boat launching facilities are available. Early spring and late fall offers better fishing.

Rock Creek enters the Medicine Bow River from the north after draining a northeastern portion of Medicine Bow Mountains. The creek inside the national forest is excellent for small brook, below the national forest the creek travels mostly through private lands, with some state land open to the public above and below the town of Arlington. Rainbow and brown averaging 9 inches are found in the lower reaches of the creek. Near the headwaters, **Sand Lake** (10,131 ft; 92 ac) is currently under repair. Repairs are scheduled to be completed in the summer of 2002, and the lake refilled with water by the spring of 2003. When the repairs are completed it is expected that Sand Lake will be restocked with rainbow to 12 inches, and splake. Boats with motors (gas) will still be allowed. Sand Lake and the upper reaches of Rock Creek can be accessed from Hwy 130 northwest of the town of Centennial on the twisting and turning FR 101 (Sand Creek Road) for 16 miles to Sand Lake. Sand Lake is southwest of the road by a short 0.25 trail. To the northeast **Crater Lake** (9,862 ft; 10 ac) has fair fishing for brook to 11 inches. To reach the lake follow FR 103, which is about 0.5 mile north of Sand Lake Trailhead, to the north. The lake requires a 1.25 mile hike on TR 105.

Diamond Lake (7,356 ft; 242 ac) east of the town of Arlington is good for small brook, cutthroat averaging 14 inches, and rainbow to 19 inches. The limit on trout is 2 fish, all fish less than 16 inches must be released. Fishing is by artificial flies and lures only. Take I-80 southeast of Arlington for 8 miles to Bengough Hill Road/Cooper Cove Road, follow this road (CR 15) 4 miles north, the lake will be on the left. Boats are helpful to catch the larger fish.

Higher on the edge of the Medicine Bow National Forest **Turpin Creek** enters the Medicine Bow River from the southwest. **Turpin Reservoir** (9,440 ft; 99 ac) has good fishing for brook to 12 inches, and splake. The reservoir is along side of FR 100 about 12 miles south of the town of Elk Mountain. Boats are allowed with motors (including gas powered) to 15 horsepower. Below Turpin Reservoir, at Bow River Campground, is **Long Lake** (8,924 ft; 31 ac), which is barren. Several of the Snowy Range Lakes are on this drainage, see the Snowy Range Lakes section in this chapter for complete descriptions.

Kortes Reservoir/Miracle Mile

Just north of Seminoe Reservoir is the 2-mile-long **Kortes Reservoir** (6,120 ft; 920 ac), which fills a deep gorge and offers only fair fishing by boat. Fishing and boat launching is extremely difficult in this narrow reservoir, caution should be used. Brown and rainbow average 15 to 18 inches; occasionally larger brown are taken. Access is from Kortes Road from the south.

Downstream from Kortes Reservoir, the North Platte River enters the famous **Miracle Mile,** which is actually about 6 miles of heavily fished water. In dry years when Pathfinder Reservoir is drawn down by irrigation demands, the Miracle Mile may extend to almost 15 miles. Despite heavy fishing pressure it usually lives up to its title, producing brown 10-20 inches and some up to 12 pounds. Cutthroat and rainbow are up to 2 pounds and sometimes larger. Snake River cutthroat in greater numbers are showing up in the river where they are not stocked, but rather swim up from stockings at Pathfinder Reservoir. In recent years the number of fish in the Miracle Mile have declined slightly, but the good news is the size of fish have increased. The Miracle Mile is easily accessible. Drive about 30 miles south of the town of Casper on Hwy 220, then south on Kortes Road another 30 miles from the town of Alcova. The Miracle Mile is also accessible from the towns of Sinclair and Medicine Bow, following the same routes to Seminoe Reservoir; follow the signs on this winding, sometimes-washed-out, dirt road that directs you to Kortes Dam or the Miracle Mile. Anglers get results with large wet flies, scud patterns, streamers and Panther Martin spinners. During the spring, when other streams are roily with run-off, the Miracle Mile is superb due to the water control of the dams. Expect a lot of company, the Miracle Mile is usually very crowded, especially on the weekends.

Another species of fish that inhabits the Mile, is the carp. Although not quite as beautiful as the trout, the carp apparently has no adverse affect on the trout population, except for crowding, according to the Wyoming Game & Fish Department. The two species are not in direct competition for food. Trout prefer insects while the carp is a scavenger, and can be found in a shallow pool where it filters the sand for food.

The North Platte River from Kortes Dam downstream to the confluence with Sage Creek (Miracle Mile) the limit for trout is 2 fish. Only 1 trout can be longer than 20 inches. The River is closed to night fishing (8PM - 6AM) during the month of April.

Pathfinder Reservoir

Below the Miracle Mile is **Pathfinder Reservoir** (5,850 ft; 20,000 ac when full, 18 miles long). This Reservoir is also subject to high winds and big drawdowns by irrigation - as much as 25-35 feet in dry years. Cutthroat and rainbow 15-18 inches are fairly common, as well as brown up to and over 21 inches. Walleye are common, with most being less than 2 pounds in weight, although a few large fish exceeding 8 pounds are caught each year. There are designated public use areas and boat-launching facilities on the east side of the reservoir. There is also a marina near the dam. Caution should be used when using lightweight boats when the wind is blowing. Trolling is best in the summer; bank fishing using lures and pop gear with worms is fair to good in the spring and fall.

To the east of Pathfinder Reservoir is **Dome Rock Reservoir** (6,695 ft; 7 ac), which is managed the Wyoming Game and Fish Department as a trophy trout fishery. At 7 acres this reservoir seems small compared to the neighbors on the North Platte River, however, it does offer outstanding fishing for large Snake River cutthroat, some to 7 pounds. The limit on trout is 1 fish and all trout less than 20 inches must be released. Artificial flies and lures only. Spring and late fall are the best time to fish Dome Rock Reservoir, which is located on the east side of Kortes Road 5 miles north of the small town of Leo.

Below Pathfinder Reservoir the **North Platte River** flows through Fremont Canyon (Cardwell Access Area) to Alcova Reservoir. Wyoming Fish and Game, and the Wyoming Flycasters have worked with the Bureau of Reclamation (BuRec) in an agreement for a minimum stream flow through the canyon. In the spring of 2002 Wyoming Game and

Rob Yingling/Bighorn Web Design Photo

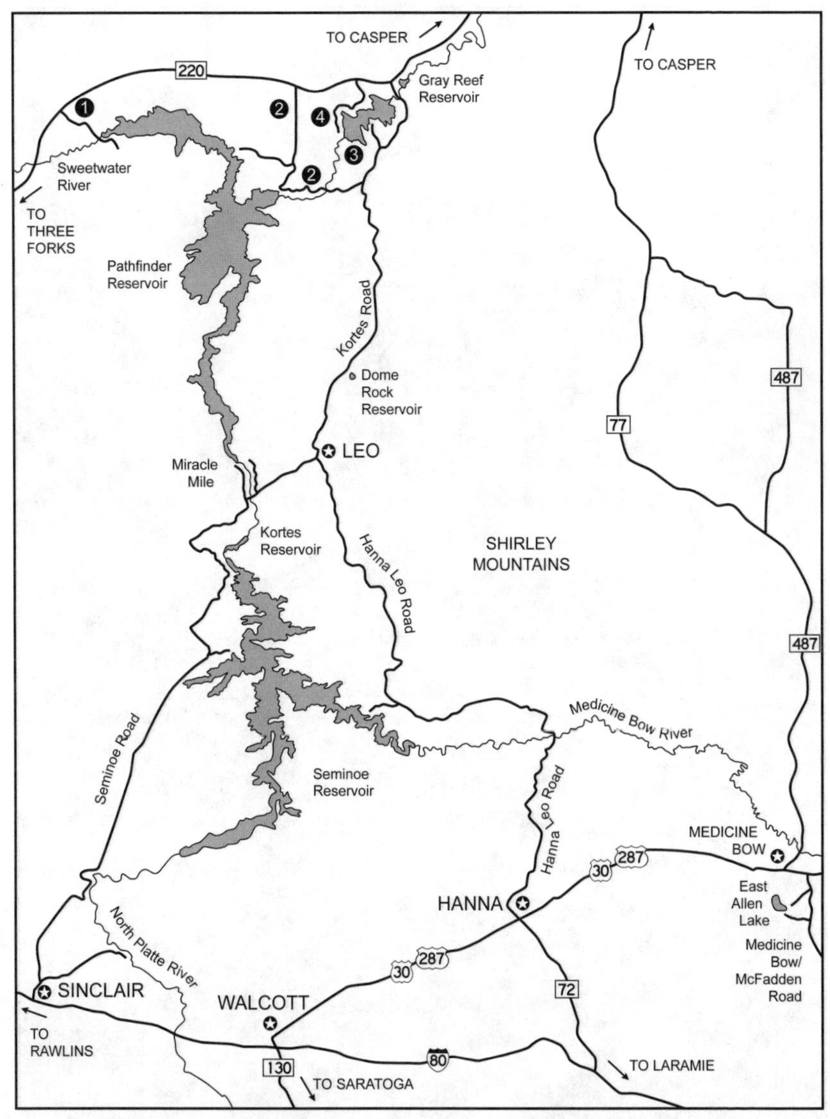

1. Buzzard Road
2. Pathfinder Road
3. Alcova Reservoir
4. Lake Shore Road
5. North Platte River

Fish will stock the river with rainbow and cutthroat, with hopes of this area becoming a trophy trout fishery.

Alcova Reservoir

Alcova Reservoir (5,500 ft; 2400 ac when full) is downstream from Pathfinder. The reservoir is 5 miles long, 2500 acres, and has several boat ramps, as well as boat rentals and supplies. The reservoir has fair fishing for rainbow that run 8-12 inches, brown 10 –16 inches, with a few cutthroat and good numbers of walleye 14-20 inches. Shore fishing for trout is best in the spring and fall; trolling with lures and pop gear with worms is good in the summer. There are several campgrounds surrounding the reservoir.

Grey Reef Reservoir (5,320 ft; 182 ac when full), 30 miles southwest of Casper on Hwy 220 to CR 412, is a regulating reservoir below Alcova Reservoir. It has difficult fishing for rainbow and brown running 12 –18 inches, with larger brown and rainbow occasionally caught. Best results are from boats. The Wyoming Game and Fish Department has a 0.25 mile Walk-in Area lease on the North Platte River above the reservoir where fishing is good for rainbow and brown averaging 13 inches. In the late fall large releases of water from the dam are common making fishing difficult, when this happens try fishing the river and reservoirs above the dam. Fishing downstream from the dam can be good for brown and cutthroat averaging 16 inches, rainbow and cutbows average 15 inches. Rainbow clearly out number the other species in this stretch of the river. There is a mile or so of public access land interspersed with private land immediately below Grey Reef on the North Platte River. Anglers can park at the reservoir immediately below the dam or at a BLM access area 2 miles below the dam.

NORTH PLATTE RIVER – GREY REEF TO CASPER

The North Platte River offers over 36 miles of quality fishing between Grey Reef Reservoir and the town of Casper. Private property predominates, however there are several major public fishing and floater put-in/take-out areas available. Floating the river is the recommended method for fishing this section of the North Platte River. While floating, signs along the river in the shape of a triangle indicate public and private lands; red for private and blue for public. The angler will find mostly rainbow averaging 15 inches, with some to 10 pounds. Brown on average are smaller, averaging 10 inches, but there are some big ones lurking in the river to 8 pounds. Cutthroat are also in the river, most average 14 inches, but occasionally cutthroat from 20 to 24 inches are caught.

From the first float launching area at Grey Reef Dam there is a float of about 8 miles down to the Lusby Access, a float of around 4 to 5 hours. The North Platte River from Grey Reef Dam downstream 8 miles to the upstream boundary of the

Lusby Public Fishing Area, the limit for trout is 1 fish. All trout less than 20 inches must be released. Fishing is with artificial flies and lures only.

From the Lusby Access it is a couple hour, 4.25 mile float, to Miles Landing (Government Bridge). From Government Bridge downstream for about 1.5 miles the west bank of the river has been leased as part of Wyoming Game and Fish Walk-in Area Program. From Miles Landing, float 2.75 miles down river to the By-The-Way Access Area, which takes about 1 hour to float. By vehicle, the By-The-Way Access is 1.25 miles north of Highway SR 220 on CR 316. The next access, Sechrist Access, requires about a 5 to 6 hour float and is 8 long miles down river. Sechrist Access is only 15 miles southwest of the town of Casper, and is 0.25 miles off of SR 220 to the north, watch for signs indicating access. The next two accesses, The Narrows and Schmitt access areas, offer primarily bank fishing access next to SR 220 about 14 miles southwest of the town of Casper. No boat ramps are available. The next put-in/take-out access is Bessemer Bend Access, 6 miles below Sechrist Access. This float averages around 2.5 to 3 hours to complete. To reach the access take SR 220 southwest out of Casper for 10 miles, turn northeast on CR 308 (Bessemer Road) for 2.5 miles to river and parking area. The North Platte River from the upstream boundary of the Lusby Public Fishing Area downstream to the Bessemer Bend Bridge (Natrona County

Road 308) the limit for trout is 2 fish. Only 1 trout can be longer than 20 inches.

Robertson Road Access, which provides bank fishing on the edge of the town of Paradise Valley, is reached from SR 220 and north 1.5 miles on CR 305 (Robertson Road) to parking area. No boat ramp is available. The next put-in/take-out below Bessemer Bend Access is Morad Park, within the city limits of Casper. Morad Park Access is located along SR 220 at Wyoming Blvd. The trip from Bessemer Bend Access to Morad Park is about a 13 mile trip, and a 6.5 to 7.5 hour float. Below Bessemer Bend Access the North Platte River to Morad Park has fishing for wary rainbow, brown and cutthroat, some of them quite large, if you can tempt them.

Between Grey Reef Reservoir and Morad Park the North Platte River does flow through private and public lands. Please respect private property and do not trespass by crossing, wading or landing on private property.

Bates Creek drains an area southwest of Casper and enters the North Platte 11 miles northeast of the town of Alcova. Turn east off Hwy 220 onto Hwy 487; after 9 miles CR 141 follows the creek east. The creek has fair fishing for brook averaging 6 inches and rainbow averaging 9 inches. Several miles of Bates Creek on 2 Wyoming Game and Fish Walk-in Areas provides access to the creek, 4 wheel drive is needed to reach both leases. One is located 1.25 miles below Bates Creek Reservoir (which shows on most maps, but rarely hold water), the other is about 4 miles below the reservoir as the crow flies. The remainder of the creek is on private land, requiring owner's permission to fish.

Twenty-four miles from Casper off of Highway 20, between the towns of Natrona and Bucknum, is **Goldeneye Reservoir** (5,502 ft; 466 ac) which has poor fishing for rainbow. Attempts to kill out the large carp population over the years have not been successful. Starting in 2001 small walleye will be introduced to feed on the carp, changing the lake over to a walleye fishery in the next few years.

LOWER NORTH PLATTE RIVER

The North Platte River from the town of Casper to the Pacific Power and Light (PP&L) Dam below Glenrock has some nice brown and rainbow in areas with good habitat, but overall fishing is only fair, as the water is warmer and picks up more silt in the lower elevations. Small cutthroat are also caught from the river as it flows through Casper. Good fishing for channel catfish is found in the public accesses below the PP & L Dam to Glendo Reservoir, an occasional walleye is also caught.

Twenty miles downstream from Casper, near the town of Glenrock, **Deer Creek** joins the North Platte from the south. It runs through a hodgepodge of state, federal and private lands from its source in the Deer

Creek Range of the Medicine Bow National Forest. It has good fly fishing for 8- to 12-inch brown and smaller rainbow, with brook in the headwaters. Avoid the lower several miles, where fishing is poor. Access to the upper reaches of the creek is by driving south from I-25 at Glenrock on the Mormon Canyon Road or the Deer Creek Road. The middle reaches of the creek can be reached by taking the Hat Six Road (2 miles east of Casper) south 20 miles to the forest boundary from I-25. Near the headwaters of the Deer Creek outside of the national forest boundaries, is a small tributary, **Curry Creek.** Wyoming Game and Fish has leased several miles of the creek, rough 4 wheel drive roads from CR 402 (Bates Creek Road) provide access.

La Prele Creek and **La Prele Reservoir** (5,495 ft; 579 ac) southwest of the town of Douglas are completely on private property, no public access is allowed.

South of Douglas along the Esterbrook Road is **La Bonte Creek**, which has fair to good fishing for 10-inch rainbow, the creeks upper portions on Forest Service land is off of CR 16 (Old Fetterman Road) and FR 658.

The North Platte River, around the town of Douglas, has several access points where fishing is fair for catfish and walleye. During the colder months of winter, November to April, fishing can also be fair for rainbow, brown, and cutthroat. An access area is located in the town of Douglas, at the West Yellowstone Street (US 20/26) Bridge. Four more access areas are along SR 94 beginning around 4.5 miles south of Douglas, watch for signs indicating public access.

Glendo Reservoir

Glendo Reservoir (4,635 ft; 12,000 acres when full) and State Park has walleye, channel catfish, largemouth bass, and perch. Glendo Reservoir is predominantly a walleye fishery with many walleye over 10 pounds. Yellow perch range from 6- to 10-inches and channel catfish average 1 to 3 pounds. Large white crappie and black crappie are found in the reservoir to 12 inches. The reservoir covers about 12,000 acres when full but, like other reservoirs on the river, is subject to dramatic drawdowns from irrigation demands. At Glendo Reservoir there is a full-service marina with boat rentals and several boat ramps. Trolling in the mornings is most productive. Ice fishing is a popular way to pass the winter months on the reservoir. There are nice rainbow in the river below Glendo Dam. Seven and 8-pound channel catfish have been caught upstream from Glendo. Boats are not allowed on the North Platte River between Glendo Dam and the Glendo Powerplant.

Flowing into the North Platte below the town of Glendo, is **Horseshoe Creek**, with fair to good fishing for brown and rainbow averaging 10 inches. Horseshoe Creek Road, 1 mile south of Glendo, follows most of the creek. Much of it is on private

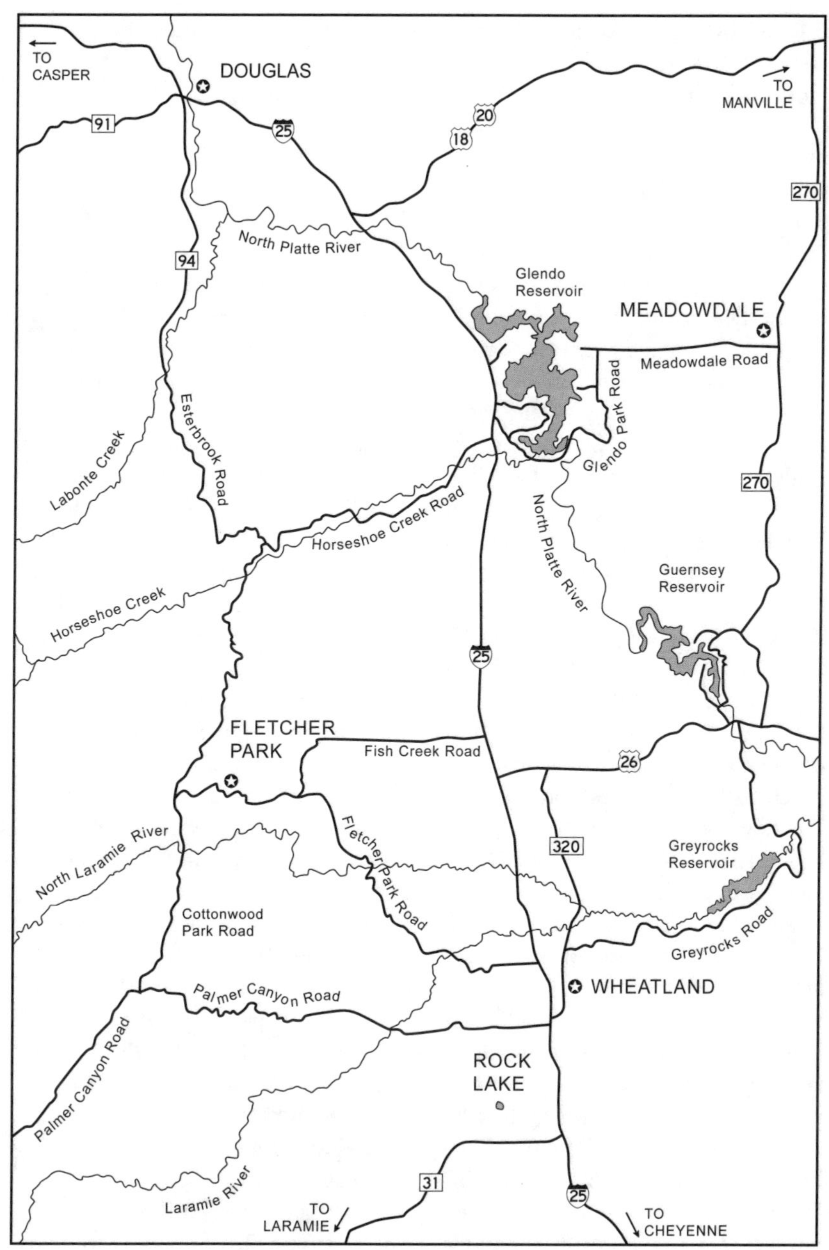

land, where permission to fish is necessary. The upper reaches are in the national forest.

Above and around Glendo there are several small tributaries that offer good angling. **Roaring Fork Creek,**

Ashenfelder Creek, and **Friend Creek** are good for rainbow and brook, especially in the spring. Much of the access to these streams is through private land and landowner permission is required for access.

The North Platte River from Glendo Reservoir to Guernsey Reservoir does harbor some nice rainbow, brown, and cutthroat. Best fishing is early spring and summer, as the river tends to run low in the fall making fishing difficult. Much of the river runs through private property, many anglers float the North Platte River from Glendo Reservoir through Wendover Canyon, where there is fair fishing for large, but wary, rainbow and brown. The BLM Wendover Access Area provides some public access to the river and a boat pull-out at the lower end of the canyon. Wendover Access Area is 2.5 miles west of the town of Guernsey on Highway 26, and then 8.5 miles northwest on Wendover Road.

Guernsey Reservoir (4,406 ft; 1843 ac) and Guernsey State Park is the last large reservoir on the North Platte River. The reservoir is a pleasant place for water skiing and other water sports activities, but not fishing, as it is an irrigation reservoir that is completely drained twice a year.

The North Platte flows another 80 miles to the Nebraska-Wyoming line, but the water and fishing quality suffers from irrigation drawdowns, and the water is too warm to support a trout population, large catfish are the predominate species here.

Hawk Springs Reservoir (4,405 ft; 843 ac) and State Recreation Area, 50 miles northeast of Cheyenne off Highway 85 and CR 186 near the Nebraska border, receives heavy fishing pressure for catfish and stocked walleye, crappie, yellow perch, and bass. All bass less than 12 inches must be released. A boat ramp is available.

A couple of reservoirs near the Wyoming/Nebraska border in the Bump Sullivan/Springer Wildlife Habitat Unit have fishing for warm water fish. These reservoirs are 15 miles south of the town of Torrington off Highway 85. **Bump Sullivan Reservoir** (4,295 ft; 400 ac) offers warm water fishing for walleye and crappie. The reservoir is closed to fishing November 1 through January 31. Also in the Springer Unit is **Springer Reservoir** (4,265 ft; 22 ac), that has fishing for stocked walleye and is closed to fishing from November 1 through January 31.

Several bodies of water dot the landscape around the border with Nebraska. These lakes and reservoirs are all below 5,000 feet in elevation and offer similar fishing for catfish, bass, crappie, and some perch and walleye. Many of the waters are on private property, or do not contain fish due to drawdowns from irrigation. Public waters of note are **Sinnard Reservoir**, **Packer Lake**, and **McMaster Reservoir.**

LARAMIE RIVER

The Laramie River flows north and east from the Snowy Mountain Range across the Laramie Plain to enter the North Platte River at Fort Laramie. The upper reaches of the river are excellent for fly fishing, although the river is heavily fished. Where access is possible there is good fishing for brown 12 to 14 inches and larger, and some rainbow. Take highway 230 west from Laramie to reach the river. The road leaves the river to follow Woods Creek up into the Medicine Bow National Forest to provide access to the small creeks that feed into the Laramie River. The headwaters of the Laramie River are in Colorado, for a complete description of the Laramie River headwaters in Colorado refer to *Kip Carey's Official Colorado Fishing Guide*.

Much of the upper reaches of the Laramie River are on private property, Wyoming Game and Fish Departments does have two access areas; one is off of SR 10 at the town of New Jelm and the other is 5.25 miles southwest of Laramie off of Hwy 230. Watch for signs indicating public access. The Laramie River, from the Wyoming/Colorado border downstream to the Pioneer Canal Diversion, all rainbow are catch and release. The limit on trout is 6 fish, only 1 can be longer than 16 inches, and all trout between 10 and 16 inches must be released. Fishing is with artificial flies and lures only.

Lake Owen (8,960 ft; 86 ac) is a popular body of water. It lies 3 miles southeast of the town of Albany as the crow flies, by road it is more like 9 or 10 miles. Lake Owen is reached by going west on Hwy 11, just past the town of Filmore, south on FR 311 about 2 miles, west on FR 517 about 3 miles and, finally, south on FR 540 about 2 miles. There is camping at Lake Owen Campground. The lake produces mostly small brook and rainbow. Boats with motors (gas) are allowed on the lake.

East of the Snowy Range, as the Laramie River meanders toward its juncture with the North Platte, there are a number of aptly named "plains" reservoirs and lakes, some of which provide good fishing. They are heavily fished and require stocking. They are often treeless, shallow and fluctuate because of agricultural drawdowns. Wind is a factor, as constant winds blow down from the Medicine Bow Mountains to the west.

Sodergreen Lake (7,370 ft; 62 ac), located along Hwy 230 about 17 miles southwest of Laramie, has fair fishing for 10-inch rainbow. The lake provides municipal water storage for Laramie.

Lake Hattie (7,263 ft; 2900 ac when full) is 18 miles west of Laramie. The lake has good fishing for large brown, rainbow, kokanee, a few lake trout and yellow perch. Lake Hattie has good feed, rainbow reach 16 to 18 inches and brown are caught in the 5 to 7 pound range, but wind can be a deterrent to anglers. There are campsites and boat launching areas. This lake is supplied irregularly with water from the Laramie River by canal, and it sometimes runs low. Access is by driving 8 miles southwest from Laramie on Hwy 230, then turning west for 7 miles on Pahlow Lane to Hanson Lane, and 5 more to the lake.

Also on Pahlow Lane, 5 miles closer to Laramie, is **Meeboer Lake**

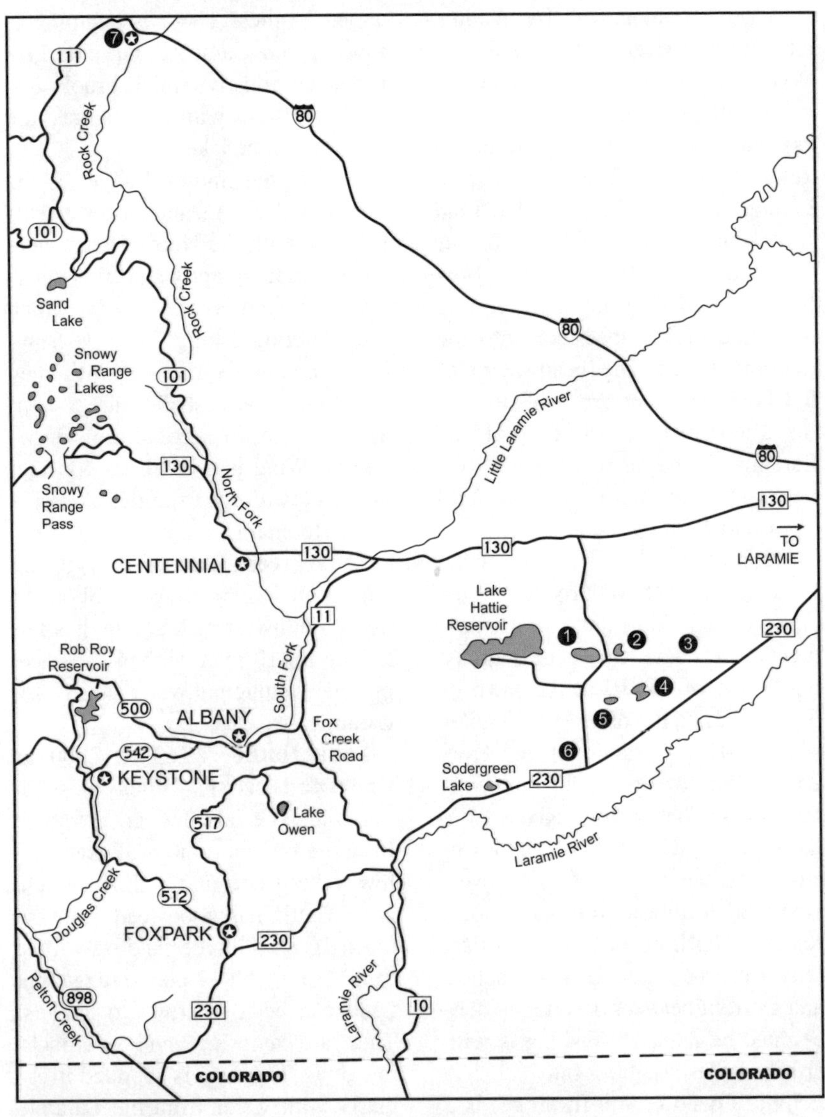

1. Twin Buttes Lake
2. Gellet Lake
3. Pahlow Road
4. Osterman Lake
5. Mortenson Lake
6. Harmony Lane
7. Arlington

(7,235 ft; 115 ac). This shallow lake has good fishing for stocked rainbow to 14 inches. A mile northwest of Meeboer is **Gelatt Lake** (7,250 ft; 34

ac) with rainbow averaging 10 inches. Best fishing is early in the spring. **Twin Buttes Lake** (7,245 ft; 326 ac) is 1 mile west of Gelatt Lake on Pahlow Lane, and it has good fishing for brown and rainbow to 18 inches.

Alsop Lake (5,000 ft; 40 ac) is 14 miles northwest of Laramie and north of I-80. To get to the lake drive 5 miles west from the town of Laramie on SR 130, then turn north on SR 12 (Herrick Lane Road) for 7 miles to the northwest. Shore fishing is limited as much of the lake is surrounded by private land. Fishing is fair for stocked rainbow. Several other lakes in the vicinity are all private lakes.

Little Laramie River flows out of the Snowy Mountain Range and the National Forest in to private property as it makes its way northeast to meet the Laramie River north of the town of Laramie. The **South Fork Little Laramie River** is almost completely outside of the National Forest and on private property. Inside the forest boundary the **Nash Fork Little Laramie River** and **North Fork Little Laramie River** drain the eastern Snowy Range lakes. Fishing on these creeks is for small brook to 10 inches, a few small rainbow might be found near the forest boundary.

SNOWY RANGE LAKES

The Snowy Range comprises more than 500,000 acres of mountainous and heavily timbered wilderness broken by grassy mountain meadows and plateaus. The sheer mountains shoot skyward with the highest reaching an elevation of 12,500 feet. Due to the altitude, most of the lakes in this area do not ice-off until at least late June. Small streams abound in this area, most of which are dammed by beavers and contain small brook. Snowy Range Pass and Snowy Range Lakes are located 35 miles west of the town of Laramie or 25 miles east of the town of Saratoga on Highway 130 (Snowy Range Highway/ Scenic Byway). A map produced by the US Forest Service, Wyoming Game and Fish Department, and the Platte Valley Chapter of Trout Unlimited, of the Snowy Range Lakes is available from the US Forest Service/Laramie office at 307-745-3200. There are numerous campgrounds, a ski area and easy access to lakes by 4 wheel drive vehicles, cars or by foot. There is heavy fishing pressure due to the population concentration in this area of the state, visitors from Colorado and the close proximity of the waters to the highways. Some of the lake fishing is maintained by stocking, but the majority contains naturally reproducing brook populations. About 32 square miles of the forest have been closed to motor vehicles. Much of the range is part of Medicine Bow National Forest, although there is some private ownership.

Several lakes lie to the south of Highway 130 east of Snowy Range Pass. Above the town of Centennial 2 miles Barber Lake Road leaves the highway to the west, along the road is **Barber Lake** (8,760; 2 ac) which is a small pond stocked with rainbow. Back on Highway 130 above Libby Creek Picnic Grounds 2.75 miles,

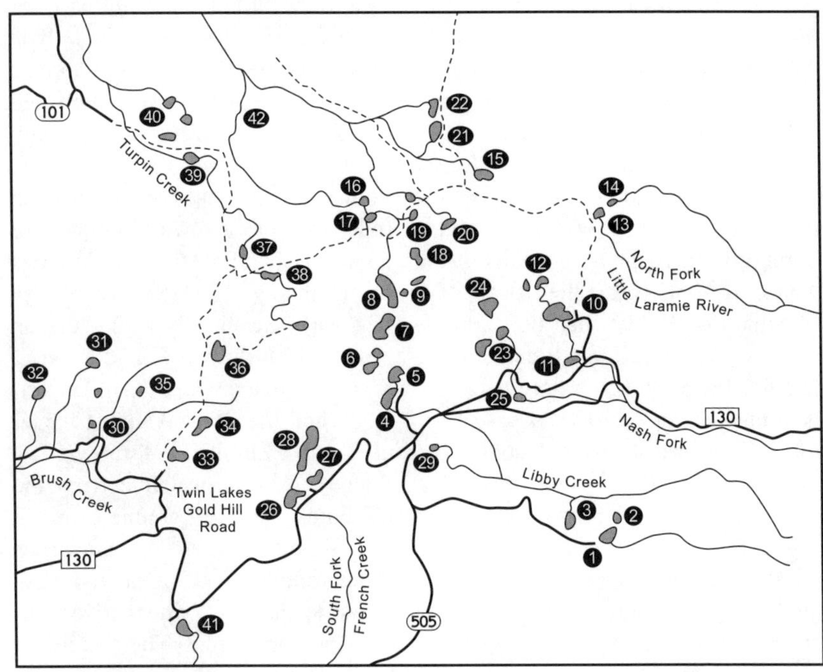

1 Silver Run Lake
2 Upper Silver Run Lake
3 Bear Lake
4 Libby Lake
5 Lewis Lake
6 Klondike Lakes
7 South Gap Lake
8 North Gap Lake
9 Shelf Lakes
10 Brooklyn Lake
11 Little Brooklyn Lake
12 Glacier Lakes
13 South Twin Lake
14 North Twin Lake
15 Sheep Lake
16 North Meadow Lake
17 South Meadow Lake
18 Crescent Lake
19 Cutthroat Lake
20 Arrow Head Lake
21 Mutt Lake
22 Jeff Lake
23 Telephone Lake
24 Lost Lake
25 Towner Lake
26 Lake Marie
27 Mirror Lake
28 Lookout Lake
29 Blackjack Lake
30 Stampmill Lake
31 Arrastre Lake
32 Phantom Lake
33 South Twin Lake
34 North Twin Lake
35 Missouri Lakes
36 Dipper Lake
37 Quealy Lake
38 Vagner Lake
39 Cascade Lake
40 Banner Lakes
41 Silver Lake
42 Medicine Bow River

and to the south of the road, is **Hanging Lake** (9,060 ft; 4 ac) which is very shallow and stocked with small seasonal rainbow. Continuing on the highway 2 miles, southwest of Nash Fork Picnic Grounds, is **Swastika Lake** (10,060 ft; 12) which is barren. **Highway 130 Lake** (10,470 ft; 5 ac) and **Hourglass Lake** (10,515 ft; 8 ac), also to the south of the highway, are both barren. Near the summit of Snowy Range Pass FR 505 (4 wheel drive) leaves the highway to the south, passes the shallow **Blackjack Lake** (10,580 ft; 4 ac) which may have small brook, and connects with FR 396 (4 wheel drive). Follow FR 396 down to **Libby Flats Lake** (10,225 ft; 3 ac) which is very shallow and contains small brook; **Silver Run Lake** (10,062 ft; 14 ac) with brook to 13 inches; **Upper Silver Run Lake** (10,065 ft; 1 ac) with book to 11 inches; and **Bear Lake** (10,105 ft; 17 ac) with fair fishing for cutthroat and brook to 10 inches.

North of the Highway 130, about 9 miles west of the town of Centennial, a well-marked road (FR 317) goes north to **Brooklyn Lakes**. After 1 mile the road forks, on the left fork is **Little Brooklyn Lake** (10,350 ft; 7 ac) with brook averaging 8 inches and some splake. Along the right fork 0.75 mile is **Big Brooklyn Lake** (10,526 ft; 36 ac) with cutthroat, splake and brook 10-12 inches. Big Brooklyn Lake is heavily fished. **Snowbank Lake** (10,560; 2 ac) shown on some maps, is barren.

One mile north of Big Brooklyn on Sheep Lake Trail (FT 389) is **South Twin Lake** (10,650 ft; 10 ac) with cutthroat to 9 inches. Just to the north is **North Twin Lake** (10,650 ft; 4 ac) which cannot sustain fish through the winter and is not stocked. Still further along the trail is **Sheep Lake** (10,770 ft; 19 ac) with brook to 13 inches and larger. To the west of Sheep Lake is **Deep Lake** (10,495 ft; 25 ac), **North Meadow Lake** (10,620 ft; 5 ac), **South Meadow Lake** (10,615 ft; 11 ac), **Reservoir Lake** (10,780 ft; 29 ac), **Garden Lake** (10,650 ft; 6 ac), **Crescent Lake** (10,850 ft; 8 ac), **Cutthroat Lake** (10,680 ft; 6 ac), and **Arrowhead Lake** (10,770 ft; 10 ac) all with fair fishing for brook. Northwest of Sheep Lake is **Mutt Lake** (10,625 ft; 16 ac) and **Jeff Lake** (10,620 ft; 7 ac) which are both barren. North still further on Sheep Lake Trail is **Sand Lake** (10,131 ft; 92 ac), which drains into **Rock Creek.** Sand Lake is currently under repair. Repairs are scheduled to be completed in the summer of 2002, and the lake refilled with water by the spring of 2003. When the repairs are completed it is expected that Sand Lake will be restocked with rainbow to 12 inches, and splake. Boats with motors (gas) will still be allowed. Sand Lake and the upper reaches of Rock Creek can be accessed from Hwy 130 northwest of the town of Centennial on the twisting and turning FR 101 (Sand Creek Road) for 16 miles to Sand Lake. Sand Lake is southwest of the road by a short 0.25 trail. East of Mutt and Jeff lakes, without a trail, is **Grassy Lake** (10,670 ft; 3 ac) with small brook and, on Trail Creek, **Golden Lake** (10,470 ft; 5 ac) with good fishing for brook and cutthroat to 11 inches, if there has not been a winterkill.

Northwest of Big Brooklyn Lake 0.5 miles on Lost Lake Trail (TR 395) is **East Glacier Lake** (10,730 ft; 7 ac), with good fishing for cutthroat to 12 inches and small brook, and **West Glacier Lake** (10,730 ft; 8 ac) where the fishing is fair for brook to 11 inches. The trail continues past the lakes 0.5 miles to **Big Telephone Lake** (10,750 ft; 9 ac) and **Little Telephone Lake** (10,700 ft; 8 ac), both with good fishing for brook to 13 inches; **Scott Lake** (11,030 ft; 2 ac) which is barren; and **Lost Lake** (10,950 ft; 17 ac) on the south side of Brooklyn Ridge, has brook. On the creek below Little Telephone Lake, southwest of Little Brooklyn Lake near Highway 130, is **Towner Lake** (10,465 ft; 9 ac) and **Mill Pond** (10,270 ft; 3 ac). Towner Lake is fair for small brook, Mill Pond is very shallow and may contain small brook.

Libby Lake (10,805 ft; 26 ac) and **Lewis Lake** (10,807 ft; 19 ac) are located 1 mile north of Hwy 130 by following a signed Sugarloaf Recreation Area road (Lewis/Libby Lake Road) just east of the summit of Snowy Range Pass. Both lakes contain small brook, cutthroat and splake. Lewis is the better of the two and may harbor some larger brown to 14 inches. There are several campgrounds in the area. This marks a popular jumping-off point for hikes to other lakes. Northwest of Lewis Lake on TR 295 are the three **Klondike Lakes – East Klondike Lake, North Klondike Lake** and **South Klondike Lake** (10,807 ft; 2-24 ac). All three are fair to good for brook and splake, West Klondike Lake also has some cutthroat. North from Lewis Lake 0.5 mile on North Gap Lake Trail (TR 108) are **North Gap Lake** (10,970 ft; 32 ac) and **South Gap Lake** (10,970 ft; 30 ac). South Gap Lake has good fishing for cutthroat and rainbow to 10 inches; North Gap Lake has fair fishing for brook to 10 inches. The four **Shelf Lakes** (10,970 ft; 1-7 ac) lie directly east of North Gap Lake on the north side of Brooklyn Ridge, where the fishing is fair to good for brook at lakes 4 and 5 and cutthroat at lakes 1 and 2.

West of the summit of Snowy Range Pass on Highway 130 is **Bellamy Lake** (10,660 ft; 1 ac), a shallow pond which may harbor some small brook. One mile west of the summit within 0.5 mile of each other are **Lake Marie** (10,500 ft; 26 ac) and **Mirror Lake** (10,530 ft; 26 ac). They both contain small brook, and rainbow averaging 10 inches, and some splake. Lying at the foot of Medicine Bow Peak (12,006 ft), at the head of South French Creek, these waters are heavily fished. Just north is **Lookout Lake** (10,630 ft; 35 ac), with small brook and slightly less pressure from anglers. Three miles west of these lakes on Hwy 130 is Silver Lake Campground and **Silver Lake** (10,715 ft; 17 ac), which is good for brook averaging 9 inches. The marked Twin Lakes-Gold Hill Road (4 wheel drive) heads north off Hwy 130 about 6 miles west of Snowy Range Pass. A mile from the highway the road forks, the left fork (FR 200) follows South Brush Creek about 2 miles to **Stamp Mill Lake** (9,900 ft; 4 ac) which is barren. FR 200-2A is a 0.5 mile further to the west, this rough road travels north to **Phantom Lake** (10,050 ft; 12 ac) which has good fishing for small brook. From Stamp Mill Lake FR 205 goes to the north 1 mile, passing the barren **Magnolia Lake** (10,185 ft; 4 ac), to **Arrastre Lake** (10,220 ft; 12 ac) which has small brook and cutthroat. The right fork, from Hwy 130 on the Twin Lakes-Gold Hill Road (FR 103), leads 0.5 mile to **South Twin Lake** (10,282 ft; 27 ac) and **North Twin Lake** (10,400 ft; 27 ac). South Twin Lake has fair fishing for splake, North Twin Lake has plenty of small brook. Southeast of the lakes, without a trail, is **Sucker Lake** (10,425 ft; 13 ac). The lake has been stocked with brook and cutthroat, but is shallow and may winterkill. Northwest of the Twin Lakes is **Lower Missouri Lake** (10,200 ft; 4 ac) with fair fishing for small brook and **Upper Missouri Lake** (10,180 ft; 6 ac), which is barren. FR 103 (4 wheel drive) continues north 1.5 miles to **Dipper Lake** (10,692 ft; 28 ac). Dipper Lake has suffered from drought conditions, the lake should have good fishing for nice-sized cutthroat when the water levels return to normal. From the north side of Dipper Lake TR 294 heads east to TR 101 and group of small lakes. **Upper Long Lake** (10,835 ft; 4 ac) is barren; **Hatchet Lake** (10,790 ft; 3 ac), **Little Long Lake** (10,625 ft; 5 ac), **Middle Long Lake** (10,715 ft; 6 ac), and **Vosseller Lake** (10,550 ft; 2 ac) are all shallow lakes with good brook fishing. **Heart Lake** (10,820 ft; 12 ac) is deeper and has slightly bigger fish. North of Dipper Lake 1.5 miles on FR 103 are the **Quealy Lakes** (10,330 ft; 2 to 10 ac), another 0.5 mile by trail leads southeast to **Vagner Lake** (10,450 ft; 11 ac). These lakes have good fishing for brook averaging 8 inches. Another 2 miles north is **Cascade Lake** (10,090 ft; 8 ac) with good fishing for brook averaging 8 inches; a mile farther is **North Banner Lake** (9,930 ft; 9 ac) with some brook to 15 inches. Nearby are **East Banner Lake** (10,050 ft; 8 ac) and **South Banner Lake** (9,950 ft; 4 ac), which have brook when they have not winterkilled. These lakes can also be approached from the north by driving south from I-80 on the Elk Mountain Road (CR 101) and into the national forest on CR 100 to within 0.5 mile of Cascade Lake. **Campbell Lake** (10,026 ft; 14 ac) with brook averaging 10 inches, and **Edwards Lake** (10,275 ft; 4 ac) with brook averaging 7 inches, are to the southwest of Cascade Lake. From Turpin Reservoir, follow CR 100 south 2.25 miles to FR 205 and FR 116 which are rough 4 wheel drive roads to the south that may have to be walked.

LOWER LARAMIE RIVER

North of Laramie, **Diamond Lake** (7,037 ft; 137 ac) is probably the most popular lake in the area and is reached by county road from US 30/287 or from I-80 at Cooper Cove exit. Diamond Lake has suffered from drought conditions, the lake should have good fishing for rainbow, cutthroat and brook when the water levels return to normal. **Long Lake** (6,985 ft; 842 ac) is barren and not stocked.

One large body of water 40 miles north of Laramie - **Wheatland Reservoir No. 2** - shows up on most maps, but public access is not allowed. The canal from the headgate on Wheatland Reservoir #2 to the canal mouth on Wheatland #3 is also closed to fishing, and boats are not allowed in this area.

Wheatland Reservoir No. 3 (6,950 ft; 630 ac), has fair fishing for walleye and rainbow to 20 inches if the water level is not too low. Cutthroat and brown are also stocked and also reach 20 inches. The reservoir can be reached from Rock River by going 1 mile north to Fetterman Road, then 18 miles east.

Johnson Creek Reservoir (6,200 ft; 8 ac) is located off of **North Fork Sybille Creek** on **Johnson Creek**. The reservoir is on the Wyoming Game and Fish Sybille Creek Experimental Unit where work to recover the Black-Footed ferret from extinction has been going on since 1985. The reservoir is open to fishing for stocked rainbow to 10 inches. Camping is available and boats without motors are allowed. Johnson Creek Reservoir is located 34 miles southwest of Wheatland via SR 34, watch for signs to the Sybille Access area, the reservoir is 1 mile north of SR 34 on a gravel road that follows Johnson Creek.

Wheatland Reservoir #1 (4,930 ft; 320 ac) is 4 miles south and 4 miles west of the town of Wheatland via SR 34 and CR 151 (Grange Road). Fishing is for walleye, catfish, and yellow perch. A boat ramp and camping is available. **Rock Lake** (4,975 ft; 38 ac), 1 mile to the south of Wheatland Reservoir #1, has bass, walleye, yellow perch, catfish, crappie, and stocked rainbow. There are no boat launching facilities, but boats can be launched from the shade-covered shorelines. **Festo Lake** (4,730 ft; 43 ac) is 3 miles northwest of Wheatland, with bass and channel catfish. Has good fishing for bass averaging 15 inches. All bass less than 12 inches must be released. The use of internal combustion motors is prohibited. **Joe Johnson Reservoir** (4,660 ft; 128 ac) 10 miles north of Wheatland has been drained and at this time does not offers any fishing opportunities.

On the Laramie River, 10 miles above its confluence with the North Platte, is **Grayrocks Reservoir** (4,367 ft; 3500 ac). This water body has walleye to 4 pounds and yellow perch to 10 inches. Grayrocks Reservoir has fishing for bass, crappie, pumpkinseeds, bluegill, tiger muskie and channel catfish. All bass less than 12 inches must be released, The limit on crappie is 15 fish. All tiger muskie less than 30 inches must be released immediately. There is camping on the south side and two boat ramps. Between the spillway and floating regulatory buoys or as designated by regulatory signing is closed to fishing. From Wheatland take SR 320 to CR 647 (Grayrocks Road) for 14 miles; or go west on SR 160 from US 26 at Fort Laramie (via SR 316/South Guernsey Road) to CR 647, to reach Grayrocks Reservoir from the east.

NORTH LARAMIE RIVER

The **North Laramie River** headwaters drain the southern side of the Medicine Bow National Forest northwest of the town of Wheatland. Near the headwaters is **Toltec Reservoir** (7,023 ft; 320 ac when full) which has good fishing for small brook, splake, and rainbow averaging 11 inches. The reservoir is 1 mile east of CR 61 (Fetterman Road), watch for signs indicating access. Toltec Reservoir and the North Fork Laramie River upstream to Kafka Reservoir are closed to fishing from April 15 through May 14. **Kafka Reservoir** is private. East of the reservoirs via FR 653 (Esterbrook Road) are the headwaters of **Bear Creek**, Wyoming Game and Fish has leased several miles of this small creek as it flows south through Green Canyon. The parking access is about 12.5 miles east of Fetterman Road.

The headwaters of the North Laramie River are in the national Forest, but quickly leave near the town of Toltec, flowing through mostly private property until the river again reaches the National Forest and a narrow canyon several miles down stream south of Fletcher Park. A trail follows the river through the upper portion of the canyon. Fishing in the canyon is for rainbow averaging 9 inches, some brown slightly larger are found in the lower end of the canyon. The North Laramie River leaves the national forest after circling around Chimney Rock and flows down to the Laramie River across private property.

CHEYENNE AREA

In the extreme southeast portion of the state, along the border of Colorado, are a few waters worth mention. **Crow Creek** drains several lakes in the Medicine Bow National Forest and Curt Gowdy State Park before its eastern departure from the state and into the South Platte River.

Crystal Lake Reservoir (6,975 ft; 109 ac) and **Granite Reservoir** (7,210 ft; 156 ac) are part of Curt Gowdy State Park, which is 25 miles west of Cheyenne via Happy Jack and Crystal roads. The reservoirs supply water for the town of Cheyenne. Both Reservoirs are heavily stocked with rainbow averaging 10 inches. Access from Highway 210 and Interstate 80 makes these waters very popular. **Upper North Crow Reservoir** (7,505 ft; 97 ac) is 5 miles to the north on CR 101 (Crow Road) and has fishing for rainbow to 12 inches. Boats without motors are allowed.

NORTHEAST WYOMING

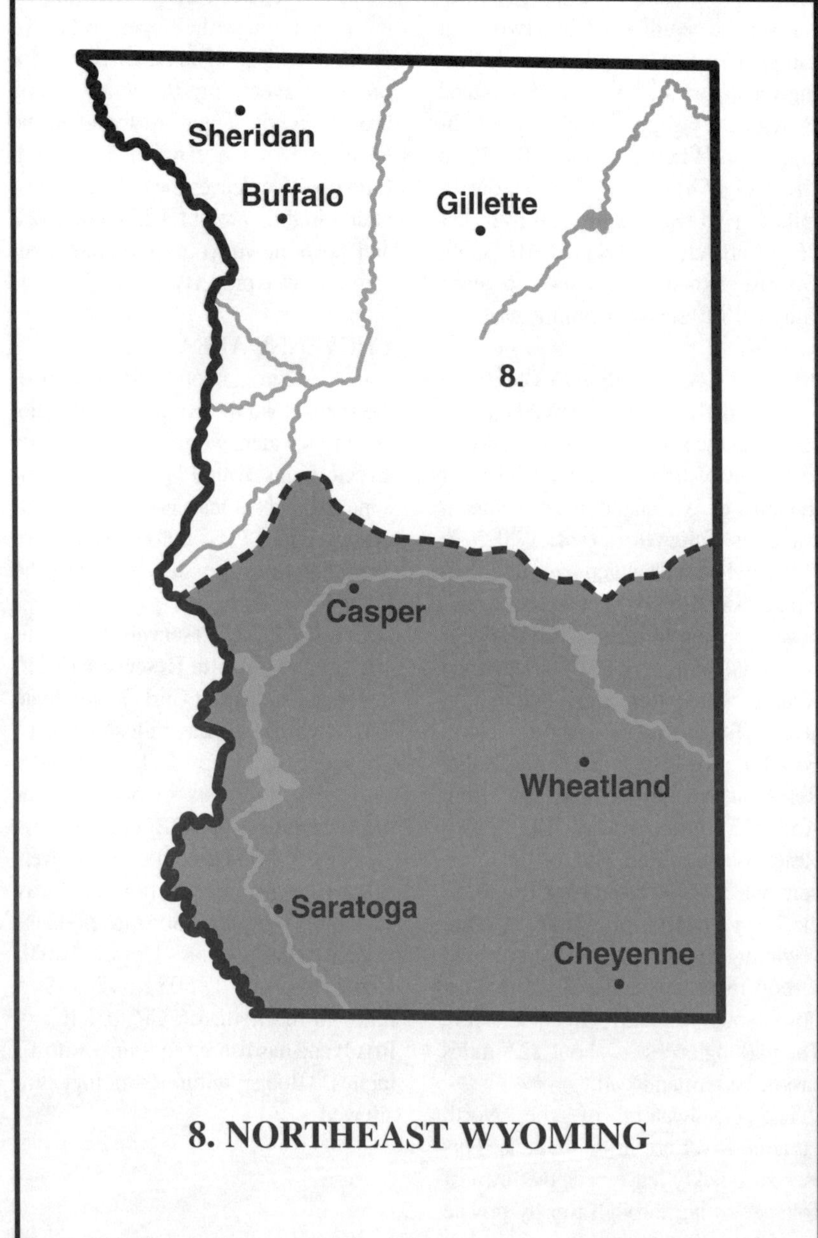

NORTHEAST WYOMING

The northeast corner of Wyoming is a land of contrast, from lofty elevations of Cloud Peak (13,167 feet) and Black Tooth Mountain (13,005 feet) in the Bighorn Mountains west of the towns of Buffalo, Story and Sheridan; to the endless Thunder Basin Grasslands south of the towns of Gillette, Moorecroft, and Upton. In the west are the high elevations of the Bighorn Mountains and Cloud Peak Wilderness, which are home to numerous alpine lakes. West of the towns of Kaycee, Story, Buffalo and Dayton, the clear waters of the Little Bighorn and Tongue rivers, Big Goose, Crazy Woman, Clear, and Piney creeks offer outstanding fishing for cutthroat, brown, rainbow, golden and brook. East of interstates 25 and 90 are the broad arid plains of the Powder and Little Powder rivers, which offers little fishing opportunities as they flow north through cattle country to the Montana border. Further east, in the northeast corner of the state, the warmer waters of the Belle Fourche River cut northeast and then east into South Dakota. Fishing opportunities in this part of the state are sparse, limited to portions of the Belle Fourche River and a few reservoirs. To the south of the river lie the Bear Lodge Mountains and Black Hills National Forest, home to the cool clear waters of Sand Creek near the South Dakota border. To the south, the low elevation landscape is characterized by flat wide open prairies and vast grasslands, but few fishing opportunities.

LITTLE BIGHORN RIVER

The **Little Bighorn River** headwaters are in the northern Bighorn Mountains. The river flows north 17 miles in Wyoming before entering into Montana 17 miles southwest of Wyola, Montana. The river has brown, rainbow and whitefish; and in the canyon area north of US 14A, the river has cutthroat from 8 to 12 inches. Above the canyon fishing is for rainbow and brook from 5 to 10 inches. Access is by taking US 14A west from the town of Sheridan until the highway begins to drop south toward the town of Greybull at Baldy Pass. Directly west of the pass FR 114 leaves the highway to the north, follow this road 0.75 miles to FR 125, and follow signs on rough roads to the headwaters. The Little Bighorn River drainage upstream from the mouth of Dayton Gulch Creek all trout (except brook) are catch and release. Fishing is with artificial flies and lures only. Three tributaries of the Little Bighorn River have fair fishing; **Wagon Box Creek**, **Dry Fork Creek** and **Pumpkin Creek**. Wagon Box Creek and Dry Fork Creek have rainbow and brook to 12 inches, Pumpkin Creek also has small cutthroat.

The Little Bighorn River on the Montana border offers good fishing for brown, rainbow, and whitefish averaging 10 inches. To reach this portion of the river drive 2 miles north of the town of Parkman on SR 345, then 16 miles west on CR 144. After crossing the State Line into Montana, a signed access road (4

Rob Yingling/Bighorn Web Design Photo

wheel drive) travels southwest back into Wyoming providing access to the Little Bighorn River and Dry Fork Little Bighorn River through private property. Trails lead up the rivers several miles providing access to public lands in the national forest.

TONGUE RIVER

The **Tongue River** drains the northern end of the Bighorn National Forest. The river flows east out of the Bighorn Mountains, through the Tongue Canyon west of the town of Dayton, and past the towns of Ranchester and Kleenburn on its way to the Montana border. Below the town of Dayton the river is mostly on private property, better trout fishing is found in the national forest to the west. Tongue Canyon Trailhead, beginning at the mouth of the canyon

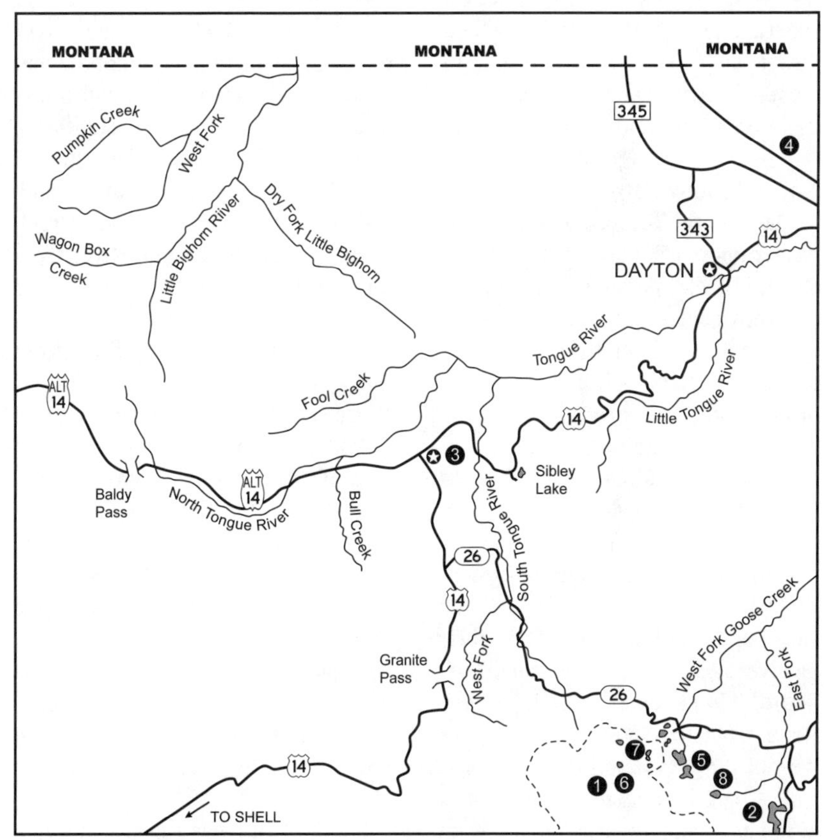

1 Cloud Peak Wilderness
2 Park Reservoir
3 Burgess Junction
4 To Sheridan
5 Dome Lake Reservoir
6 Coney Lake
7 Stull Lakes
8 Weston Reservoir

west of the town of Dayton provides access to trails upstream onto national forest lands. West of the town of Dayton, take River Road to the mouth of the canyon, watch for signs indicating access to Tongue Canyon and Tongue Canyon Trailhead. From the mouth of the canyon to the confluence of the North and South Forks of the Tongue River fishing is good for large rainbow, brown, and whitefish. **Fool Creek** north of Burgess Junction via FR 15 is fair for cutthroat and rainbow averaging 11 inches. The river receives heavy fishing pressure throughout the summer.

North Tongue River

The **North Tongue River** is the westernmost tributary of the Tongue River, US 14A parallels the river and provides access. The North Tongue River has excellent fishing for cutthroat, and fair fishing for rainbow, brown and some brook. The North Tongue River drainage upstream of the mouth of Bull Creek is restricted to catch and release for all trout except brook. Fishing can be excellent for cutthroat averaging 14 inches. Fishing is permitted with artificial flies and lures only. The river receives heavy fishing pressure.

Bull Creek enters North Tongue River from the south about 4 miles west of Burgess Junction on US 14A. Bull Creek is a small stream that is also catch and release on all trout except brook. Fishing with artificial flies and lures only. The fishing is also excellent for cutthroat up to 14 inches. **Big Willow Creek** enters the North Tongue River west of Burgess Junction. It is a small stream with fair fishing for brook in its upper reaches, and small rainbow and cutthroat in its lower reaches.

South Tongue River

East of Burgess Junction, the **South Tongue River** stretches about 15 miles from the south to enter the Tongue River proper north of Pine and Prune Creek campgrounds on US 14. The South Tongue River offers good fishing for rainbow and brown to 14 inches, and small brook nearer to the headwaters. The South Tongue forks about 7 miles south of US 14 at Dead Swede Campground. Eastward along US 14, **Prune Creek** enters the South Tongue River from the east. Prune Creek has fair to good fishing for brown, brook, and rainbow to 9 inches. Seven miles from the confluence of South Tongue River and Prune Creek, **Sibley Lake** (7,938 ft; 33 ac) is along the south side of US 14 as the highway turns northward. It offers fishing for stocked rainbow and brown. A few cutthroat are also stocked, and the lake contains small brook. The lake receives heavy fishing pressure. Pay campsites are available, and boats with motors are not allowed. Prune Creek, above the lake, has fair to good fishing for small brook and cutthroat.

South of Burgess Junction a rough 4 wheel drive FR 233 leaves the highway heading east 2.5 miles to **Duncan Lake** (9,220 ft; 9 ac), which offers good fishing for rainbow aver-

Rob Yingling/Bighorn Web Design Photo

aging 10 inches. Some small brook are also present.

East Fork South Tongue River also has several tributaries including **Graves Creek, Mohawk Creek** and **Woodchuck Creek**, which are small creeks with fair fishing for brook to 8 inches. Access to the creeks is by turning south on US 14 at Burgess Junction, and traveling about 5 miles to Owen Creek Campground. At Owen Creek Campground, turn east on FR 16 to Tie Flume Campground where the road turns south and crosses the creeks. **Calvin Lake** (9,550 ft; 3 ac), lays to the west of FR 226 (4 wheel drive) as it gets ready to make its way over Woodchuck Pass and down to the Shell Creek drainage of the Bighorn River. A rough 4 wheel drive FR 268 leads 0.5 miles to the lake, which has fishing for cutthroat to 10 inches. May have to hike the last .25 mile as road may be impassable even for 4 wheel drive vehicles.

Further northwest, the **West Fork South Tongue River** has several tributaries including **Prospect Creek** and **Bruce Creek**. These small creeks are rated fair for small brook. Access is by turning south at Burgess Junction and driving 8 miles. The tributaries are on the northeast side of Granite Pass.

North of the confluence of the West and East Forks, **Bonanza Creek, Sucker Creek, Copper Creek, Owen Creek** and **Sheeley Creek** enter the South Tongue River. These streams are fair to good fishing for small rainbow, with brook in their upper reaches.

The **Little Tongue River**, just east of South Tongue River, meanders northeast and enters the Tongue River at the town of Dayton from the southwest. About half of the stream is on private land and has good fishing for brown, brook, and rainbow. The upper reaches are on public land in the national forest and can be reached by foot to the south of Highway 14.

Little Goose Creek

The principal tributary of the Tongue River proper is **Goose Creek**, which enters the river from the south just north of the town of Sheridan. Lower reaches of the Tongue River and Goose Creek have very limited access due to private property. At the town of Kleenburn are the two **Kleenburn Ponds** (3,630 ft; 5 ac each) which have fair fishing for crappie, catfish, and bass. At the confluence of the Tongue River and Goose Creek the Wyoming Game and Fish Department has leased part of Padlock Ranch to provide Walk-in Access fishing for brown and rainbow in both the creek and the river.

To the southwest, **Big Goose Creek** flows through 20 miles of rough country. It offers good fishing for brown and rainbow west of the town of Beckton (10 miles west of Sheridan on Hwy 331) to the headwaters of East and West Forks Big Goose Creek in the Bighorn Mountains.

East Fork Big Goose Creek flows from the south to enter Big Goose Creek about 7 miles southwest of the town of Beckton. From its confluence with Big Goose Creek to its headwaters, East Fork Big Goose

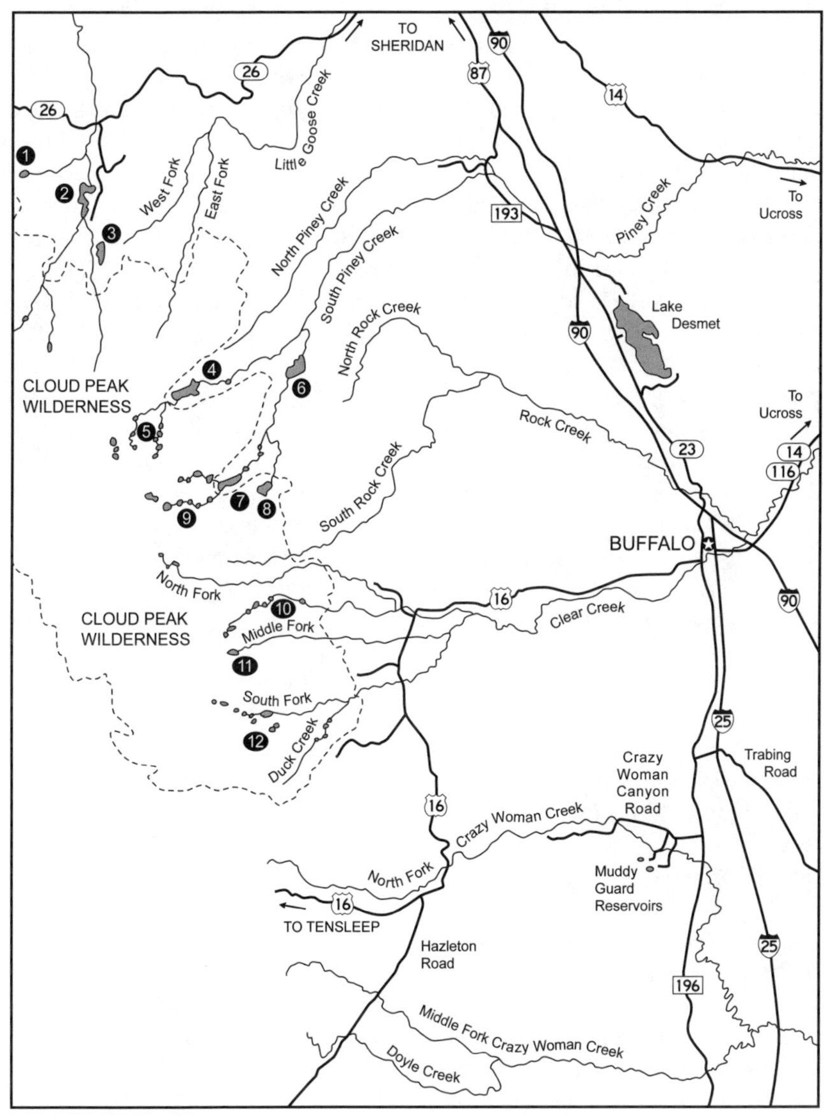

1. Weston Reservoir
2. Park Reservoir
3. Bighorn Reservoir
4. Kearny Reservoir
5. Loomis Lake
6. Willow Park Reservoir
7. Cloud Peak Reservoir
8. Elk Lake
9. Diamond Lake
10. Seven Brothers Lakes
11. Lake Angeline
12. Firehole Lakes

Creek offers about 20 miles of good fishing for rainbow to 10 inches and small brook.

Access to the headwaters of East and West Forks of Big Goose Creek, and numerous high mountain lakes in the Cloud Peak Wilderness at their headwaters, is by way of FR 26 from the town of Bighorn to the east; or from the west via FR 26 from Highway 14 south of Burgess Junction.

At the headwaters of East Fork Big Goose Creek, inside the Cloud Peak Wilderness, are several lakes. The trailhead for these lakes is at Coffeen Park, which is 3.5 rough 4 wheel drive miles above Park Reservoir. Most anglers park below Park Reservoir on FR 293 and hike the road to the trailhead. West of Coffeen Park 0.5 miles, 0.75 by Rinehart Trail, are the two **Rinehart Lakes** (lower 8,933 ft; 5 ac, upper 8,983 ft; 6 ac), which have been stocked with rainbow. Above the upper lake 1.25 miles is **Hope Lake** (9,580 ft; 14 ac) which has fair fishing for cutthroat. From Coffeen Park follow the Geneva Pass Trail along East Fork Big Goose Creek for 1.5 miles to Duncan Lake Trail. **Duncan Lake** (8,896 ft; 6 ac) is 0.5 miles to the east and has good fishing for small golden to 10 inches. The Gevena Pass Trail along the creek continues 2 miles to **Lake Geneva** (9,286 ft; 27 ac), which is good for brook, rainbow, and lake trout. The trail continues above Lake Geneva to **Crystal Lake** (9,696 ft; 6 ac), which is fair to good for small rainbow, and from there over Geneva Pass into the North Paint Rock Creek drainage of the Bighorn River.

Also above Coffeen Park is **Edelman Creek,** a small tributary of the East Fork Big Goose Creek rated good for small brook. The creek enters the East Fork Big Goose Creek 1 mile above Coffeen Park. Edelman Pass Trail follows the creek into the Cloud Peak Wilderness. About 2 miles up the creek a spur trail leads south across the creek 0.25 miles to **Thayer Lake** (9,215 ft; 4 ac) which is good to excellent for small brook. To the west of Thayer Lake 1.25 miles, without a trail, is **Lost Wilderness Lake** (9,940 ft; 9.5 ac) where there is good fishing for large cutthroat and brook. The Edelman Pass Trail continues along the creek 0.75 miles to **Devils Lake** (9,406 ft; 2 ac) where there is good fishing for cutthroat and brook. **Lake Golden** (10,025 ft; 2 ac) is southwest of Devils Lake 0.75 miles, and is shallow, but reported to have cutthroat to 16 inches. Edelman Pass Trail continues over Edelman Pass and onto Emerald Lake in the Shell Creek drainage of the Bighorn River.

Park Reservoir (8,265 ft; 300 ac), outside the wilderness, fluctuates greatly. It is rated fair for brook, with some rainbow and cutthroat. The reservoir is south of FR 26 on Park Reservoir Road (FR 293). On the northeast side of the reservoir, **Patricia Lake** (8,307 ft; 3 ac) is fair to good for 10-inch cutthroat. **Granger Reservoir** (8,260 ft; 12 ac) is fair for brook and brown.

At Park Reservoir, **Cross Creek** enters the East Fork Big Goose

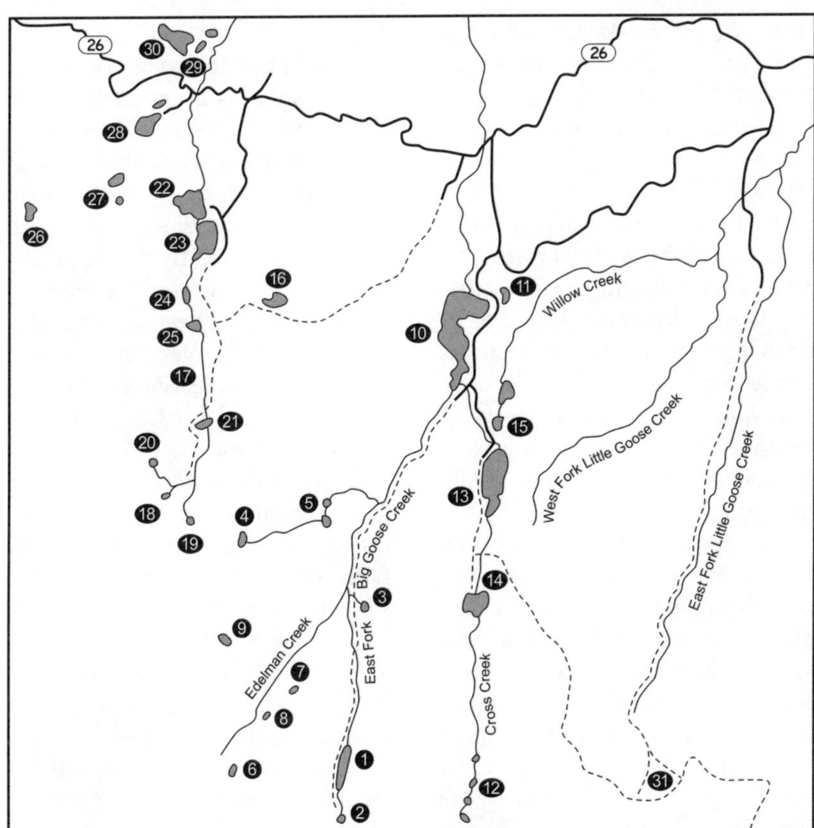

1. Lake Geneva
2. Crystal Lake
3. Duncan Lake
4. Hope Lake
5. Rinehart Lakes
6. Lake Golden
7. Thayer Lake
8. Devils Lake
9. Lost Wilderness Lake
10. Park Reservoir
11. Granger Reservoir
12. Cross Creek Lakes
13. Bighorn Reservoir
14. Cross Creek Reservoir
15. Last Chance Reservoir
16. Weston Reservoir
17. West Fork Big Goose Creek
18. Lake Buffalo
19. Lake Shamrock
20. Lake Alibi
21. Geddes Lake
22. Dome Reservoir Lake
23. Dome Lake
24. Heart Lake
25. Crescent Lake
26. Coney Lake
27. Stull Lakes
28. Twin Lakes
29. Sawmill Lakes
30. Sawmill Reservoir
31. Highland Park

Creek. At the headwaters of Cross Creek are the **Cross Creek Lakes** (9,951 to 10,143 ft, 2 to 4 ac), which are good for brook and rainbow to 10 inches. **Cross Creek Reservoir** (9,005 ft; 27 ac) is fair to good fishing for brook, rainbow and brown to 12 inches. **Bighorn Reservoir** to the south is surrounded by private property. **Weston Reservoir** (8,862 ft; 27 ac) to the west of Park Reservoir has fishing for grayling. The 4.5-mile trail, which starts out as a 4 wheel drive road, to the reservoir leaves to the south from Big Goose campground.

West Fork Big Goose Creek offers fishing for rainbow to 10 inches and small brook. There are several lakes at the headwaters of West Fork Big Goose Creek. **Geddes Lake** (9,310 ft; 13 ac) offers excellent fishing for small brook; **Lake Mirage** (9,280 ft; 1 ac) is barren. **Lake Buffalo** (9,870 ft; 1.5 ac) has good fishing for small brook. **Lake Shamrock** (9,905 ft; 1.5 ac) is shallow and barren. **Lake Alibi** (10,070 ft; 2 ac) has good fishing for stocked brown. Access to the lakes is difficult, start out at Weston Lake and hike west almost 1 mile to pick up old 4 wheel road leading south along West Fork Big Goose Creek. Geddes Lake is a 1.75 mile hike upstream, the other lakes are within a 0.5 mile of Geddes Lake and require difficult hikes on small tributaries.

Dome Lake, **Dome Lake Reservoir, Heart Lake** and **Crescent Lake**, near Twin Lakes Campground, are private and closed to fishing.

Twin Lakes Reservoir (8,583 ft; 46 ac), which is accessed from FR 285 to Twin Lakes Picnic Grounds. A short walk is necessary to reach the reservoir, which is good for 10 to 12 inch cutthroat, small brook, and an occasional lake trout. The reservoir supplies water for the town of Sheridan. Several years ago the two Twin Lakes reservoirs were converted into one larger reservoir, hence the name Twin Lakes. **Coney Creek** enters the West Fork Big Goose Creek from the west at Twin Lakes Picnic Grounds. At its headwaters inside the wilderness are **Coney Lake** (9,258 ft; 19 ac), good for small brook to 10 inches, and **Stull Lakes** (lower 8,820 ft; 15, upper 8,890 ft; 3 ac). The larger Stull Lake is good for brook and rainbow to 10 inches, and the smaller is good for small brook. The trailhead for these lakes is along FR 26 between West Fork Big Goose Creek and Sawmill Pass; Stull Lakes are a 1.75 mile hike, Coney Lake is about 3.75 miles from the road.

Sawmill Creek enters the West Fork Big Goose Creek north of FR 26 from the west. The stream is rated good to excellent for small brook. A 0.75 hike to the north from FR 26 at West Fork Goose Creek on FT 22 provides access to the two **Sawmill Lakes** (8,148 and 8,175 ft; 5 and 8 ac). The lakes have small brook, and cutthroat to 15 inches with the average being about 10 inches. Above the two Sawmill Lakes a few hundred feet, **Sawmill Reservoir** (8,180 ft;

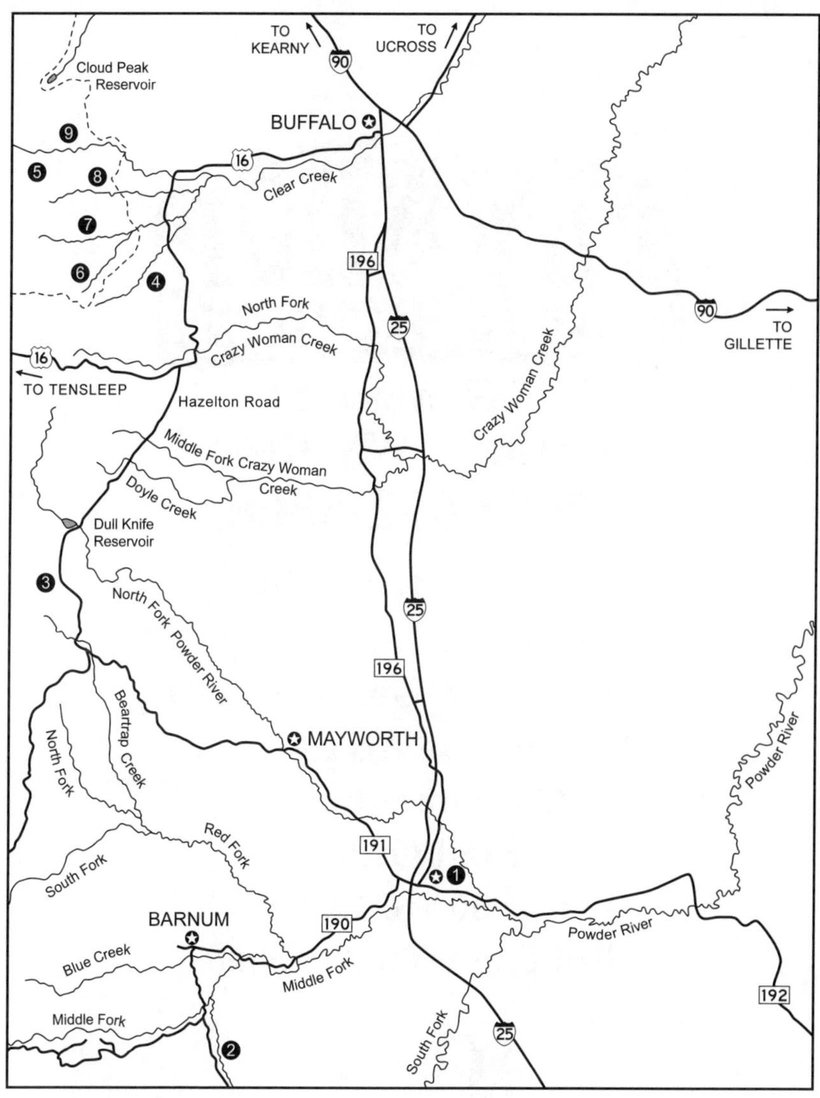

1. Kaycee
2. Buffalo Creek
3. Hazelton Road
4. Sourdough Creek
5. Cloud Peak Wilderness
6. Duck Creek
7. South Fork Clear Creek
8. Middle Fork Clear Creek
9. North Fork Clear Creek

56 ac) contains plenty of small brook and has been stocked with splake.

POWDER RIVER

Streams flowing east out of the Bighorn Mountains offer sparse fishing because of limited public access. West of Kaycee, via Hwys 190 and 191, some good fishing can be found in the upper reaches of the Middle Fork Powder River and North Fork Powder River. The South Fork Powder River's headwaters lie 55 west of the town of Casper and flow north through desolate country to meet the Middle and North Fork Powder rivers east of the town of Kaycee.

The **South Fork Powder River** and its tributaries are shallow and are not considered a viable fishery. Near the headwaters, northwest of the town of Powder River is **Burlington Reservoir** (5,670 ft; 29 ac), which is shallow and can occasionally winterkill. Fishing is good for small stocked rainbow. The reservoir is closed to fishing September 1 through April 30, and the use of gas powered motors is prohibited. **33 Mile Ponds** (5,375 to 5,520 ft; 7 to 28 ac) are actually made up of several small reservoirs near the town of Merino. To reach the reservoirs follow Highways 20/26 for 15 miles northwest from Casper to CR 125 (Bucknum Road), after 10 miles this road becomes CR 110 (33 Mile Road). Continue north, the reservoirs

Rob Yingling/Bighorn Web Design Photo

are accessed off CR 110 (33 Mile Road) and CR114 (Long Canyon Road), watch for access signs. Fishing is fair for stocked rainbow, brook, and cutthroat to 12 inches.

To the southeast of the town of Kaycee 12.25 miles is **J Bar U Reservoir** (4,905 ft; 9 ac) with fishing for largemouth bass averaging 10 inches. Boats are allowed, but there is not a boat ramp. Only small craft are recommended. Access to this Wyoming Game and Fish Walk-in Area is via the frontage Road at Exit 246 (South Fork Powder Road) off of I-25, then southeast along the Interstate. Watch for signs indicating public access to reservoir.

The **Middle Fork Powder River** west of the town of Kaycee has limited fishing due to private property. Outlaw Canyon on the Middle Fork Powder River is one of the few stretches of the river on public land. Access to the canyon is west on Barnum Road (SR 190) to Bar C Road, south to Outlaw Cave Road which follows the river to the west. A short, but steep, hike is required to reach the river. Fishing is mostly for rainbow and brown to 16 inches, larger brown are caught in the fall. The Middle Fork Powder River, from Bachaus Creek downstream to the Bar C Road (Johnson County Road 238) on the Bar C Ranch (approximately 8.5 miles); the limit on trout is 6 fish, only 1 can be longer than 16 inches; and, all trout between 10 and 16 inches must be returned to water. Fishing is by artificial flies and lures only. **Buffalo Creek, Blue Creek, Beartrap,** and **Red Fork Creek** are tributaries of the Middle Fork and have fishing for rainbow and brown to 10 inches, and small brook near the headwaters. Buffalo Creek is paralleled by Buffalo Creek Road (CR 105) to near its headwaters. Several miles of North Fork Buffalo Creek have been leased as a Walk-in Area by the Wyoming Game and Fish Dept. below FR 109 (Bighorn Mountain Road). Fishing is limited on **Beaver Creek** by private property.

The **North Fork Powder River**, reached from Hwy 191 north of Kaycee, has good fishing but, once again, is predominantly on private land. It has a canyon area that offers good fishing. The canyon area itself is on public land but is surrounded by private land, so ask permission before fishing. The North Fork is fair for 8- to 12-inch rainbow and brown. Near its headwaters in the national forest, **Dull Knife Reservoir** (8,146 ft; 108 ac) is a fluctuating irrigation reservoir surrounded mostly by private land. Dull Knife Reservoir is rated fair for 10- to 15-inch brown and rainbow. Access the reservoir by taking US 16 west from Buffalo about 27 miles to the Hazelton Road intersection. Turn south and drive 12 miles to the reservoir.

Pass Creek and **Dry Creek**, tributaries of the North Fork Powder River, are usually dry by summer and offer no fishing.

Several tributaries enter the Powder River below the town of Kaycee. They may look promising on a map, but **Salt Creek, Fourmile Creek,**

Rob Yingling/Bighorn Web Design Photo

Soldier Creek, Willow Creek, Ninemile Creek, Pumpkin Creek and **Deadhorse Creek** are fishless.

CRAZY WOMAN CREEK

The headwaters of **Crazy Woman Creek** lie just north of the headwaters of the North Fork Powder River. Lower Crazy Woman Creek and **South Fork Crazy Woman Creek** offers poor fishing for catfish and shovel-nose sturgeon which can be caught on lower Crazy Woman and Clear creeks as they come up to spawn. Below I-90, Crazy Woman Creek is excellent for channel catfish.

Middle Fork Crazy Woman Creek meanders about 10 miles through mostly private land. It has beaver ponds and good fishing for brown. The creek can be reached by I-25 and Hwy 196 from where they cross the creek. Remember to seek landowner permission. At higher elevations in the national forest, **Doyle Creek**, **Poison Creek**, and the Middle Fork offer good fishing for small brook and brown to 8 inches. The headwaters and small tributary streams are accessible from Hazelton Road in the national forest, about 30 miles southwest of Buffalo.

North Fork Crazy Woman Creek, with its headwaters in Bighorn National Forest, offers good fishing for 8- to 10-inch brook. Crazy Woman Canyon has good fishing for brook, and occasionally small rainbow and brown. Access to the lower end of the canyon is from Hwy 196 about 12 miles south of Buffalo via Crazy Woman Canyon Road. The upper end of the canyon is 25 miles southwest of the town of Buffalo on

Hwy 16, turn east for 5 miles on FR 33.

South of Buffalo 13 miles, off the Crazy Women Canyon Road and Muddy Creek roads are the two Muddy Guard reservoirs. **Muddy Guard Reservoir #1** (5,272 ft; 16 ac) is managed as a trophy rainbow and brown reservoir, where fish to 23 inches are possible. The limit on trout is 2 fish under 18 inches, fishing is with artificial flies and lures only. **Muddy Guard Reservoir #2** (5,295 ft; 31 ac) is stocked heavily with rainbow and brown, with brown to 5 pounds possible. Fishing is good early and late in the season. Boats are allowed on both reservoirs, with a 15 horsepower limit.

CLEAR CREEK

The headwaters of **Clear Creek** lie north of the Crazy Woman Creek headwaters. Clear Creek has good fishing for brown and rainbow from 8 to 12 inches. West of the town of Buffalo, Clear Creek flows through several miles of mostly public land to the national forest boundary. Some private property does exist.

The headwaters of the North, Middle, and South forks of Clear Creek are in the Cloud Peak Wilderness west of the town of Buffalo on Highway 16. Trails follow each of the forks to high alpine lakes with fishing for rainbow, brook, golden, and cutthroat. Access to North Fork Clear Creek drainage in the Cloud Peak Wilderness is by way of Hunters Trailhead on Hunter Creek Road (FR 19); rough 4 wheel drive roads (FR 394 and FR 395) continue past the trailhead to the wilderness boundary. Lakes in the wilderness on the Middle and South Fork Clear creeks are via FR 20, and the Circle Park Trailhead.

South Clear Creek is crossed by US 16 about 15 miles west of the town of Buffalo. The stream is good for rainbow and brown to 8 inches, and small brook at higher elevations. At the creeks headwaters are several lakes in the Cloud Peak Wilderness, Circle Park Trailhead provides access to the numerous lakes in the drainage. To reach the trailhead take FR 20 (Circle Park Road) west from Highway 16 for 2 miles, follow the left fork in the road for 0.5 miles to the trailhead. The trail reaches Shred Lake after 1.75 miles. **Shred Lake** (8,780 ft: 3 ac) is stocked with cutthroat. North from Shred Lake, a trial drops over into the Oliver Creek drainage, 0.5 miles upstream along Oliver Creek is **Long Lake** (8,925 ft; 2 ac) and **Ringbone Lake** (8,970 ft; 7 ac). Both are fair for wary cutthroat. Further upstream 0.5 miles is **Romeo Lake** (9,195 ft; 3 ac), **Martin Lake** (9,352 ft; 3 ac) and **Willow Lake** (9,315 ft; 8 ac). These small lakes are fair for small cutthroat, and Willow Lake is good for grayling to 12 inches.

From Shred Lake the Circle Park Trail makes a big loop to the South Clear Creek drainage and back again. To the west on the trail 1.25 miles is **Rainy Lake** (9,385 ft; 3 ac) which is barren. A spur trial to the northwest goes almost a mile to Willow Lake and the Oliver Creek drainage. Con-

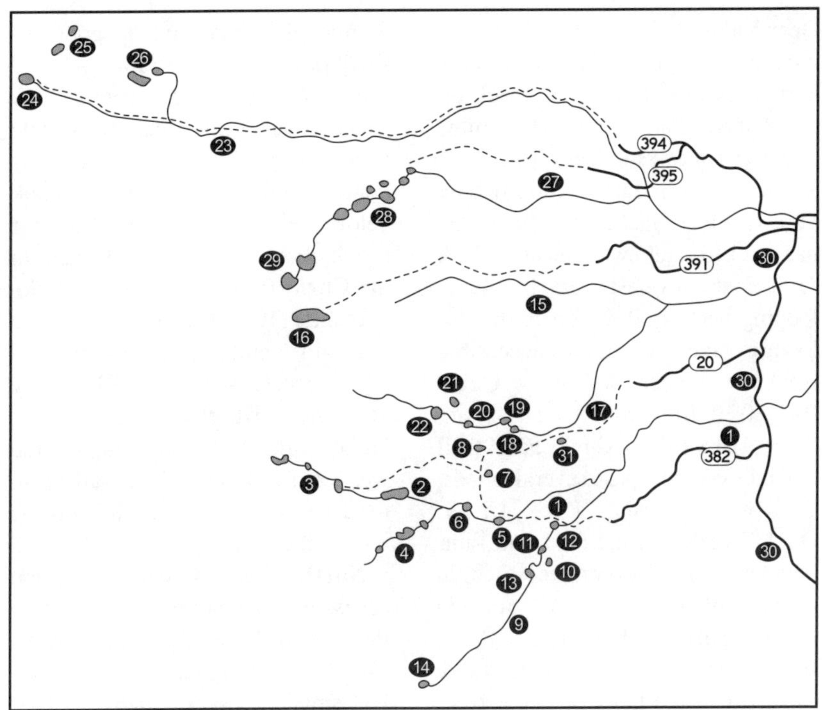

1. South Fork Clear Creek
2. Lame Deer Lake
3. Chill Lakes
4. Firehole Lakes
5. Her Lake
6. Old Crow Lake
7. Otter Lake
8. Rainy Lake
9. Duck Creek
10. Brown Bear Lake
11. Magdalene Lake
12. Trigger Lake
13. Mabel Lake
14. Paradise Lake
15. Middle Fork Clear Creek
16. Lake Angeline
17. Oliver Creek
18. Long Lake
19. Ringbone Lake
20. Romeo Lake
21. Martin Lake
22. Willow Lake
23. North Fork Clear Creek
24. Florence Lake
25. Golden Lakes
26. Powell Lakes
27. Seven Brothers Creek
28. Seven Brothers Lakes
29. Frozen Lakes
30. Hwy 16
31. Sherd Lake

tinuing past Rainy Lake on the Circle Park Trial the trail turns south 0.5 miles to **Otter Lake** (9,238 ft; 3 ac), with good fishing for small brook. To the south 0.5 miles a trail heading to the west goes up the South Clear Creek drainage to **Old Crow Lake** (9,310 ft; 2 ac), which is good for brook; and further up the drainage to the **Firehole Lakes** (9,480 to 9,510 ft; 4 to 15 ac). The Fire Hole Lakes have lake trout to 17 inches, rainbow, brook and Firehole Lake #2 has fair fishing for golden. Nearby **Lame**

Deer Lake (9,596 ft; 22 ac) has good fishing for rainbow; **Chill Lakes** are barren. Below these lakes, back on the Circle Park Trail, 0.5 miles downstream is **Her Lake** (9,185 ft; 2.5 ac) which is fair to good fishing for brook to 10 inches. Her Lake also has stocked rainbow. The Circle Park Trail continues east from Her Lake looping back to Shred Lake, the following lakes are more accessible from the southern leg of the Circle Park Trail from Shred Lake. From Shred Lake follow Circle Park Trail 2.5 miles south, past several ponds, then west crossing Duck Creek. **Duck Creek** is good for small rainbow and brook. Several lakes, within a mile of the trail, are on this drainage; **Brown Bear Lake** (8,985 ft; 1.5 ac) and **Magdalene Lake** (8,945 ft; 6 ac) have cutthroat from 10 to 14 inches, and **Trigger Lake** (8,840 ft; 2 ac) has 10- to 12-inch cutthroat. **Mabel Lake** (9,060 ft; 6 ac) and **Paradise Lake** (10,090 ft; 3.5 ac) are barren. These lakes can also be accessed from FR 382 (4 wheel drive) which ends at the wilderness boundary to the east of Duck Creek, a trail connects to road to Circle Park Trail.

Tie Hack Reservoir (7,380 ft; 25 ac) and campground is to the east of Highway 16 via FR 21. Tie Hack Reservoir supplies water for the towns of Sheridan and Buffalo. Fishing is improving in this newer reservoir and is rated fair for small stocked rainbow, cutthroat, and brook. **Sourdough Creek** is a southern tributary of South Clear Creek, Sourdough is rated fair to good for small brook and some rainbow.

Middle Clear Creek enters Clear Creek about 3 miles east of Middle Fork Campground. The stream is good for rainbow, brown and brook below the campground and good for brook above it. At its headwaters in the Cloud Peak Wilderness is **Lake Angeline** (10,554 ft; 56 ac). The lake is good for cutthroat and rainbow 10 to 14 inches. Access from Highway 16 is by 4 wheel drive FR 391 to Weber Park, and hiking 6 miles to the west on FR 473413. The trail up to the lake is steep and up hill all the way to the lake.

North Clear Creek has good access by road and then by trail into the Cloud Peak Wilderness Area. The stream has rainbow to 10 inches, and small brook. A small tributary, **Hunter Creek**, has good fishing for brook. At the headwaters of North Clear Creek are several lakes near the center of the wilderness area. Access to these high alpine lakes is by way of Hunters Trailhead on Hunter Creek Road (FR 19). Passenger cars can drive to the trailhead; rough 4 wheel drive roads FR 394 (which is an extremely rough 4 wheel drive road) and FR 395 continue past the trailhead to the wilderness boundary. Most anglers start at the Hunter Trailhead. **Seven Brothers Creek** enters North Fork Clear Creek from the southwest. This stream is overpopulated with small brook averaging 5 inches. At the headwaters of Seven Brothers Creek are the **Seven Brothers Lakes** (9,485 to 9,560 ft; 5

to 21 ac). The lakes have lake trout and rainbow, lake #6 has cutthroat. FR 394, from the wilderness boundary requires a 1.75 mile hike to reach the lakes; the Hunter Trailhead, following FR 395 to the wilderness boundary, requires a hike of 5.5 miles. **Frozen Lakes** (lower 10,200 ft; 21 ac, upper 10,345 ft; 23 ac) are no longer stocked with golden and are barren.

Near the headwaters of the North Fork Clear Creek drainage are several lakes accessible from Florence Pass Trail. From the Hunter Trailhead, follow FR 394 west for 5.5 miles to Trail Park; from Trail Park to the west 4.25 miles up Powell Creek are the **Powell Lakes** (10,622 to 11,026 ft; 3 to 11 ac). Only the lower two lakes have fish and are good for cutthroat 10 to 16 inches. Further up the Florence Pass Trail 2.25 miles is **Florence Lake** (10,860 ft; 18 ac), which has good fishing for cutthroat from 9 to 14 inches. Above the lake the trail continues over Florence Pass and into the West Ten Sleep drainage. Higher in the drainage **Golden Lakes** (11,232 and 11,378 ft; 2 and 4 ac) are no longer stocked with golden and are now barren.

French Creek enters Clear Creek from the west, less than 5 miles east of Buffalo. The lower reaches are on private property and the upper reaches are in the national forest. The stream is rated fair to good for rainbow and brook to 12 inches. Check locally for access.

Rock Creek flows from the northwest to meet Clear Creek just east of Buffalo. Rock Creek is primarily a brown stream, and most of it flows through private property. The upper forks, **North Rock Creek** and **South Rock Creek**, have small brook.

Healy Reservoir (4,430 ft; 141 ac) 3.75 miles northeast of I-90 on US 16 is good for large rainbow, brown, and cutthroat. The limit on trout is 2 fish; fish over 15 must be released. Fishing is by artificial flies and lures only. Boats are not allowed.

PINEY CREEK

South Piney Creek, North Piney Creek and **Kearny Creek** in the national forest offer fishing for rainbow to 10 inches and small brook. Lower reaches of these creeks, outside the national forest boundaries, are on private property. To reach the headwaters of these creeks in the national forest and Cloud Peak Wilderness require long, and sometimes steep, hikes in very scenic country. There are several trails into the wilderness, all of them are up hill. The most direct, but steepest, way into the high country is via Little Goose Creek on Little Goose Trail. From FR 26 take FR 314 (4 wheel drive only) south to Hazel Park, from there hike south 6 mile to Highland Park, and then 2.75 miles to Kearny Lake. Another route is from the town of Story, FT 33 leads west 5.5 miles to join up with FT 320 (which is closed to motorized traffic), which leads another 9.5 miles to Kearny Lake. An alternate route into this area is by driving about 29 miles from Sheridan through Big Horn on the Red Grade Road (FR 26) to Big

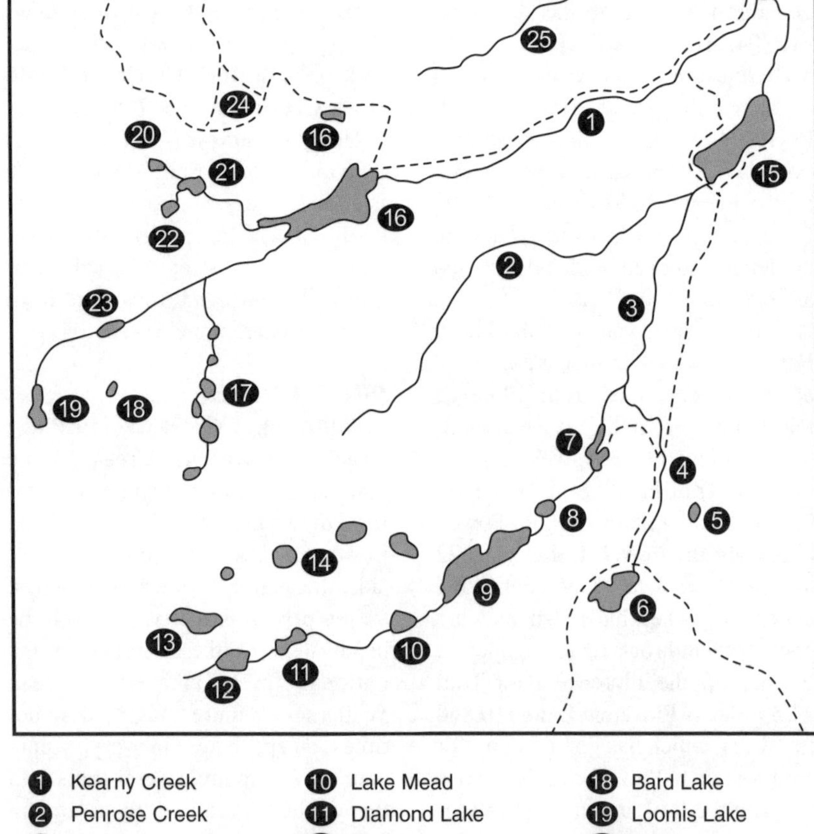

Goose Campground, then south to Bighorn Reservoir (some 4 wheel drive vehicles can drive as far as Bighorn Reservoir), from the lower end of Park Reservoir a hike west of about 14 miles to Kearny Lake is required. Another way to access this area (southern drainages) is from the Hunter Trailhead on the Clear Creek drainage. From the trailhead follow FR 394 for 2.5 miles to FR 365, then 5 miles to the north to Elk Lake;

Cloud Peak Reservoir is over a low ridge to the northwest, Willow Reservoir is downstream 4.25 miles.

At the headwaters of Kearny, and North and South Piney creeks, are several lakes that are in the Cloud Peak Wilderness boundary. Lakes on the headwaters of Piney creeks include: **Diamond Lake** (10,535 ft; 18 ac) and **Glacier Lake** (11,493 ft; 45 ac) which are barren; **Lake Mead** (9,845 ft; 22 ac) has rainbow and brook; **Cloud Peak Reservoir** (9,721 ft; 162 ac) has excellent fishing for cutthroat, rainbow, and small brook; the four **South Piney Lakes** (10,164 to 11,096 ft; 4 to 27 ac) and **Flatiron Lake** (9,543 ft; 14 ac) with cutthroat and brook to 11 inches; **Frying Pan Lake** (9,384 ft; 21 ac) with 7- to 10-inch cutthroat and rainbow. **Sapphire Lake** (10,770 ft; 28 ac) and **Gem Lake** (9,895 ft; 7 ac) are barren. **Elk Lake** (9,870 ft; 77 ac) has a few brook and cutthroat. Cloud Peak Reservoir, Frying Pan Lake, Flatiron Lake, and Gem Lake are outside of the wilderness boundary. These lakes can be accessed from the Hunter Trailhead on the Clear Creek drainage. From the trailhead follow FR 394 for 2.5 miles to FR 365, then 5 miles to the north to the lake. Cloud Peak Reservoir is over a low ridge to the northwest.

Lakes on the headwaters of Kearny Creek include; **Kearny Lake Reservoir** (9,177 ft; 188 ac) with lake trout, cutthroat, brook and rainbow. Inside the wilderness area are the five **Sawtooth Lakes** (10,134 to 10,718 ft; 3 to 17 ac), the lower 2 lakes have rainbow; **Bard Lake** (10,379 ft; 4 ac) and **Loomis Lake** (10,574 ft; 27 ac) with cutthroat; **Spear Lake** (9775 ft; 12 ac) with brook to 10 inches; **Myrtle Lake** (9,810 ft; 9 ac), **Highland Park Lake** (9,659 ft; 14 ac) and **Peggy Lake** (9,815 ft; 9 ac) with brook and rainbow. **Lake Winnie** (9,675 ft; 8 ac) winterkills and is barren. East of that group of lakes and outside the wilderness area, **Willow Park Reservoir** (8,615 ft; 186 ac) is one of the largest lakes in the area, but can fluctuate greatly due to irrigation drawdowns. It is on South Piney Creek and is fair to good fishing for brook and rainbow to 10 inches.

LAKE DESMET

Lake DeSmet (4,573 ft; 3600 ac) is just east of I-90, 10 miles northeast of the town of Buffalo. The lake is 110 feet deep and has good fishing for rainbow, brown to 2 pounds are in the lake, but most are around 14 inches. The lake contains populations of rock bass and yellow perch, and cutthroat are occasionally caught. The lake has 2 boat ramps. Fishing is best by trolling, but fishing from shore works as well. The best fishing occurs in the spring and early summer. **Shell Creek**, from west of the Game and Fish markers at its confluence with Lake Desmet to a designated point above the State spawning trap is closed to fishing from March 1 through May 31.

POWDER RIVER AND THE LITTLE POWDER RIVER

Between the Bighorn Mountains and Keyhole Reservoir lie the

rolling, grassy prairie and the **Powder River**. Although shallow, this stream is very underrated. It has excellent channel catfish populations, as well as goldeye, and on years of high spring flows, shovelnose sturgeon. All access to private property must be by permission of private landowners, respect the rights of others and do not trespass. Wyoming Game and Fish has a few Walk-in Area leases in the lower drainage near the town of Spotted Horse, **South Brown Reservoir** (4,030 ft; 5 ac) and **Odegard Reservoir** (3,950 ft; 7 ac). South Brown Reservoir is 3.25 miles west of the town of Spotted Horse on Highway 14/16, then north about 5.75 on S A Road to Matz Road. The reservoir is a 0.5 mile walk down to the west. To reach Odegard Reservoir drive east 6 miles from the intersection of Highway 14/16 and SR 341, reservoir is on a dirt road 0.75 miles to the north. Fishing in both reservoirs is for stocked rainbow averaging 10 inches. Another unnamed reservoir (3,940 ft; 5 ac) (Powder River Area # 3 in the 200-2001 Wyoming Game and Fish Walk-in pamphlet) is also stocked with small rainbow. From the intersection of Highway 14 and SR 341 drive east 9.5 miles on highway 14/16 to Ivy Creek Road (CR 57), follow this twisting road 3.75 miles to the north to access parking. Reservoir is a 0.5 mile walk to the southwest.

The **Little Powder River**, about 30 miles east of the Powder River, is 40 miles long and flows through private property. The tributaries are usually dry and the main stream offers only marginal fishing for channel catfish, and only with landowner permission.

BELLE FOURCHE RIVER

Farther east, the **Belle Fourche River**, stretching about 100 miles to the northeast, flows east of the town of Gillette toward the famed Black Hills and into South Dakota. Access to the river is limited due to private property, public access is provided on state owned land southwest of Hwy 212 near the town of Colony and a portion of the river inside Devil's Tower National Monument northeast of Keyhole Reservoir. Warm water fishing is considered only fair for catfish, sunfish, bass, and stonecat. Catfish up to 10 pounds are found in some portions of the river.

In the town of Gillette, **Gillette Fishing Lake** (4,525 ft; 11 ac), in Dalby City Park, has fishing for catfish, bass, brook, and stocked rainbow.

Sand Creek flows out of the Black Hills and into Redwater Creek, which then flows into the Belle Fourche River near the town of Beulah. Sand Creek has big brown and rainbow, although most average 12 inches. The limit on this spring-fed stream, at the Ranch 'A' Public Fishing Area down to Interstate 90, is 12 brown only 1 may exceed 12 inches, all other trout must be released. Fishing is with artificial flies and lures only on the Ranch 'A' Public Fishing Area. Turn south off I-90 at Beulah

Rob Yingling/Bighorn Web Design Photo

Rob Yingling/Bighorn Web Design Photo

and take the well-marked Sand Creek Road. Public fishing is signed and begins about a mile south of town and continues upstream for about 2 miles. Sand Creek Country Club is closed to fishing, Ranch 'A' is adjacent to the club and is about 6 miles south of the town of Beulah. The fish in Sand Creek are very spooky, it can be a tough place to fish despite the exceptional numbers of trout. **Hay Creek, Raven Creek** and **Inyan Kara Creek** offer little fishing opportunities.

Keyhole Reservoir (4,090 ft; 8000 ac), northeast of Moorcroft; is rated fair for walleye, northern pike, crappie, bluegill, yellow perch, smallmouth bass. Keyhole Reservoir is the only place in Wyoming where northern pike are found. All northern pike less than 30 inches in length must be released immediately. The north shore and around the sandbars in Deer Creek Bay are good for walleye, which average 15 inches. Smallmouth Bass can reach 15 inches. Campgrounds, boat ramp, bait, tackle, supplies and boat rentals are available. This is a State Park, which charges a small entrance fee. From Gillette, take I-90 east about 29 miles to the town of Moorcroft; turn north on Hwy 14 for 8 miles to State Road

113, which skirts the southern side of the lake or from I-90 take exit 165, then north 6 miles to the State Park Entrance.

Northeast of Keyhole Reservoir in the Bear Lodge Mountains is **Cook Lake** (4,735 ft; 19 ac) with good fishing for 10 inch brown, and rainbow averaging 11 inches. Catfish and bluegill are also present. Boats with motors are not allowed. Accessible from Highway 14 via Alladin Junction 12 miles east of the town of Sundance, then north 3 miles to FR 843 for about 10 miles.

Northeast of the town of Sundance is **Medicine Lake** (4,480 ft; 17 ac), which is stocked with rainbow and brook. Follow Highway 14 northeast 4 miles from Sundance to dirt access road to the north. Medicine Lake is leased through the Wyoming Game and Fish Walk-in program.

LAK Reservoir (4,380 ft; 71 ac) is 5 miles east of Newcastle off of Beaver Creek Road. The reservoir is a private reservoir that is open to the public, and requires a permit. Permit available at Hardware Hank's, 219 W. Main St., Newcastle (307-746-9391). The reservoir is not a beautiful place to fish but it does offer excellent fishing for rainbow, brown, walleye, tiger muskie, sunfish, and bass. This lowland lake has fishing for tiger muskie averaging 20 inches, rainbow and brown averaging 12 inches, and small bass. All tiger muskie less than 30 inches must be released immediately.

In the town of Wright, **Panther Pond** (4,960 ft; 3 ac) has fishing for sunfish, bass, catfish, and stocked rainbow. Southeast of Wright, **Little Thunder Reservoir** (4,775 ft; 20 ac) is rated fair for catfish, bass, bluegill, and stocked rainbow. The reservoir is located on Hilight Road 2 miles south of SR 450. Signed access and a rough dirt road lead 1 mile west to the reservoir.

A few waters of note are found near the border with South Dakota; **Black Hills Power and Light Reservoir** is 1 mile east of the town of Osage has fishing for bass and stocked brown and rainbow, **Turner Creek Reservoir** is about 7 miles northeast of Osage and has fishing for bass, **MW Reservoir** which is 18 miles south of Newcastle has fishing for bluegill and stocked rainbow and brook, and **East Iron Creek Reservoir** which is northeast of the town of Upton is good for bluegill, bass, catfish and stocked rainbow. Many other small lakes and reservoirs dot the landscape and maps on the eastern plains of northeastern Wyoming. Most are on private property or do not offer any fishing opportunities due to water drawdowns for irrigation needs. The lakes that do have fish all offer similar fishing for bass, bluegill, and catfish.

Streams also cover the map in eastern Wyoming which might harbor a catfish or two, but the best advice here is to stick to the high country fishing found in the Bighorn Mountains or try the Black Hills of South Dakota.

INDEX

A

A & M Reservoir: 201

Abosko Lake: 141

Adelaide Lake: 78

Adler Lake: 106

Agate Creek: 110

Alcova Reservoir: 219

Alice Lake: 37

Alpine Lake: 58

Alsop Lake: 227

Alum Creek: 108

Amethyst Creek: 114

Amphitheater Creek: 114

Amphitheater Lake: 138

Anchor Reservoir: 67

Anderson Creek: 77

Angle Lakes: 135

Antelope Creek: 110

Archie Creek: 194

Arizona Creek: 132

Arizona Lake: 132

Arnica Creek: 106

Arrastre Lake: 231

Arrow Canyon Creek: 118

Arrowhead Lake: 184, 229

Arrowhead Pool: 138

Ashenfelder Creek: 224

Aster Creek: 122

Aster Lake: 122

Astringent Creek: 107

Atlantic Creek: 51, 53, 105

Atlantic Creek Lake: 53

August Lake: 175

B

Bacon Rind Creek: 99

Badger Creek: 104, 149

Baer Lake: 48

Bailey Creek: 132, 145

Bailey Lake: 145

Baker Lake: 153

Baldy Creek: 172

Baldy Lake: 172

Baptiste Lake: 59

Barbara Lake: 168

Barber Lake: 176, 229

Bard Lake: 255

Barnes Lake: 172

Barren Lake: 182

Basin Creek: 121

Basin Creek Lake: 121

Bass Lake: 63

Bates Creek: 221

Battle Creek: 195

Battle Lake: 195

Beach Lake: 107

Beach Springs Lake: 107

Bear Creek: 40, 107, 233

Bear Lake: 48, 70, 155, 229

Bear River: 194

Bearpaw Lake: 130

Beartooth Lake: 86, 88

Beartrap: 248

Beauty Lake: 87

Beaver Creek: 79, 121, 184, 186, 248

Beaver Dam Creek: 104

Beaver Lake: 117, 182

Bechler River: 125

Beck Lake: 83

Becker Lake: 87

Belford Lake: 172

Bell Lake: 172

Bellamy Lake: 230

Belle Fourche River: 256

Bench Lake: 153

Bergman Reservoir: 149

Beula Lake: 125

Bewmark Lake: 177

Big Atlantic Gulch: 199

Big Bear Lake: 101

Big Brooklyn Lake: 229

Big Creek: 206

Big Goose Creek: 240

Big Milky Lake: 44

Big Moose Lake: 90

Big Sandy Lake: 183

Big Sandy Reservoir: 184

Big Sandy River: 183

Big Sheep Mountain Lake: 157

Big Stough Creek Lake: 51

Big Telephone Lake: 230

Big Thumb Creek: 106

Big Willow Creek: 238

Bighorn Lake: 84

Bighorn Reservoir: 244

Bighorn River: 65, 66, 67

Billy's Lake: 182

Bitch Creek: 149

Black Butte Creek: 99

Black Hills Power and Light - Reservoir: 259

Black Joe Lake: 183

Blackjack Lake: 229

Blackrock Creek: 136

Blackrock Lake: 51

Blacks Fork: 190

Blackstone Lake: 91

Blacktail Deer Creek: 112

Blacktail Pond: 112

Blanket Lakes: 37

Blucher Creek: 199

Blucher Lake: 197

Blue Creek: 248

Blue Lakes: 134

Blue Miner Lake: 139

Blueberry Lake: 42, 175

Bluff Park Creek: 165

Boarder Waters: 195

Bob Creek: 56

Bob Lakes: 56

Bob's Lake: 177

Bog Lake: 40

Bog Lakes: 40

Bomber Lake: 39

Bonanza Creek: 240

Bone Draw: 184

Bonneville Lake: 179

Boone Creek: 77, 148

Boone Lake: 37

Borum Lake: 167

Boulder Creek: 174, 175, 177

Boulder Lake: 174

Boulter Lake: 182

Boundary Creek: 125

Box Lake: 145

Boysen Reservoir: 60

Bradley Lake: 138

Brewster Lake: 141

Bridge Creek: 106

Bridger Creek: 167

Bridger Lake: 105, 168

Broad Creek: 110

Brooklyn Lakes: 229

Brooks Lake: 33

Brooks Lake Creek: 35

Brown Bear Lake: 252

Bruce Creek: 240

Buck Lake: 114

Bucking Mule Creek: 85

Bucklin Reservoir #1: 201

Bucklin Reservoir #2: 201

Bucklin Reservoirs: 201

Bud's Lake: 42

Buffalo Bill Reservoir: 80

Buffalo Creek: 67, 115, 248

Buffalo Fork River: 134

Buffalo Lake: 125

Bugle Lake: 90

Bull Creek: 56, 238

Bull Lake: 56

Bull Lake Creek: 56

Bump Sullivan Reservoir: 224

Burlington Reservoir: 247

Burnt Creek: 110

Burnt Lake: 174

Burnt Timber Lake: 37

Butte Creek: 105

C

Cabin Creek: 104, 106

Cache Creek: 114

Cache Lake: 113

Calfee Creek: 113

Calvin Lake: 240

Camp Creek: 190

Camp Lake: 44

Campanula Creek: 100

Campbell Lake: 231

Canyon Creek: 68, 93

Carmondy Lake: 199

Carnelian Creek: 110

Carson Lake: 37

Cascade Creek: 108

Cascade Lake: 108, 231

Cathedral Lake: 48

Cedar Creek: 79

Chain Lakes: 93, 172

Chalcedony Creek: 114

Chateau Lake: 141

Cheyenne Area: 233

Chickadee Lake: 106

Chill Lakes: 252

Chipmunk Creek: 106

Chittenden Bridge: 108

Christian Pond: 132

Christina Lake: 53

Christine Lake: 175

Christmas Lake: 91

Cirque Lake: 130

Clark Creek: 79, 155

Clark Lake: 155

Clarks Fork Yellowstone River: 85, 86

Claw Lake: 88

Clear Creek: 104, 107, 134, 155, 250

Clear Creek Lake: 134

Clear Lake: 110, 155, 183

Clearwater Creek: 80

Clendenning Lake: 35

Cliff Creek: 105, 145

Cliff Lake: 48, 74, 93

Cloud Peak Reservoir: 255

Cloverleaf Lake: 48

Cold Creek: 113

Columbine Creek: 104

Conant Creek: 149

Coney Creek: 244

Coney Lake: 244

Cook Lake: 48, 259

Coon Lake: 49

Copper Creek: 240

Copper Lakes: 86

Corral Creek: 147

Corral Creek Lake: 147

Cottongrass Creek: 108

Cottonwood Creek: 67, 79, 112, 138, 139, 181, 184, 206, 208, 210

Cottonwood Lake: 147, 181

Cougar Creek: 100

Coulter Creek: 121

Cow Creek: 77, 210

Cow Creek Reservoir: 210

Cow Lake: 132

Cowan Creek: 103

Coyote Creek: 112

Coyote Lake: 138, 163, 175

Crag Lake: 99

Crandall Creek: 85

Crane Lake: 87

Crater Lakes: 75, 136, 215

Crawfish Creek: 121

Crazy Creek: 90

Crazy Woman Creek: 249

Crescent Lake: 99, 157, 179, 229, 244

Crevice Creek: 112

Crevice Lake: 112

Crompton Reservoir: 194

Crooked Creek: 120

Cross Creek: 244

Cross Creek Lakes: 244

Cross Creek Reservoir: 244

Cross Lake: 175, 179

Crow Creek: 145, 233

Crow Creek Lakes: 145

Crystal Creek: 114, 139

Crystal Lake: 39, 242

Crystal Lake Reservoir: 233

Cub Creek: 104, 107, 134

Cub Lake: 42

Current Creek: 194

Curry Creek: 222

Cutoff Creek: 115

Cutthroat Lake: 51, 167, 229

Cygnet Lakes: 103

Cygnet Pond: 132

D

Dad's Lake: 182

Dale Lake: 155

Daly Creek: 99

Daniel Fishing Easement: 158

Daphne Lake: 155

Darby Creek: 149

Deacon Lake: 37

Dead Indian Creek: 85

Deadhorse Creek: 249

Dean Lake: 165

Deaver Reservoir: 84

Deep Creek: 49, 68, 110

Deep Creek Lakes: 49

Deep Lake: 91, 141, 183, 229

Deer Creek: 85, 221

DeLacy Creek: 123

DeLacy Lakes: 123

Dell Creek: 145

Delta Lake: 138

Delusion Lake: 106

Dempsey Creek: 190

Dennis Lake: 44

Devil's Hole Creek: 190

Devils Lake: 242

Dewdrop Lake: 108

Diamond Lake: 183, 215, 232, 255

Diamond Springs Reservoir: 199

Dickinson Creek: 46

Dinwoody Lakes: 42, 56

Dipper Lake: 231

Divide Creek: 177

Divide Lake: 98, 134, 177, 182

Dollar Lake: 93, 141, 170

Dome Lake: 244

Dome Lake Reservoir: 244

Dome Rock Reservoir: 216

Don Lake: 42, 172

Donald Lake: 182

Double Lake: 42

Douglas Creek: 205

Downs Lake: 42

Doyle Creek: 249

Dream Creek: 177

Dream Lake: 177

Dry Basin Lake: 139

Dry Creek: 42, 248

Dry Fork Creek: 235

Dry Fork Granite Creek: 79

Dry Piney Creek: 186

Dryad Lake: 107

Duck Creek: 100, 161, 252

Duck Lake: 93, 106

Dudley Lake: 130

Dull Knife Reservoir: 248

Duncan Lake: 238, 242

DuNoir Creek: 35

Dutch Oven Lake: 46

Dyke Lake: 38

E

Eagle Creek: 80

East Allen Lake: 214

East Banner Lake: 231

East DuNoir Creek: 35

East Fork Big Goose Creek: 240

East Fork Creek: 79

East Fork Lakes: 183

East Fork River: 181

East Fork South Tongue River: 240

East Fork Sweetwater River: 199

East Fork Wind River: 39

East Glacier Lake: 230

East Iron Creek Reservoir: 259

East Newton Lake: 83

East of Jackson Lake: 132

East Ten Sleep Creek: 68

East Ten Sleep Lake: 68

East Torrey Creek: 39

Echo Lakes: 48, 87

Edelman Creek: 242

Eden Reservoir: 184

Edmond Lake: 175

Edwards Lake: 231

Eklund Lake: 168

Elbow Creek: 153, 167

Elbow Lake: 167

Eleanor Lake: 107

Elk Antler Creek: 108

Elk Creek: 112

Elk Fork Creek: 80

Elk Lake: 40, 58, 90, 255

Elk Park Pond: 141

Elk Ranch Reservoir: 136

Elk Tongue Creek: 115

Emerald Lake: 40, 78, 91

Emma Lake: 172

Emma Matilda Lake: 132

Encampment River: 208

Enos Lake: 58, 134

Ernest Lake: 149

Escarpment Creek: 105

Europe Creek: 176

Ewe Lake: 88

F

Fairy Creek: 103

Faler Lake: 155

Fall Creek: 145, 174

Fall Creek Lakes: 174

Falls River: 124, 148

Fan Creek: 98

Fantan Lake: 93

Farney Lakes: 141

Fawn Creek: 116, 145

Fawn Lake: 53, 116

Fayette Lake: 170

Feather Lake: 103

Fern Lake: 110

Ferry Lake: 134

Festo Lake: 232

Fiddlers Creek: 51

Fiddlers Lake: 51

Finger Lake: 88

Firehole Canyon: 102

Firehole Lakes: 176, 251

Fish Creek: 139, 141, 186, 190

Fish Creek Lakes: 140

Fish Lake: 37, 148, 182

Fisherman Creek: 145

Fishhawk Creek: 80

Fishing Bridge: 108

Flake Lake: 87

Flaming Gorge Reservoir: 192

Flat Creek: 141

Flat Creek Lake: 143

Flat Lake: 141

Flatiron Lake: 255

Flint Creek: 114

Floating Island Lake: 112

Florence Lake: 42, 253

Flume Creek: 188

Fontenelle Creek: 188

Fontenelle Lakes: 188

Fontenelle Reservoir: 186

Fool Creek: 238

Footprint Lake: 51

Forest Creek: 121

Forest Lake: 121

Forget-me-not Lakes: 138

Fort Lake: 93

Fortress Lakes: 71

Foster Lake: 114

Foster Reservoir: 83

Fourmile Creek: 248

Fox Creek: 118, 149

Francis Lake: 182

Fremont Creek: 168

Fremont Lake: 165

French Creek: 206, 253

Friend Creek: 224

Frost Lake: 113

Frozen Lake: 35, 87

Frozen Lakes: 184, 253

Frye Lake Reservoir: 51

Frying Pan Lake: 255

Full Moon Lake: 176

Funnel Lake: 46

G

Gadsby Lake: 155

Gallatin Lake: 96

Gallatin River: 96

Garden Lake: 229

Gardner Lake: 91

Gardner River: 116

Gaylord Lake: 46

Geddes Lake: 244

Gelatt Lake: 226

Gem Lake: 255

Gibbon River: 101, 102

Gilbert Creek: 191

Gillette Fishing Lake: 256

Glacier Lake: 91, 176, 255

Glacier Trail: 39

Glade Creek: 128

Glen Creek: 117

Glendo Reservoir: 222

Glimpse Lake: 165

Gneiss Creek: 100

Golden Lake: 42, 44, 135, 153, 230, 253

Goldeneye Reservoir: 221

Goodwin Lake: 143

Goose Creek: 240

Goose Lake: 103

Gooseberry Creek: 67

Gorge Lake: 168

Gottfried Lake: 167

Grace Lake: 73

Granger Reservoir: 242

Granite Creek: 144

Granite Lake: 75, 90, 141, 153

Granite Reservoir: 233

Grass Lake: 37

Grassy Lake: 42, 229

Grassy Lake Reservoir: 148

Grave Lake: 46

Gravel Creek: 132

Gravel Lake: 132

Graves Creek: 240

Grayling Creek: 100

Grayling Lake: 88

Grayrocks Reservoir: 232

Grebe Lake: 101

Green Lake: 40

Green River: 151, 153, 188

Green River Lakes: 153

Grey Reef Reservoir: 203, 219

Greybulll River: 76

Greys River: 145

Grizzly Bear Lake: 138

Grizzly Lake: 117, 139

Gros Ventre River: 139

Grouse Creek: 106

Grouse Lake: 170

Guernsey Reservoir: 224

Gunboat Lake: 71

Gus Lake: 88

Gustave Lake: 53

Gypsum Creek: 157

H

Halfmoon Lake: 88, 170

Halls Creek: 176

Halls Lake: 176, 177

Hams Fork River: 188

Hanging Lake: 229

Hardpan Creek: 79

Hardpan Lake: 79

Harebell Creek: 121

Harlequin Lake: 101

Harrington Reservoir: 76

Hatchet Lake: 58, 231

Hauser Lake: 93

Hawk Springs Reservoir: 224

Hay Creek: 258

Hay Pass Lakes: 44

Healy Reservoir: 253

Heart Lake: 87, 120, 167, 231, 244

Heart River: 120

Hebgen Lake: 100

Hellroaring Creek: 112

Helmet Lake: 46

Henrys Fork: 192

Henrys Fork River: 192

Her Lake: 252

Hering Lake: 125

Heron Pond: 132

Hidden Creek: 105

Hidden Lake: 39, 48, 58, 149, 161, 174

High Lake: 99

High Meadow Lake: 48

Highland Park Lake: 255

Highway 130 Lake: 229

Hoback River: 143

Hobble Creek: 194

Hobbs Lake: 168

Hog Park Creek: 208

Hog Park Reservoir: 208

Hogan Reservoir: 86

Holly Lake: 138

Holster Lake: 46

Honeymoon Lake: 42

Hope Lake: 242

Horse Creek: 37, 78, 79, 184

Horseshoe Creek: 222

Horseshoe Lake: 73, 88, 141, 174

Hourglass Lake: 229

Howard Lake: 176

Howe Lake: 177

Howell Creek: 104

Hunter Creek: 252

I

Ice Creek: 49

Ice Lakes: 49, 58, 101

Iceflo Lake: 138

Indian Creek: 117

Indian Lake: 138, 149

Indian Pond: 107

Ink Wells Lakes: 42

Inlet Creek: 87

Inyan Kara Creek: 258

Iron Spring Creek: 102

Island Lake: 53, 87, 168

Ivy Lake: 90

J

J Bar U Reservoir: 248

Jack Creek: 77, 145, 199, 210

Jackpine Creek: 149

Jackson Lake: 128, 130

Jagg Creek: 139

Jakey's Fork Creek: 37

Jasper Creek: 114

Jeff Lake: 229

Jenny Lake: 136

Jensen Reservoir: 201

Jessie Lake: 181

Jim Creek: 181

Jim Harrower Lake: 179

Jim Lake: 181

Joe Johnson Reservoir: 232

Joffe Lake: 116

Johnson Creek: 135, 232

Johnson Creek Reservoir: 232

Johnson Lake: 181

Jojo Creek: 77

Jojo Lake: 77

Joy Peak Lake: 136

Junco Lake: 148

Junction Lake: 170, 176

K

Kafka Reservoir: 233

Kearny Creek: 253

Kearny Lake Reservoir: 255

Kemmerer City Reservoir: 190

Kendall Warm Springs: 157

Kendall Warm Springs Creek: 157

Kevin Lake: 155

Keyhole Reservoir: 258

Kirkland Lake: 56

Kisinger Lake: 35

Kleenburn Ponds: 240

Klondike Lakes: 230

East Klondike Lake: 230

North Klondike Lake: 230

South Klondike Lake: 230

Knob Lakes: 179

Kortes Reservoir: 215

L

La Barge Creek: 186

La Bonte Creek: 222

La Prele Creek: 222

La Prele Reservoir: 222

LAK Reservoir: 259

Lake Alibi: 244

Lake Alice: 194

Lake Angeline: 252

Lake Arden: 78

Lake Bastow: 145

Lake Buffalo: 244

Lake Cameahwait: 63

Lake Creek: 90, 163, 206

Lake DeSmet: 255

Lake Elsa: 74

Lake Ethel: 175

Lake Eunice: 75

Lake Geneva: 242

Lake George: 174

Lake Golden: 242

Lake Hattie: 225

Lake Heebeecheeche: 58

Lake Helen: 70

Lake Isabella: 176

Lake Kagevah: 58

Lake Louise: 39, 44

Lake Marie: 230

Lake Marion: 70

Lake McClain: 68

Lake Mead: 255

Lake Mirage: 244

Lake of the Crags: 138

Lake of the Woods: 117, 141, 148

Lake Owen: 225

Lake Polaris: 58

Lake Prue: 176

Lake Sequa: 174

Lake Shamrock: 244

Lake Solitude: 58, 73, 138

Lake Susan: 176

Lake Taminah: 138

Lake Vera: 176

Lake Victor: 176

Lake WGN: 93

Lake Whitney: 42

Lake Winnie: 255

Lake Winona: 176

Lake Wyodaho: 125

Lakes of the Rough: 78

Lamar River: 113, 114

Lamb Lake: 88

Lame Deer Lake: 251

Lander Creek: 197

Landslide Creek: 113

Laramie River: 224

Laurel Lake: 138

Lava Creek: 117

Lead Creek: 184

Lee Lake: 177

Leg Lake: 51

Legion Lake: 182

Leidy Creek: 136

Leidy Lake: 136

Leigh Creek: 149

Leigh Lake: 138

Lewis Lake: 122, 230

Lewis River: 121

Lewis-Shoshone Channel: 123

Libby Flats Lake: 229

Libby Lake: 230

Lightning Lakes: 179

Lily Lake: 73, 90

Lilypad Lake: 125

Little Atlantic Lake: 53

Little Bear Lake: 87

Little Bighorn River: 235

Little Bob Lake: 56

Little Brooklyn Lake: 229

Little Buffalo Creek: 112

Little Copeland Lake: 90

Little Cottonwood Creek: 112

Little Dad's Lake: 182

Little Divide Lake: 177

Little Fall Creek: 174

Little Firehole River: 102

Little Goose Creek: 240

Little Greys River: 145

Little Halfmoon Lake: 170

Little Lamar River: 113

Little Laramie River: 227

Little Long Lake: 231

Little Medicine Bow River: 214

Little Milky Lake: 44

Little Moccasin Lake: 59

Little Moose Lake: 90

Little Moss Lake: 46

Little Popo Agie River: 51

Little Powder River: 255, 256

Little Red Creek: 194

Little Robinson Creek: 125

Little Sage Creek: 211

Little Sandy Creek: 184

Little Sandy Lake: 184

Little Sawtooth Lake: 93

Little Seneca Lake: 168

Little Shell Lake: 78

Little Snake River: 195

Little Soda Lake: 165

Little Stough Creek Lakes: 51

Little Sweetwater Creek: 199

Little Telephone Lake: 230

Little Thunder Reservoir: 259

Little Tomahawk Lake: 53

Little Tongue River: 240

Little Valentine Lake: 46

Little Washakie Lake: 46

Little Wind River: 60

Littlerock Creek: 91

Loch Leven Lake: 46

Lonesome Lake: 48, 88

Long Lake: 37, 48, 59, 87, 168, 176, 215, 232, 250

Lookout Lake: 230

Loomis Lake: 255

Loon Lake: 149

Losekamp Lake: 91

Lost Camp Lake: 165

Lost Creek: 68, 112

Lost Lake: 38, 59, 73, 90, 110, 136, 168, 230

Lost Soldier Lake: 201

Lost Twin Lakes: 70

Lost Wilderness Lake: 242

Louis Creek: 51, 53

Louis Lake: 53

Lovatt Lake: 175

Lovell Lakes: 84

Lower Basin Lake: 103

Lower Bighorn River: 75

Lower Cook Lake: 172

Lower Copper Lake: 86

Lower Crater Lake: 75

Lower Deep Creek Lake: 49

Lower Glacier Lake: 44

Lower Green River Lake: 153

Lower Jade Lake: 35

Lower Jean Lake: 170

Lower Laramie River: 232

Lower Lizard Head Lake: 48

Lower Lost Twin Lake: 70

Lower Medicine Lodge Lake: 73

Lower Missouri Lake: 231

Lower North Platte River: 221

Lower Paint Rock Lake: 74

Lower Saddlebags Lake: 53

Lower Sheepeater Lake: 87

Lower Silas Lake: 53

Lower Silver Lake: 179

Lower Slide Lake: 139

Lower Sunshine Reservoir: 77

Lower Sweetwater River: 199

Lower Sylvan Lake: 179

Lower Titcomb Lake: 170

Lunch Lake: 141

Lupine Creek: 118

Lydle Lake: 58

Lynx Creek: 104

M

Mabel Lake: 252

Mackinaw Lake: 135

Macon Lake: 46

Macs Lake: 175

Madison Lake: 102

Madison River: 99, 100

Maes Lake: 182

Magdalene Lake: 252

Magnolia Lake: 231

Magpie Creek: 103

Maki Creek: 184

Mallard Lake: 103

Mammoth Beaver Ponds: 118

Maple Creek: 100

Marion Lake: 38, 138

Mariposa Lake: 118

Mark's Lake: 42

Markham Reservoir: 83

Marm's Lake: 182

Marmot Lake: 88

Marston Creek: 79

Marten Creek: 153

Marten Lake: 42, 153

Martin Lake: 250

Mary Lake: 103

Maybelle Lake: 68

McBride Lake: 115

McMaster Reservoir: 224

Meadow Creek: 104, 174

Meadow Lake: 93, 174

Meadowlark Lake: 68

Medicine Bow River: 214

Medicine Lake: 259

Medicine Lodge Creek: 71

Medicine Lodge Lakes: 73

Medina Lake: 175

Meeboer Lake: 225

Meek's Cabin Reservoir: 190

Meeks Lake: 181, 183

Mica Lake: 138

Middle Boone Creek: 149

Middle Bull Lake Creek: 44

Middle Clear Creek: 252

Middle Cloud Peak Lake: 73

Middle Copper Lake: 86

Middle Creek: 107

Middle Deep Creek Lake: 49

Middle Depression Reservoir: 63

Middle Fork Boulder Creek: 176

Middle Fork Crazy Woman Creek: 249

Middle Fork Lake: 177

Middle Fork Popo Agie River: 49

Middle Fork Powder River: 248

Middle Fork Wood River: 77

Middle Lake: 48

Middle Long Lake: 231

Middle Piney Creek: 185, 186

Middle Piney Lake: 186

Middle Ten Sleep Creek: 70

Mile Long Lake: 39

Milky Lakes: 44

Mill Pond: 230

Miller Creek: 113

Miller Lake: 170, 184

Miner Lake: 168

Mink Lake: 138

Miracle Mile: 215

Mirror Fork Timothy Creek: 113

Mirror Lake: 70, 91, 113, 182, 230

Mist Creek: 113

Mistake Lake: 170

Mistymoon Lake: 71

Moccasin Lake: 59

Mohawk Creek: 240

Mol Heron Creek: 113

Monroe Lake: 179

Moon Lake: 37

Moose Creek: 123, 149

Moose Lake: 42, 149, 179

Moraine Lake: 58

Morgan Lake: 134

Mosquito Lake: 157

Moss Lake: 46, 132

Mountain Ash Creek: 125

Mountain Creek: 104

Mountain Sheep Lake: 49

Movo Lake: 58

Mud Lake: 78, 170, 181

Muddy Creek: 88, 195, 206

Muddy Guard Reservoir #1: 250

Muddy Guard Reservoir #2: 250

Mule Lake: 88

Murray Lake: 35

Mutt Lake: 229

MW Reservoir: 259

Myrtle Lake: 255

Mystery Lake: 134

N

Nash Fork Little Laramie River: 227

Native Lake: 42, 88, 157

Needles Lake: 197

Neil Lake: 167

New Cody Reservoir: 83

New Fork Lakes: 161

New Fork River: 161

Newton Lakes: 83

Nez Perce Creek: 103

Night Lake: 87

Ninemile Creek: 249

No Name Lakes: 167

Norman Lakes: 175

North Banner Lake: 231

North Beartooth Creek: 88

North Boone Creek: 149

North Buffalo Fork Creek: 136

North Clear Creek: 252

North Fork Barrett Creek: 206

North Fork Boulder Creek: 176

North Fork Crazy Woman Creek: 249

North Fork Dry Creek: 42

North Fork Lake: 175

North Fork Little Laramie River: 227

North Fork Little Snake River: 195

North Fork Little Wind River: 58

North Fork Popo Agie River: 46

North Fork Powder River: 248

North Fork Shoshone River: 79

North Fork Spring Creek: 210

North Fork Sybille Creek: 232

North French Creek: 208

North Gap Lake: 230

North Lake: 184

North Laramie River: 233

North Meadow Lake: 229

North Mullen Creek: 206

North Paint Rock Creek: 73

North Piney Creek: 185, 186, 253

North Piney Lake: 186

North Platte River: 203, 205, 216, 219

North Rock Creek: 253

North Spring Creek Lake: 210

North Three Forks Creek: 145

North Tongue River: 238

North Twin Lake: 229, 231

Nowlin Creek: 143

Nowood Creek: 67

Nowood River: 67

Nuthatch Lake: 107

Nymph Lake: 101

O

Obsidian Creek: 117

Obsidian Lake: 117

Ocean Lake: 59

Odegard Reservoir: 256

Old Crow Lake: 251

Opal Creek: 114

Open Creek: 105

Otter Creek: 68, 108

Otter Lake: 251

Outlet Creek: 120

Outlet Lake: 120

Ouzel Creek: 125

Owen Creek: 240

Owl Creek: 67

Oxbow Creek: 112

P

Pacific Creek: 132

Packer Lake: 224

Paint Rock Creek: 71

Paint Rock Lakes: 73

Painter Reservoir: 194

Palisades Reservoir: 147

Palmer Lake: 165

Panther Creek: 116

Panther Pond: 259

Paradise Lake: 58, 93, 252

Park Lake: 49

Park Reservoir: 242

Pass Creek: 105, 211, 248

Pass Lake: 46, 167

Passage Creek: 106

Pathfinder Reservoir: 216

Patricia Lake: 242

Peak Lake: 155

Peat Lake: 38

Pebble Creek: 114

Peggy Lake: 255

Pelham Lake: 35

Pelican Creek: 107

Pelton Creek: 206

Penny Lake: 165

Perry Lake: 175

Pete's Lake: 49

Peter Lake: 172

Phantom Lake: 112, 231

Phelps Lake: 139

Phillips Lake: 42

Phlox Creek: 104

Phyllis Lake: 48

Pilgrim Creek: 132

Pilot Butte Reservoir: 59

Pine Creek: 165

Pine Island Lake: 177

Piney Creek: 253

Pinto Lake: 38, 49

Pipestone Creek: 176

Pipestone Lakes: 176

Pixley Creek: 153

Plateau Creek: 118, 120

Pocket Creek Lake: 181

Pocket Lake: 123

Poison Creek: 249

Poison Lake: 51

Pole Creek Lake: 172

Polecat Creek: 123, 128

Popo Agie Wilderness Area: 44

Porcupine Creek: 84, 194

Poston Lake: 182

Powder River: 247, 255, 256

Powell Lakes: 253

Promise Lake: 87

Proposition Creek: 125

Prospect Creek: 240

Prune Creek: 238

Pumpkin Creek: 235, 249

Pyramid Lake: 183

Q

Quartz Creek: 110

Quealy Lakes: 231

R

Raft Lake: 58

Raid Lake: 179

Rainbow Lake: 35, 75, 93, 113, 135, 163, 177

Rainy Lake: 250

Rambaud Lake: 175

Ramsheild Lake: 138

Ranger Creek: 46

Ranger Lake: 125

Rapid Lake: 184

Raven Creek: 107, 258

Ray Lake: 59

Raymond Creek: 194

Red Creek: 121, 194

Red Fork Creek: 248

Red Wing Lake: 37

Reese Creek: 113

Renner Reservoir: 67

Reno Lake: 90

Reservoir Lake: 229

Reynolds Creek: 161

Ribbon Lake: 110

Richards Creek: 100

Riddle Lake: 106

Rim Lake: 37, 211

Rimrock Lake: 138

Rinehart Lakes: 242

Ring Lake: 38

Ringbone Lake: 250

Roaring Fork Creek: 51, 157, 223

Roaring Fork Lake: 51

Roaring Fork Little Snake River: 195

Rob Roy Reservoir: 206

Roberts Lake: 58

Robin Lake: 75

Robinson Creek: 125, 190, 208

Robinson Lake: 125

Rock Creek: 91, 125, 157, 186, 199, 214, 229, 253

Rock Creek Reservoir: 199

Rock Lake: 53, 232

Rocky Creek: 104

Romeo Lake: 250

Rose Creek: 114

Ross Lake: 39

Round Lake: 73, 163

Ruff Lake: 175

S

Sage Creek: 191, 211

Salt Creek: 248

Salt River: 147

Sand Creek: 46, 256

Sand Creek Lake: 46

Sand Lake: 214, 229

Sand Mesa Reservoir #1: 63

Sand Mesa Reservoir #2: 63

Sandpoint Lake: 177

Sandra Lake: 38

Sapphire Lake: 255

Saratoga Lake: 210

Sauerkraut Lakes: 167

Savage Run Creek: 206

Savery Creek: 195

Sawmill Creek: 244

Sawmill Lakes: 244

Sawmill Reservoir: 244

Sawtooth Lake: 93, 255

Scab Creek: 177

Scaup Lake: 102

Scott Lake: 153, 230

Section Corner Lake: 163

Sedge Creek: 107

Sedge Lake: 99

Seminoe Reservoir: 208, 213

Seneca Lake: 168

Sentinel Creek: 103

Seven Brothers Creek: 252

Seven Brothers Lakes: 252

Seven Lakes: 141

Shadow Lake: 182

Shallow Creek: 110

Shallow Lake: 88

Sheeley Creek: 240

Sheep Lake: 40, 179, 229

Sheepherder Lake: 74

Sheet Lake: 184

Shelf Lake: 48, 99, 230

Shell Creek: 78, 255

Shell Lakes: 78

Shell Reservoir: 78

Sheridan Creek: 35

Sheridan Lake: 121

Shirley Basin Reservoir: 214

Shirley Lake: 155

Shoal Lake: 51

Shoe Lake: 59

Shoshone Creek: 48, 123

Shoshone Lake: 48, 58, 123

Shoshone River: 79

Shred Lake: 250

Shrimp Lake: 114

Sibley Lake: 238

Sickle Creek: 120

Silas Creek: 51, 53

Silver Lake: 210, 230

Silver Run Lake: 229

Simpson Lake: 37

Sinnard Reservoir: 224

Skull Lake: 182

Slate Creek: 139

Slide Creek: 155

Slide Lake: 118, 155

Slough Creek: 114

Smith Lake: 48

Smiths Fork: 191

Smiths Fork Bear River: 194

Snake Lake: 163

Snake River: 118, 121, 127, 128, 130, 143

Snow Lake: 40, 87

Snowband Lake: 39

Snowbank Lake: 229

Snowdrift Lake: 138

Snowy Range Lakes: 227

Snyder Lake: 87

Soapstone Lake: 37

Soda Butte Creek: 114

Soda Fork Creek: 136

Soda Lake: 141, 165, 185

Sodergreen Lake: 225

Solar Lake: 93

Soldier Creek: 249

Solfatara Creek: 101

Solution Creek: 106

Sonnicant Lake: 58

Sour Creek: 108

Sourdough Creek: 252

South Banner Lake: 231

South Boundary Lake: 123

South Brown Reservoir: 256

South Clear Creek: 250

South Cottonwood Creek: 185

South Fork Boulder Creek: 177

South Fork Buffalo Creek: 134

South Fork Crazy Woman Creek: 249

South Fork Fish Creek: 140

South Fork Little Laramie River: 227

South Fork Little Wind River: 44,

46, 58
South Fork Powder River: 247
South Fork Sage Creek: 83
South Fork Shoshone River: 79
South Fork Spring Creek: 210
South Fork Wood River: 77
South Forks Lakes: 46
South Gap Lake: 230
South Meadow Lake: 229
South Mullen Creek: 206
South Piney Creek: 185, 186, 253
South Piney Lakes: 255
South Rock Creek: 253
South Spring Creek Lake: 210
South Tongue River: 238
South Twin Lake: 229, 231
Sparhawk Lake: 93
Spear Lake: 255
Spearpoint Lake: 46
Specimen Creek: 99
Spider Lake: 172
Splake Lake: 42
Sportsman Lake: 113
Spread Creek: 136
Spring Creek: 102, 210
Springer Reservoir: 224
Spruce Creek: 103, 171
Spruce Lake: 172
Squirrel Lake: 51
Stamp Mill Lake: 231
Star Lake: 42, 179
Steamboat Lake: 58
Steer Creek: 77
Stephens Creek: 113
Stockade Lake: 91
Stonehammer Lake: 155
Stough Creek: 51
Stough Creek Lakes: 51
Straight Creek: 117
String Lake: 138
Stull Lakes: 244
Stump Lake: 145
Sturrey Lake: 171
Sucker Creek: 240
Sucker Lake: 231
Suicide Lake: 168
Sulphur Creek: 195
Sulphur Creek Reservoir: 194
Summer Ice Lake: 170
Summit Lake: 103, 167

Sunlight Creek: 85, 86

Sunrise Lake: 177

Sunshine Creek: 77

Sunshine Reservoirs: 77

Surprise Creek: 120, 174

Surprise Lake: 174

Swamp Lake: 86

Swan Lake: 117, 132

Swastika Lake: 229

Sweeney Creek: 170

Sweeney Lakes: 170

Sweetwater River: 197, 199

Sylvan Lake: 104, 107

T

T Lake: 88

Taggart Lake: 138

Talus Lake: 130

Tanager Lake: 123

Tayo Creek: 49

Teal Lake: 103

Teardrop Lake: 90

Temple Lake: 184

Ten Sleep Creek: 68

Tepee Creek: 157

Tern Lake: 110

Teton Creek: 149

Teton Reservoir: 211

Texas Lake: 182

Thayer Lake: 242

The Six Lakes: 139

33 Mile Ponds: 247

Thistle Creek: 108

Thomas Fork: 194

Thorofare Creek: 105

1000 Island Lake: 172

Three Elk Lake: 177

Thumb Lake: 53

Tie Hack Reservoir: 252

Tigee Lake: 58

Tillery Lake: 148

Timberline Lake: 138

Timico Lake: 174

Timothy Creek: 113

Toadstool Lake: 51

Toboggan Lakes: 177

Toltec Reservoir: 233

Tomahawk Lake: 53

Tongue River: 237

Top Lake: 93

Toppings Lakes: 136

Torrey Creek: 38

Torrey Lake: 38

Tosi Creek: 157

Tower Creek: 110

Towner Lake: 230

Townsend Creek: 51

Trail Creek: 106, 153, 190

Trail Lake: 35, 38, 58, 88, 106, 167

Trapper Lake: 130, 163

Trappers Creek: 104

Tri-County Lake: 136

Triangle Lake: 139, 168

Trigger Lake: 252

Trilobite Lake: 117

Trophy Lake: 172

Trout Creek: 68, 85, 108, 194

Trout Creek Lake: 35

Trout Lake: 114, 135

Turbid Lake: 107

Turner Creek Reservoir: 259

Turpin Creek: 215

Turpin Reservoir: 215

Turquoise Lake: 39, 145

Twin Buttes Lake: 227

Twin Lake: 42, 49, 58, 91, 117, 155, 167, 182

Twin Lakes Reservoir: 244

Two Ocean Lake: 132

U

Union Lake: 37

Upper Brooks Lake: 35

Upper Cook Lake: 172

Upper Copper Lake: 86

Upper Crater Lake: 75

Upper Crescent Lake: 157

Upper Deep Creek Lake: 49

Upper Golden Lake: 44

Upper Green River Lake: 153

Upper Jade Lake: 35

Upper Jean Lake: 170

Upper Long Lake: 168, 231

Upper Lost Twin Lake: 70

Upper Medicine Lodge Lake: 73

Upper Missouri Lake: 231

Upper North Crow Reservoir: 233

Upper Paint Rock Lake: 73

Upper Phillips Lake: 42

Upper Ross Lake: 39

Upper Sheepeater Lake: 87

Upper Silas Lake: 53

Upper Silver Lake: 181

Upper Silver Run Lake: 229

Upper Slide Lake: 139

Upper Sunshine Reservoir: 77

Upper Sylvan Lake: 179

Upper Titcomb Lake: 170

Upper Toadstool Lake: 51

V

V Lake: 183

Vagner Lake: 231

Valentine Lake: 46

Valiate Lake: 155

Valley Lake: 175

Venus Creek: 77

Vernal Lake: 59

Viva Naughton Reservoir: 189

Vosseller Lake: 231

W

Wagner Lake: 147

Wagon Box Creek: 235

Wagon Creek: 157

Walker Jenkins Lake: 214

Wall Lake: 87, 172

Wapiti Lake: 110

Warbonnet Lake: 179

Wardel Reservoir: 76

Warm Spring Creek: 35

Warren Bridge Fishing Easement: 158

Washakie Creek: 182

Washakie Lake: 46

Washakie Reservoir: 59

Watkins Lakes: 35

Weasel Creek: 106

West DuNoir Creek: 35

West Fork Big Goose Creek: 244

West Fork Iron Springs Creek: 103

West Fork Smiths Fork: 194

West Fork South Tongue River: 240

West Glacier Lake: 230

West Newton Lake: 83

West Ten Sleep Creek: 68, 70

West Ten Sleep Lake: 70

West Torrey Creek: 39

Weston Reservoir: 244

Wheatland Reservoir #1: 232

Wheatland Reservoir No. 2: 232

Wheatland Reservoir No. 3: 232

White Lake: 110

Widgit Lake: 148

Wiggins Fork: 40

Wilderness Lake: 176

Willet Lake: 79

Willett Creek: 78

Willow Creek: 113, 147, 163, 191, 199, 249

Willow Lake: 163, 250

Willow Park Reservoir: 255

Wilson Creek: 58

Wind River: 33

Wind River Canyon: 63

Wind River Indian Reservation: 54

Wind River Lake: 33

Windy Lake: 53

Winegar Lake: 125

Winter Creek: 117

Witch Creek: 121

Wolf Lake: 101, 181

Wolverine Creek: 121

Wood River: 77

Woodchuck Creek: 240

Woodruff Narrows Reservoir: 194

Worthen Meadows Reservoir: 51

Wrangler Lake: 108

Wykee Lake: 58

Y

Yellowstone Lake: 105, 106, 107

Yellowstone River: 103, 104, 107, 110

Yellowtail Reservoir: 84

Z

Z Lake: 87

Zigzag Lake: 51